Human Resilience

of related interest

Early Experience and the Life Path
Ann Clarke and Alan Clarke
ISBN 1 85302 858 4

Vulnerability and Resilience in Human Development
A Festschrift for Ann and Alan Clarke
Edited by Barbara Tizard and Ved Varma
ISBN 1 85302 877 0 pb
ISBN 1 85302 105 9 hb

Children's Rights and Power
Charging Up for a New Century
Mary John
ISBN 1 85302 659 X pb
ISBN 1 85302 658 1 hb
Children in Charge 9

Children in Exile
Therapeutic Work in the Community and the Clinic with Child Survivors of
Political Violence and War
Edited by Sheila Melzak
ISBN 1 85302 585 2

Psychology and Social Care
Edited by David Messer and Fiona Jones
ISBN 1 85302 762 6

Human Resilience

A Fifty Year Quest

Ann Clarke
and Alan Clarke

Jessica Kingsley Publishers
London and New York

First published in the United Kingdom in 2003
by Jessica Kingsley Publishers Ltd
116 Pentonville Road
London N1 9JB, England
and
29 West 35th Street, 10th floor,
New York, NY 10001-2299, USA
www.jkp.com

Copyright © Ann Clarke and Alan Clarke 2003

Library of Congress Cataloging in Publication Data
Clarke, Ann M. (Ann Margaret)
    Human resilience : a fifty year quest / Ann Clarke and Alan Clarke.
        p.cm.
    Includes bibliographical references.
    ISBN 1-84310-138-6 (alk paper) -- ISBN 1-84310-139-4 (pbk : alk paper)
    1. Child development. 2. Resilience (personality trait) in children. 3. Developmental psychology. 4. Children with mental disabilities. 5. Nature and nurture. I. Clarke, A. D. B. (Alen Douglas Benson) II. Title.

RJ131.C555 2003
155.4'1824--dc21   2003041607

British Library Cataloguing in Publication Data
A CIP catalogue record for this book is available from the British Library

ISBN 1 84310 139 4 Paperback
ISBN 1 84310 138 6 Hardback

Printed and Bound in Great Britain by
Athenaeum Press, Gateshead, Tyne and Wear

Contents

In memory of our parents

Laura Gravely (1895–1967)
and Frederic Henry Gravely (1885–1965)

Mary Lizars Clarke (1885–1936)
and Robert Benson Clarke (1878–1949)

and of Jack Tizard (1919–1979) pioneer and friend

Personal Profile
Ann and Alan Clarke*

Barbara Tizard

A good place to start the story of their rise to international fame would be their meeting as students in 1946. It was not at all a case of love at first sight. Alan was 24, straight from army service as an officer in the Signals Corps. He had been involved in secret work concerned with the D-Day landings, was used to taking command, and was, according to both Ann and himself, arrogant, abrupt and aloof. (This is hard to credit, since his manner is now gentle, courteous and kind.) Ann was 17, very pretty, but, according to Alan, schoolgirlish and naive. (Others remember her as extraordinarily poised and self-confident.) The attribution of naivety is given some credence, though, by Ann's own comment to me that until she met Alan she had no idea that people could be agnostic; she thought that everyone belonged to some religious group. Her mother was a Danish missionary who had met her father, a Quaker, and Director of the Madras Museum, in India, where Ann grew up. She was mainly taught at home by her parents and a governess, and her father instilled in her the importance of complete honesty and of searching for the truth. It was, she says, a gloriously happy childhood.

*   This article first appeared in 2001 in the *Child Psychology and Psychiatry Review* 6, 4, pp.191–193. Reprinted from the *Child Psychology and Psychiatry Review* by permission of the author, the journal and the Association for Child Psychology and Psychiatry.

Alan was the son of a successful, well-to-do solicitor, who had fought his way up from a working-class background by determination and ferociously hard work. Alan had a very close relationship with his father, which helped him when, at 14, his mother suddenly died. What didn't help him was the training from his parents and his school, which he has never completely overcome, in not embarrassing people by showing feelings. Still, he was very happy at his High Church public school, Lancing College, doing the minimum of work to get by. His real interest from the age of 9 was geology, pursued with such passion and effect that at 15 he discovered a previously unknown fossil coral, now in the Natural History Museum. At 16 he became an agnostic and also a communist supporter, influenced like many others by the Spanish Civil War and by the left-wing views of his older sister and one of his teachers. These new beliefs did not, he says, upset either his father or his house at school, where a number of the boys (but not Alan) were pacifists. I suspect that he did not make a big issue of his opinions either then, or later in the army. Alan remained, discreetly, a member of the Communist party until 1955, Ann joining somewhat reluctantly after their marriage.

Despite rather different backgrounds, both Alan and Ann were brought up with a sense of duty, honour and obligation to those less fortunate than themselves. It transpired that both were also unusually determined, well organized, and extremely hard working. Alan, who had done the first year of a science degree before joining up, was persuaded by his brother-in-law, Monte Shapiro, to switch to psychology. Alan insisted that he should be allowed to join the second year of the honours psychology course, and, determined to get a first class degree, formed a self-support study group with another ex-serviceman, George Granger. They divided the syllabus between them, and each explained to the other the parts they had not studied. Ann, who had chosen psychology because her mother thought it would be useful to her as a teacher, persuaded the men to allow her to join their group. All three graduated with first class honours and, led by Alan, enrolled at the Institute of Psychiatry to work for PhDs under the supervision of Hans Eysenck. The Institute was then an exciting place, which left its mark on all who worked there, including the Clarkes. The Director, Aubrey Lewis, was a deeply sceptical thinker. A charismatic, rather awe-inspiring figure, he insisted on rigorous scientific methodology and constant critical analysis. The atmosphere was intensely competitive.

In 1950 Ann and Alan, then aged 21 and 28, were awarded their PhDs and, having finally fallen in love, were married. They at once set about looking for jobs where they could work together in some socially useful but also academic capacity. This was a tall order, since jobs as psychologists were in short supply, and employers, including universities, were generally unwilling to appoint a married couple to their staff. Eventually they learned that two psychologists were needed at the Manor Hospital, Epsom, an institution for those then called mental defectives. Reluctantly, since they feared the work would consist mainly of routine IQ testing, and might damage their career prospects as academics and researchers, they decided to apply, thinking that they need only stay for a year or two. In the event, they stayed for 12 years, during which time they made a major contribution to the scientific study of intellectual disability, greatly improved the lot of the inmates, and changed the status of clinical psychology.

The Manor Hospital at that time held approximately 1400 people, all compulsorily detained, the sexes rigidly separated. About 70 per cent were deemed 'mildly retarded'. Many were not intellectually retarded at all, but had been seen by the authorities as a public nuisance because of a combination of petty crime and school failure. Their family background was often one of great poverty, cruelty and neglect. Some were kept occupied in old-fashioned workshops, where brooms and the like were handmade; others worked in the hospital as gardeners and maids. It was a place without hope, where nothing new happened, and staff soon became apathetic and institutionalized themselves. To the Clarkes, this was a challenge. The National Council for Civil Liberties was currently campaigning against the compulsory detention of these patients, but the Clarkes preferred the scientific approach. After demonstrating that the initial skills of the inmates could be greatly improved by training, they set up a programme of rehabilitation in new industrial workshops, subcontracting from local industry. This enabled the 'higher grades' to move on to normal jobs in the community at normal rates of pay. They showed that even 'imbeciles', with IQs in the 30s, then thought completely untrainable, could, with appropriate training, perform fairly complex industrial tasks, which would enable them to be employed under sheltered conditions.

An unexpected and important finding was that young people of 'higher grade' who came from exceptionally unfavourable social backgrounds made much better progress than those from less deprived backgrounds. Even the unstimulating but orderly life in the hospital was an improvement on their previous environment, and allowed substantial gains in IQ and social functioning. Within three years of arriving at the hospital the Clarkes published these initial findings in an article in *The Lancet*, entitled 'How constant is the IQ?', also challenging the accepted notion of developmental constancy in the general population. This article, which was discussed in an editorial in the same issue, was a watershed in their lives, bringing them public recognition. In a later article, in 1958, they were probably the first to suggest the need to investigate why some are resilient in the face of misfortune, others are vulnerable.

As their fame spread they acquired more staff, and formed links with the Institute of Psychiatry. Psychologists and PhD students came to work with them, a film was made of their work, and foreign visitors poured in. One psychologist who spent a few months there told me of the excitement the Clarkes' enthusiasm generated: 'There was a feeling that they were totally committed, and were going to make the world a better place.' Their work amounted to a de-medicalization of mental deficiency, a demonstration that the patients' problems were primarily in dealing with their lives, and in learning, and were thus the province of psychologists. They took this message outside the hospital through their research-based textbook, *Mental Deficiency: The Changing Outlook*, which was to run into four editions. In 1960 Alan was one of the three organizers of the first international, multidisciplinary conference on mental retardation. This led to the formation of the International Association for the Scientific Study of Mental Deficiency (IASSMD), of which Alan became successively Secretary, President and Honorary Life President.

None of this satisfied Alan's academic ambitions. When he was 30 he had decided that he wanted to become a professor by the time he was 40, and in 1962, aged 40, he successfully applied for a Chair in psychology in Hull. It was the first time a psychologist had ever been appointed to a University Chair of psychology from a clinical post in an institution, let alone one for the mentally retarded. In 1966 he became Dean of the Faculty of Science, and from 1968–71 he was Pro-Vice-Chancellor at Hull. Further honours followed: the Presidency of the British Psychological Society, an honorary Doctorate of Science, an Honorary Fellowship of the Royal College of Psychiatrists, a CBE. But the Clarkes did not abandon their concern with intellectual disability. Alan, for example, was Chairman of the Training Council for Teachers of the Mentally Handicapped from 1969–74, and they continued to bring out new editions of their famous textbook. In 1982 both received the Distinguished Achievement Award for Scientific Literature from the IASSMD.

Ever since their first discovery of IQ changes in adult life the Clarkes had been searching for further evidence that the whole of the life path provides potential for change. This view ran counter to received opinion from Plato onwards, with both ethologists and psychoanalysts currently stressing the critical role of the earliest years. John Bowlby, for example, was then claiming that maternal deprivation in the first three years of life 'may entirely cripple the capacity to make relationships with other people' (Bowlby 1951). But the Clarkes, though appearing in most ways to be a conventional middle-class couple, have in their work advanced quite subversive notions, which they have held firmly, with total conviction, against widespread opposition. (See the Burt scandal, below). There are some who feel that, as scientists, their convictions should not be quite so strongly held, but the Clarkes would argue that they always base themselves on extensive evidence, after considering counter-evidence.

By 1975 they decided they had found enough evidence to make a sustained case that there is no known adversity from which at least some children have not recovered if moved to a better environment, and that a child's future is not shaped once and for all by events in the early years. The received opinion to the contrary, they argued, derives from the fact that early effects, whether good or bad, tend to be reinforced for a number of reasons, including continuity in the environment. Thus a chain of good or bad effects is created. The book that resulted, *Early Experience: Myth and Evidence*, made an immediate impact, eventually modifying received opinion among psychologists, although the myth is still in common currency. Last year the Clarkes, then aged 78 and 71, updated their evidence and somewhat qualified their position in a new book, *Early Experience and the Life Path*.

Women reading this profile may have noticed that Alan's name has been mentioned more often than Ann's. This is because Alan has always been, so to say, the public face of the Clarkes: initially, perhaps, because of his seven years' seniority; partly, Ann says, because she did not like public life. So it was Alan who gave public lectures, spoke at conferences and served on committees, thus collecting many of the honours. No one who knows Ann, however, would doubt her academic brilliance. People have often speculated on the relative contribution of Ann and Alan to their work. They themselves say that everything was always discussed between them, and that one or other might take the lead in writing, according to circumstances. Work spilled over into family life, but (sceptics may be incredulous) they insist that although they might argue, they never quarrelled. Very unusually for her generation, despite having two children Ann always worked full-time and for long hours, except for the year when her first son was born, and their first year in Hull. A superb organizer, with the help of a Danish au pair – for a time, two au pairs – her house was always immaculate, her meals delicious. After moving to Hull, although much of their writing continued to be together, Ann held separate research grants and in 1972 moved to the Educational Studies Department, where in 1985 she was appointed to a personal Chair – the first time that Hull University had given this award to a woman.

It was Ann who, with a colleague, in 1974 first became puzzled by, and then suspicious of, Cyril Burt's research. Alan was soon involved. At first, they thought Burt had merely cut corners in an unacceptable way in order to support his belief in the major role of heritability in determining intelligence. After lengthy and detailed investigations they concluded that he had invented both his IQ data and the correlations supposedly derived from them, probably from the start of his career. The resulting scandal made headlines both here and in the USA, though a somewhat esoteric knowledge of statistics is required to follow the arguments. The Clarkes have continued to hold to their position strongly, in the face of considerable opposition and sometimes vicious personal attacks. It has been suggested that their motivation was political, or driven by their belief in the power of environmental influences. In fact, the Clarkes' political views had for many years been middle of the road, and their position on the heritability of the IQ is not too dissimilar to Burt's. What motivated them was the affront to their deeply held moral principles of discovering that an eminent psychologist should have departed, they believed, so far from standards of scientific integrity.

In 1984 Hull University was on the verge of bankruptcy and needed to shed a large number of staff. Characteristically, Alan not only volunteered to retire, but continued to do his full teaching load, unpaid, for seven years. Ann retired a few years after Alan. In 1992 they moved to Barnet to be near their elder son's family, and to help care for their beloved grandchildren. They have continued to write together and, in Alan's case, until recently to teach in the University of Hertfordshire and to serve on committees. This extraordinarily close and successful partnership in work and marriage has lasted over 50 years and is still going strong.

References

Bowlby, J. (1951) *Maternal Care and Mental Health*. Geneva World Health Organization.

Clarke, A. and Clarke, A.M. (1953) 'How Constant is the I.Q.?' *The Lancet*, 877–884.

Clarke, A.M. and Clarke, A.D.B. (eds) (1958, 1965, 1974) *Mental Deficiency: The Changing Outlook*. (4th edn with J.M. Berg [1985].) London: Methuen. New York: The Free Press.

Clarke, A.M. and Clarke, A.D.B. (2000) *Early Experience and the Life Path*. Lodnon: Jessica Kingsley Publishers.

Preface

Researchers have the possibility of two main strategies. First, they may follow earlier work, developing it further. Second, if lucky, an original observation may suggest a line of enquiry not previously encountered. We have been fortunate in pursuing both strategies.

More specifically, our own research aims, evolving over time, started with 1. studies showing that resilience was measurable and important. 2. Analysing its precursors and consequences. 3. Determining the extent to which our findings with an unusual population generalized widely. 4. Moving on, it was clearly necessary to study the nature–nurture problem, and in turn 5. to examine the effects of formal intervention programmes. These had received a boost in the early 1960s and onwards during a period of uncritical environmentalism. It also became obvious 6. that there is a wide range of individual differences both in the biosocial hazards in development and the individual responsiveness to these influences, whether benign or malevolent. 7. We also became interested in developing critical reviews of broad areas, and lastly, 8. in studying human development it seemed that there were a number of simplistic ideas which needed elucidation because they were used almost as purblind slogans. We refer to notions such as 'maternal deprivation', 'critical periods', 'regression to the mean' or 'sleeper effects'. These latter were spin-offs from our major studies.

We have selected 18 chapters or articles for reprinting in this book, these being a small percentage of our total output over the last 50 years. The criteria for inclusion have been that each must have some continuing relevance or historical interest, and that some major theme should connect them. They reflect, therefore, our interest in resilience and in the absolute and relative changes in individual development. These may be 'natural' or accelerated by some form of intervention. We have added three entirely new chapters.

The eagle-eyed reader will notice, here and there, repetitions of material from earlier publications. We make no apologies in drawing attention to this, for different aspects of the general theme have common elements. An alternative would have been to truncate the material, but this would have robbed the particular chapter of its internal logic.

Although the possibility of this book has been at the back of our minds for several years, it was the specific suggestion of Professor Barbara Tizard that gave it renewed impetus. We are also grateful to Jessica Kingsley for her continuing interest in our work over the last decade, to our current editor, Amy Lankester-Owen and to our Development Editor, Jane McGill, for their enthusiastic support and advice.

October 2002
Ann Clarke and Alan Clarke

Acknowledgements

We are very grateful to the following journals or publishers for permission to reprint articles or chapters in this book. Full details of journal dates, volume and page numbers of each will be found in the facsimiles or commentaries.

Academic Press, *British Journal of Psychology, British Journal of Psychiatry, Bulletin of the British Psychological Society, Child Psychology and Psychiatry Review,* Elsevier Science, *Intelligence* and Professor D.K. Detterman, *International Society for the Study of Behavioural Development* and Professor R.K. Silbereisen, Jessica Kingsley Publishers, *Journal of Child Psychology and Psychiatry, Journal of Experimental Child Psychology, The Lancet,* Psychology Press, Routledge (Methuen), Royal College of Psychiatrists, Taylor and Francis, and University Press of New England.

We are most grateful to the Earl and Countess of Harewood for their generosity in allowing us to use a picture of Jacob Epstein's 'Adam' on the front cover of this book.

CHAPTER 1

Genesis

This book tells the story of a voyage of discovery, starting half a century ago. In January 1951, we were appointed to reopen a psychology department, recently abandoned by three psychologists, at the Manor Hospital, Epsom. This catered for about 1400 'mental defectives', of whom three-quarters were 'high grade'. At that time all were held legally under the 1913 Mental Deficiency Act (repealed in 1959 and replaced by the Mental Health Act). The 1913 Act had two requirements; first, the individual had to be shown as suffering from 'arrested or incomplete development of mind, existing before the age of eighteen years'. Second, it was necessary to prove that the child or adult was 'subject to be dealt with'; the criteria for the latter were wide, but in the main related to social problems which had arisen or which were predicted to occur (e.g. moral danger). The young people who were incarcerated at that time would now no longer be placed in such facilities, which have mostly been closed down.

At this time the role of psychologists in the clinical field was extremely limited. They were seen as psychological testers who would save the psychiatrists time with IQ tests, estimates of brain damage or of personality disorders. There was no national salary scale for them in the NHS; they were just technicians. In setting up rehabilitation schemes for young men and women, we were soon to alter that situation. However, we had been attracted to this apparently unpromising field solely because there were no other jobs available. We expected to remain for a couple of years and then, like our predecessors, move on to something more exciting.

The general view of human development at that time was represented by the constancy model. This maintained that, either through the effects of genetics, or by the predeterministic role of early experience, people did not alter with respect to their age group. All this was underpinned by tradition, by psychoanalysis and by early behaviourism. Thus prediction of individual development was straightforward and simple; the child was father to the man in every sense. In the field in which we now found ourselves the phrase 'once a defective, always a defective' prevailed and thus reflected the constancy model.

A word now about those of 'high grade', the majority in the hospital. Mostly adolescents and young adults, they were largely drawn from conditions of adversity or severe adversity. Although traditionally IQ 70, or thereabouts, was considered to be the upper limit for such patients, in fact half were functioning above this figure, with many in the 1970s, 1980s and even 1990s. Nowhere in the 1913 Act was intelligence mentioned and those who wished to defend this situation emphasized that 'arrested and incomplete development of mind' was a wider concept than intelligence alone. Thus social problem cases who posed an existing or predicted concern found themselves at the end of the road, certified as mentally deficient. In the main they were illiterate or semi-literate, unstable and unmotivated, except to achieve, usually after many years, discharge from care. Work schemes outside the hospital involved poorly paid kitchen work for men, while the women were sent into domestic service. The risk of exploitation was great, and the so-called social workers were ex-nurses, male and female.

It seemed to us to be urgent that proper habilitation schemes should be set up, and following the early work of Tizard and O'Connor we initiated industrial units in which subcontract work was sought so that industrial skills and work discipline comprised the programmes. We did not start these units as a research study, but as a service. Nevertheless, it was clear that the time needed to achieve discharge from care was relatively rapid (around four years) compared with the lengthy process which had been usual in the past. Programmes of literacy were initiated and every attempt made to assist the individual in his or her factory job. So, over the years, we noted that much could be done for seemingly unpromising material.

Before this work on habilitation had begun we were required to assess most of the patients in the hospital, a long and tedious task lasting about a year. Our first shock was to discover that a number of adolescents and young adults had shown marked increases in IQ, and later in social adaptation, over a few years. We set out to discover how often this happened and why. We found that these changes were typical for those from the very worst backgrounds of cruelty and neglect. The first reprinted article in this book, 'How constant is the IQ?', outlined our initial findings and was accompanied by a very positive editorial in *The Lancet*. This article began to answer our questions and also raised the general issue of IQ changes, which until then had neither been recorded nor addressed in this country. Trawling through American literature from the 1930s and 1940s, we found a lot of relevant material in the early long-term studies of individuals. Thus we were able to place our results in a wider context. Our article caused something of a storm, so wedded were people to the constancy model (see, for example, Burt's patronising critique, Chapter 2).

Two points stand out from this initial work. First, questions about this unusual population could be answered, giving a different picture than the traditional one. Second, such studies could raise more general issues of equal concern. These twin outcomes were again and again apparent during succeeding decades.

We had entered the field of clinical psychology with the hope that such work would be socially useful and indeed found it so to be. Thus we remained in it for 12 years, rather than the two originally envisaged. Indeed, the issues that our early studies raised have provided a focus for part of our lives' work.

We have selected some 18 publications for reproduction out of a very much larger number, to illustrate a major aspect of what is now termed life-span developmental psychology. Three entirely new chapters have been added. We stress the present, practical relevance of research in this field. The book is divided into five parts, and here we will merely comment very briefly on each.

Some of those who know our work may be surprised that we are not including here a section on learning disabilities, especially since our early work in this field proved to be so fruitful in stimulating our own thinking. But its separate inclusion would have made this book unwieldy and detracted from its broader theme. In any event Chapters 2, 3 and 17 concern the mildly retarded and the more severe cases are touched upon in Chapter 16, and in the second part of Chapter 18 (the 42nd Maudsley Lecture).

Part I contains a number of articles on a fundamental problem which our earliest findings suggested. To what extent do people remain constant in their development in relation to their age peers? In other words, from earlier measures is individual development predictable? We find that for normal individuals reared under humane circumstances, there is a fair amount of change in relative position, but the case must not be overstated; most remain within fairly wide bands. Thus the bright child may remain equally bright, or somewhat brighter, or somewhat less bright. So, too, with the dull child there is a range of possibilities. And in personality the shy child may remain equally shy, or less so or more so. In abnormal early development, however, there is a greater constancy in some conditions. For those reared under adversity the prospects are potentially very different, if rescued and placed in a markedly better situation. Then a break in the otherwise expected life path is likely to occur.

These studies all underline the immense complexity of the interacting influences which impinge upon the individual's own characteristics. There is, indeed, for some, a principle of developmental uncertainty.

In **Part II** we look at a number of developmental research problems, first at some catch-phrases which seem to explain something but which are essentially descriptive. It is possible to unravel the behavioural implications behind these often used terms. Second, we outline common problems and solutions.

Part III includes articles with a bearing on the nature–nurture interactions, including an examination of the ways in which cognitive structures are built up in early life. The interactions, genetic and environmental, in IQ as well as the problem of parent–child resemblances are considered. In this latter case, the 'suspiciously perfect' regression results arose in the fraudulent work of Cyril Burt. In this case, he got the right results from the wrong model. Another article suggests that the claims for the long-term effects of early intervention lack the support their authors suggest, unless a continuing intervention arises.

Part IV includes articles challenging the notion that early experiences predestine the child's future. From Plato onwards, and endorsed by early psychologists and by John Bowlby's early work, there was a failure to record what had happened to the child, whether good, bad or indifferent, after the early situation. Among other things, this led to an underestimation of what could be done for early damaged children[1]. Finally we consider possible modifications to our theme.

Part V summarizes some main findings, adding an overview of factors promoting resilience, as well as personal and contextual influences preventing its expression. Here we must offer a disclaimer. This book, by its very nature, does not aim to review all the major studies of resilience, a research area increasingly recognized as important. However, we do look at the recent work of Sir Michael Rutter and his team in Chapter 20, which strikes us as of the greatest importance in following children who have experienced the most extreme forms of global privation.

Each reprinted article in this book is preceded by a brief commentary concerning the findings, the context in which they were written and their continuing relevance. We track the emergence of increasing knowledge of the broader questions about human development and the individual life course.

By some 45 years ago, we had become persuaded that our early findings (see Chapter 2) could be generalized to other deprived persons, implicitly demanding the initiation of a large area of research. Thus we began to draw attention 'to the whole problem of human resilience' (Chapter 17). We asked about differences in 'human susceptibility to early psychological damage and resilience thereafter, and what is their nature? Why is it that some children are

utterly overwhelmed by adverse conditions while others are apparently stimulated by them? We have no real estimate of the proportion which escapes
relatively unscathed, simply because we tend only to study problem cases, but
it may well be larger than we think' (p.58). Our then ignorance about the
nature of human resilience, the importance of its general role, its antecedents,
its consequences and constraints, has given way over the years, through the
work of many other researchers, to a corpus of information, added to from time
to time, which has utterly transformed this area. We can confidently expect
further discoveries. Finally, how should this concept be defined?

Interest in resilience has increased markedly since the 1950s, and a number of definitions of this process now exist. Moen and Erickson (1995) have a
brief definition. 'Resilience', they write, 'can be defined as the capacity to cope
with life's setbacks and challenges' (p.170), and they examine the developmental course of resilience, and whether current adult experiences moderate
the effects of early experience and how such adult experiences are themselves
shaped by earlier experiences. They suggest that the seeds of early socialization may shift in importance with adults' own changing roles, responsibilities
and attainments (p.175).

Rutter (1999) defines the term as one 'used to describe relative resistance
to psychosocial risk experiences'. He goes on to point to the enormous variation in children's responses to such experiences. Multiple risk and protective
factors are involved. Children vary in their vulnerability as a result of both
genetic and environmental influences. Chain reactions influence the extent to
which the effects of adversity persist over time, and new experiences opening
up new opportunities can provide beneficial turning points (p.119).

An often quoted suggestion by Fonagy *et al.* (1994) that 'resilience is *normal* development under difficult circumstances' (p.223) is unsatisfactory.
Although resilience can be exhibited under such circumstances, development
may still not be normal; it may have shifted but still be retarded. Further, more
often it occurs *after* difficult circumstances. Hence a more accurate definition
would indicate that 'resilience is apparent when, against common expectancies, children maintain development within, or accelerate markedly after,
adverse situations. What is clear is that both personal inborn characteristics
and the effects of the social context interact to promote – or diminish – resilience' (Clarke and Clarke 2001) This, then, is the definition which most
closely describes the findings we have reviewed and is thus our preference.

References

Clarke, A.M. and Clarke, A.D.B. (2001) 'Early adversity and adoptive solutions.' *Adoption and Fostering 25*, 24–32.

Fonagy, P., Steele, M., Higgitt, A. and Target, M. (1994) 'The Emanuel Miller Memorial Lecture, 1992: The theory and practice of resilience.' *Journal of Child Psychology and Psychiatry 35*, 231–257.

Moen, P. and Erickson, M.A. (1995) 'Linked lives: A transgenerational approach to resilience.' In P. Moen, G.H. Elder and K. Luscher (eds) *Examining Lives in Context.* Washington DC: APA.

Rutter, M. (1999) 'Resilience concepts and findings: Implications for family therapy.' *Journal of Family Therapy 21* 119–144.

Note

1   Months after the present volume had been delivered to the publisher, we were sent J.T. Bruer's very positive and learned reviews of out last book (2000), published in Contemporary Psychology (2000). Intrigued, we traced his work and, in particular, his *The Myth of the First Years*, published in New York by The Free Press in 1989. In it, he indicates, as we have, the enviromental component of the 'myth', but argues in addition that misinterpretations of early neuro-anatomical development are a further source of error in concerning the supposed significance of the first few years.

PART I

Constancy and Change in Human Development

CHAPTER 2

How Constant is the IQ?

Commentary

In the 1950s, the 'mental deficiency' services in England and Wales were the responsibility of the Ministry of Health under the umbrella of the 1913 Mental Deficiency Act. It was appropriate, therefore, to offer our first research paper to the prestigious medical journal, *The Lancet*. We wanted to indicate to doctors who relied on often poorly administered intelligence tests that even a proper IQ assessment was subject to 'error' because sometimes developmental changes occurred between one occasion and a later one. Further, it had been necessary to place our findings in a wider context which was revealed when we discovered the then unquoted early American longitudinal studies of IQ, especially the results of the Harvard Growth Study. These all suggested that in normal populations, IQ change over time was fairly common. Little did we then know that our initial results, which had sought us rather than vice versa, would dictate both directly and indirectly much of our lives' research.

These twin results – our preliminary study and its wider context – caused something of a storm because the controversy over the 11-plus educational selection was at its height. This selection involved an intelligence test and scholastic measures, so that those above the borderline found themselves in academic grammar schools, with the remainder, those below the borderline, being allocated to the less ambitious 'secondary modern' schools. In effect both types of schools trained their pupils to fulfil the selectional prediction and thus justify selection. It was a long time before it was recognized that, particularly around the borderline, errors would occur – that is, some who achieved grammar-school status would fail to succeed while others from the secondary modern schools would later have been successful had they had the opportunity.

We now come to Sir Cyril Burt (see also Chapter 15). As graduate students we had been taken on by Eysenck who was to act as our supervisor. We were

27

then not to know of Burt's enmity to Eysenck, Sir Aubrey Lewis and the Maudsley Hospital. He had tried to prevent the initiation of a Maudsley Psychology Department and Eysenck himself was prevented from having formal university-recognized teaching status. After some months of PhD research it dawned on us that we had heard nothing from the University of London. Eysenck should on our behalf have tried to regularize the situation. Instead, he told us to write to Burt and ask him to deal with the matter. So Burt took us on, and only later did we appreciate that he regarded us as Trojan horses in Eysenck's stable. By then we had been informed of Burt's devious and unethical ways, so his letter attacking our article came as no great surprise. We print below his letter to *The Lancet* together with our reply. A few weeks later another contributor deplored Burt's smear about these 'young investigators', indicating that age should be irrelevant to scientific credibility. Those who studied the correspondence felt that Burt had not come out of it well, and a personal letter from him suggested that the discussion need not be taken further!

Letter to *The Lancet* from Sir Cyril Burt and a letter in reply

Vagaries of Intelligence*

SIR, – The pronouncements on the constancy of the IQ in your issue of Oct 24 have been widely quoted in the press, and I should therefore be grateful if I might remove one or two misconceptions.

The criticisms of the IQ brought forward by the three young investigators whom you mainly quote are by no means as new as they suppose. Dr and Mrs Clarke declare that 'the fact of IQ variability can no longer be disputed'. But who has ever disputed it? In criticizing previous views they refer, among other publications, to an LCC report of my own, and add: 'these investigators…rarely if ever submit their hypotheses to experimental proof'. The report was first published, not in 1947, but in 1921. Results were then given for cases retested annually for five years, and I emphasized that the constancy of IQ 'is but imperfectly realized'. In later reports data were given for cases followed up for 25 or 30 years. The 'experimental proof' of Dr and Mrs Clarke covers an average period of two years three months only.

In an earlier report (1917) I insisted that 'for scientific work the employment of the standard deviation (or its equivalent – the percentile) seems indisputably the best device', and merely proposed a quotient or ratio because it could

---

be rapidly calculated and seemed more intelligible to magistrates and medical officers. 'The quotient,' it was explained, 'assumes as a first approximation that the changes in mean mental age and in the standard deviation are rectilinear, whereas in fact they are curvilinear.' This simplification is the main (but not the only) cause of the inconstancy. Your contributors seem to be wholly unaware that psychologists, not only demonstrated the existence and amount of error to be expected, but showed how it could largely be corrected by adopting a more complex formula. This entails a statistical analysis of a rather elaborate type: the most recent suggestions will be found in an article by Dr Fraser Roberts,[1] based on tests applied at Stoke Park Colony and the Royal Eastern Counties Institution. Every psychologist will therefore welcome what you say in your leader on the need for 'publicizing the value of statistical research'.

One important cause of variation is not mentioned by your contributors – the fact that so many of those who employ (and criticize) intelligence tests have never been trained in their administration and interpretation. Dr Tizard states that an IQ of less than 70 is very widely accepted as evidence of mental subnormality, sometimes on the basis of a single test. Presumably he is referring to the standard proposed for certifying special-school cases in the days when such cases had to be certified. Possibly some medical officers have relied on a single test. But no trained psychologist relies on tests alone – much less on a single test – in any doubtful case.

In your leading article you seem to confuse three different concepts that psychologists have carefully distinguished: first, the innate general cognitive factor (γ); second, the estimates obtained for such factor measurements (g); third, the vague qualities called 'intelligence' in everyday speech. To prove that the last can be altered by education, or that the second provides only rough and fallible assessments, is not to demonstrate that the first – an entirely abstract and hypothetical component – is subject to variability. The psychologist, like the physicist, has adopted a popular word to avoid pedantic symbols and circumlocutions; but, in criticizing what he says about 'intelligence' as he has defined it, arguments based on some other interpretation seem (if I may say so) merely to confuse the issue.

Cyril Burt
University College
London WC1

Vagaries of Intelligence*

SIR, – We note that Sir Cyril Burt, in his letter of Nov 7, does not disagree with the main general conclusion of our article. He confines himself to removing 'one or two misconceptions', some of which seem (if we may say so) to be of his own creation.

He states that the criticisms we made of the IQ are by no means new, and asks who has ever disputed IQ variability. Surely he must be aware that there is a widespread belief, both in uninformed and informed circles, that the IQ, as currently used, is virtually constant; and this belief is supported by many reputable textbooks.

He makes the important statement that the formula for calculating the IQ, suggested by himself and others, is based on a fallacy – i.e., that the changes in mean mental age and in the standard deviation are rectilinear, whereas in fact they are curvilinear. He then goes on to say that this formula is the main cause of IQ inconstancy, but that it can largely be corrected by 'adopting a more complex formula'. He does not mention such findings as those of the Harvard Growth Study, the results of which are not expressed in terms of the usual IQ formula, but as observed means and observed distributions. Does he seriously suggest that the changes in intellectual status demonstrated by Dearborn and Rothney, or even in our own small experiment, are mainly statistical artifacts? In the latter study it was quite clear that those who had made the larger IQ increments could deal more effectively with reality, as sampled by their greater success in solving objective and standardized test problems. In addition, of course, the Wechsler test overcomes the difficulties implicit in the use of the conventional IQ formula, as is indicated in Dr Wechsler's book on the subject.

Sir Cyril says that we criticize previous views, including his own, and he quotes us as saying: 'These investigators…rarely, if ever, submit their hypotheses to experimental proof.' He has omitted the key phrase of the sentence, which reads: 'These investigators, *however, while offering hypothetical explanations for the changes in intellectual level which they demonstrate*, rarely, if ever, submit their hypotheses to experimental proof.' He thus implies that we criticized himself and others for not proving IQ inconstancy; on the contrary, we quoted his experiment as supporting our thesis. Our only criticism, as the full quotation clearly indicates, is that the investigators, having demonstrated the fact of IQ variability, failed to take their work a stage further by verifying the

---

*   Reprinted from *The Lancet*, 21 November 1953, p.1096

often important hypotheses which they advanced to explain it. (For example, 'some happy change in home conditions seemed responsible' for some IQ increments, was one of Sir Cyril's own hypotheses.)

Sir Cyril observes that one reason for IQ inconstancy is that so many who employ intelligence tests 'have never been trained in their administration and interpretation'. This is undoubtedly (and very unfortunately) a feature of some administrative and clinical practice; our article, however, confined discussion to researches carried out by well-established psychologists. He also points out that no trained psychologist 'relies on tests alone – much less on a single test – in any doubtful case'. Unfortunately, however, decisions about an individual's future are sometimes made (whether the psychologist likes it or not) by the authorities concerned, on the basis of a single test score, which may have been assessed by someone with the lack of training which Sir Cyril properly deplores, and under conditions which may be by no means ideal.

In brief, it is not infrequently observed that bright children may in time show less promise than had been hoped, or that dull children may sometimes blossom to a level which surprises those who knew them. Individuals are not static, but capable of change, within limits which are as yet imperfectly understood. We are sure that Sir Cyril will agree that we need to identify the factors which influence such changes, in order to play a more positive role than that of passive spectators who merely record them, as and when they occur.

A.D.B. Clarke
A.M. Clarke
Manor Hospital
Epsom, Surrey

How Constant is the IQ?[*]

A.D.B. Clarke and A.Clarke

Since the early years of this century intelligence tests have been used as measures of general intellectual capacity, and an immense body of published work has grown up around the subject. Nowadays the intelligence quotient (IQ) is widely employed in educational, selection and clinical procedures, and there is no doubt that intelligence tests provide a method more valid than subjective or clinical judgement in assessing a person's intellectual level. Not only is the IQ

[*]   This article first appeared in *The Lancet*, 1953, ii, p.877–880.

used as an estimate of a person's present intellectual status, but the additional assumption has developed that this remains sufficiently constant during the life of the individual for fairly accurate predictions to be made about his future ability. In other words, a person's intelligence at, for example, the age of 5, would be the same, relative to others of his age group, at later ages; thus the young genius would always be a genius, the average child would always be average, and the defective would remain defective. Such are the implications of a belief in a constant IQ, a belief which within broad limits seems to be in accord with common observation. Nevertheless, how broad such limits may be is of great importance at present, when the IQ is so widely used in selection (e.g., of schoolchildren at the age of 11); and in this paper we consider this point.

Mental growth in normal people

In the United States there have been many studies of IQ constancy which have as yet received little publicity in this country. It is not our aim to provide a comprehensive bibliography, but the few references given will enable the interested reader to trace several hundred researches bearing on the problem.

Nemzek (1933) and Thorndike (1940) summarize in all 359 studies carried out before 1940; and such researches show consistently that: (a) the predictive value of the IQ (as measured by test–retest correlation) decreases as the interval between the tests lengthens; and, as a corollary, (b) although the group or population average may not alter greatly, there will be considerable change of status of some individuals within that group (subsequent retests showing that to varying extents some subjects increase in IQ, some decrease, and some remain constant); and (c) mental tests given to children during the preschool years have usually little predictive value, and that assessments during infancy have no relationship with later status (except of course in such clear-cut clinical entities as mongolism, microcephaly, and the like).

To illustrate the first two conclusions, the practical implications of commonly observed test–retest correlations may be considered. Reviews by Nemzek (1933), Thorndike (1933) and Thorndike (1940) have shown that retest correlations are rarely as high as 0.95, and that on *immediate* retest the most probable value is 0.9.

Shapiro (1951) demonstrates the implications of this second finding as follows:

> Let us assume that we have a test with a test–retest correlation of 0.9 and a standard deviation of 16. These data mean that, out of every three children obtaining an average score of 100, one would obtain a retest score above 107

or below 93. On the basis of the same data, out of every 10 children obtaining an average score on the first test, one child would obtain a score above 112 or below 88 on the second test. (These illustrations assume that no learning has taken place.)

IQ changes may, of course, occur for a number of reasons: errors of measurement as well as genuine alterations in the rate of intellectual growth may account jointly or separately for lack of perfect reliability.

Over time intervals of several years, test–retest correlations are usually much lower than 0.9. Honzik *et al.* (1948) found a retest correlation of about 0.6 for a time interval of 12 years, after following up a representative sample of urban children from infancy to the age of 18 years.

They tested over 150 children at the ages of 6 and 18, and found that the IQs of 58 per cent changed 15 or more points; the IQs of 35 per cent changed 20 or more points; and the IQs of 9 per cent changed 30 or more points. In only 15 per cent of cases was the change 9 points or less. Individual IQ constancy over this period was thus the exception rather than the rule. The group averages, on the other hand, showed a maximum shift in IQ, over this period, of only 5 points. The maximum IQ change for any individual was 50 points. Similarly, Hilden (1949), who is in process of studying the intellectual growth of 100 children, has reported findings on 30 of those examined from early childhood to late adolescence. In this small sample, too, individual variability in IQ was often found.

Dearborn and Rothney (1941) have reported findings from the important Harvard Growth Study in which both mental and physical development in children were investigated over many years; their book gives results from many different researches on several hundred children. They conclude that

> prediction of growth at various ages is extremely hazardous, but is particularly so during the period of adolescence...marked variability in individual growth curves appear throughout the course of the growth period... The principle of individual variability goes right to the root of such problems as constancy of the IQ...We have established the fact that variability rather than consistency of growth is the rule, that prediction except for average of groups is extremely hazardous...

To illustrate conclusion (*c*), namely that mental tests in the preschool years have little predictive value, Honzik *et al.* (1948) can again be cited.

Tests at 21 months correlate less than 0.1 with the results at the age of 18 years. Similarly, Bayley (1940) found that mental scores derived from tests at 7, 8 and 9 months, while correlating highly with scores a few months later, had a relationship in the region of zero with all measurements after the age of 30 months. Indeed, in at least three researches quoted by Jones (1946), small negative correlations were found between intelligence scores in infancy and test scores in later life. As age increases, however, so does the correlation with later intellectual status. Thus, Bayley (1949) found that for 27 children tested from infancy onwards, the correlations with the test score at the age of 18 years became positive from the age of 2, and by the age of 4 had become 0.52.

From the wealth of available data it is clear that, in the general population, the concept of a rigidly constant IQ is contradicted by the facts; IQ constancy over long periods of time during the years of mental growth is the exception rather than the rule. Moreover, this conclusion is based on the findings of researches in which individual rather than group tests were used for the most part; all that has been said applies with even greater force to group-tests (widely used for selection), which are in general less satisfactory than individual intelligence tests.

Intellectual changes in mental defectives

The general thesis advanced above can be further illustrated by some work we have done recently with mental defectives. This has led us to ask: 'How permanent is intellectual subnormality? Is "once a defective, always a defective" true?'

In the past there have been several studies, almost exclusively of feeble-minded, non-organic defectives, in which IQ changes – often large – have been reported. Such writers as Burt (1947), McKay (1942), Roberts (1945), Spaulding (1946), Sarason (1949), and Guertin (1949) have described IQ increments, some as large as 43 points. These investigators, however, while offering various hypothetical explanations for the changes in intellectual level which they demonstrate, rarely, if ever, submit their hypotheses to experimental proof. The same criticism can be applied to the studies of normals already quoted.

We have retested with the Wechsler test (form I) over 100 adolescent and adult certified defectives.[2] The population from which they were drawn has already been described by MacMahon (1952). As a result of routine intelligence-testing we observed that some patients who had been examined a year or more before with the same test showed large IQ increments; and we planned a research to elucidate these IQ changes, and to determine the frequency of their occurrence.

The main experiment entailed the retesting of a group of 59 subjects after an average of 27 months had elapsed since the original test; 27 of these patients increased their scores by 8 points or more, 17 by 10 points or more, and seven by 15 points or more, the maximum increment being 25 points. The remaining 32 patients showed small increases or decreases. Increments were general throughout the subtests of the Wechsler intelligence scale, and were not merely confined to a few of these. The test–retest correlation was 0.90.

In order to determine the maximal effect of test practice, errors of measurement, and underestimation at the time of the first test (since many certified feeble-minded patients are emotionally unstable their intelligence may occasionally be underestimated when they are tested), a control group of 29 mentally subnormal subjects, mostly new admissions to the Manor Hospital, was matched with the main group for initial IQ and age, and was retested after a short time interval (average three months).

On retest these subjects showed an average increase of 4 points, the majority showing changes between plus and minus 4 points; only six had increments of 8 points or more, and only one of these had an increment of over 10 points (13 points). The distribution of these changes may be seen in Table 2.1. The control group data, therefore, indicate that the average increment of 4 points upon retest represents the average maximal effect of test practice, errors of measurement, and initial underestimation. In terms of test–retest correlation – 0.94 – the reliability of the test is quite high on this population.

Several hypotheses were advanced to account for the increase in IQ shown by the members of the main group.

Table 2.1 Distribution of IQ changes						
Change (IQ points)	Very bad homes (25 cases)		Remainder (34 cases)		Control group (29 cases)	
	No.	%	No.	%	No.	%
−7 to 0	1	4	8	24	4	14
+1 to +7	6	24 } 100	17	50 } 100	19	65 } 100
+8 or more	18	72	9	26	6	21
+10 or more	12	48	5	15	1	3
+15 or more	7	28	0		0	
+25	1	4	0		0	

Each of these hypotheses was critically examined, but in all cases but one the evidence was such that they had to be rejected. The exception was that there was a strong relationship between very adverse early home conditions and subsequent IQ increases. Twelve clearly defined criteria of adverse home conditions were formulated – NSPCC intervention, orders appointing some-one as 'fit person' to have charge of the child, parental attitude antagonistic towards the child, home conditions very bad, home dirty and neglected, child considerably neglected, no fixed abode, irregular school attendance due to parental neglect, gross poverty, deficiency diseases, child found begging or wandering, and parents or sibs with criminal records. These were applied to the 59 case-histories under consideration, and the presence of two or more of these somewhat overlapping criteria was taken as clearly indicating very bad home circumstances. It was found that those who had been subjected to such adverse early environments were mainly those who made large IQ increases. An external investigator (Dr J. Tizard of the Medical Research Council's Unit for Research in Occupational Adaptation), who had no knowledge of either the patients or their test scores, independently analysed the case-histories; he agreed with our assessments of home conditions in 55 of the 59 cases; in the remaining four cases his rating was accepted as final. Evidence of very bad home conditions was found in 25 case-histories, while in the remaining 34 there was either no evidence of really adverse conditions, or a complete lack of data regarding early home life, or (in only six cases) clear evidence of a good home. Tables 2.1 and 2.2 show the main results of the investigation.

Table 2.2 Changes between test and retest in full scale IQ points			
—	Very bad homes (25 cases)	Remainder (34 cases)	Total group (59 cases)
Mean change	+9.7	+4.1	+6.5
Standard deviation	6.3	4.9	6.2

$t = 3.86$, significant beyond 0.1% level

IQ range at first test = 35–98   mean = 66.2   SD = 14

IQ range at retest = 49–97   mean = 72.7   SD = 13.4

Age range at retest = 14–50 years   mean = 23.5   SD = 8.1 years

(Only nine patients were aged over 30)

Period between test and retest: mean = 26.9 months   SD = 6 months

Range of IQ changes   –7 to +25 IQ points

The difference between the gains made by the 'very bad home' group and the remainder is significant beyond the 0.1 per cent level, which shows very clearly the strong association between early adverse environment and IQ increase many years later. It is consistent with this finding to suggest that the environment which is really antagonistic towards the child retards mental development for many years. Later, however, after removal from such conditions this retardation begins to fade, and IQ increments occur, often at ages when mental growth is commonly assumed to have ceased.

Retrospective validation, such as has been described, carries with it the possibility of error as a result of chance relationships in the records of those investigated. It was necessary, therefore, to ascertain whether the criteria of bad homes were equally effective in predicting IQ changes as they had been in discriminating retrospectively.

There remained at the hospital only about 20 patients who had been tested two years before and who had not already been retested for the various experiments included in the research; from these, six cases were selected whose records clearly indicated adverse home conditions, and a further five were found who had come from homes which seemed unlikely to have been very bad. Increments were predicted in the former, but not in the latter, and it was only after definite predictions had been made that retests were undertaken. The changes in IQ points for those for whom increments had been predicted were: +14, +9, +10, +10, +4, +5, average +8.7 points; the changes for those for whom increments were not predicted were: −5, −2, +7, −1, +4, average +0.6.

It will be noted that on this very small group the criteria show some predictive value; it would, of course, be desirable that this finding should be checked on a larger group, and independently, as was the retrospective validation.

The IQ changes in this investigation were largely in the upward direction, whereas in some researches already quoted the variability was equal in both directions. This, however, is probably the effect of the very adverse backgrounds of the certified feeble-minded, and it is not suggested that the factor shown to be associated with IQ changes in this research is necessarily the only one underlying changes in general. Other investigators have suggested both this factor and others in relation to the problem of IQ inconstancy. As already noted, however, these hypotheses seem never to be carried to the stage of experimental validation.

The results show clearly that intellectual retardation among such deprived people as have been studied here is not necessarily a permanent and irreversible condition. Obviously, too, the increases demonstrated over a period of two years will not represent, in most cases, the total change which the individual has already made or will make in the future. As Honzik *et al.* (1948) point out, some subjects show consistent trends in IQ changes over a long period.

Conclusions

It is evident from the work of many different investigators that, group averages apart, considerable changes in intellectual level may take place during the course of individual development; and that the question is not so much 'Is the IQ constant?' but rather 'How constant is it?' As Honzik *et al.* (1948) put it:

> Whereas the results for the groups suggest mental test stability between 6 and 18 years, the observed fluctuations in the scores of individual children indicate the need for the utmost caution in the predictive use of a single test score, or even two such scores. This finding seems to be of special importance since many plans for individual children are made by schools, juvenile courts, and mental hygiene clinics on the basis of a single mental test score.

The fact that all longitudinal studies of intellectual growth show a decline in predictive ability of the IQ with increase of time implies change in individuals. The IQ, percentile grade, or standard score must be regarded as an objective estimate of a person's present intellectual status; and it is certainly better (even for predictive purposes) than subjective judgement or unstandardized examinations. When we use the IQ for prediction, however, we must realize that errors are inevitable, and that these errors may have far-reaching and serious consequences for individuals selected by the tests for particular purposes.

The fact of IQ variability can no longer be disputed, and the evidence is rich in implications. Let us consider merely one example: it has been shown that a group of socially deprived, mentally subnormal people tend, when removed from adverse conditions, to advance towards intellectual normality. Can such relatively spontaneous changes be accelerated and improved? These and many other related problems invite the psychological and psychiatric investigator to a clear field for research.

We wish to thank Dr J.F. MacMahon, physician-superintendent of the Manor Hospital, for his help and encouragement during this research; Mr M.B. Shapiro, senior lecturer, in the psychology department of the Maudsley Hospital, for stimulating suggestions and criticisms; Dr J. Tizard for help in an essential part of the experiment; Mr A. Ehrenberg, of the statistical laboratory of the Maudsley Hospital, for useful advice; and Mr G.J.F. Singleton for the statistical computations.

Notes

1   Roberts. J.A.F. (1952) *British Journal of Statistical Psycholory 5*, 65.

2   This study has already been reported to meetings of the Mental Deficiency
Section of the Royal Medico-Psychological Association (5 November 1952)
and of the British Psychological Society (13 April 1953).

References

Bayley, N. (1940) *Yearbook of the National Society for the Study of Education.* 39, 11.

Bayley, N. (1949) *Journal of Genetic Psychology 75*, 165.

Burt, C. (1947) *Mental and Scholastic Tests.* London.

Dearborn, W.F. and Rothney, J.W.M. (1941) *Predicting the Child's Development.*
Cambridge, Mass.

Guertin, W.H. (1949) *Journal of Clinical Psychology 5*, 414.

Hilden, A.H. (1949) *Journal of Psychology 28*, 187.

Honzik, M.P., Macfarlane, J.W. and Allen, L. (1948) *Journal of Experimental
Education 17*, 309.

Jones, H.E. (1946) 'Environmental Influences on Mental Development.' In
L. Carmichael (ed) *Manual of Child Psychology.* London: Chapman and Hule.

MacMahon, J.F. (1952) *British Medical Journal ii*, 254.

McKay, B.E. (1942) *American Journal of Mental Deficience 46*, 496.

Nemzek, C.L. (1933) *Psychological Bulletin 30*, 143.

Roberts, A.D. (1945) *American Journal of Mental Deficiency 50*, 134.

Sarason, S.B. (1949) *Psychological problems in Mental Deficiency.* New York: Harper.

Shapiro, M.B. (1951) *Journal of Mental Science 97*, 748.

Spaulding, P.J. (1946) *American Journal of Mental Deficiencey 51*, 35.

Thorndikc, R.L. (1933) *Jounal of Educational Psychology 24*, 543.

Thorndike, R.L. (1940) *Psychological Bulletin 37*, 167.

CHAPTER 3

Cognitive and Social Changes
in the Feeble-minded
Three Further Studies

Commentary

As in our first study of cognitive changes in adolescent and young adult learning disabled persons, the following three reprinted here were 'clean'. That is to say that although the words 'experimenter effect' had not appeared in the literature, it was well known that researchers should not directly test their own hypotheses. Thus, as before, social histories were evaluated by a colleague, using very strict case-note criteria, who had no knowledge of previous test scores nor of present assessments. Another colleague, who was ignorant of previous test scores, nor knew the social histories, carried out the reassessments. Only then was it appropriate to bring together the two streams of information.

This study showed that over a six-year time interval the IQs had on average increased by a little over a standard deviation if the backgrounds had been very adverse, whereas those from lesser adversities had improved on average by two-thirds of a standard deviation. Social increments were reflected in differences in availability of members of each group. Many more of the original group from very bad homes had by then been discharged from care, compared with the remainder, and were thus unavailable to us.

The second study used a four-and-a-half year time interval between assessments. Here the size of the increments was smaller than for the longer interval, but the differential remained.

The third study was concerned with the graduates of our rehabilitation scheme who had been trained and placed in normal industrial employment. We had expected that, regardless of social history, background IQs would be similar in improvements for members of the two community groups. We were wrong! Thus differential improvements between these two new groups were much the same as they would have been if they had remained in hospital, rather than working in the community. Hence the increments were not an effect of their new life paths, but rather a fading of earlier unfortunate influences, the 'self-righting tendency' outlined by the geneticist, Waddington (1966).

Cognitive and Social Changes in the Feeble-minded: Three Further Studies[*]

Earlier papers have described researches showing that IQ increments in adolescent and young adult persons certified as feeble-minded occur not infrequently, cannot be explained as artifacts, and appear to be linked with early very adverse environmental experiences. The present three studies indicate that IQ increments can be large over long periods of time, are correlated with changes in social adjustment, but cannot be shown to be induced by special environmental stimulation; in the present age range and type of subject, they tend to occur in any reasonable environment. Results imply that a necessarily poor outcome cannot be predicted for children with IQs in the 50s, 60s or 70s if they also come from very adverse conditions. Test reliability, statistical regression and a review of some relevant literature are discussed; theoretical problems concerning intellectual development are presented; and attention is directed to individual differences in susceptibility to environmental damage and to the whole problem of human resilience.

Introduction

In earlier papers (Clarke and Clarke 1953, 1954b, 1955) the general problem of IQ inconstancy was considered and, specifically, the variability of the IQ among adolescents and young adults certified as feeble-minded was discussed. A two-year study indicated that IQ increments were of frequent occurrence, particularly in cases characterized by extreme deprivation in early life. In a population drawn, on the whole, from very adverse socio-economic conditions, those from the worst had made an average increment of 9.7 points, while a residual group from somewhat less unfavourable conditions made an average increase of 4.1 points. This latter was similar in amount, though not necessarily of the same nature, as the gains arising from the maximal effects of test

[*]   This article first appeared in May 1958 in the *British Journal of Psychology 49*, 2, pp.144–157.

practice and errors of underestimation in a control group retested after a short time interval. Cognitive changes in the certified feeble-minded differed from those occurring in normals in that:

1. they tended to be mainly in the direction of improvement

2. in relation to time interval between test and retest, they tended to be rather large and

3. they took place at ages when intellectual growth is commonly assumed to have ceased.

The general picture which emerged from this and other studies was that many high-grade defectives showed temporary arrest of intellectual growth, while later reverting towards (and sometimes achieving) normality.

When the earlier work (which throughout the present paper will be termed the *original research*) was completed, it was decided to plan longer-term investigations which might throw further light on the determinants and limits of these increments, and which might have further implications for our understanding of mental deficiency. Objective psychometric assessments have been carried out at this hospital since 1949, and it was considered that by 1955–6 sufficient data would be available to make such longer-term research possible. In all, three new studies are reported here.

First study

Cognitive changes

The first experiment was designed to follow-up those members of the *original research* who were still available. The original subjects had, in 1952, been allotted either to a group from very bad homes (based on the presence of two or more of 12 criteria[1] in the case-history) or to a residual group from less adverse circumstances; this rating had been carried out independently by an external investigator who knew neither the patients nor their test scores. It seemed clear that the 28 available at the end of 1955 (from an original 59) were, in the main, the less satisfactory members of the sample, since a large proportion (54%) of the remainder had by now been discharged either as being 'no longer mentally deficient within the meaning of the Act' or as being sufficiently competent socially to warrant this action or, alternatively, were on distant licence and likely to achieve discharge in the near future. Table 3.1(a) and (b) indicate that the present subjects were, both in 1949 and in 1952, on the average less intelligent than the remainder of the sample now no longer available, and this fact adds support to the belief that these were indeed the less satisfactory members

Table 3.1 Test–retest data, Wechsler, Form I,[2] over six years						
	1949, Full Scale IQ	1952, Full Scale IQ	1955, Full Scale IQ	Diff 1949–52	Diff 1952–55	Diff 1949–55
(a) Group from very bad homes						
Mean	59.6 (66.4)	70.7 (76.1)	75.8	11.1 (9.7)	5.1	16.2
SD	9.7 (14.1)	11.4 (13.4)	10.3	4.2 (6.3)	5.0	6.1
N	9 (25)	9 (25)	9	9 (25)	9	9
t (1-tail test)	—	—	—	7.929	3.059	7.969
Significant at	—	—	—	0.1%	1%	0.1%

IQ range: 1949, 47–72; 1952, 58–86; 1955, 64–91.

Age at final retest: mean 26.4   SD 5.5 years

Period between first and final test: mean 70.9 months,   SD 2.5 months

Range of IQ changes: +3 to +22 points (10 points and above: 8/9=89%; 15 points and above: 7/9=78%)

(b) Group from less adverse homes						
Mean	62.3 (66.1)	66.8 (70.1)	72.5	4.5 (4.1)	5.7	10.2
SD	13.4 (14.1)	13.0 (13.1)	13.3	4.4 (4.9)	5.1	6.6
N	19 (34)	19 (34)	19	19 (34)	19	19
t (1-tail test)	—	—	—	4.460	4.872	6.737
Significant at	—	—	—	0.1%	0.1%	0.1%

IQ range: 1949, 35–87; 1952, 40–89; 1955, 48–100.

Age at final retest: mean 27.9   SD 9.5 years

Period between first and final test: mean 74.2 months,   SD 5.3 months

Range of IQ changes: –2 to +21 IQ points (10 points and above: 10/19=53%; 15 points and above: 5/19=26%)

t (between group from very bad homes and group from less adverse homes) = 2.403 (significant above 2.5% level, 1-tail test).

of the original sample. Thus, the results of a follow-up of those remaining would be expected to give a minimal estimate of the IQ change over a period of six years for patients of this age, type and social background. Table 3.1 (a) and (b) show the test and retest data on Wechsler, Form I, for the members of the two groups. The figures in brackets indicate the relevant data for the original groups of which the present subjects formed a part.

It will be noted that the IQs of those from very bad homes present a substantially different cognitive picture in 1955 from that in 1949, having, on the average, increased by about one standard deviation. The IQs of those from less adverse home circumstances had changed by about two-thirds of a standard deviation, and it is clear that in their case the change had been slower, smaller in amount, and had been roughly equal in the two equivalent time periods, 1949–52 and 1952–5. Members of the former group, however, had shown the maximum change in the earlier part of this period, thereafter improving less rapidly. This does not conflict with the earlier hypothesis that IQ increments seemed to be the effect of a fading of 'intellectual scars' induced by bad home conditions, and occurred more as a result of *removal from* such conditions rather than of entry into relatively better ones. Those with the greater damage due to deprivation made the greater recovery (often many years later) and they made it more rapidly.

Social changes

A significant social factor is reflected by the difference between the two groups in terms of present availability; at the end of 1955 only nine of the original 25 from very bad homes were still available, whereas a larger proportion, 19 out of 34, from less adverse conditions were still under the care of the hospital. Since many of the remainder had been discharged, this adds support to the generalization that, in this type of population, the worse the social background, the better the prognosis from all points of view. Moreover, of the nine remaining from the original group from very bad homes, eight were already working in the community although still under certificate, and one was receiving industrial training prior to community placement. Only four of the 19 remaining from the original group from less adverse circumstances were in a similar position at the end of 1955.

It is unlikely that IQ increments play a major part in *causing* improved social adaptation, since the correlation between IQ and social competence at this level is not very high. These increases must therefore be regarded as one facet of a process of more or less total personality development which is also likely to be associated with the same general causation.

Second study

Cognitive changes

The second study followed up all patients of feeble-minded grade first admitted to this hospital in 1951 who were still available at the beginning of 1956. The purpose of this investigation was to find out whether, among other things, IQ changes in this population and age range were a direct function of time interval between test and retest, as is sometimes implied for normals (see Eysenck 1953). Retesting these subjects in 1955–6 gave an interval between tests of four-and-a-half years, roughly double that of the *original research*; it was thus possible to ascertain whether the average increments would also be doubled. Of an original 60 patients admitted in 1951, 32 were still available, and, as before, it seemed likely that they were the less promising members of the original sample.

The following methodology was employed. An independent investigator from another hospital examined in detail the 32 case-histories, using the 12 criteria evolved in the *original research* (see Note 2) and divided them into a group from very adverse homes and a residual group from less adverse conditions. As before, this latter contained many from bad homes, though not exceptionally bad, and very few from good homes. The external investigator knew neither the patients nor their test scores. It was then predicted that members of the former group would tend to make the larger increments. Subsequently, the retesting was carried out by one of us (S.R.) who was ignorant of the patients, their social histories, the group to which they had been allotted, the prediction which had been made, and their earlier test scores. The results are shown in Table 3.2.

It will be seen that once again the subjects from very bad homes tended on the average to make the larger increments, although in this sample the discrepancy between the *average* increments by the two groups is less marked than in the *original research*. With roughly double the original time interval, it is clear that, on the one hand, the present group from very bad homes did not increase greatly their average increment compared with that achieved by the original group (mean increment 11.5 compared with 9.7 points). Clearly, therefore, the amount of gain in this group is not a direct function of the length of time between test and retest. On the other hand, it will be seen that members of the residual group from less adverse conditions almost doubled their mean increment over the doubled time interval (mean increment of 7.2 compared with 4.1 in the *original research*). Thus their gains are much more a direct function of the test–retest time interval. This is consistent with findings in the present *First Study* in which the maximal gain for the group from very bad homes occurred in the first two to three years, with a relatively slow increase thereafter, while those from less adverse conditions made a steady increase over the six-year period. Thus, the difference between the gains made by both the groups is

	Table 3.2 Patients admitted in 1951, retested 1955–6					
	Group from very bad homes			*Group from less adverse homes*		
	Wechsler Full Scale IQ, 1951	Wechsler Full Scale IQ 1955–6	Diff	Wechsler Full Scale IQ 1951	Wechsler Full Scale IQ 1955–6	Diff
Mean	63.1	74.6	11.5	69.0	76.2	7.2
SD	15.0	15.2	6.3	13.9	14.6	6.6
N	13	13	13	19	19	19
t (1-tail test)	—	—	6.894	—	—	4.926
Significant at	—	—	0.1%	—	—	0.1%
IQ ranges:	1951, 37–90; 1955–6, 54–99			1951, 42–94; 1955–6, 55–101		
Age at retest:	Mean 23.0, S.D. 5.9 years			Mean 23.6, S.D. 6.1 years		
Period between test and retest:	Mean 53.6 months, SD 3.8 months			Mean 51.6 months, SD 5.0 months		
Range of IQ changes:	0 to +18 points (10 points and above: 9/13=69%; 15 points and above: 7/13=54%)			−7 to +20 points (10 points and above: 8/19=42%; 15 points and above: 1/19=5%)		

t (between group from very bad homes and group from less adverse homes) = 1.925, significant at the 5% level (1-tail test). This difference is much less significant than in the *original research*, and probably arises from a combination of four factors: 1. Total *N* is much smaller. 2. One patient in the group from less adverse homes showed a very atypical gain of 20 points, which alone was responsible for depressing statistical significance from the 2.5% to the 5% level; at the time of first testing it had been noted that she was unusually disturbed emotionally, and came from a background which, though not quite conforming to the necessary criteria, was far from adequate. 3. The only patient in the group from very bad homes who did not change at all was later found to have been suffering from a right temporal malignant tumour during the material period. 4. Selective wastage had almost certainly occurred since 1951, since rehabilitation and discharge rates have accelerated greatly since then. Consequently, there has probably been a tendency for the better members of the group from very bad homes to have left the institution.

maximal at the beginning of the period in which increments have been studied, and subsequently because the growth rate of the bad home group tends to decelerate sharply (see Table 3.1), while the residual group maintains a steady progress, the difference between the average gains decreases.

Social changes

The present sample on the average had been under care of this hospital a shorter time than any of the others and was younger. Nevertheless, social changes had already begun to be apparent, and differences, as yet small, between the two groups were noticeable. Thus seven out of the 13 from very bad homes were either undergoing intensive training prior to community placement (see next study) or were already in outside employment, while only six out of the 19 from the less adverse homes were similarly placed.

Third study

This study was devoted to a special problem; the *original research* had suggested that IQ changes resulted as an effect of removal from very adverse conditions rather than from entry into relatively better ones; that is, absence of such unfavourable circumstances enabled intellectual scars to fade. An important problem then envisaged was to determine whether special environmental conditions would aid this apparently natural process of recovery. A group of patients was readily available for the testing of this hypothesis.

For some years the psychology department has been responsible for running two small rehabilitation units for selected high-grade patients. These are taught industrial skills in small workshops, develop good work habits, receive educational aid and experience of the community, eventually being placed in local industry at standard wages and in normal jobs. During their initial period outside they return to the hospital nightly but after a time may graduate to lodgings and obtain their discharge. Observation, and their success rate, suggested that many undergo radical changes under these conditions, and the question thus became whether these involved intellectual aspects of personality, and, if so, whether these gains were environmentally induced. The scheme briefly mentioned has been described in detail elsewhere (Clarke and Clarke 1954a).

At any one time about 20 to 25 patients so trained are at work in the community, and these formed the subjects of the present experiment. All had at some time during the last few years been given Wechsler, Form I, and this enabled retest results to be compared with their earlier scores. During the period between test and retest all had had at least six months intensive training, and at least six months' in the community (and often more), both of which involved considerable change of circumstances for these persons. Social histories before admission were again assessed by the external investigator who knew neither the patients nor their test scores, and retesting was carried out by one of us (S.R.) who knew neither the patients, nor their early histories, nor their earlier test scores. Table 3.3 shows the relevant data for both groups.

The first point of note is the rather higher proportion than usual of the whole group (a little over half, compared with about 42 per cent in a more random sample) who came from very bad homes; this is likely to be the result of a selection factor, namely that such persons tend to do better socially than others and are therefore more likely to be chosen for special training and rehabilitation. Once again, the larger increments tended to occur in these patients, although the difference did not reach an acceptable level of significance; this may have resulted from a selection factor favouring the more promising patients from the less adverse conditions. While in both groups the average increase is rather large, it is not so very different from what would be expected under ordinary hospital conditions. We are able to compare these data with the results of the *Second Study*, Table 3.2. The average test–retest time interval is similar, and in the *Second Study* the average gain of those from very bad homes was 11.5 points, SD 6.3, while in the present study the similar group increased on the average by 14.1 points, SD 6.0. Similarly, the group from less adverse homes in the *Second Study* made an increment of 7.2 points, SD 6.6, compared with an average of 10.4, SD 6.3, from the similar group in the present investigation. The average difference between the gains in the *Second* and *Third Studies* is thus a rough measure of the effect of special environmental conditions; for the groups from bad homes the difference is 14.1 minus 11.5=2.6 points, and for the remaining group 10.4 minus 7.2=3.2 points. These are then the maximum effects which can be ascribed to environmental difference, and they are clearly small.

As has been stated, subsequent IQ increment seems to occur as a long-term effect of removal from a traumatic environment, and there can be no doubt that the earlier intellectual deficit resulted, partly at least, from *negative* environmental effects in childhood. The present study has indicated that fairly clear environmental differences in this age group do not exert much of a *positive* effect upon the IQ. There are two possible explanatory factors. First, the difference between the ordinary institutional environment and the one provided by intensive training in special units followed by community experience may not be as large as thought. On the other hand, it must be noted that the difference is certainly large enough to produce considerable social changes, resulting in

Table 3.3 Wechsler full-scale test–retest results on persons specially trained in rehabilitation units and placed in the community in normal employment

	Group from very bad homes			Group from less adverse homes		
	Test IQ	Retest IQ	Diff	Test IQ	Retest IQ	Diff
Mean	64.8	78.9	14.1	75.1	85.5	10.4
SD	13.7	13.1	6.0	13.4	12.4	6.3
N	11	11	11	10	10	10
t (1-tail test)	—	—	7.772	—	—	5.547
Significant at	—	—	0.1%	—	—	0.1%
IQ ranges:	First test, 49–94; Retest, 64–105			First test, 63–108; Retest, 68–112		
Age at retest:	Mean 24.2, SD 3.9 years			Mean 27.6, SD 6.9 years		
Period between test and retest:	Mean 54.6 months, SD 17.6 months			Mean 47.0 months, SD 17.6 months		
Range of IQ changes:	+5 to +20 IQ points (10 points and above: 9/11=82%; 15 points and above: 7/11=64%)			+2 to +19 IQ points (10 points and above: 5/10=50%; 15 points and above: 3/10=30%)		
Time in training:	Mean 10.6 months, SD 6.2 months			Mean 12.4 months, SD 5.2 months		
Time in employment	Mean 13.2 months, SD 10.4 months			Mean 16.4 months, SD 11.7 months		

t (between group from very bad homes and group from less adverse homes) = 1.449, not significant (1-tail test).

greater success and more rapid discharge, so that there is little doubt that the environment is a specially stimulating one.

Second, it is possible that the findings reflect both an initial *negative* effect in childhood and a *masked positive* effect in adolescence and early adult life. It may be that any environment, other than an adverse one, will stimulate the apparently natural recovery process, and that the effects of environmental differences are small simply because all – even the institutional environment – have a *positive* effect. That environmental effects cannot themselves be measured needs stressing; only the effects of environmental differences are measurable. Precisely this same point has been made about the classic studies of identical twins brought up apart; in only a few cases was each twin in a radically different environment and thus the variable 'environment' was seldom accessible for full measurement.

Another source of evidence bearing out the present conclusions emerges from a comparison of the results of the *First Study* with this one. The time intervals are not quite similar, but it will be noted that the members of both groups from very bad homes made very similar mean increments. Eight of the nine members of this group in the *First Study* were employed in the community in jobs traditionally provided for the mentally deficient and for which they had no special training; yet their IQ gains were closely similar to those in the present study. So, too, with the members of both groups from less adverse homes; those who had had no special training and the majority of whom had had no experience of outside employment (*First Study*) made similar increments to those who had had both. There was no doubt, however, that special training and normal experiences had induced profound social changes in the patients of the present study. They were all holding good jobs with wages ranging from £3 0s 0d to £8 2s 0d per week with an average of £5 17s 0d. All were expected to gain their discharge, and to become reasonable and self-supporting citizens.

Summing up, it seems clear that intellectual retardation or arrest can and does occur in conditions really antagonistic to mental health in childhood. And it is precisely these conditions from which the vast majority of the certified feeble-minded are drawn. Entry into any better environment seems equally able to stimulate increments in IQ and to allow the damage to fade. This, however, is a long-term process which will be discussed in detail in the next section.

Discussion

Variability of the IQ

At this stage, brief discussion of the causes of IQ variability is appropriate. Spurious changes can be subsumed under the first three of the following headings.

1. *Errors of measurement* which in most cases represent *personal fluctuations* (e.g. alterations in mood, misunderstanding of the instructions, chance decisions, fatigue, boredom, anxiety and changes in motivation on the part of the subject, and errors in scoring, instructions, or in the establishment of rapport on the part of the tester). These combine to reduce test–retest correlation from a theoretical +1.0 to an average of 0.9 on immediate retest (Thorndike 1933). Similarly, standardization differences (e.g.

varying SNs on the 1937 Stanford–Binet at different ages) will, if uncorrected, produce spurious changes.

2. *Test practice and coaching* have well-known effects (see Vernon 1954).

3. *Incorrect testing* by persons unqualified in psychometrics may clearly produce errors resulting in excessive IQ variability upon retest.

4. *Variation in the rate of intellectual growth.* In general, as the interval between tests lengthens, so the retest correlation decreases, often steadily (Eysenck 1953; Nemzek 1933; Thorndike 1940). There is no reason to suppose that errors of measurement (whether arising from personal fluctuations in respect of subject or tester, or standardization errors) are likely to be steadily cumulative, and thus a decreasing correlation coefficient must be primarily a reflection of some real change of status of members of the group.

In this connection, it is necessary to discuss 'test reliability' since confusion tends to arise over this concept. Test reliability relates to two factors: first, whether the test measures the same quality in the same way on different occasions; and second, whether the quality measured itself alters. The first point has been discussed under 'errors of measurement', and the second might well be termed 'unreliability of persons' since, as we have seen, the fact of decreasing correlation with increase of time implies just that. It is this in particular which produces difficulties; it is by no means uncommon to hear or read the following tautological argument: 'over several years test results change because of imperfect correlation or test unreliability'. It is further implied that such changes are statistical, reside in the test rather than in the person tested, and therefore have no psychological significance. Obviously, however, the test unreliability or lowered correlation over several years is more likely to be a reflection of change of status of individuals rather than vice versa.

Statistical regression towards the mean is another concept frequently used to account for IQ changes; where this concerns errors of measurement on the same or different tests, or where different tests have a low initial correlation when given within a day or two of each other, then this is entirely correct. In such cases, regression of extreme scores is inevitable and of no psychological significance. In a cogent discussion of regression, McNemar (1940), agreeing that it is a descriptive rather than an explanatory concept, points out that an inferior or superior group will not move towards the general population mean on retest unless it has been specifically selected on the basis of initial test results (e.g. Terman's group of gifted children, selected on the basis of IQ 140 and above). Within a group not so selected, regression effects will occur around the group mean, be it superior or inferior. We have already seen that, granted proper standardization and test reliability (i.e. small errors of measurement) a steadily decreasing correlation coefficient tends to occur with increase of time, such that after five years it may be about 0.7. This implies some changes of as much as 15–20 points, and it would be quite incorrect to say that these are 'due to regression' with consequently no psychological meaning. Yet such statements are not uncommonly made, and in effect there appears to be a tendency to regard statistical expressions as somehow primary to behavioural data, with curious results. Regression cannot explain such large changes which reflect primarily an alteration in response to the test situation; naturally the implications of such variations are not necessarily obvious and must be interpreted with caution.

At the risk of labouring this point, let us see why in the *original research* and the present studies, the concept of regression cannot explain the major part of the increments.

First, the groups were not chosen for study or follow-up on the basis of initial test score. Second, the *original control group* retested after a short time interval made an average increment of only 4 points, which must be a maximal estimate of errors of measurement including regression effects for this type of sample. Stating the same point differently, the Wechsler test has a very high immediate retest reliability, hence regression effects must be small. Third, such wastage of subjects as occurred in the *First* and *Second Studies* was for reasons other than initial test results. Fourth, the two groups which formed the main sample in the *original research* were initially equal in IQ. Yet by the time that investigation was complete, and even more so now, different cognitive and social trends had occurred, and regression cannot account for such differences in initially equated groups. Fifth, statistical regression is psychologically meaningless. Throughout all our studies, however, there has been a consistent tendency for the amount of 'regression' to be related to psychologically meaningful external criteria, the record of early experiences. It is hardly likely that the purely statistical would be so linked with the purely behavioural. Thus on all counts, statistical regression cannot explain the major portion of the IQ increments.

The present findings

The increments noted both in the *original research* and in the present studies are likely to have been largely the effect of 'unreliability of persons', that is, of variations in the rate of late intellectual maturation. All four investigations underline the better prognosis for the feeble-minded person from bad social conditions; they tend to have larger IQ increments, to enjoy a greater success within the hospital, to be selected for intensive training by virtue of their other qualities, to respond to training a little more rapidly and to be tried in the community earlier and more often than those from rather less adverse social conditions. They also tend to achieve discharge from care more rapidly and more often, and although sometimes they may have a lower IQ in adolescence than the other patients, they tend to catch up and overtake them within a few years. Indeed they present a substantially different picture in many spheres after, say, six years, and often these changes occur at relatively late ages. In general, these results are strongly supported by the social findings of Charles (1953) in which a very long-term follow-up, conducted with exemplary care, of children originally judged mentally deficient showed that they had not developed according to a rigid stereotype. Many at the ages of 30 and above were in the normal or dull normal range and were holding their own in the community. The outcome for the majority was far better than would have been predicted at the time of their attendance in the 'opportunity rooms' of Lincoln, Nebraska, schools. Similarly, any person reading the case-histories of many of the present subjects cannot fail to be struck by the discrepancy between the gloomy predictions of psychologists and psychiatrists made within the last ten years, and the actual progress made. Delayed personality maturation may well be a factor explanatory of Penrose's (1949) observation that the incidence of high-grade deficiency decreases sharply from the age of 15 onwards.

What, then, are the precise mechanisms of these changes? Earlier papers (Clarke and Clarke 1954b, 1955) argued that at all stages the obtained IQs were relatively accurate measures of the then intellectual status of the subjects, rejecting the hypothesis of pseudo-feeble-mindedness, which, as will be seen, really begs the question. The work of Hebb (1949) is clearly relevant; adverse conditions in early life would be likely to interrupt or seriously damage the formation of 'phase sequences', and the more adverse these conditions the greater the deficit to be made good. It appears that improvement may not commence until adolescence and may continue well into the twenties. In many cases there thus appears to be a period of latency, during which growth rates may show little acceleration, lasting from childhood and infancy when the damage occurred, until adolescence. We possess far less data on this period, however, and this view is inferred from several sources: (a) the few children studied with similar backgrounds to those of our older subjects appear to change little; (b) the case-histories of our subjects do not imply, in most cases, a level in childhood very much inferior to their status in adolescence; and (c) most of the early investigators believed that intellectual growth in the feeble-minded ceased several years earlier than in the normal. Our own results suggest precisely the opposite for many such persons, but it is a reasonable assumption that this original view about intellectual development in the feeble-minded sprang from the fact that children were mainly being studied at that time, and it may be that over late childhood there is a developmental plateau which, when it begins, suggests a cessation of growth. While this latency period is a hypothesis, it seems to be a reasonable one, and at all events it seems quite certain that in childhood these persons do not change as rapidly as later. Removal of most feeble-minded children from traumatic conditions usually took place years before entry into a mental deficiency hospital, the interim period being spent in residential schools for the emotionally subnormal (ESN), children's homes or orphanages. Then, perhaps at age 16, certification took place as the last link in a long chain of official intervention.

All one can say in explanation of this hypothetical latency period is that it may be needed to make good the foundations upon which subsequent development depends, and to establish or re-establish some integration of personality – that perhaps five or ten years are needed to give the developmental basis normally gained during the first few years of life. Certainly future investigations must be concerned with studying such persons at a much earlier age, and as soon as possible after removal from adverse homes.

A further and necessary hypothesis requiring some discussion is that there must be limits to the change which occurs; these limits may be set by the basic resources of the central nervous system, genetically determined, and also, perhaps, by the amount and quality of the damage produced by negative environmental influence. The largest increment ever noted in this hospital on the same test was 29 points but this was over about seven years; this then appears to be the maximum over a similar time period in adolescence and early adult life among such subjects. Over the whole of a person's life span, however, the limits to change may be slightly greater, say, a maximum of 40 points (see Vernon 1955); obviously, however, the majority of the feeble-minded may never make changes of this order. Not only do the amounts of change differ in different subjects but also the rates of change. We have seen in the *First Study* that those from really adverse conditions tended to make a large initial gain over about three years, which on the average was halved during the next three years; those from less adverse homes (but nevertheless bad ones) tended to make a steady gain over the six-year period. The first interpretation mentioned was that the rate of recovery depended upon the severity of initial damage. The concept of limits may, however, also provide an explanation. It may be that the members of the group from very bad homes were reaching their limits of change and therefore growth rates were decelerating. Longitudinal research over about ten years might elucidate this important point.

The main implications of the cognitive and social findings reported here seem clear; we cannot predict a necessarily poor outcome for children with IQs in the 50s, 60s and 70s if they also come from very adverse environments. While there is no doubt much truth in Bowlby's thesis that separation from the mother may have very unfortunate effects on the child, we must not interpret this finding too rigidly for, as Hilda Lewis (1954) points out, it may be even more disastrous to leave some children with unsuitable parents. Moreover, findings such as these suggest that feeble-minded persons, most of whom come from bad or very bad conditions, are within limits far from being the hopeless propositions which until recent years was generally accepted; already a much more positive attitude towards them is emerging.

Relevance of other work to the present findings

That environment can exercise a stimulating or depressing effect upon intellectual function is now generally accepted (see Vernon 1955), although there is still a dearth of knowledge about precise mechanisms, the limits to, and the factors limiting, such changes. So far as the mentally deficient are concerned, however, the concept of pseudo-feeble-mindedness continues often to be used to explain away IQ increments among them. Perhaps the best statement of this view is that of Porteus (1941): 'Very wide differences in intellectual status merely indicate that the first diagnosis was wrong. Any child who finally functions at a normal level proves thereby that he never was feebleminded.' In effect, Doll's attitude (1941) is similar; essential incurability is suggested as a necessary criterion of mental defect; one might, therefore, have to wait 20 years to find out whether a child improved and hence no firm diagnosis of a high-grade case could be made in childhood. Both writers express an outlook firmly rooted upon the concept of a fairly rigid constancy of the IQ, a view to which few would now subscribe. Elsewhere (Clarke and Clarke 1955), we have argued that the concept of pseudo-feeble-mindedness is now untenable in cases showing deferred maturation, since most studies show that initial testing gave no indication of underestimation at the time, and must be considered a true picture of the then present status of the person. Thus Porteus's view that *mistaken diagnosis* has occurred must be rejected; rather, the clinician has made a *mistaken prognosis*. And the present studies have shown that it is possible to predict IQ changes by an external criterion. It is important to realize, therefore, that arrest in intellectual development, or a decelerated growth rate, may be permanent or impermanent to varying degrees. In both types, the symptoms (e.g. social incompetence, behaviour disorder or low IQ) may be similar, but it is a truism that the same symptom may arise from different causes.

Previous researches on IQ changes in the mentally deficient have been critically reviewed elsewhere (Clarke and Clarke 1958). Here, it is proposed to discuss only one specific study relating to English feeble-minded patients, and two others with broader implications.

1. Mundy (1955), in studying environmental influences on the IQ, used an experimental and control group each consisting of 28 adult feeble-minded women, and believed that the two groups were initially equated on a number of important variables. The interval between test and retest was two years, during which time the controls remained within a good institution (a convent) while the members of the experimental group enjoyed normal life experiences, mostly in residential wage-earning employment. On retest, the control group showed an average increment on the Wechsler test of 2.25 points, and on the Progressive Matrices of 3.46 points. The average gains made by the experimental group, however, were 11 and 9.82 IQ points, respectively. Mundy believed that these results indicated that present environmental differences induced differential gains, but the validity of this conclusion clearly rests upon whether control and experimental groups were in fact *initially equal in all respects*. We are told, however, that there was no clinical selection by the hospital for outside employment, and that 'any able-bodied patient who wished for outside work was found suitable employment as soon as this was feasible'. This suggests that the members of the experimental group had all, through drive, ambition and initiative, asked for outside employment and hence gained it, while for several years at least the members of the control group had been content to remain within a good institution: there was thus a difference between the groups in terms of 'self-selection'. It should be added, however, that in a personal communication the author has stated that some cases were in effect originally transferred to employment for administrative reasons; this would reduce the amount of 'self-selection' but it might well be an indication of selection by the hospital. A further reason for believing that the control group contained atypical patients was the extraordinary stability of their test scores over the two-year period; 25 out of the 28 remained within 0 and plus 4 IQ points of their initial

Wechsler result, and no patient increased by more than 6 points. This would imply a much higher test–retest correlation than is reported elsewhere in the literature. Because of these two factors, therefore, Mundy's conclusion is open to some doubt, and, in view of our own findings, it may well be that the IQ changes would have occurred differentially in any reasonable environment. Where her research and our own agree, however, is that early very adverse experiences played a part in retarding intellectual and general development. (See also Mundy 1957.)

2. Some striking parallels with our own findings emerge from experimental work in an entirely different field of deprivation, although these analogies ought not to be pressed too far. Widdowson and McCance (1954) studied the effects of different food diets on undernourished German orphanage children. Among other things, their growth in height, weight and ossification were investigated. The most striking observation was that following the period of undernourishment, these children grew even better than normal children of the same age, in spite of the very simple diet provided, which contained little milk or animal protein, and up to 75 per cent of its calorie value in the form of flour products. It may be either that the flours of different extraction rates were equally nutritious or that the differences between them were masked by the exceptionally rapid growth rates of undernourished children when receiving a diet adequate in calories. Even the addition of a special milk supplement did not increase further these already accelerated rates of increase. In an appendix to this report (p.80) J.O. Irwin indicated that alternative viewpoints are equally possible. Because of original underfeeding, these children might have grown on any diet not grossly inadequate, the response to different amounts of vitamins would therefore be largely non-specific, and specific differences might still be detected in children with a more normal nutritional history on similar diets. On the other hand, others might be more struck with the fact that these children grew equally well on all the diets and at a faster rate than normally. The similarity between these concepts and those relating to our own study of environmental effects is very close. Another interesting finding, so far as weight increases were concerned, was that initial increases were more rapid than later ones (see our *Second Study*). It is of some consequence that unusual

> growth rates (with respect to normals) after malnutrition should in
> some ways be analogous with unusual increments in cognitive and
> social development in persons who suffered a different form of
> deprivation.

3. The work reviewed by Bowlby (1951) is too well known to need
    summary; it is highly relevant to our thesis that early adverse
    environmental influences have played a part in producing mental
    deficiency. His monograph is, however, almost entirely concerned
    with studies of children or young adolescents. In general, Bowlby
    is pessimistic about their recovery from early psychological
    damage, particularly in the absence of psychotherapy. Yet our own
    subjects, the majority of whom could scarcely have suffered worse
    childhood experiences (followed by institutional upbringing in
    many cases) being therefore *par excellence* a deprived group, have
    on the whole done much better than might have been expected,
    and none has received formal psychotherapy. Similarly, some of the
    social studies such as that of Charles (1953) have indicated that
    persons who were originally high-grade defectives in childhood
    do not develop according to a rigid stereotype, that a wide range
    of individual differences is maintained, with many eventually
    functioning in adult life at dull-normal or normal levels. There is
    no way of knowing what our subjects would have been like had
    they enjoyed normal conditions from birth onwards, but there is
    no doubt that in adult life they are, on the whole, very much less
    impaired than would have been expected from Bowlby's original
    theory.

Two very important general questions arise. First, to what extent are the main
variables those of human susceptibility to early psychological damage and
resilience thereafter, and what is their nature? Why is it that some children are
utterly overwhelmed by adverse conditions while others are apparently stimulated by them? We have no real estimate of the proportion which emerges
relatively unscathed, simply because we tend only to study the problem cases,
but it may well be larger than we think. For example, often two or three children in a family come to the notice of the authorities while their other siblings
do not, and we know next to nothing about the latter. Second, is it possible
that, when more deprived children are followed up through adolescence and
adult life, it will be found that, in many, the initial psychological damage, as
with our own deprived population, tends steadily to be repaired to varying
extents? This, if true, would represent a need for modification of the 'maternal

deprivation' thesis, and it is of great interest that Bowlby, Ainsworth, Boston and Rosenbluth (1956) have already begun to re-formulate some aspects of it.

The writers are greatly indebted to Dr J.F. MacMahon, Physician Superintendent, for his many suggestions and constructive criticism; to Dr Gordon Claridge for having made independent assessments of social histories; and to Dr H.R. Beech for statistical advice and for the computations.

Notes

1   The main point in each of these criteria was as follows: NSPCC intervention, parental attitude antagonistic, no fixed abode, 'Fit Person' Order, home conditions bad, considerable neglect, irregular school attendance due to neglect, home dirty and neglected, gross poverty, crime in parents, rickets, child found begging.

2   Fifty patients drawn from the present three studies were, in addition, given the Progressive Matrices test to confirm their present levels. These correlated to the extent of 0.81, with a mean difference of 2.67 points between them in favour of the Wechsler.

References

Bowlby, J. (1951) *Maternal Care and Mental Health*. Geneva: World Health Organization.

Bowlby, J., Ainsworth, M., Boston, M. and Rosenbluth, D. (1956) 'The effects of mother-child separation: a follow-up study.' *British Journal of Medical Psychology* 29, 211–47.

Charles, D.C. (1953) 'Ability and accomplishment of persons earlier judged mentally deficient.' *Genetic Psychology Monographs 47*, 3–71.

Clarke, A.D.B. and Clarke, A.M. (1953) 'How constant is the IQ?' *Lancet ii*, 877–880.

Clarke, A.D.B. and Clarke, A.M. (1954a) 'A rehabilitation programme for the certified mental defective.' *Mental Health 14*, 4–10. London: NAMH.

Clarke, A.D.B. and Clarke, A.M. (1954b) 'Cognitive changes in the feebleminded.' *British Journal of Psychology 45*, 173–179.

Clarke, A.D.B. and Clarke, A.M. (1955) 'Pseudo-feeblemindedness–some implications.' *American Journal of Mental Deficiency 59*, 507–509.

Clarke, A.M. and Clarke, A.D.B. (eds) (1958) *Mental Deficiency: The Changing Outlook*. London: Methuen.

Doll, E.A. (1941) 'The essentials of an inclusive concept of mental deficiency.' *American Journal of Mental Deficiency 46*, 214–219.

Eysenck, H.J. (1953) *Uses and Abuses of Psychology*. London: Penguin.

Hebb, D.O. (1949) *The Organisation of Behavior*. London: Chapman and Hall.

Lewis, H. (1954) *Deprived Children*. London: Oxford University Press.

McNemar, Q. (1940) 'A critical examination of the University of Iowa studies of environmental influences upon the IQ.' *Psychological Bulletin 37*, 63–92.

Mundy, L. (1955) 'Environmental influences in intellectual function as measured by intelligence tests.' London University, unpublished MSc Thesis.

Mundy, L. (1957) 'Environmental influence on intellectual function as measured by intelligence tests.' *British Journal of Medical Psychology 30*, 194–201.

Nemzek, C.L. (1933) 'The constancy of the IQ.' *Psychological Bulletin 30*, 143–168.

Penrose, L.S. (1949) *The Biology of Mental Defect.* London: Sidgwick and Jackson.

Porteus, S.D. (1941) *The Practice of Clinical Psychology.* New York: American Book Co.

Thorndike, R.L. (1933) 'The effect of the interval between test and retest on the constancy of the IQ.' *Journal of Educational Psychology 24*, 543–549.

Thorndike, R.L. (1940) '"Constancy" of the IQ.' *Psychological Bulletin 37*, 167–186.

Vernon, P.E. (1954) 'Symposium on the effects of coaching and practice in intelligence tests. V. Conclusions.' *British Journal of Educational Psychology 24*, 57–63.

Vernon, P.E. (1955) 'The assessment of children.' In *Studies in Education*, no. 7. University of London Institute of Education.

Waddington. C.H. (1966) *Principles of Development and Differentiation.* New York: Macmillian.

Widdowson, E.M. and McCance, R.A. (1954) 'Studies on the nutritive value of bread and on the effect of variations in the extraction rate of flour on undernourished children.' *Special Report Series Medical Research Council London 287*. London: HMSO

CHAPTER 4

Predicting Human Development
Problems, Evidence, Implications

Commentary

This British Psychological Society Presidential Address (1978) tackles the problem of constancy and change in a much broader way than was possible in Chapter 2 written 25 years earlier. As indicated, from a consideration of a large range of research areas, the data suggest 'an ongoing determinism rather than a one-off predeterminism, with the individual as an active agent in his own development. This awareness of a degree of open-endedness requires a much closer look at the macro- and microsocial factors which construct or maintain stabilities or promote change'.

Prediction Human Develpment:
Problems, Evidence, Implications[*]

A.D.B. Clarke[1]

Past presidents of this Society have tackled the subject matter of their addresses in different ways. Some have offered a sort of 'state of the Union' evaluation, whether of psychology in general, or of the Society in particular. Others have discussed a particular area of research which attracts them. This latter is my own choice, and I shall touch lightly upon some broad issues in the hope that these will be of greater interest than a narrower yet deeper analysis.

Now accurate prediction is the most obvious hallmark of a successful science. Quite apart from its general scientific and theoretical importance,

[*]   This article first appeared in 1978 in the *Bulletin of the British Psychological Society 31*, pp.249–258.

effective prediction in psychology might allow us specifically in applied fields to set up conditions that 1. might encourage the predicted outcome, making it more certain; or 2., equally important with deviant or handicapping conditions, might discourage the fulfilment of the forecast. Third, good prediction, used as a baseline, would allow us to assess the relative merits of alternative interventions (R. Flynn, personal communication). I shall remind you, however, that, except in crude terms, long-term prediction of *individual* human development is not very impressive; in *group* terms it is rather better. This is so whatever measure one uses to forecast a later score, or other outcome. Figure 4.1 indicates some typical predictive paradigms.

I propose to tackle the issue of prediction in four sections: 1. historical; 2. interpretative and methodological; 3. longitudinal data from fairly static situations; and 4. quasi-experimental or experimental studies of naturally occurring or contrived changes in environment and their effects. Finally, I shall attempt to draw the threads together.

Historical background

To put my subject matter into context, it will be necessary to dip selectively into the history of psychology over the last 70 years, to notice the origin and evolution of present debates and, with hindsight and its attendant wisdom, to notice our errors and misperceptions.

I return, then, to the beginning of this century. The overwhelming orientation of contemporary developmental psychology was to see man as possessed of instincts, fixed dispositions or abilities. Thus Spearman, who thought that intelligence would be most efficiently assessed by measuring simple psycho-physical responses, believed that it became fully developed by the ninth year or possibly even earlier, thereafter normally never changing even into extreme old age. Exactly the same predeterminism was emerging from the psychoanalytic school; the child's future was predestined even earlier, for his experiences in the first five years were regarded as crucially formative. Long-term fixations from difficulties at different stages of development were seen as common and unmodifiable, except through very lengthy transactions with the analyst. It was necessary, metaphorically speaking, to be born again, or at least to rerun the oral, anal or oedipal phases.

In 1912 Watson's manifesto launched Behaviourism, and with it a retreat into the animal field. Watson did not stay there too long, however, particularly after his brief encounter with Little Albert. Indeed, he became a strange bedfellow of Sigmund Freud. 'But once a child's character has been spoiled by bad handling, which can be done in a few days, who can say that the damage is ever repaired?...some day the importance of the first two years of infancy will be fully realized... At 3 years of age the child's whole emotional life has been laid down, his emotional disposition set' (Watson 1928). This was Watson's last book, which you may think was just as well.

The only person who stood out against this trend was Binet (1905) who attacked Spearman's concept of an unchanging intelligence. Noting Spearman's claim that teachers' judgements of children and the results of simple sensory experiments were almost identical, Binet stated that 'We ourselves are profoundly astonished at this because of the very defective character we find both in the sensory experiments...(of Spearman)...and also in his method of estimating...the total intelligence' (Wolf 1973). The battle lines were drawn up, then, some seven years before Stern and Burt, using Binet's own mental test contributions, proposed the IQ and guessed its constancy over time. And indeed, foreseeing all this before his premature death in 1911, Binet pronounced with contempt 'Some recent philosophers appear to have given their moral support to the deplorable verdict that the intelligence of the individual is a fixed quantity, a quantity which cannot be augmented... We shall endeavour to show that it has no foundation whatever...' (quoted by Skeels and Dye 1939).

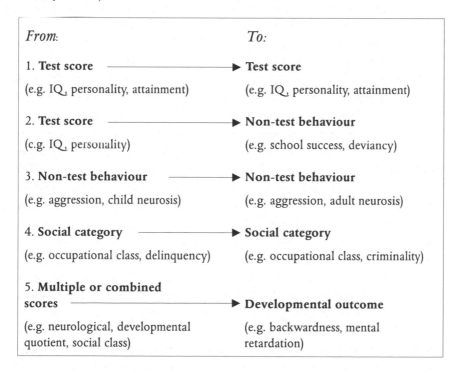

From:

1. **Test score** ──────────▶ **Test score**

(e.g. IQ, personality, attainment)

2. **Test score** ──────────▶ **Non-test behaviour**

(e.g. IQ, personality)

3. **Non-test behaviour** ──────▶ **Non-test behaviour**

(e.g. aggression, child neurosis)

4. **Social category** ────────▶ **Social category**

(e.g. occupational class, delinquency)

5. **Multiple or combined scores** ──────────▶ **Developmental outcome**

(e.g. neurological, developmental quotient, social class)

To:

(e.g. IQ, personality, attainment)

(e.g. school success, deviancy)

(e.g. aggression, adult neurosis)

(e.g. occupational class, criminality)

(e.g. backwardness, mental retardation)

Figure 4.1 Typical sources for long-term prediction

Summarizing, it is clear that during the first quarter of this century the predominant orientation was towards a conception of human characteristics, whether of hereditary or experiential origin, as fixed and irreversible from an early age. This model of human development, originally based on little more than guesswork, became widely held and influences our perceptions even today.

But already this extreme view carried within it the empirical seeds of its own destruction. Dearborn, himself at first a firm believer in IQ constancy (1928), gradually shifted his position with successive follow-ups of the Harvard Growth Study. By 1941, Dearborn and Rothney had concluded that 'prediction of growth is hazardous', and they disagreed, too, with the traditional view that intelligence tests measured innate capacity.

By the 1950s and later we again move into a general debate with wider implications than the study of intelligence. How much constancy and how much variability occurs in the development of human characteristics? In the early 1960s both Bloom (1964) and Kagan and Moss (1962) gave quite firm answers. The former offered what he saw as empirical support for the notion of the long-term influences of early development. Unfortunately, his interpretations were marred by his apparently imperfect comprehension of the meaning of correlation coefficients. One of his three minimal requirements for the existence of a stable attribute was a correlation of only 0.5 over a lengthy period. Another consequence was his use of the term 'half-development' (perhaps influenced by atomic physics) for the evolution of a characteristic, that point in time when a 0.7 correlation with adult status is achieved. But of course 0.7 only accounts for half the variance at adulthood, and anyway, the notion of half-development is meaningless without a common linear scale of measurement, having both zero and terminal points. Kagan and Moss (1962), dealing with a whole range of cognitive and personality variables derived from the Fels study, also concluded that continuity was the rule. But a decade later, reviewing similar data and finding consistent evidence of correlations decreasing steadily over time, we concluded that individual variability was as impressive as consistency. Moreover, where marked environmental change occurred, personal changes always followed, although individual differences, probably constitutional in origin, were reflected in different degrees of individual change (Clarke and Clarke 1972). Later, we pointed to the likelihood that, contrary to common theory, development was not purely incremental, but included substantial discontinuities as well as incremental continuities for particular processes (Clarke and Clarke 1977, 1978). It is of interest that Kagan has recently substantially changed his earlier views on consistency. Indeed, in a speech which preceded the paper by Kagan and Klein (1973) courageously he said of his earlier work that he had 'uncovered fragile lines that seem to travel back and forth in time…I rationalized the modest empirical support for continuity by arguing that although behaviours similar in manifest form might not be stable over long term periods, the underlying structures might be firmer'.

Interpretation and methodology

Before proceeding further, it may be worth glancing at some of the problems of interpretation of data and methodology which beset the field of prediction.

I turn first to the correlation coefficient, so often used as a shorthand method of describing relationships over time, and hence consistency or otherwise of the characteristic. The following simple points must be made: 1. on its own, a correlation tells us nothing about means or variances or about mean shifts or variance changes; 2. misinterpretation of the meaning of correlation coefficients is still common, and many psychologists are unused to accounting for proportions of variances which a given coefficient implies. Thus a recent article on an achievement motivation test quotes a split-half correlation of 0.54; this indicates that each half accounts for only 29 per cent of the variance of the other. Three months later the overall retest correlation was 0.45, test or retest accounting for only 20 per cent of the other's variance. The author (Opolot 1977) notes that 'although these correlations are not very high, they are encouraging', but surely these results are profoundly discouraging. Even a retest r of 0.9 fails to account for about a fifth of the variance; moreover, such a very strong relationship can conceal large changes over time in a minority of individual scores; and an imperfect test–retest correlation on its own tells us nothing about the developmental curves of the individuals making up the sample; 3. correlation coefficients reflect ordinal position, and as implied in 1. above, ordinal position could remain for an individual quite similar across a considerable mean shift. Is one merely interested in ordinal position? Rank order, in a very homogeneous group, matters little; it of course takes on importance in heterogeneous groups. This is what Magnusson (1974, 1976) calls 'relative consistency'. But there is also 'absolute consistency' (e.g. degree of anxiety expressed across different situations) as well as 'coherence'. Magnusson (1974, 1976) defines the latter as behaviour that is inherently lawful and hence predictable; it may indeed show variability across situations but is lawful nonetheless, and the person's rank order may remain similar. In other words, consistency does not necessarily imply cross-situational invariance of behaviour; variability across situations may be entirely lawful and appropriate – but different – when the situation is different. An eminent predecessor in his presidential address to this Society bared his soul by indicating great consistency in last-minute completion of important academic commitments (such as the preparation of inaugural or presidential lectures) as against what he termed his notorious and obsessional planning of holidays months in advance. Here we have, anecdotally, a beautiful example of cross-situational inconsistency and within-situational consistency. Commonly all these differing meanings of consistency are confused; 4. where large samples are involved, correlation coefficients expressing an overall relationship may obscure the existence of subgroups (e.g. male and female) in which well-marked but different and even opposite trends occur.

Turning now to common methods of studying human development, one must note that longitudinal data are costly to collect and, with very few exceptions, are subject to sample attrition. In at least some senses such loss must be selective (Labouvie *et al.* 1974). Nor is it necessarily of great comfort to show, as many have tried to do, that lost subjects were, at the start, insignificantly different from those who remained. To be equal at the beginning of a race doesn't preclude later individual differences. There are many examples in the literature of longitudinal studies where the wastage is primarily from the 'worst' end of the sample. A few others are from the 'best', but the former appear to be in a majority.

So do cross-sectional studies have an advantage? At least they represent an economy in time and effort and allow total samples to be studied. But here again there are very large problems; for example, their results never correspond with those of longitudinal investigations, and obviously individual development can never be tracked. Perhaps the main sources of difference between longitudinal and cross-sectional studies may reside in 1. the increasing sample wastage over time of longitudinal samples, 2. the effect of constant retesting, and 3. secular trends in the variables under scrutiny. These latter have been well discussed by Labouvie *et al.* (1974). These authors argue that the concurrent assessment of children and adults, as is usual in standardizing psychometric instruments, draws its age samples from different birth epochs. This may involve different levels of the function tested because of secular differences in the different birth year cohorts. An especially hazardous variant has been provided by Fisher and Zeaman (1970). Using an extended cross-sectional study over a two-year span ('semi-longitudinal') they assessed *concurrently* the abilities, at different ages, of a large institutional sample of the mentally retarded, in order to arrive at general mental growth curves. Nowhere did they mention the absolute certainty that the constitution of the subsamples would differ in different age groups, being more pathological and more damaged in the younger children, and losing their brighter members into the community in late adolescence or early adult life.

Both longitudinal and cross-sectional studies are of course necessary, but the longitudinal method seems the more satisfactory, and in a few cases of very small samples (e.g. Skeels 1966) there has been no sample loss. But in very few large studies is attrition a negligible problem, and we may be too ready, either through lack of resources or lack of persistence, to allow sample attrition, with distorting consequences.

A further problem is that psychologists all too often employ single predictive measures. In a multi-causal world this is seen as limiting prediction possibilities. This view is less cogent than it appears, for sometimes the single measure (e.g. social class) itself implies a multiple correlation of many individually less powerful components. We live in a world where everything seems to have some relation with everything else; it is exceedingly difficult to avoid nature's favourite correlation coefficient, about 0.35. It is because of this that the employment of many variables, additively or in weighted combination, normally fails to improve prediction very greatly. After the combination of two or three variables, the law of diminishing returns nearly always operates.

There are a lot of other problems but there is no time to explore them.

Longitudinal data from fairly static situations

Here I want to outline some findings in two areas which represent quite a range of prediction problems, first personality and second intelligence.

Even in the 1920s there were hints that trait theories were not wholly satisfactory, and that there was a good deal of situational specificity in behaviour. These notions were reincarnated in the work of Bandura and Walters (1963) and particularly in Mischel's book of 1968. He challenged the very existence of 'stimulus-free highly generalized behavioural sets', saying that although behaviour patterns may be stable, they are usually not highly generalized across situations. Behaviours depend on highly specific events but remain stable when the consequences to which they lead, and the evoking conditions, remain similar (1968, p.282). Since behaviour depends on stimulus conditions, regularities in them lead to predictable behaviour. Thus the study of environmental stabilities is likely to be profitable. Here it may be interjected that for the historical reasons already outlined, developmental psychologists have devoted much work to what they have seen as intra-individual dispositions, and very little to quantifying the environment. Mischel also reviewed evidence suggesting that people's self-categorized labels, as well as constructions about others, tend to persist longer than the behaviour which elicited them. Further, global personality labels tend to be so wide that it is very difficult to disconfirm them. 'To the extent that exact learning conditions in the environment are not taken into account, accurate forecasts are unrealistic hopes.' Moreover, in ordinary life many determinants are accidental and hence unpredictable by any science. 'Individuals are constantly confronted with choices, and each choice, in turn, places the chooser under new contingencies and produces new consequences' (1968, p.299). 'Indeed, traits and states are too crude and global to encompass the complexity of human behaviour...a more adequate conceptualization must take account of man's extraordinary adaptiveness and capacities for discrimination, awareness, and self-regulation...' (p.301). These were fighting words which, not surprisingly, sparked off a major controversy which yet rumbles on. Different authors have reacted to Mischel's challenge in different ways. Fiske (1974) has responded with pessimism. Personality lies in the eyes of the beholder; it is a perception, interpretation and construction about other people's behaviour. We are close to the limits of the conventional science of personality. Bem and Allen (1974) revived Allport's (1937) calculation that there are 18,000 trait or trait-like words in our lexicon which assist our implicit personality theories imposed upon the behaviour of others. Our observations are narrow and selective, and we overgeneralize from those consistencies which are in fact present. We can look only for consistencies in *some* of the people for *some* of the time. For Magnusson (1976) consistency is to be found not in stable rank orders but in lawful idiographic patterns of stable and changing behaviour across situations. But again the perception of the beholder is emphasized.

Bowers (1977) is one of the most active critics of Mischel. There is a confusion of personality phenomena and their explanation. Depending upon one's interests and criteria, the same data may be interpreted as showing consistency or variability. The reconciliation, however, lies in interactions. When the subject × treatment statistic is large, the generality of main effects (i.e. the person or the situation) is obviously qualified. And as Bowers showed earlier (1973) in summarizing 11 studies that utilized analysis of variance to account for main effects and interactions, neither the trait nor the situationist predictions were borne out. The percentage of variance on average accounted for by the person is about 13 per cent; on average for situations it is 10 per cent. In fact the interaction of persons × settings accounts for a higher proportion of the variance than either main effect in 14 out of 18 possible comparisons; in 8 out of 18, interaction accounts for more than the sum of both main effects. It also appears that person effects are greater in disturbed than in normal persons. And indeed we would hazard a guess that extremes of personality dimensions, possibly for transactional reasons, show considerable stability over time.

So far we have mainly been discussing cross-situational consistencies. What about longitudinal consistency of personality? Kagan and Moss (1962) have already been cited, but there is something of a dearth of long-term studies. For example, I can find no such investigations of Eysenck's Personality Questionnaire. In recent years, however, much has been made of Block's (1971) *Lives Through Time* which used a Q-sort method to describe each of 150 subjects in the Oakland and Berkeley Guidance Studies at Junior High School, Senior High School and in their mid-30s. Different judges used different data at each of the three age checkpoints to Q-sort the same person. This method is said to allow an appreciation of personality organization to emerge from the accumulation of independent decisions. Inter-judge reliability averaged about 0.75 from Junior to Senior High School and about 0.55 from Senior High School to adulthood: 'over a span of 15 years or so, it represents an impressive degree of personal consistency' writes Bowers (1977). Some persons were more consistent than others. But overall this latter correlation indicates that 70 pent cent of the adult variance was unaccounted for from Senior High School measures. To me this is unimpressive, except as indicating considerable change. This is, however, a statement of averages; some subjects showed great stability over time, others showed marked personality changes.

Jean Macfarlane (1964) reviewed the outcome of the 30-year Berkeley Guidance Study, which represented rather more than half Block's sample; one must note, too, her surprised interpretation, working as she did from an implicit hypothesis that people do not change.

> Many of our most mature and competent adults had severely troubled and confusing childhoods and adolescences. Many of our highly successful children and adolescents have failed to achieve their predicted potential... As children and adolescents, they were free of severe strains, showed high abilities and/or talents, excelled at academic work and were the adulated images of success... One sees among them at age 30 a high proportion of brittle, discontented and puzzled adults whose high potentialities have not been actualized, at least as of now...(but) we were not always wrong! We did have several small groups whose adult status fulfilled theoretical expectations' (i.e. strong continuities). It rather sounds as if sooner or later most people in this sample had a bad time, but not sooner *and* later!

Or again, consider the New York Longitudinal Study by Thomas and Chess (1976) of 136 subjects from infancy to adolescence. This prospective longitudinal research, using a middle- and upper-class volunteer group, permitted investigations both of behavioural constancies and the evolution of behaviour disorders. Mild reactive behaviour disorders were quite common in the preschool and early school years. By adolescence, almost half had recovered and about 12 per cent improved, a small percentage were unchanged, about 19 per cent were mildly or moderately worse, and 16 per cent became markedly worse. Those who recovered were probably assisted by guidance given to the parents. They were in adolescence no different from those who had not shown behaviour disorders in childhood. The major picture then is of *inconstancy* of characteristics; the vast majority of those who had childhood disorders either got better or worse, they did not stay the same. And the earlier hope of identifying 'primary reaction patterns' which would hold up over time was not fulfilled (Thomas and Chess 1977). Correlations over short periods proved to be unimpressive.

There are many other authors whose work is relevant to these problems (e.g. Hogan, De Soto and Solano 1977; Magnusson and Endler 1977; Schaie and Parham 1976; Stagner 1977), but time presses, and I will merely return to Mischel and outline the ways in which his views have now been modified (1977). He summarizes the lessons which should have been learned: first, there is multiple determinism of behaviour and a continuous interaction both within the person and in the situation. A focus on either the person alone or the environment alone is highly misleading. Specificity may occur because of the large number of different ways that different people may react to the 'same' treatments and re-interpret them, and because their impact may be easily changed by co-existing conditions. There is a need to qualify generalizations about human behaviour, whether one is searching for generalized person-free situation effects or situation-free personality variables. Then there is the problem of different goals in personality research, e.g. person-centred versus norm-centred. A vast amount of work has been carried out on norm-centred approaches for screening or research purposes. A minority like M.B. Shapiro in this country, and Kelly in the United States, and more recently, of course, the behaviour modifiers, have attacked individual problems by entirely different strategies. Mischel clearly sees the latter approaches as more valuable.

The second main lesson which Mischel outlines is that, by now, what others have called the transactional model of man is strongly supported (Sameroff and Chandler 1975). He writes that 'we continuously influence the "situations" in our lives as well as being affected by them in a mutual organic interaction', and goes on to say that the settings people select may provide clues to their personal qualities.

A third lesson advanced by Mischel is that our subjects' passive role as testees should give way to a more active association as collaborators in the development of descriptions and predictions. He agrees with Bem and Allen (1974) that there is consistency for *some* people at least in *some* areas of behaviour. While some may show consistency of relative position on some traits, virtually no one is consistent on all traits. On the whole, those subjects who predicted their own consistency were the ones who proved to be consistent.

Fourth, we need to develop a taxonomy of environments. Fifth, when information about situations is absent or unclear, knowledge of person variables becomes essential.

For Mischel, the picture of man is of 'an active, aware problem-solver, capable of profiting from an enormous range of experiences and cognitive capacities, possessing great potential for good or ill, actively constructing his or her psychological world, and influencing the environment but also being influenced by it in lawful ways...'. (Mischel 1977) This is in sharp contrast to simplistic views of behaviour as the outcome of narrow sets of determinants, whether habits, drives, reinforcers, constructs, instincts or genes, whether inside or outside the person.

I can deal briefly with the much more familiar IQ data. The belief in a necessary constancy of IQ began to be eroded as a result of longitudinal studies in the 1930s. The two laws then evolved, *which seem to apply to all behavioural data*, were 1. the earlier the measure, the less the long-term reliability; and 2. the longer the period predicted, the less the reliability.

It is now generally agreed that, except in extreme cases (e.g. severe subnormality), early measures have no long-term predictive value. This probably results from a combination of (a) different processes being measured early compared with later measures; (b) the fact that development is proceeding fast in early life and fluctuating fairly rapidly; and (c) a number of important processes have not yet appeared at all in the early years, so that the basis for their prediction is lacking.

For later measures, while there are always significant correlations, these decrease over time to a marked extent, and one can only conclude that variability is as striking as consistency. But of course much depends on how you define these terms. Certainly, however, the declining accuracy of prediction over time, whether ordinal or absolute, cannot primarily be ascribed to errors of measurement. It must therefore mainly reflect genuine personal change. Some recent unpublished data from the longitudinal study of Hindley and Owen are worth considering. They identify six major patterns of IQ change in their sample, and a seventh where no special trend is obvious. For example, there is a group with a steady downward trend between preschool measures and age 17. Here not only is there a change in ordinal position of the group's members but, more important, a declining absolute value of IQ, all the more interesting because groups who are retested on several occasions are usually thought to show practice effects. In general Hindley and Owen's study rather challenges the view of Sontag, Baker and Nelson (1958) that the course of individual growth is always idiosyncratic. One awaits with interest further reports from Hindley and Owen on factors associated with individual IQ variation.

It is clear from this and from much other work, then, that the individual IQ is not necessarily constant, and that both in ordinal position and absolute terms the individual may show a fair amount of change over a decade or more, even in adult life. What does this mean? It could be that these changes are entirely genetically programmed. It could also be that these are responses to subtle changes in the environment of the individual, or most likely it could be the result of both. But whatever the mechanism is does not seem primarily to reside in the measuring instrument, even though in such monstrosities as the 1937 Stanford–Binet, used in research and practice for 25 years, errors due to defective construction and standardization produced gross distortions at ages 2½, 6 and 12 (Clarke 1958).

The effects of naturally occurring or contrived environmental changes

So far, the data indicate rather poor prediction, both of individual ordinal position and also of absolute value of characteristics over long periods of time. Since errors of measurement are unlikely to be cumulative, these findings indicate, primarily, changing rates of development. It is usually quite unclear from correlational data, however, whether such changes are genetic/constitutional or reflect subtle or gross environmental factors, or both. Moreover, the earlier reliance on main effect models (genetics vs environment) has given way to interactionist or transactionist models. So future prediction studies need to be based much more on investigations of interactions, and transactions. The experimental or quasi-experimental method, however, tells us much more firmly about individual change, and crude predictions, particularly when environmental alteration has been considerable, can be made with some confidence, whether in contrived experiments or studies in natural settings. This area of research is likely to be much more profitable than the correlational or psychometric. It has the potential, as yet largely unrealized, for telling us exactly what is happening. As the late Walter Dearborn said to his young student Urie Bronfenbrenner, 'if you want to understand something, try to change it' (Bronfenbrenner 1977). I want to quote just a few studies on the gross effects of environmental change, and it may help if I first offer, as a signpost, the conclusions which can be drawn from such studies. These show that: 1. changes in psychological characteristics always move, on average, in the direction of environmental shift. Their amount depends upon the degree of shift, its nature and duration. There are nevertheless always individual differences, a range of reaction probably constitutional in origin, around mean group changes; 2. the amounts of such alterations are not primarily related to the age of the child; they can occur at any stage even into late adolescence or early adulthood – and just possibly even later. In general, therefore, there are no critical periods of psychological development, although there may be sensitive periods in childhood and even in adulthood (for detailed documentation, see Clarke and Clarke 1976); 3. all this suggests that within limits, human development *may be regarded as somewhat open-ended, at least potentially so.* This is, of course, in no sense to deny the powerful influences of genetic and constitutional factors, but, as is well known, a given genotype may have a variety of phenotypic expressions.

Now let me summarize in telegraphese a few studies, representative of another 50 or so we have reviewed elsewhere (Clarke and Clarke 1976).

Lewis (1954) studied 500 children with poor backgrounds, the worst in Kent, admitted to a reception centre, mostly over 5 years of age. Whereas 40 per cent were in good or fair condition on admission, only two years later this had increased to 75 per cent after exposure to better conditions.

Clarke and Clarke (1954) *and Clarke, Clarke and Reiman* (1958) studied over a six-year period two large samples of mildly retarded, unstable, semi-literate adolescents and young adults, drawn in the main either from bad or exceedingly bad homes. Social histories and IQs were independently collected, indicating large average IQ and social increments in those with the worst backgrounds. These occurred between adolescence and age 30. There was selective sample wastage of the better subjects, hence estimates were conservative.

Bowlby et al. (1956) reported on 60 ex-TB sanatorium children followed up in middle and late childhood. Contrary to prediction these did not become subaverage, affectionless psychopaths although they did show 21 per cent excess maladjustment, some of which, as the authors indicate, is to be attributed to adverse environmental factors other than separation.

Kadushin (1970). Large sample of healthy children, typically coming from large families in substandard circumstances, often below poverty level, and suffering physical neglect. Natural parents showed a picture of promiscuity, mental deficiency, alcoholism, imprisonment and psychosis. At average age 3½, the children had been legally removed from their homes, and after an average of two to three changes of foster home were placed for adoption just over average age 7, and followed up at an average of almost 14 years. Adoptive parents older than natural parents and of a considerably higher socioeconomic level. Outcome was far better than would have been predicted 1. from social history; 2. after several foster changes; and 3. following very late adoption.

The *Koluchová* (1972, 1976) reports on twin boys, isolated, neglected and cruelly treated from 18 months to 7 years, are very detailed. These were severely subnormal, rachitic and virtually without speech upon discovery. Now in a most unusual adoptive home, they are cognitively and emotionally normal and have caught up scholastically. Now aged nearly 18, they have graduated to a technical high school and aim to become electricians. Nor can it be said that their first 18 months of life were ideal. Shortly after birth they were taken into care for a year following the mother's death. Transferred to a maternal aunt for the period 12–18 months, they were then handed over to the sadistic stepmother who banished them to a cellar for the next five-and-a-half years.

Another late intervention programme has been reported by *Feuerstein and Krasilowsky* (1972) and *Feuerstein et al.* (1976) in Israel. Various groups of immigrant adolescents exhibiting IQs between 60 and 90 at the start, with illiteracy or semi-literacy, and sometimes personality disturbances, were exposed to various forms of treatment, intensive training and usually residence in a kibbutz. The external validation of these programmes was derived from Army data on several characteristics some four years later. The means of all groups for a variety of characteristics then lay either a little above or a little below the national Army means, even though originally the subjects were well below average both intellectually, academically and emotionally.

Then there are a large number of training studies which induce development of particular processes in a relatively short time. These may or may not parallel what happens in ordinary life which stimulates development in a much more leisurely way, but at least such studies have a bearing upon the modifiability of development and indicate a particular way in which it can be accelerated.

Summary and conclusions

Let me now summarize. We have glanced at some of the trends apparent at the beginning of the century. Although very different, these had a common philosophical background, in so far as they reflected a one-off, predetermined development, rather than an ongoing determinism. Either at conception, or in the so-called formative years of infancy or early childhood, human characteristics were formed, fixed and predestined. Such views lacked any substantial data base and they suggested that accurate long-term prediction would be easily achieved. They were strengthened by – and in turn justified and reinforced – contemporary social policies, e.g. the use of the IQ to exclude immigrants to the United States, and the passing in this country of the 1913 Mental Deficiency Act to protect us, among other things, from national degeneracy by reducing breeding of 'bad stock'.

Hence the hunt was on – and really still remains on – for stabilities, consistencies and continuities in human characteristics. Yet the accumulation of data over half a century made such an extreme view increasingly untenable. Books by Bloom (1964) and Kagan and Moss (1962) represented final last-ditch attempts to find continuities to the exclusion of variability, as in effect Kagan now points out.

We looked briefly at methodological problems, identifying the ubiquitous and simple correlation coefficient, the main coinage of developmental research, as an ill-understood and tempting seducer. Sample attrition was also seen as a common, and sometimes avoidable, distorter of findings.

Next, we dipped into the field of personality, reviewing evidence that suggested a good deal more behavioural specificity than common sense recognizes. The extremes of situationism on the one hand and trait theory on the other were outlined. Personality seems to be a many splendoured thing, and susceptible to greater change than IQ over long time periods, both being characterized by much more variability than is commonly recognized.

Lastly, we glanced at experimental studies, whether using natural or contrived environmental change as independent variables. All these show an average shift of characteristics in the direction of the change, depending on its amount and duration, with a wide range of individual differences in responsiveness.

Let me now conclude. The rather poor long-term predictions of individual development which except for extreme conditions (e.g. autism) characterize our science do not primarily rest upon inadequacies in our methods of measurement, whether these are test results or social categories. They lie in development itself. No science can predict accurately qualities which have not yet made any appearance in the development of the preschool child, whether these be genetically programmed or dependent upon future transactions between constitution and environment. No science can predict those chance encounters, opportunities or calamities which 20 years ahead can act as strong determinants of stability or change. So we have *to some extent*, and *potentially*, an open-endedness of human development. Yet some of this open-endedness may be more apparent than real, reflecting the strong influence of unfolding genetic programmes, perhaps especially powerful in early life and old age. But even if this so, open-endedness is certainly much greater when a powerful and prolonged environmental change takes place.

But these changes in characteristics clearly have limits which differ markedly between individuals: some maintain rock-like stability in the face of environmental alterations which affect the majority; others show an equally marked capacity for change. And there seems little doubt that this open-endedness declines with age, either because this is intrinsic to the organism or because the individual seeks only the situations which enhance the stabilities which are personally or culturally desirable, or because society puts the person in his place.

Although, as I have argued, we should not expect exact predictions of individual human development, data are now accumulating which enable us to forecast within a broad accuracy the range of reaction that may occur within groups exposed to environmental change, or groups in relatively unchanging circumstances. For example, we know that, for several reasons, children of mildly retarded mothers when adopted by above-average families have a good chance of normality. Under certain circumstances late adopted children do well. On average, neurotic disorders of childhood do not show continuity; sociopathy does in the main but with exceptions. Although specifying a range of possibilities remains crude, it is still of importance, in many cases giving unexpected and valuable indications of future potentialities, and the need for particular social policies. But we know nothing of the processes involved in stability or change.

There is a growing and, I think, very healthy dissatisfaction with the past and present in developmental psychology. 'We lack a substantial science of naturalistic developmental processes', writes McCall (1977). Much contemporary work, says Bronfenbrenner (1977), represents 'the science of the strange behaviour of children in strange situations with strange adults for the briefest periods of time'. Or, for me, much experimental research has represented the pursuit of elegance at the expense of relevance. Moreover, the definition of development embodies a focus on change over time (Wohlwill 1973), yet, as McCall indicates, most developmental psychology is developmental in name only; it is a study of static organisms in static situations (McCall 1977). And as we have stated (Clarke and Clarke 1976) 'There has been a disproportionate amount of time and effort devoted to the earliest years... Far too little is as yet known, in a detailed way, about cognitive and social behaviours at later stages, or their biological and environmental correlates. Developmental research requires effort over a broad spectrum of time if it is to be of any significance,' a point echoed by Bronfenbrenner (1977), who indicates that with less and 'less information through middle childhood and adolescence...[developmental psychology] then becomes virtually silent for decades, until the organism begins to decline, when there is again a spurt of scientific activity'.

We have been dominated too long by notions of fixed characteristics, strong continuities and stability of the ordinal position of individuals. The more balanced view which modern data increasingly demand is of some stabilities, often attenuating over time, and some discontinuities and changes during human development. It suggests an ongoing determinism rather than a one-off predeterminism, with the individual as an active agent in his own development. This awareness of a degree of open-endedness requires a much closer look at the macro- and microsocial factors which construct or maintain stabilities or promote change. Some of the real-life experimental studies recently reported suggest that the prospects ahead are very exciting. Snapshot experimentation now needs to be balanced by a greater investment in long-term process-orientated prospective research.

Note

1   The author is indebted to his wife, Dr Ann Clarke, whose thinking and researches are frequently reflected in this paper; he alone, however, is responsible for its imperfections. Gratitude is also expressed to R.G.B. Clarke for helpful comments upon a preliminary draft.

References

Allport, G.W. (1937) *Personality: A Psychological Interpretation.* New York: Holt, Rinehart & Winston.

Bandura, A. and Walters, R.W. (1963) *Social Learning and Personality Development.* New York: Holt, Rinehart & Winston.

Bem, D.J. and Allen, A. (1974) 'On predicting some of the people some of the time: The search for cross-situational consistencies in behavior.' *Psychological Review 81*, 506–520.

Binet, A. (1905) 'Analyse de C. Spearman "The proof and measurement of association between two things" et "General intelligence objectively determined and measured".' *L'Annee psychologique 11*, 623–624.

Block, J. (1971) *Lives Through Time.* Berkeley, California: Bancroft Books.

Bloom, B.S. (1964) *Stability and Change in Human Characteristics.* London: Wiley.

Bowers, K.S. (1973) 'Situationism in psychology: An analysis and a critique.' *Psychological Review 80*, 307–336.

Bowers, K.S. (1977) 'There's more to Iago than meets the eye: A clinical account of personal consistency.' In D. Magnusson and N.S. Endler (eds), *Personality at the Crossroads: Current Issues in Interactional Psychology.* Hillsdale, NJ: Erlbaum.

Bowlby, J., Ainsworth, M.D., Boston, M. and Rosenbluth, D. (1956) 'The effects of mother–child separation: A follow-up study.' *British Journal of Medical Psychology 29*, 211–247.

Bronfenbrenner, U. (1977) 'Towards an experimental ecology of human development.' *American Psychologist 32*, 513–531.

Clarke, A.D.B. (1958) 'The 1937 Revision of the Stanford–Binet Scale – a critical appraisal.' *Bulletin of the British Psychological Society 35*, 11–13.

Clarke, A.D.B. and Clarke, A.M. (1954) 'Cognitive changes in the feebleminded.' *British Journal of Psychology 45*, 173–179.

Clarke, A.D.B. and Clarke, A.M. (1972) 'Consistency and variability in the growth of human characteristics.' In W.D. Wall and V.P. Varma (eds) *Advances in Educational Psychology*, vol. I, 33–52. London: University of London Press.

Clarke, A.D.B., Clarke, A.M. and Reiman, S. (1958) 'Cognitive and social changes in the feebleminded – three further studies.' *British Journal of Psychology 49*, 144–157.

Clarke, A.M. and Clarke, A.D.B. (eds) (1976) *Early Experience: Myth and Evidence.* London: Open Books.

Clarke, A.M. and Clarke, A.D.B. (1977) 'Problems in comparing the effects of environmental change at different ages.' In H. McGurk (ed) *Ecological Factors in Human Development*, 47–58. Amsterdam: North Holland.

Clarke, A.M. and Clarke, A.D.B. (1978) 'Early experience: Its limited effect upon later development.' In D. Shaffer and J.F. Dunn (eds), *The First Year of Life.* New York: Wiley (In press).

Dearborn, W.F. (1928) *Intelligence Tests: Their Significance for School and Society.* Boston: Houghton Mifflin.

Dearborn, W.F. and Rothney, J.W.M. (1941) *Predicting the Child's Development.* Cambridge, Mass: Sci-Art Publications.

Feuerstein, R., Hoffman, M., Krasilowsky, D., Rand, Y. and Tannenbaum, A.J. (1976) 'The effects of group care on the psychosocial habilitation of immigrant adolescents in Israel, with special reference to high-risk children.' *Intersational Review of Applied Psychology 25*, 189–201.

Feuerstein, R. and Krasilowsky, D. (1972) 'Interventional strategies for the significant modification of cognitive functioning in the disadvantaged adolescent.' *Journal of the American Academy of Child Psychiatry 11*, 572–581.

Fisher, M.A. and Zeaman, D. (1970) 'Growth and decline of retardate intelligence.' In N.R. Ellis (ed) *International Review of Research in Mental Retardation*, vol. 4, 151–191. New York: Academic Press.

Fiske, D.W. (1974) 'The limits for the conventional science of personality.' *Journal of Personality 42*, 1–11.

Hindley, C.B. and Owen, C.F. (1978) 'Individual patterns of DQ and IQ curves from 6 months to 17 years.' *British Journal of Psychology.*

Hogan, H., De Soto, C.B. and Solano, C. (1977) 'Traits, tests and personality research.' *American Psychologist 32,* 255–264.

Kadushin, A. (1970) *Adopting Older Children.* New York: Columbia University Press.

Kagan, J. and Klein, R.E. (1973) 'Cross-cultural perspectives on early development.' *American Psychologist 28,* 947–961.

Kagan, J. and Moss, H.A. (1962) *Birth to Maturity.* New York: Wiley.

Koluchová, J. (1972) 'Severe deprivation in twins: A case study.' *Journal of Child Psychology and Psychiatry 13,* 107–114.

Koluchová, J. (1976) 'A report on the further development of twins after severe and prolonged deprivation.' In A.M. Clarke and A.D.B. Clarke (eds) *Early Experience: Myth and Evidence* 55–66. London: Open Books.

Labouvie, E.W., Bartsch, T.W., Nesselroade, J.R. and Baltes, P.B. (1974) 'On the internal and external validity of simple longitudinal designs.' *Child Development 45,* 282–290.

Lewis, H. (1954) *Deprived Children.* London: Oxford University Press.

Macfarlane, J.W. (1964) 'Perspectives on personality consistency and change from the guidance study.' *Vita Humana 7,* 115–126.

Magnusson, D. (1974) *The Person and the Situation in the Traditional Measurement Model.* Report of the Department of Psychology, University of Stockholm, no. 426.

Magnusson, D. (1976) *Consistency and Coherence in Personality: A Discussion of Lawfulness at Different Levels.* Report of the Department of Psychology, University of Stockholm, no. 472.

Magnusson, D. and Endler, N.S. (eds) (1977) *Personality at the Crossroads: Current Issues in Interactional Psychology.* Hillsdale, NJ: Erlbaum.

McCall, R.B. (1977) Challenges to a science of developmental psychology. *Child Development 48,* 333–344.

Mischel, W. (1968) *Personality and Assessment.* New York: Wiley.

Mischel, W. (1977) 'On the future of personality measurement.' *American Psychologist 32,* 246–254.

Opolot, J.A. (1977) 'Reliability and validity of Smith's quick measure of achievement motivation scale.' *British Journal of Social and Clinical Psychology 16,* 395–396.

Sameroff, A.J. and Chandler, M.J. (1975) 'Reproductive risk and the continuum of caretaking casualty.' In F.D. Horowitz, E.M. Hetherington, S. Scarr-Salapatek and G.M. Siegel (eds) *Review of Child Development Research,* vol. 4. Chicago: University of Chicago Press.

Schaie, K.W. and Parham, I.A. (1976) 'Stability of adult personality traits: Fact or fable?' *Journal of Personality and Social Psychology 34,* 146–158.

Skeels, H.M. (1966) 'Adult status of children with contrasting early life experiences: A follow-up study.' *Monogaphs of the Society for Research in Child Development,* 105, 3.

Skeels, H.M. and Dye, H.B. (1939) 'A study of the effects of differential stimulation on mentally retarded children.' *Proceedings of the American Assocication on Mental Deficiency 44,* 114–136.

Sontag, L.W., Baker, C.T. and Nelson, V.L. (1958) 'Mental Growth and Personality Development: A Longtudinal Study.' *Monogaphs of the Society for Research in Child Development,* 68, 2.

Stagner, R. (1977) 'On the reality and relevance of traits.' *Journal of Genetic Psychology 96,* 185–207.

Thomas, A. and Chess, S. (1976) 'Evolution of behavior disorders into adolescence.' *American Journal of Psychiatry 133,* 539–542.

Thomas, A. and Chess, S. (1977) *Temperament and Development.* New York: Brunner/Mazel.

Watson, J.B. (1928) *Psychological Care of Infant and Child.* New York: Norton.

Wohlwill, J.F. (1973) *The Study of Behavioral Development.* New York: Academic Press.

Wolf, T.H. (1973) *Alfred Binet.* Chicago and London: University of Chicago Press.

CHAPTER 5

Developmental Discontinuities
An Approach to Assessing Their Nature

Commentary

Our 1976 book, *Early Experience: Myth and Evidence*, was widely read in the USA and led to an invitation to speak at the University of Vermont conference on the Primary Prevention of Psychopathology in the summer of 1981. This chapter is the text which one of us offered on that occasion.

Our thesis is that while there can be a strong *correlation* between early experience and later personality attributes, we did not consider that there is a necessary *causal* connection between the two. It was argued that later events during development, themselves continuing the earlier influences, were at least equally effective in determining the outcome. It follows that adoption of seriously disadvantaged children into superior adoptive homes is probably the best solution for children removed from their families. This would prevent the many problems which would otherwise continue.

The chapter starts with a critique of a very famous study by Skeels and his collaborator, Marie Skodak, the latter being present at the conference. This research, which would have been entirely familiar to the audience, is elaborated here since it was sketchily outlined in the lecture. It remains important though it has been misunderstood both by Skeels, the main author, and everyone else.

Skeels had worked in, among other facilities, a very austere orphanage in Iowa with very deprived infants who, under the terrible regime, became seriously mentally disabled. Two infants, functioning as very retarded, were removed and placed in a 'colony' for the learning disabled. As the only infants present, they were looked after in a ward for moderately and mildly retarded women in this state institution. Six months later, Skeels visited and enquired about the infants and was amazed at their progress, intellectually and in other ways, which he attributed to their having become 'pets' of the retarded women. This led to an experiment when 11 other children from the orphanage were deliberately moved to the 'colony' in view of their poor prognosis. It was expected that, as further 'pets', they would be stimulated by the inmates and the ward attendants. They, too, responded and in due course were offered for late adoption, leaving the institution for good. Followed up some 25 years after the last contact, they proved to be normal citizens, attributed by Skeels to the *early* influences upon them in the state 'colony' rather than their experiences later in adoptive homes. We can again illustrate our viewpoint by the case study of one infant, selected as unpromising, left behind in the orphanage and placed in a contrast group. His strange life history had an unexpected outcome. When he entered school he was found to have a moderate hearing loss, so was transferred to a residential school for the deaf at the age of eight. Here the matron took a fancy to him as one of the youngest who had no family. She thus provided him with all the things which he earlier had lacked. At follow-up in adulthood he had a skilled job, a stable marriage, four intelligent children, owning a house in a middle-class area and was earning as much as all the rest of the 11 contrast persons. His experiences after the age of 8 had redeemed him.

Late adoption is then considered in the lecture as a way of creating discontinuity. Also reviewed are studies of cumulative deficit, and finally there are comments on some intensive, but expensive, early intervention programmes. The results of such endeavours are still to some extent being debated, but seem to have resulted in rather modest gains for their participants.

Developmental Discontinuities: An Approach to Assessing their Nature[*]

Ann M. Clarke[1]

Two unrelated streams of work, starting at the turn of the century, have made a powerful and ongoing impact upon our model of human development. Both stressed continuities in development, whether through genetic factors or through the formative role of the early environment. The first stream – Galton, Pearson, Spearman – led to the explicit statement that the IQ was constant. At the same time Freud and his followers suggested that affective development

[*]   From L.A. Bond and J.M. Joffe (eds) (1982) *Facilitating Infant and Early Childhood Development*, pp.58–77, by permission of the University Press of New England, Hanover, NH, USA

was fixed for good or ill in the first few years, to be modified, if at all, by later psychotherapy.

I have been asked to write about discontinuities, and although my husband and I were among the first to discuss this topic (Clarke and Clarke 1972, 1977), I should make it clear that I neither deny nor underestimate the continuities that exist; accounting for them is more difficult; some *discontinuities* are likely to be genetically caused, and in other cases we lack adequate measuring tools to determine in a precise way developmental patterns.

Developmental discontinuity, whether for individuals or groups, may best be defined under a number of headings:

- The emergence of an entirely new characteristic not present earlier, for example, the onset of schizophrenia, stammering or formal reasoning.

- The disappearance or inhibition of an habitual characteristic, for example, the disappearance of crawling as a preferred mode of mobility, loss of a school phobia, the burning out of an emotional disorder of childhood.

- A significant shift in the ordinal position of an individual (let us say arbitrarily by a standard deviation or more) on a second or later assessment of status on a particular characteristic, for example, a large IQ increment or decrement, a large change in degree of extra version at adolescence. Such a shift would normally imply either a change in the level or relative level of the characteristic (Clarke 1978).

- Reflecting the point immediately above, a significant change in the test–retest correlation for groups, implying large changes in ordinal position for at least some subjects in the sample. A change in average *level* for the sample may or may not be implied.

Such discontinuities may be sudden and large, or slow and small, with everything in between these extremes. They may occur in response to environmental change, or they may arise within some environmental constancy. Thus we shall be looking both at discontinuities in relation to environmental change and also in the more-or-less constant micro-environment. A constant micro-environment should not be construed as a static one – obviously the social environment changes as a young child matures. But certain socioeconomic and psychological factors within a family and neighbourhood can meaningfully be viewed as predictable. Contrast this usual rearing situation, however, with the effects of rescue on a socially isolated child, and it is clear that a real distinction between constant and inconstant environments can validly be made.

Apart from these brief introductory remarks, this paper will be divided into three sections: first, some problems central to measurement and evaluation; second, empirical research; and third, concluding discussion. A vast and indigestible amount of material could be packed into the allotted space but, instead, the empirical data will merely be exemplified.

Some problems concerned with measurement

Two problems should be outlined. The first is really strategic or philosophical. If your model of development stresses continuities, you do not search for discontinuities. Hence although some popular stage theories are really discontinuity theories, remarkably little notice has been taken of their implications. Take, for example, the vast number of longitudinal correlational studies of various human characteristics, particularly IQ. Early papers by Nemzek (1933) and Thorndike (1940) summarized several hundred studies on this theme. They showed: 1. that preschool tests had little, if any, long-term predictive value; 2. that at all ages, the longer the test–retest time interval, the lower the correlation, that is, the greater the change of ordinal position of individuals. Recently updated literature analyses confirm these findings (Jensen 1980; McAskie and Clarke 1976). We can assume that the correlation between ages 3 to 5 with adult intelligence is around 0.4, increasing to around 0.7 in middle childhood (6 to 9 years). By contrast, the correlation for height between age 6 and adulthood is 0.8; a commensurate correlation for IQ is only attained in late adolescence. With height, one is measuring the same dimension in early childhood as later, but with cognitive skills one is assessing *qualitatively* different behaviours in these two life periods. Thus it can be noted that it is not possible from any early behavioural measures during the period of considerable brain growth to predict adult ability to think abstractly (except in rare, extreme cases). This appears to represent a real discontinuity both in quality and in the individual's ordinal position of cognitive functions between preschool and later. An analogy might be with the metamorphosis of the butterfly – is the sequence caterpillar, chrysalis, butterfly to be regarded as evidence for continuity or discontinuity?

The second problem relates to difficulties in comparing levels of individual performance of psychological characteristics across time and space as a result of one or more of the following factors: 1. inadequate standardization of an instrument; 2. differences in the content of tests; and 3. secular trends (Jensen 1980; McAskie and Clarke 1976). To track cognitive or social development across the life span using either longitudinal or cross-sectional data always involves changing the measuring device along the line. Our task in assessing continuities or discontinuities is not helped by the fact that our tools are subject to often considerable errors of measurement. Please note, I am *not* referring to test bias.

My generation slowly discovered that the 1937 Stanford–Binet had different means at different ages, but, worse still, standard deviations that varied between 12 and 20 points. These errors ensure that a *constant* IQ for a bright or retarded child would, for example, appear grossly *inconstant* between ages 6 and 12, by as much as 24 points. The even greater horrors in the standardization of the 1916 Binet have been buried in the mists of time and have to be seen to be believed. We carried out a recent exhumation and with great difficulty secured from across the Atlantic the original standardization data. There can be no doubt that adolescent and adult IQs are seriously underestimated (e.g. Mitchell 1941) and that IQ levels (though not correlations) in some of the still widely quoted nature–nurture papers (e.g. Skodak and Skeels 1949) are in need of reinterpretation. A number of earlier and more sophisticated researchers, however, appreciated this problem and fiddled the Chronological Age (CA) denominator. Nor do our difficulties with this test stop after the first two revisions. The recent Texas Adoption Study (Horn, Loehlin and Willerman 1979) used the 1960 norms for younger children and ended up having to subtract 7 points from each IQ. Scarr and Weinberg (1976), using the 1972 norms, apparently avoided this problem.

Note that these problems are important in considering *level* of performance but are relatively unimportant in studies where only *ordinal position* is evaluated, as Outhit (1933) so elegantly demonstrated. But level of performance is often crucially important in developmental psychology. To have to rely solely on correlations is hampering, to say the least.

Nor is it only IQ where there may be measurement difficulties. Take the assessment of that many-splendoured thing, personality. Here the problems are that: 1. many personality tests consist of self-report – what individuals *say* they are or do (whereas cognitive tests assess what they actually do); 2. much of the information on child characteristics relies on ratings which tend to have a much lower reliability; and 3. there is a degree of situational specificity to personality expression. This is notably less than the situationists imply but more than could be predicted from trait theories. Attempts to identify basic and early expressions of temperament that would hold up over time have been similarly unsuccessful (Thomas and Chess 1977).

Empirical research

The prevention of psychopathology involves understanding its causes and assessing the efficacy of intervention programmes. Psychopathology is concerned with deviant development, which in turn involves a focus on the nature and causes of human differences.

This is by no means to deny the importance of commonalities in development such as those which Piaget has investigated, nor the fact that nature and nurture are essential and interlocking processes. It may well also be that heritability indices are a latter-day philosopher's stone: in any case their sample dependence leads to widely different estimates, some of which have been collated by Vandenberg (1971) in connection with twin studies. But it has appeared to me that some psychologists, in their urgent desire to get away from painful, politically emotive issues of individual differences, have hoped that if they focused their attention on process models of development such as Piaget's, the differences would go away. Unfortunately, however, when various subgroups of the American and British populations were assessed on Piagetian tasks, the disparities across social classes (or ethnic subgroups) were, if anything, greater than on conventional IQ tests. Teachers and social workers are still going to have to cope with children whose characteristics vary enormously; these cannot be obscured.

In an attempt to make sense of a great deal of apparently controversial material, which has vexed those interested in developmental abnormalities for years, I have undertaken detailed analyses of studies in the following areas:

- studies of infants adopted soon after birth
- studies of later adopted children
- case studies of children rescued from severe deprivation
- studies of cumulative deficit
- social factors affecting attainment and adjustment
- the outcome of experimental intervention programmes, notably those by Skeels and by Heber and Garber (the Milwaukee project).

They will be briefly considered, one by one.

Early adoption

The many studies of very early adopted children show quite uniformly: 1. average or above average intellectual status; 2. correlations with the natural parent's status; and 3. low correlations with the adopted parent's status, which can often be accounted for by 4. evidence of selective placement. In interpreting the first point, too rarely is account taken of selective factors that determine which children are considered for adoption and the timing of adoption. However, there is a great deal of evidence, acknowledged in the Scarr and Weinberg (1976) transracial study, that these are important in interpreting the outcomes of early and later adoptions. As you may know, I do not believe that there is any reason to assume that lack of secure and stimulating early environment has by itself negative implications for later development, provided there follows a total ecological change into a greatly superior environment (Clarke and Clarke 1976). These points will be illustrated by referring in the first instance to two studies that have had a seminal and probably distorting effect on our view of early development.

Behind many attempts to help disadvantaged children and behind some of the thinking on importance for later development of early environmental events looms the figure of that great humanist Harold Skeels. He and his colleague Marie Skodak are best known for two research projects: one reported the outcome for a large sample of infants adopted in the first six months of life whose mothers were said to be of low intelligence (Skodak 1939; Skodak and Skeels 1945; Skodak and Skeels 1949); the second (Skeels 1966) was entitled, 'Adult status of children with contrasting *early* life experiences' (present author's italics). It will be assumed that readers are familiar with both studies, but that, unlike ourselves, they have not spent weeks pursuing all the relevant documents and combing through them to establish whether the implications attributed by the authors and many later commentators are necessarily justified.

Probably all the important points can be made by reference to the 1966 paper. This contrasted the fortunes in adult life of 13 young children in the Iowa Soldiers' Orphan Homes in the 1930s, supposedly rehabilitated in an institution for the mentally retarded, with a group who remained in the orphanage. This gives evidence of very considerable and intensive screening by the various adoption agencies, no doubt reflecting the requirements of potential parents, of *all* children who were adopted in Iowa during the relevant period. It is clear from the various papers on the early adopted children that there was selective placement; common sense demands that there was likely to be very careful selection *into* adoption in the first place. And this is in fact very well documented:

> Since study homes or temporary care homes were not available to the state agency at that time, the choice for children who were not suitable for immediate placement in adoptive homes was between, on the one hand, an

unstimulating, large nursery with predictable mental retardation or, on the other hand, a radical iconoclastic solution, that is, placement in institutions for the mentally retarded in a bold experiment to see whether retardation in infancy was reversible... Children whose development was so delayed that adoptive placement was out of the question remained in the orphanage. (Skeels 1966, p.7)

At the ages when adoptive placement usually occurred, nine of the children in the contrast group had been considered normal in mental development. All 12 were not placed, however, because of different circumstances: five were withheld from placement simply because of poor family histories, two because of other health problems and one because of possible mental retardation. (Skeels 1966, p.11)

The contrast-group members remained in the orphanage until placement. One was returned to relatives, but in most instances the children were eventually transferred to an institution for the mentally retarded as long-term protected residents. A few of the contrast group had been briefly approved for adoptive placement, and two had been placed for short periods. None was successful, however, and the children's decline in mental level removed them from the list of those eligible for adoption. (Skeels 1966, p.12)

While it is true that the very incomplete histories of the biological families of the two groups showed relatively little difference, it is also apparent that none of these children was eligible for placement in adoptive homes before the age of 6 months. It further appears from the honestly reported medical histories, that among the 12 contrast children there were more with possible neural damage than in the experimental group.

It is evident from Skeels's (1936) first paper that 1. the Bureau of Welfare required that a child remain in a foster home at least 12 months before adoption was permitted, and 2. On 1 February, 1934 a policy was established whereby no child could be adopted until a psychological examination had been made.

As already noted, examination of the standardization of the 1916 Stanford–Binet makes clear that it underestimated the IQs of adults and that, therefore, we have no way of accurately estimating the intelligence level of biological mothers of adopted children in Iowa in the 1930s (see Mitchell 1941). My conclusion from all I have collated is that in the early adoption study the biological mothers were in the average range. I also conclude that an unknown number of children were returned by the adopting homes as unsuitable. All of which adds up to a highly selected sample of infants who became the subjects of the world's most famous adoption study.

Shall we return to the children who, at Skeels's request, were sent as house guests to the Glenwood State School after varying periods in the orphanage? Of the 13, 11 surmounted the obstacle race into adoptive homes and were not returned; two failed and remained in the institution for the mentally retarded. Both of these women were later discharged and at the time of follow-up were in modest jobs, one of them having married. The remaining 11 adoptees were on the whole more successful. It should also be noted that all of these children had spent time in the orphanage whose facilities for infants were, to say the least, very meagre; they were then moved into an institution for retarded people where, according to Skeels, they were actively encouraged to make a close relationship with one person, and then at ages varying from 13 months to 82 months, averaging 37 months, all but two were removed from these loving mother figures and placed in adoptive homes to start making relationships all over again. On the whole, however, the outcome in adult life was good. For my money this progress was very marginally due to the early life experiences and massively due to the later prolonged period of security in permanent homes.

Meanwhile, the 12 contrast children had failed in the obstacle race into adoption and remained in the orphanage, with the exception of one boy (case 19). His ancestry was relatively impeccable, but he had a hearing loss and his IQ was, during the critical period, on a downward course. However, having survived the orphanage for eight years, during the latter period being given special educational help, he was transferred to a residential school for the deaf where he made good all-round progress and completed 12th grade. At follow-up in adulthood he was totally atypical of the contrast group, more closely resembling the better members of the experimental group. Surely his progress was related both to his natural endowments and his circumstances in later life?

Late adoption

What might some of the seminal factors be in determining outcome for late adoptees? Kadushin (1970) has sensitively documented his views, based on his own and other research workers' experiences as he described a cohort of late-adopted children removed from deplorable circumstances adapting to the social and academic expectations of their new homes.

It is true that in this study, as in other adoption studies, there was selection: nobody with an IQ below 80 was offered. Nevertheless the fact remains that these children came from very low status families and many of them had had an incredibly rough time; they had been removed from their parents by court order and had been in several foster homes. 'Outcome was positively related to parents' acceptance of the child, in their perception of him as a member of the family, and negatively related to self-consciousness by parents regarding adoptive status' (Kadushin 1970, p.210).

Kadushin did not feel the need to offer evidence on the IQs of his late-adopted children. He felt it was sufficient to look deeply into the social and emotional adjustment of the children to their new parents and the outcome in terms of achievement at school. In seeking to identify the factors responsible for the resilience which so many children have shown in recovery from earlier traumas, he offers two. First, of course, the security of the home and the relationships within it, but in addition and very important, he suggests that the wider social context plays a significant part in the recovery process. He points out that these children had made *two* important shifts in moving from their own seriously disadvantaged backgrounds via foster homes to the adoptive contexts. They made a change from homes that offered little in the way of meeting their needs in terms of affection, acceptance, support, understanding, and encouragement to the adoptive homes that offered some measure of these essential psychic supplies. They also changed from deprived lower-class, multi-problem contexts to respectable, status-conscious, middle-class homes.

The child 'now receives messages which proclaim his acceptability, and support, reinforce, and strengthen whatever components, however limited, of self-acceptance he has been able to develop as a result of whatever small amount of affection he received in his former home. The effect of positive parent–child relationships within the home are now buttressed by social relationships outside the home rather than vitiated by the contradiction between the acceptance of the lower-class child in the lower-class home and his rejection by the community' (Kadushin 1970, p.222).

My own conclusion is that older children adapt towards the academic and behavioural norms of their domestic community whatever these may be. They may adapt up or they may adapt down, but the general ecology in which children are reared has almost certainly an important impact on their achievement and their adjustment: their motivation is bound to be affected as goals change.

Case studies of children rescued from severe deprivation

There are a few well-documented case studies of children rescued from conditions far more deprived and depraved than those which are normally considered in studies of deprivation. I am aware that the outcome is not equally happy in all cases, but hope I may be forgiven for not diverting from my course to contrast Genie, for example, with Isabelle or the Koluchová twins. My purpose here is to present evidence that we must take into account in considering developmental discontinuity. Many of you will already be familiar with the history presented by Mason (1942) and Davis (1947) of a 6-year-old child, Isabelle, rescued from lifelong isolation with a deaf-mute mother. When discovered she was rachitic, without speech, and apparently severely retarded. She received prolonged specialist treatment and at follow-up when she was 14 was regarded as normal.

The Czechoslovakian twins documented by Koluchová (1972, 1976) were reared first in an institution, then with a maternal aunt until the age of 18 months. They were then isolated and cruelly treated in the home of their father and stepmother. On discovery at the age of 7 they were severely rachitic, without speech, emotionally disturbed, and had IQs of around 40. A prolonged specialist rehabilitation programme which included placement at the age of 9 in a most carefully selected adoptive home resulted in recovery into cognitive, academic and emotional normalcy.

Recently because of our known interest in cases of this kind we were approached by a research worker, Angela Roberts of Manchester University, who is an unusually qualified nurse. She spent a period in Bogota, Colombia, associated with a missionary orphanage that catered for a small group of abandoned illegitimate babies or infants given up because their parents could not cope. The illegitimate were usually the babies of young teenage servants and sometimes were literally foundlings. One little boy, Adam, was abandoned at 4 months and first received into a reformatory for girls. Our colleague visited him there and describes the conditions as appalling. His main diet was a watery vegetable soup and porridge, and he remained in a bleak, bare, windowless room in perpetual darkness, unless the door was open.

On admission to the mission orphanage Adam, aged 16 months, weighed only 12 lb, 12 oz. He had the physical signs of nutritional marasmus, his head was infested, he had scabies, a fungal rash, and numerous sores. His abdomen was grossly distended. Emotionally he was completely withdrawn; he could not sit, crawl or walk. His development appeared similar to that of a 3 month infant. A local doctor diagnosed him as an extremely malnourished, mentally retarded spastic. By 23 months of age his weight was 23lb, he could sit up from a prone position, could stand holding furniture, could imitate two words together, and could feed himself with a spoon. A month later he could stand without support for a few seconds and could walk around his cot holding on with one hand. At 26 months, ten months after admission, he weighed 26lb, took his first independent steps, had improved emotionally and in other ways, and at 32 months was adopted by a North American family. There were, of course, problems, but by the age of 5 Adam was essentially average both mentally and physically. At the age of 7¾ Adam is in the second grade and is evaluated by his teacher as an average 7-year-old, who is showing signs of specific talents.

Case studies of this kind illustrate in a tragic but dramatic way the effect of physical and social deprivation on developing humans, together with later recovery granted very special help and complete removal from the depriving circumstances. Some of you may wonder if I believe their recovery to be complete? Might they be even more able and stable had they not been subjected to these dreadful experiences? The answer of course is that I cannot be sure, but as some kind of Popperian I think we have here two alternatives, either to face the possibility that this is a hypothesis which is unfalsifiable or to make a stab at a solution. If we follow the psychoanalytic argument I think we will find that none of us is functioning at an optimal level – whatever that might be. My tentative solution is as follows: one should be able to make an actuarial prediction of the probable outcome for deprived children had they been reared in more normal circumstances with biological relatives (in the case of the Koluchová twins by their simple-minded father and mother who died). Sibling controls offer a potentially helpful solution but the data are not always available.

Studies of cumulative deficit

This familiar concept seems to have had its roots in a study by the Englishman, Gordon (1923), who found that canal-boat children averaged an IQ of 87 at age 6 and of 60 at age 12. The correlation between age and IQ was –0.76. Subsequently considerable research has been carried out, much of it in the United States, with controversy about the cause of declining IQs in children reared in disadvantaged circumstances.

Jensen (1974, 1977) has published two studies using older and younger sibling comparisons. The first, in California, found a significant age decrement in verbal but not in non-verbal IQ among black elementary school children. This difference averaged only 2 IQ points for an average sibling age discrepancy between about 19 and 31 months in the age range 5 to 12. Jensen raises the possibility that this small decrement may reflect reading differences on the verbal test.

The second study took place in rural Georgia and again used older and younger sibling comparisons. Significant and substantial linear IQ decrements, both verbal and non-verbal, between 5 and 16 years occurred in blacks but not in whites. There was an average decrement of 1.62 verbal IQ points per year and 1.19 non-verbal IQ points, over the age range 6 to 16. Jensen believes that an environmental explanation seems reasonable in this case. Kamin (1978), while not claiming to invalidate the notion of cumulative deficit, raises the possibility that the younger siblings may have been responding to general social and educational improvements that were taking place during the relevant period.

Heber's (1968) first study in Milwaukee seems to me to offer impressive cross-sectional evidence for cumulative deficit. Among the important factors to which he and his colleagues drew attention was that socioeconomic status is a rather poor guide to the familial processes that result in cumulative deficit. It will be recalled that he was able to differentiate between families living in the same slum, showing an average considerable deficit occurring in children whose mothers' IQs lay below 80 but no deficit among the children whose mothers' IQs lay above 80.

I would like to draw some conclusions from the material I have presented so far. It seems to me that studies of early-adopted children rather clearly show genetic effects and fail to show commensurate correlations with the rearing environment after account has been taken of selective placement. This is not altogether surprising in view of the selection both of infants and of adopting families. There is one French adoption study, however, which is an exception. Schiff, Duyme, Dumaret, Stewart, Tomkiewicz and Feingold (1978) employed an entirely novel method that I hope will be followed by others. They searched the files of six public adoption agencies to find children of lower-class origin adopted into high-status homes who also had a sibling or half-sibling reared by the biological mothers. There are some problems with the presentation of the data, which make me cautious in interpreting the findings. However 32 adopted children were located, born to mothers and fathers who were unskilled workers; only 20 siblings were found, reared by their own mothers. The 20 home-reared children had average IQs of 94.5 and the 32 adoptees of 110.6, or on another test 95.4 and 106.9 respectively. In terms of school attainment the authors state that the two groups were typical of their rearing environments. Certainly the home-reared children were very much more likely than their adopted siblings to have presented educational problems. Only two out of 20 adopted had repeated a grade or been in a special class, whereas 13 out of 20 home-reared siblings had. None of the adopted had IQs below 85 and only five lay between 85 and 102. Among their disadvantaged siblings, three had IQs below 85 and only five were above 102 (Schiff, personal communication). This study clearly needs replication for, among other things, the extent to which such adopted children are accelerated by the positive features of the environment or the home-reared depressed by negative aspects remains unclear.

My second conclusion is that cumulative deficit among socially disadvantaged families is a very real phenomenon. It appears to affect a minority of developing children. Taking the data together there appears to be good evidence for the social environment operating as a threshold phenomen. The majority of the children growing up in an advanced nation almost certainly lie above that threshold; for them the physical and social environment is sufficiently adequate for genetic effects to show up as major causes of differences. Below the threshold it seems likely that there are various degrees of deficit which will be related to the severity of family pathology. There is as yet little direct evidence for this: I present it simply as a hunch. However if we were to accept varying degrees of pathology leading to varying degrees of deficit, the chances are that we may have to think in terms of a substantial minority of our children who may be subject to effective environmental deprivation.

My third conclusion is that late-adopted children represent a different sample in terms of family background to the early adopted and that removing those reared in very adverse conditions to superior homes results in normal development.

Attainment, adjustment and intervention programmes

The question of creating discontinuity through intervention with socially disadvantaged children is exceedingly important. Here may I say that despite the evidence recently published by Willerman, Horn and Loehlin (1977) suggesting that achievement is no more subject to social influences than is the IQ, a great deal of other evidence persuades me that this may not be the case. Admittedly some of it comes from studies of the gifted, with particular reference to the over-representation of first-born children in areas of academic distinction, which are beyond the scope of this paper. However a recent longitudinal study by Rutter, Maughan, Mortimore and Ouston (1979) conducted in inner London schools serving below-average adolescents provides evidence of a very significant differential influence of schools on attainment and adjustment after allowance has been made for pre-entry differences in verbal reasoning and parental status. School variables that appeared to be irrelevant to outcome were those indices related to material factors, for example, size or age of school or amount of resources. Variables that were found to be important include the balance of intellectual intake (but not social or ethnic), academic emphasis and teacher behaviour, and positive attitudes among the staff toward their pupils. This study shows how schools may differentially contribute to discontinuities in those areas of competence that society most values; both family and school process variables are likely to affect outcome.

So far as intervention with the disadvantaged is concerned, the majority of programmes so far have been made available to preschool children whose IQs, as already noted, are not usually more than minimally predictive of cognitive status in later life. Furthermore, advantages in IQ for experimentally treated children are usually lost fairly rapidly (Bronfenbrenner 1974; Zigler and Trickett 1979).

These points are exemplified in the two recent reports of the Consortium for Longitudinal Studies (Lazar and Darlington 1978; Lazar, Hubbell, Murray, Rosche and Royce 1977). The major finding was that before inception into these specially designed, high-quality programmes, the treatment and control children did not differ in IQ. At age 6 treatment children scored significantly higher than controls and this superiority continued for at least three school years after the end of the preschool programmes. At the time of the latest follow-up in adolescence, however, there was no significant difference between treatment and control children on WISC-R scores for the vast majority of these projects. Very sensibly the researchers, perhaps influenced by Edward Zigler, gathered data on school achievement. They found that children who had attended preschool were only about half as likely as control children to be attending special education classes. They were also less likely to be retained in grade. However on achievement test scores, although there was a significant difference between mathematics scores of treatment and control children, the reading scores did not differ. Furthermore, although I do not wish to devalue the importance of the work and the care with which the follow-up was conducted, we are dealing here with differences among children for whom the general level is low. The Consortium monitored the long-term outcome of programmes that were limited in the amount of time devoted to the children and indeed to their families, and there was, in the end, no difference shown between one kind of excellent programme and another. Nor was there any relation between outcome and age of entry to the preschool programme or time spent within it. Although evaluation of the admittedly limited gains is hazardous, it seems likely that the mediating mechanism may well have been the mothers' contacts with intelligent, informed and devoted people who encouraged somewhat higher aspirations for the children than they otherwise would have had. Perhaps even longer support for these families and enrichment programmes for the children as they go through school might result in an even better outcome.

One of the most imaginative and courageous experiments was started in Milwaukee in the mid-1960s (e.g. Garber and Heber 1977, 1978; Heber 1968; Heber, Garber, Harrington, Hoffman and Falender 1972). This programme was designed to provide maximum intervention short of removing the children altogether from their families. The intervention effectively started at the birth of the children included in the experimental group in that those who were later to stimulate and enrich the infants were in contact with their mothers. Formal intervention started at the age of 3 months on a full-day basis and lasted until the children entered school at the age of 6. From 24 months to 72 months the experimental group maintained an advantage over the control subjects of between 20 and 34 IQ points. Intervention terminated at school entry, which was at the mean age of 72 months. At this point the experimental group's mean IQ was 120.7 (SD=11.2) compared to the control group's mean IQ of 87.2 (SD=12.8), a difference of over 30 IQ points. The authors of this programme have repeatedly enjoined us not to over-interpret these IQ values *per se*, for both experimental and control groups were subjected to a programme of testing such as no children in any other longitudinal study have experienced. Thus Heber and Garber caution that test-taking skills for both groups have been enhanced. What is to be viewed as of significance is the differential in performance between these two groups. However I would like to comment that Ramey and Campbell (1979) presented results from a somewhat similar long-term intervention programme, the Abecedarian Project (Ramey, Collier, Sparling, Loda, Campbell, Ingram and Finkelstein 1976), which showed much less striking IQ differences (12 points at age 4 and 8 points at age 5) than the Milwaukee project and furthermore their control group was at a similar level to the Milwaukee controls. There could be a number of explanations for these disparities which include: a situation in which the Abecedarian Experimental Group did not reach the dizzy heights of the Milwaukee children perhaps because they were tested less often or because they did not have a maternal habilitation programme, but the control children appear remarkably similar to the repeatedly tested Milwaukee controls, perhaps because they had nutritional supplements, although my inclination is to reject this as an explanation.

Garber and Heber (1978) have followed the children for nearly four years past intervention and in the last report the experimental group had a mean IQ of 105 as compared to the control group mean of 85. Thus there still continued to be a 20-point gap, reduced from an earlier maximum of over 30, between these groups and the experimental group continued to be above the national average. The picture is very much less rosy for scholastic achievement. On the Metropolitan Achievement Test the experimental group was significantly superior to the control group on all subtests through the first two years. For the first year the distribution of the experimental group approximates the national profile, while the performance of the control group was markedly depressed. The performance of the experimental children since then has further declined, first to the lower level of the city of Milwaukee and then to the still lower one of their inner-city schools. It is perhaps small comfort that they remain one grade ahead of the controls and are significantly superior in reading (Garber, personal communication).

Although the difference in outcome as measured on standardized intelligence tests between the Abecedarian and Milwaukee programmes remains to be resolved, we cannot but accept the evidence in terms of scholastic achievement as an indication that Heber's enormously important and expensive intervention project has failed to safeguard its participants against deficit in those skills required for success in school. It is possible that later intervention would have been more effective; or that whatever the timing of intervention, subtle processes within the family and neighbourhood will always determine major outcomes in attainment and adjustment. On the other hand, possibly new strategies of intervention for selected groups of high-risk families may be required; once again my advocacy would be for long-term intensive support by specially qualified teams. It is highly unlikely that the pervasive effects of severe environmental deprivation can be counteracted without exceptional effort by exceptional people. And, finally, it would be well to remember that as yet we have no evidence from adoption studies concerning the potential outcome for children selected as being at serious risk for mental retardation, as the participants in the Milwaukee project were.

Conclusions

From the evidence reviewed, buttressed by data beyond the scope of this paper, I make the following conclusions. First, there exist natural discontinuities under normal conditions of development, although inadequacies of our measuring instruments make it difficult to monitor these with precision. Such changes also occur in some deviant conditions (e.g. many cases of reactive behaviour disorders or juvenile delinquency). In some other cases discontinuities appear rarely (e.g. serious conduct disorders in late childhood) or very rarely (e.g. childhood autism) or not at all (e.g. moderate to profound retardation). It is often difficult to establish the extent to which continuities are intrinsic or represent an environmental feedback effect that maintains and strengthens earlier deviancy. Children are to a significant extent active agents in creating their own environments, and hence their behaviour.

Second, there is substantial reason to postulate a biological trajectory from which individuals may deviate when environmental deprivation is severe, but to which they will return when these stresses are removed or significantly diminished.

Third, there is also a social trajectory determined within broad limits by accident of birth and alterable by chance or design. Normally the two trajectories are interlocking, but in studies of deviant development they may not be so. The two trajectories are helpful conceptually in explaining apparently spontaneous recovery from deprivation. The idea is derived from the work of the British geneticist, Waddington (1957, 1966), who has drawn attention to a 'self-righting tendency' which pushes deprived children towards normality whenever circumstances allow. Perhaps this represents the most optimistic finding in the whole field of discontinuities from pathology. In addition, as we and others have shown (Clarke and Clarke 1974), the majority of earlier identified mild mental retardates merge into the working-class community in adulthood, partly as a result of prolonged social learning and adjustment and partly as a result of relief from educational pressures. And even studies of multi-problem families, of which the British research of Tonge, James and Hillam (1975) seems outstanding, indicate that at least half the children escape the intergenerational cycle of disadvantage, especially females who 'marry out'. But each generation, while losing members to normality, recruits further replacements anew. We know very little about the mechanisms of these natural discontinuities. They probably include genetic factors, modelling behaviour especially in a normal adult work environment, and chance opportunities or misfortunes to which individuals react differentially. It does not take much imagination to assume that the number and variety of lucky chances are disproportionately distributed in middle-class social environments, as may also be the abilities required to exploit them.

Fourth, studies of adopted children give us considerable encouragement concerning the outcome for disadvantaged children who experience total ecological change even at a relatively late date, although so far we lack evidence on the adoptive outcome for children selected as at risk for mild retardation. Selective processes into adoption appear to be rather thorough, although of recent years an increasing number of families have proved willing to adopt deviant or potentially deviant children.

Fifth, some preschool intervention programmes yield evidence for limited later benefit which may be in large measure attributable to changed attitudes and motivations on the part of the parents. This applies to the Milwaukee project as it does to the Consortium studies.

Sixth, accelerating young children in terms of cognitive skills appears relatively easy but of little later consequence. We do not as yet know what the outcome might be of acceleration starting at later stages of development and await the results of the second phase of the Abecedarian project, as well as further developments in Haywood's work (1979) based on Feuerstein's Instrumental Enrichment programme, which appears to have been successful in Israel (Feuerstein, Rand, Hoffman and Miller 1980). Part of the evidence suggests that such a policy might be more successful in that after the age of 6 the biological trajectory is sufficiently advanced to make children potentially more receptive to social and educational intervention. However, conflict between the domestic social trajectory and the aims of even modest intervention programmes may be an uneven battle. The best hope may in the end prove to be for ecological change to be encouraged by informed, responsible and caring citizens.

Seventh, in my country at least, it appears that social processes within schools contribute differentially to the outcome for inner-city adolescents in terms of achievement and adjustment, although Rutter (1980) is cautious about the extent to which these findings can be generalized to the United States.

Eighth, I believe there is evidence to suggest that the effects of serious environmental disadvantages are very hard indeed to shift permanently within the context of their origin and that as yet we do not understand how to proceed. I do not believe that the disappointing long-term outcomes of preschool intervention programmes necessarily demonstrate that powerful genetic factors are overwhelming influences on the deviant academic and social development of these children, although it would be imprudent to discount them. I also believe that we have learned a great deal from those research workers who have mounted and monitored the programmes.

It seems clear that unless intervention is greatly prolonged, or possibly total, then effects tend to fade, either very considerably or entirely. In the latter case they will also tend to swing over into deficit, intellectually, scholastically, and emotionally. While some brief interventions appear to promote desirable discontinuities, they have to be perpetuated over many, many years if their effects are not to be swamped by adverse social forces bearing upon individuals; for these life is an anti-Head Start programme. It is important to realize, however, that potentially the disadvantaged have a greater range of possible phenotypic outcomes than is normally apparent. But the practical, ethical, and political difficulties of promoting on a large scale a psychologically healthier society are very considerable. To have potential solutions or part-solutions is one thing; to put them into practice is another. However, I have one practical suggestion to make. The Abecedarian programme includes provision for one phase in which children will receive preschool day care to be followed by further support both in the home and in the school for a few years after the age of six. At present it is not envisaged that this support will continue into adolescence, and I suggest that it could be important to do this experimentally within the context of this well-established programme.

The final general point which an examination of the literature has forced upon me is that the whole of life-span development is important and some of the principles which I have discussed in the context of childhood deviance appear to be equally relevant to adult development.

Note

1   I acknowledge with gratitude the help and support which my husband, Alan Clarke, has provided in the preparation of this paper.

References

Bronfenbrenner, U. (1974) *A Report on Longitudinal Evaluations of Pre-school Programs. (Vol. 2) Is Early Intervention Effective?* Washington, DC: DHEW Publications No. (OHD) 74-25.

Clarke, A.D.B. (1978) 'Presidential address: Predicting human development: Problems, evidence, implications.' *Bulletin of the British Psychological Society 31,* 249–258.

Clarke, A.D.B. and Clarke, A.M. (1972) 'Consistency and variability in the growth of human characteristics.' In W.D. Wall and V.P. Varma (eds) *Advances in Educational Psychology.* London: University of London Press.

Clarke, A.M. and Clarke, A.D.B. (eds) (1974) *Mental Deficiency: The Changing outlook* (3rd edn). London: Methuen.

Clarke, A.M. and Clarke, A.D.B. (eds) (1976) *Early Experience: Myth and Evidence.* London: Open Books.

Clarke, A.M. and Clarke, A.D.B. (1977) 'Problems in comparing the effects of environmental change at different ages.' In H. McGurk (ed), *Ecological Factors in Human Development.* Amsterdam: North-Holland Publishing Co.

Davis, K. (1947) 'Final note on a case of extreme isolation.' *American Journal of Sociology 52,* 432–437.

Feuerstein, R., Rand, Y., Hoffman, M.B. and Miller, R. (1980) *Instrumental Enrichment: An Intervention Program for Cognitive Modifiability.* Baltimore: University Park Press.

Garber, H. and Heber, R. (1977) 'The Milwaukee Project: Indications of the effectiveness of early intervention in preventing mental retardation.' In P. Mittler (ed) *Research to Practice in Mental Retardation (Vol. 1).* Baltimore: University Park Press.

Garber, H., and Heber, R. (1978) *The Efficacy of Early Intervention with Family Rehabilitation.* Paper delivered at the Conference on Prevention of Retarded Development in Psychosocially Disadvantaged Children. Madison, Wisconsin.

Gordon, H. (1923) *Mental and Scholastic Tests among Retarded Children.* (Education Pamphlet 44, Board of Education, London). London: HMSO.

Haywood, H.C. (1979) *Modification of Cognitive Functions in Slow-learning Adolescents.* Paper presented at the Fifth Congress of the International Association for the Scientific Study of Mental Deficiency. Jerusalem, August.

Heber, R. (1968) 'The role of environmental variables in the etiology of cultural-familial mental retardation.' In B.W. Richards (ed) *Proceedings of the First Congress of the International Association for the Scientific Study of Mental Deficiency.* Reigate, England: Michael Jackson.

Heber, R., Garber, H., Harrington, S., Hoffman, C. and Falender, C. (1972) *Rehabilitation of Families at Risk for Mental Retardation. Progress Report.* Madison: University of Wisconsin.

Horn, J.M., Loehlin, J.C. and Willerman, L. (1979) 'Intellectual resemblance among adoptive and biological relatives: The Texas Adoption Project.' *Behavior Genetics 9,* 177–201.

Jensen, A.R. (1974) 'Cumulative deficit: A testable hypothesis?' *Developmental Psychology 10,* 996–1019.

Jensen, A.R. (1977) 'Cumulative deficit in IQ of blacks in the rural South.' *Developmental Psychology 13,* 184–191.

Jensen, A.R. (1980) *Bias in Mental Testing.* London: Methuen.

Kadushin, A. (1970) *Adopting Older Children.* New York: Columbia University Press.

Kamin, L. (1978) 'A positive interpretation of apparent "cumulative deficit".' *Developmental Psychology 14,* 195–196.

Koluchová, J. (1972) 'Severe deprivation in twins: A case study.' *Journal of Child Psychology and Psychiatry 13,* 107–114.

Koluchová, J. (1976) 'A report on the further development of twins after severe and prolonged deprivation.' In A.M. Clarke and A.D.B. Clarke (eds) *Early Experience: Myth and Evidence.* London: Open Books.

Lazar, I. and Darlington, R.B. (1978) *Lasting Effects After Preschool. Further Analyses of Longitudinal Studies.* The Consortium for Longitudinal Studies, Washington DC: DHEW Publication No. (OHDS) 79-30178.

Lazar, I., Hubbell, V.R., Murray, H., Rosche, M. and Royce, J. (1977) *The Persistence of Preschool Effects: Analysis and Final Report.* The Consortium on Developmental Continuity, Washington, DC: DHEW Publication No. (OHDS) 78-30130.

Mason, M. (1942) 'Learning to speak after six and one half years of silence.' *Journal of Speech Disorders 7,* 295–304.

McAskie, M. and Clarke, A.M. (1976) 'Parent–offspring resemblances in intelligence: Theories and evidence.' *British Journal of Psychology 67,* 243–273.

Mitchell, M.B. (1941) 'The Revised Stanford–Binet for adults.' *Journal of Educational Research 34,* 516–521.

Nemzek, C.L. (1933) 'The constancy of the IQ.' *Psychological Bulletin 30,* 143–168.

Outhit, M.C. (1933) 'A study of the resemblance of parents and children in general intelligence.' *Archives of Psychology 23,* 1–60.

Ramey, C.T., and Campbell, F.A. (1979) *Educational Intervention for Children at Risk for Mild Retardation. A Longitudinal Analysis.* Paper presented at the Fifth Congress of the International Association for the Scientific Study of Mental Deficiency, Jerusalem, August.

Ramey, C.T., Collier, A.M., Sparling, J.J., Loda, F.A., Campbell, F.A., Ingram, D.L. and Finkelstein, N.W. (1976) 'The Carolina Abecedarian project: A longitudinal and multidisciplinary approach to the prevention of developmental retardation.' In T. Tjossem (ed) *Intervention Strategies for High-risk Infants and Young Children.* Baltimore: University Park Press.

Rutter, M. (1980) 'School influences on children's behavior and development: The 1979 Kenneth Blackfan Lecture, Children's Hospital Medical Center, Boston.' *Pediatrics 65*, 208–220.

Rutter, M., Maughan, B., Mortimore, P. and Ouston, J. (1979) *Fifteen Thousand Hours: Secondary Schools and Their Effects on Children.* London: Open Books.

Scarr, S. and Weinberg, R.A. (1976) 'IQ test performance of black children adopted into white families.' *American Psychologist 31*, 726–739.

Schiff, M., Duyme, M., Dumaret, A., Stewart, J., Tomkiewicz, S. and Feingold, J. (1978) 'Intellectual status of working-class children adopted early into upper-middle-class families.' *Science 200*, 1503–1504.

Skeels, H.M. (1936) 'Mental development of children in foster homes.' *Journal of Genetic Psychology 49*, 91–106.

Skeels, H.M. (1966) 'Adult status of children with contrasting early life experiences: A follow-up study.' *Monographs of the Society for Research in Child Development 31*, 105, 3.

Skodak, M. (1939) 'Children in foster homes.' *University of Iowa Studies in Child Welfare.* Iowa: University of Iowa, Institute of Child Welfare.

Skodak, M. and Skeels, H.M. (1945) 'A follow-up study of children in adoptive homes.' *Journal of Genetic Psychology 66*, 21–58.

Skodak, M. and Skeels, H.M. (1949) 'A final follow-up study of one hundred adopted children.' *Journal of Genetic Psychology 75*, 82–125.

Thomas, A. and Chess, S. (1977) *Temperament and Development.* New York: Brunner/Mazel.

Thorndike, R.L. (1940) '"Constancy" of the IQ.' *Psychological Bulletin 37*, 167–186.

Tonge, W.L., James, D.S. and Hillam, S.M. (1975) *Families Without Hope: A Controlled Study of 33 Problem Families.* British Journal of Psychiatry Special Publication No. II. Ashford, Kent: Headley Brothers.

Vandenberg, S. (1971) 'What do we know today about the inheritance of intelligence and how do we know it?' In R.J. Cancro (ed) *Intelligence: Genetic and Environmental Influences.* New York: Grune and Stratton.

Waddington, C.H. (1957) *The Strategy of Genes.* London: George Allen and Unwin.

Waddington, C.H. (1966) *Principles of Development and Differentiation.* New York: Macmillan.

Willerman, L., Horn, J.M. and Loehlin, J.C. (1977) 'The aptitude-achievement test distinction: A study of unrelated children reared together.' *Behavior Genetics 7*, 465–470.

Zigler, E. and Trickett, P.K. (1979) 'The role of national social policy in promoting social competence in children.' In M.W. Kent and J.E. Rolf (eds) *Primary Prevention of Psychopathology, Volume 3: Social Competence in Children.* Hanover, NH: University Press of New England.

CHAPTER 6

Constancy and Change in the Growth of Human Characteristics

Commentary

This article was based on the first Jack Tizard Memorial Lecture, an ongoing series in honour of the man who contributed so richly to the fields of learning disabilities and to developmental psychology. It discusses in detail the meaning of constancy and change, problems of measurement, correlational studies and research on changing developmental levels. Attention is also given to intergenerational change and the problems of cycles of deprivation, their maintenance as well as factors associated with 'escape'. As noted, evolution seems to have shaped us in such a way that we possess a degree of constancy in development but also a potential for change in changing circumstances. To maintain constancies, whether benign or malevolent, importance must be ascribed to long-term consistent influences.

Constancy and Change in the Growth of Human Characteristics[*]

A.D.B. Clarke and Ann M. Clarke

Introduction

Four years after his death many of Jack Tizard's friends continue to feel a sense of loss; seldom has anyone been held in such widespread affection and esteem. Our own debt to him has been twofold. We enjoyed his friendship for 30 years, and his research, representing as it did a determined effort to apply rigorous scientific methods to important social problems, remains an inspiration.

This article allows us to return to a theme forced upon us 30 years ago to which from time to time we have returned. Our undergraduate and postgraduate studies had suggested a constancy of development for biological reasons, and in the early 1950s the terrible, apparently long-term consequences of early maternal deprivation with the same predeterministic implications received wide publicity. Our own findings with a very disadvantaged adolescent and young adult population at that time led us to challenge these beliefs.

This article is not primarily concerned with the obvious fact that development implies change, but rather with individual constancy, across time, in relative status with respect to age peers. It therefore relates to predictability of individual characteristics as they progress through the developmental sequence. There will be virtually no discussion of these sequences (or stages if a Piagetian viewpoint were adopted), nor the mechanisms which underlie their occurrence – this is a related, but rather different, issue. Rather, we shall approach the question of how far individuals remain consistent within a framework of behavioural characteristics which are themselves inevitably changing.

It may be helpful to make some preliminary remarks concerning constancy and change, about which there are two approaches. First, correlational research enables us to track the degree to which changes in ordinal position of a group's members have occurred. The use of correlation coefficients is a shorthand, and often ill-understood, way of describing the average situation for individuals. Second, we can describe changing levels for the characteristic in question, whatever the underlying mechanisms of change might be.

The two approaches, by correlation or by level, are not necessarily synonymous. Figure 6.1 illustrates this point. The first example, for four persons only, shows individual changes in ordinal position and level over a lengthy period of time; the average level, however, remains constant, but the correlation between scores in 1965 and 1984 is low and negative (Figure 6.1a).

A second hypothetical example is illustrated in Figure 6.1b. Four persons show no change in ordinal position yet considerable improvements in level and thus in average level. The correlation between 1965 and 1984 scores is

*   This article first appeared in 1984 in the *Journal of Child Psychology and Psychiatry 25*, 2, pp.191–210.

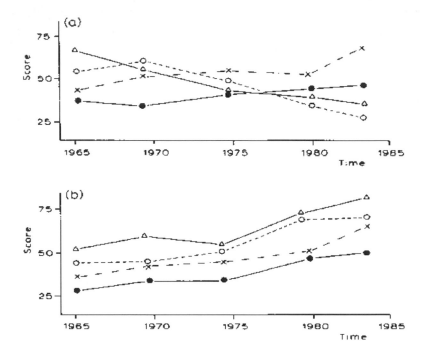

Figure 6.1 This illustrates, for four persons only, two extreme hypothetical examples relating to ordinal position and level: (a) shows no change in average level from 1965 to 1984, but considerable change in individual ordinal position and individual level; (b) indicates no change in ordinal position throughout the period, but large increases in individual and, therefore, average levels

perfect. Such a correlation implies constancy of individual rank position, yet inconstancy of level. The lesson in interpreting correlation coefficients is that the raw data should always be examined.

Constancy can thus have two meanings, whether for the individual or for the group. It can refer to a relatively unchanging individual ordinal position within a group, or it can refer to an unchanging level for an individual or for a group.

Obviously the particular definition of constancy will also affect the evaluation of extent to which individuals remain constant with respect to their peers, as well as the degree to which their level remains the same. We define constancy in rather narrow terms, as did the originators of the idea. If over a period of a decade an individual remains within plus or minus half a standard deviation of a properly established baseline, then clearly his position is constant. In fact, excluding the volatile period of infancy, only a minority display such consistency. If, however, constancy is defined as remaining within plus or minus one standard deviation of a proper baseline, then it would be obvious that most people remain constant. But such a definition of individual status would, of course, include some very wide variations which, depending upon the characteristics measured and the reliability of the measurement, might in some cases have meaningful life consequences. It is therefore rejected here.

The constancy models of human development proposed by Spearman (1904), Watson (1928) and Freud (1949) arose at a time when developmental theorists had very little empirical data at their disposal, and when modern multifactorial models had yet to be elaborated. It was more likely then than now that a theoretical position would be espoused with offered explanations of development in terms of one (or perhaps two) overriding factor: e.g. heredity; social environments across time; critical environmental experiences in infancy. Of these the first and last offered apparent support to the notion of constancy across time; only the second hypothetical factor operating alone might, if carefully considered, suggest discontinuity (Binet 1920). However, such views nowadays appear completely antediluvian, with the acceptance by an increasing body of researchers of evidence for powerful hereditary factors in the development of intelligence and personality interacting with physical environmental influences before, during and after birth and, later, social factors.

In the 1920s, 1930s and 1940s, longitudinal studies began to indicate clearly that changes in ordinal position over time were very common, as were changes in individual level, yet the constancy theory persisted, with few altering their views. The model was robust, and it remains so even today, even among teachers. As a headmaster once said, 'I don't believe in late developers, and I'm not having one in my school.'

This illustrates the point that with the usual selectivity of perceptual and conceptual processes, if one searches for constancies, they will certainly be found. Similarly, a search for changes is rewarding. Only if both are considered will a balanced view be likely to be achieved. And, of course, it is a feature of all sciences that models are commonly retained in the face of contrary evidence long after they have outlived their utility, if any.

Another common error is the belief that human genetic potential unfolds in a linear manner; the growth of physical stature is a spectacular reminder that it does not. Plomin (1983) puts this point well:

Nearly all...texts discuss genetic influences in an early chapter...thus strengthening the mistaken belief that genetic influences are locked on at full throttle at the moment of conception. However, genes do, in fact, turn on and off during development...we need to prise apart the close association that the adjectives 'genetic' and 'stable' have come to share: longitudinally stable characteristics are not necessarily genetic, nor are genetically influenced characters necessarily stable over time...

Just as genetically controlled characteristics may change over time, so too can environmental influences, even extreme ones. Wedge and Essen (1982) analysed some of the NCDS data on a nationally representative sample at age 11 and then followed this up at 16. A small proportion were very severely deprived at both ages, but they were not all the same children. Some had moved out of, and some into, severe deprivation between these ages. Moreover, thanks to the important insights and empirical work of Thomas and Chess (1957) it is increasingly realized that children play some part in creating their own environments, thus unwittingly affecting their development. For example, it is known that highly intelligent children evoke different responses from significant adults than those elicited by dull children, with, in some cases, serious consequences. The difficult child elicits antagonistic responses from his environment, the well-behaved receives signals of approval, and in both cases these factors reinforce the child's existing characteristics. These two extremes could receive quite different responses from an apparently identical situation.

As one of us (Clarke 1982) has put it, there is substantial reason to postulate a biological trajectory from which individuals may deviate when environmental stresses are severe, but to which they will return when these are removed or diminished; there is also a social trajectory determined within broad limits by accident of birth and alterable by chance or design. Normally these two paths interlock, but in studies of deviant development they may not do so.

Here a word about chance may be helpful. Chance can cause a shudder in the scientist because of its unpredictability, and its tendency to mess up neat equations. By chance, of course, one means events with a deterministic potential which are totally unpredictable. Anyone of mature years can look back in his own development and identify such factors. Psychologists have only recently begun to come to terms with this anticonstancy notion that to some extent individual human development, for this and other reasons, is somewhat unpredictable. In a recent paper Bandura (1982) grasps the nettle. In a chance encounter, he says, the separate chain of events have their own causal determinants, but their interaction occurs fortuitously rather than through deliberate plan. Some fortuitous encounters touch only lightly, others leave more lasting effects and still others branch people into new life paths. A science of psychology cannot shed much light on the occurrence of chance encounters, but it can provide the basis of predicting the impact they will have on human lives. And Bandura goes on to give evidence for this belief.

One might add that accidents of birth, social status and personal qualities may well govern both the amount and quality of chance encounters and the individual's capacity to profit from them. Higher occupational groups, as usual, are likely to be at an advantage, and the old lag's common excuse, 'I never 'ad a chance guv'nor', may sometimes have a ring of truth about it.

So there are at least four interacting and transacting headlines in human development: the biological trajectory, the social trajectory, the effect of the individual on his environment which, by a feedback cycle, acts upon him and, finally, the chance event. All these interactions tend to militate against the idea of constancy in the rate of human development. As one of us has argued elsewhere (Clarke 1977), this suggests *to some extent* a potential open-endedness in human development. That this is *potential* must also be stressed, for very often social pressures, personal interests or choice put the individual into a closed and, to some extent, predetermined path.

Developmental changes may be slow and progressive, incrementing, decrementing or merely fluctuating, with periods of change followed by constancy. They can occur in fairly constant environments, as well as in response to environmental or biological change. In the former, one is bound to believe that, like increases in stature or the cessation of growth, these alterations are maturational in origin. Moreover, change can also be rapid: e.g. the onset of some cases of schizophrenia, or of stammering. Other characteristics, equally, may disappear: e.g. crawling as the preferred mode of mobility in infants, or the loss of a school phobia.

When a marked environmental change occurs, then it is followed on average by a corresponding change in certain characteristics. It is necessary to stress 'on average' because there is a wide range of reaction to environmental change. Most of the documented changes have been from adversity to an improved situation; little is known about the converse.

It should be added that it is something of a convenience to act on the assumption that children or adults do not change very much, that the labels applied to their particular characteristics, or indeed to ourselves, tend to stick, thus maintaining a belief in constancy – the aggressive child will remain aggressive, the bright child will become an equally bright adult, the retarded will remain equally retarded. Moreover, society tends to prescribe developmental paths for the individual quite early in life, and it is therefore something of a defeat for these social pressures when a marked change occurs. Many of us know mature students who were written off at school but who in adult life developed an intellectual curiosity, as well as other abilities, which brought them to university.

Before turning to empirical evidence, there is one final point to be made. Those who cling to the constancy model yet are faced with a record of significant personal change, whether in ordinal position or level, or both, face a dilemma. This can be resolved in three ways. The first example might be termed 'denial'. In the 1930s, 1940s and 1950s, clinicians increasingly came to be aware that persons who at school age had been deemed mildly retarded later proved to be dull-normal or even normal. The way out of this difficulty was to believe that the earlier diagnosis had been wrong and so retrospectively they were assessed as having been pseudoretarded – they had apparently changed, but since people don't change, they hadn't!

A second example of resolving the dilemma of personal change is to suggest that even though an individual characteristic appears to be new, it is derived from the earlier one and represents no real change. This is the 'heads I win, tails you lose' model. Thomas (1981) has put this very elegantly in reviewing our own and similar research:

> ...the influential psychodynamic developmental concepts make it possible to identify later behavior with earlier behavior even when they appear to be strikingly dissimilar. The passive, clinging three-year-old has not really changed if he becomes an aggressive adult... He is only displaying a reaction formation against the same unconscious dependency needs that determine his behavior now as in the past... Within this closed conceptual scheme, continuity over time is guaranteed... (p.593)

Kagan (1980) makes a rather similar point; developmental ideologies of the past 'ascribed general qualities to the young child and assumed that the child possessed an internal disposition that was preserved but took different disguises during different periods in ontogeny...' and he laments that he 'spent 20 years trying to generate quantitative proof that the differences in behaviour seen during the first two years of life were preserved in some way for the next decade', likening himself and others to Don Quixote (p.322). And he goes on to say that many scientists held a tape-recorder view of ontogeny, implying that every experience that was registered was preserved (p.235).

A third reaction to the growing awareness that there is a good deal of variability in human development is to believe that we are measuring the wrong things, and if only the right things could be identified then we would find greater constancy. This was the original hope of Thomas and Chess when they identified nine 'basic' temperamental qualities in infancy. Gradually, however, they came to recognize that these, too, showed change over time (Thomas and Chess 1977). This is the 'if only...' model.

Problems of measurement: the instrument and the person

All measurement involves a degree of error, whether in physics, astronomy or psychology. The reliability of the measuring device in the latter can best be assessed by repeated testing a short time later (perhaps days, weeks or even a few months). A very high correlation then indicates a considerable degree of constancy of rank position and a limited amount of change.

The study of human development frequently involves longitudinal assessment. One of the most robust findings in the area is that correlations decrease progressively as the interval between assessments lengthens. There are three reasons accounting for imperfect correlations between a baseline measurement and later assessments.

1. The measuring instrument may have been badly standardized, thus distorting scores at different ages. The 1916 Binet is a horrific example, and the 1937 Revision not much better, with its different means and standard deviations at different ages. This results in, for example, a child assessed at age 6 and reassessed at age 12 having vastly different IQs at these ages for reasons of test error alone. These are genuine errors of measurement, that is, errors residing in the test instrument.

2. Short-term personal fluctuations in behaviour account for less than perfect correlations between test and immediate retest. These could include the results of motivation, fatigue, boredom etc. Traditionally they have been termed errors of measurement; they should really be called errors of persons.

3. There is no reason to suppose that errors of measurement or of persons as in 1. and 2. above should steadily increase over time. A steadily decreasing correlation after 'immediate' retest thus involves different phenomena for any group reassessed after various time intervals. In turn, this implies genuine changes in the ordinal position of individuals within this group, the amount of change being reflected in smaller correlation coefficients: the smaller the r, the greater the likelihood of individual change in rank order.

Thus in longitudinal studies it is important to know the immediate retest reliability of the measuring device; the extent to which this correlation falls short of +1.0 is likely to yield a fair estimate of the effects of test practice and errors of persons (see 2. above). Progressively lower coefficients from such a baseline will reflect genuine and long-term changes in development, which will usually involve both changing levels and changing rank position.

The foregoing applies to measurement of such functions as intelligence, attainment or motor skills. In the case of ratings of other behaviour (e.g. aggressiveness, dependency or loquacity) it is essential to show a high concurrent interrater agreement if a proper baseline is to be established.

Correlational studies

Longitudinal studies are often described in correlational terms, and have been with us for a long time. Hundreds of reports illustrate two general laws originally advanced in relation only to IQ but which, with very rare exceptions, also apply to the development of all psychological characteristics (e.g. temperament, attainments, personality). First, measures of infant behaviour scarcely predict later ordinal position within a group. There are probably two reasons for this: these scores must inevitably relate to qualities which may have little overlap with those exhibited in later childhood or adult life. Moreover, many important characteristics have not yet emerged, even incipiently, and so are not available for predictive measurement.

The second law (as noted) is that, regardless of age, the longer the period over which assessments take place, the lower the correlation is likely to be, that is, the greater the change in ordinal position of individuals within a group. Numerous studies of intelligence, attainment and personality were reviewed by Bloom (1964), although some of his interpretations of the data (especially the dubious notion of 'half-development') have been widely criticized (e.g. Clarke and Clarke 1976).

Taken together, these two laws imply that over long time periods (e.g. a decade) correlations will be only moderate. Exceptions, of which there have recently been three examples, indicate that the use of the same type of test structure and content employed at different periods will tend to increase the stability of scores. Thus Yule *et al.* (1982) undertook a longitudinal study of a normal sample of Isle of Wight children assessed for intelligence on the WPPSI at 5½ and retested 11 years later at 16½ on the WISC-R. The correlation between the scores was 0.86, an astonishingly high figure; the more usual is around 0.5. There was only a 10 per cent chance of children varying by more than 13 points from their original score. The authors do not offer further data on the distribution of changes but we can roughly estimate some of these from Shapiro's (1951) calculations. About 30 per cent will have varied by more than half a standard deviation either way, still an unusually low figure for this long time interval. A second example is offered by Tew and Laurence (1983), reporting a 0.92 correlation between IQs at 5 and 16 for spina bifida children. Nearly 30 per cent varied by more than 10 points and 16 per cent by more than one standard deviation over this 11-year period. This is rather more understandable in children, some of whom were clearly organically impaired. The lesson is, of course, that very high correlations do not necessarily imply constancy of ordinal position or level for all members of a sample. Another recent study (Wilson 1983) using the same tests and a similar interval yields a 0.67 correlation, accounting for much less variance, namely 45 per cent as opposed to Tew and Laurence's 85 per cent.

There are even greater problems in considering the extent to which personality characteristics remain constant during development. First, there are many different methods of assessment, ranging from the 'objective', sometimes physiologically based, to ratings or interview data, which may have different degrees of reliability. Second, it seems clear that the expression of personality is to some extent situationally determined (e.g. Mischel 1968, 1977). The conflict between the extremes of situationism and trait theory has diminished over the years, as Mischel in particular has modified his claims. Epstein (1983) notes:

> situationists and trait theorists can both prove that they are right. The problem is that each group believes that because it is right, the other group must be wrong. The paradox lies in the fact that the following three statements are all true: (a) behavior is situationally specific; (b) behavior is cross-situationally general; and (c) there are stable, broad response dispositions, or traits. In any one situation, behavior is apt to be determined primarily by the situation but it also reflects a small cross-situationally general component. By aggregating behavior over sufficient situations, thereby compounding the cross-situational component and canceling out the situationally unique component, broad response dispositions can be revealed.

The above is perhaps sufficient to hint at the problems. It is, nevertheless, possible to arrive at certain, perhaps crude, conclusions concerning the stability over time of personality characteristics, whether assessed by tests, observations or ratings. Kagan and Moss (1962), for example, indicated that only between ages 6 and 10 and not earlier did significant correlations occur between personality assessments within that age range and those repeated in adulthood; and the correlations were only moderate, averaging about 0.5.

In more recent years much has been made of Block's (1971) *Lives Through Time*, which used a Q-sort method to describe each of 150 subjects in the Oakland and Berkeley Guidance Studies at Junior High School, Senior High School and in their mid-30s. Different and very experienced raters studied diverse data at each of the three age checkpoints to Q-sort the same person. This method allows an appreciation of personality organization to emerge from the accumulation of independent decisions. Interjudge agreement averaged about 0.75 from Junior to Senior High School and about 0.55 from Senior High School to adulthood: 'over a span of 15 years or so, it represents an impressive degree of personal consistency,' writes Bowers (1977). Some personalities changed little while others showed marked changes. But overall this latter correlation indicates that 70 per cent of the adult variance was un-accounted for from Senior High School measures. This indicates to us both some constancy and also considerable change. However, since interjudge concurrent reliability is always less than perfect (in this study ranging between 0.72 and 0.78 for composite ratings), part of the changes noted will undoubtedly have arisen for subjective reasons and thus represent 'errors of measurement'.

Macfarlane (1964) commented upon the outcome of the 30-year Berkeley Guidance Study, which represented rather more than half of Block's sample: her interpretation was one of surprise, working as she did from an implicit hypothesis that people do not change.

> Many of our most mature and competent adults had severely troubled and confusing childhoods and adolescences. Many of our highly successful children and adolescents have failed to achieve their predicted potential... As children and adolescents, they were free of severe strains, showed high abilities and/or talents, excelled at academic work and were the adulated images of success...
>
> One sees among them at age 30 a high proportion of brittle, discontented and puzzled adults whose high potentialities have not been actualized, at least as of now...(but) we were not always wrong! We did have several small groups whose adult status fulfilled theoretical expectations. (i.e. strong continuities).

It rather sounds as if sooner or later most people in this sample had a bad time, but not sooner *and* later! Block himself (1980) plays down Macfarlane's statement as subjective commentary. We do not, because subjective commentary that notes a failure of deeply held expectancies to be realized is in itself impressive.

Or again, consider the New York Longitudinal Study by Thomas and Chess (1976, 1977) of 136 subjects from infancy to adolescence. This prospective longitudinal research, using a middle- and upper-class volunteer group, permitted investigations both of behavioural constancies and the evolution of behaviour disorders. Mild reactive behaviour disorders were quite common in the preschool and early years. By adolescence, almost half had recovered and about 12 per cent improved, a small percentage were unchanged, about 19 per cent were mildly or moderately worse and 16 per cent had become markedly worse. Those who recovered were probably assisted by guidance given to the parents. In adolescence they were no different from those who had not shown behaviour disorders in childhood. The major picture, then, is of *inconstancy* of characteristics; the vast majority of those who had childhood disorders either got better or worse, they did not stay the same. Also, the earlier hope of identifying 'primary reaction patterns' which would hold up over time was not fulfilled (Thomas and Chess 1977). Correlations over short periods proved to be unimpressive. A similar point is made in Giuganino and Hindley's (1982) study of personality characteristics between 3 and 15 years. These authors consider that personality measures are less constant than IQ.

Some of the issues discussed so far, as well as others which have not been covered, have been reviewed in detail in Brim and Kagan's (1980) text, which offers a wide-ranging and important review.

Studies of changing levels

Changes under normal conditions

Similar findings inevitably emerge if one considers not only the shorthand of correlation coefficients but what they may reflect, namely changing individual levels. Several examples could be outlined, of which the most thorough recent work is by Hindley and Owen (1979), who state that a prime consideration in studying the development of any measurable characteristic is to employ methods which serve to reveal, rather than conceal, the course of change in individual subjects. With a careful, statistically sophisticated method of computer analysis they sought to examine the extent to which there is evidence of non-random, or systematic, changes in IQ scores in individual subjects using a London-based sample of children who were originally recruited from ante-natal clinics and represented widely differing social backgrounds. The subjects were tested at 6 and 18 months with the Griffiths Scale of Infant Development; at 3 and 5 years with the 1937 Stanford–Binet; at 8 and 11 years with the starred items from the 1960 Stanford–Binet; and at 14 and 17 years with the AH 4, administered individually. Correlations between adjacent ages after the age of 3 years were sufficiently high to indicate well over 50 per cent of common variance and, after correction for attenuation, around 70 per cent or more between underlying variables. Before the age of 3 years correlations between adjacent ages were sufficiently low to conclude that tests were only to a limited degree measuring related dimensions, or that subjects' scores were very labile, or both.

Across the entire age range (from 6 months to 17 years) there were seven striking and consistent trends in individual growth curves that could not be attributed to random fluctuations. The authors believe that changes in IQ scores follow systematic patterns that differ between subjects with implications for the interpretation of IQ scores taken at any particular point in time. One of the patterns showed complete constancy, another showed a steady increase over time and yet another showed a steady decrease.

The authors are careful to point out that their work is descriptive and as yet has not proceeded to the extent of identifying correlates of the differing growth curves. Their further reports are awaited with great interest, since to date speculations concerning social environmental correlates of changes in individual IQ scores across time in non-deviant populations have not stood the test of cross-validation.

It may well be that, for the majority of children, changes in IQ are the result of genetic influences that come into operation at various points in time. A growing body of research strongly suggests that it is not before adolescence or early adulthood that the full effect of hereditary influences can be observed. Wilson (1983), who has conducted a longitudinal study of a large sample of MZ and DZ twins and their siblings, states

> The message from these results seems clear: there is a strong developmental thrust in the growth of intelligence that continues through adolescence, and is guided by an internal template or ground plan. The template is rooted in genetic processes that act throughout childhood and adolescence. The effects are most dramatic in early childhood, when the rate of gain is sharpest and the spurts and lags most pronounced. But even during adolescence, as the integrative power of the brain approaches its maximum level, the end-phase of this protracted sequence is still subject to maturational processes that are gene-controlled.

This conclusion was based on the findings that differing patterns of intellectual growth were much more highly correlated in MZ subjects than in the DZ sample or in singleton siblings. If this is correct, then one must predict that Hindley's search for environmental correlates of different growth patterns will prove unrewarding. The only exception may be the group which shows a steady decline; this may possibly represent an environmentally induced cumulative deficit (Clarke 1982; Jensen 1977). This phenomenon is to be found in some, but by no means all, minority populations in the United States, and recently in England (Scarr *et al.* 1983).

As implied in the section on correlational studies, individual changes in personality measurements over lengthy periods of time are also common under normal conditions.

Changes after major environmental shifts

So far the development of groups or individuals in moderately constant situations has been considered. While these certainly include some environmental change, the studies sample the ordinary range of circumstances in which children and adults find themselves.

To look at the effect of grosser environmental changes is important for three reasons. First, it enables an estimate of the limits of change in individuals to be made. Second, it permits an assessment of the theoretical prospects of upgrading the functioning levels of various deprived groups. Third, it allows one to determine whether or not particular periods are 'formative'. If a large change for the better takes place in a child's life at the age of 5 after an infancy and early childhood of gross deprivation, and this is not followed by recovery at all, then one could truly say that the first five years were critically formative. These notions may be explored, beginning with horrific examples and moving to lesser degrees of adversity. These have been reviewed in detail elsewhere (Clarke and Clarke 1976) but can be outlined very briefly.

Koluchová's (1972, 1976) reports on twin boys isolated, neglected and cruelly treated from 18 months to 7 years are very detailed. Shortly after birth they were taken into care for a year following the mother's death. Transferred to a maternal aunt for the period 12–18 months, they were then handed over to a sadistic stepmother who banished them to a cellar for the next five-and-a-half years. These were severely subnormal, rachitic and virtually without speech upon discovery. Now in a most unusual adoptive home, they are cognitively and emotionally normal and have caught up scholastically. Aged 23, they have graduated from a technical high school and are working as electricians.

A further example concerns a child called Adam, abandoned by his mother in Bogota and then grossly neglected in a reformatory until the age of 16 months. He was rescued by a British nurse/psychologist, Angela Roberts, but because of his general condition was diagnosed by a doctor as being mentally retarded, malnourished and spastic. He responded to proper nutrition, was adopted by an American family at the age of 32 months and transplanted to a new culture and new language. There were, of course, severe problems, but on the most recent assessment two years ago he was regarded as a normal 9-year-old at school and had an IQ of 113 (Clarke 1982).

The researches of Dennis (1973) on adoption in the Lebanon are badly faulted methodologically and will not be commented on. However, one aspect of his investigation appears to be free of major problems. Foundlings in Beirut were housed under very adverse conditions in an orphanage. At the age of 6 their IQs averaged in the 50s. Girls were then transferred to an equally bad institution and boys to a good one. By adolescence the girls' IQ again averaged in the 50s and the boys' at about 80, a clear indication of environmental effects following age 6.

Clarke and Clarke (1954) and Clarke et al. (1958) studied over a six-year period two large samples of mildly retarded, unstable, semi-literate adolescents and young adults, mainly drawn from bad or exceedingly bad homes. Social histories and IQs were independently collected, indicating large average IQ and social increments in those with the worst backgrounds. These occurred between adolescence and age 30, and seemed to represent recovery from the effects of early adversity. There was selective sample wastage of the better subjects, hence estimates were conservative. Recent replications, but with much longer time intervals, have been reported by Svendsen (1982, 1983), both on similar and rather brighter samples.

Lewis (1954) studied 500 children with poor backgrounds, the worst in Kent, admitted to a reception centre, mostly over 5 years of age. Whereas 40 per cent were in good or fair condition on admission, only two years later this had increased to 75 per cent after exposure to better conditions.

Kadushin (1970) reported on a group of healthy children, typically coming from large families in substandard circumstances, often below poverty level and suffering physical neglect. Natural parents showed a picture of promiscuity, mental deficiency, alcoholism, imprisonment and psychosis. At an average age of 3½ the children had been legally removed from their homes, and after an average of 2–3 changes of foster homes were placed for adoption at an average age of just over 7, and followed up at an average of almost 14 years. Adoptive parents were older than natural parents and of a considerably higher socioeconomic level. Outcome was far better than might have been predicted 1. from social history; 2. after several foster changes; and 3. following very late adoption.

Bowlby et al. (1956) reported on 60 ex-TB sanatorium children followed up in middle and late childhood. Contrary to prediction, these did not become subaverage, affectionless psychopaths, although they did show 21 per cent excess maladjustment, some of which, as the authors indicate, was to be attributed to adverse environmental factors other than separation.

There are about another 50 studies of this type which are relevant to our theme, and in the very rare cases where negative findings emerge, that is, where environmental changes are not followed by at least some degree of personal change, plausible reasons can be advanced.

Intergenerational changes

A very important question related to individual consistency/change across the years is that of intergenerational constancy. We have seen that there are powerful genetic programmes underlying the environmental potentiation of personal characteristics. These will determine both similarities and, of course, differences within families, and link one generation with another. However, it is equally possible that social disadvantages or advantages in one generation might be transmitted environmentally, so that some intergenerational links might be of a non-genetic but familial nature.

In June 1972, Sir Keith Joseph, the Secretary of State at the DHSS, announced at once a problem, a hypothesis and a means of testing that hypothesis. The problem lay in the persistence of poverty and deprivation in our society despite general economic development and the growth of social services. The hypothesis was the existence of a cycle of deprivation whereby deprivations and maladjustments might be transmitted from generation to generation through patterns of parenting and other familial processes. The mechanism was to be a joint DHSS/SSRC working party, funded by the former, which would commission and monitor research in this area.

The ten-year programme supported some 23 studies and more than a dozen reviews of world literature bearing upon the theme of transmitted deprivation. It has been admirably evaluated by Brown and Madge (1982). Among the important conclusions, it seems apparent that the processes leading to disadvantage and to cycles of disadvantage are multifactorial, and that there is a natural 'escape' rate as well as fresh recruitment. Brown (1983) summarised the evidence very well in stating that:

> Cycles of deprivation exist – but they do not inevitably exist...individuals do defy predictors and so continuities are never absolute... The individual's experience of deprivation, and his response to it, are determined by the interaction of his natural endowment and family resources within the socio-economic structure of society, and the network of unequal opportunities and life chances that the structure maintains... The final report... documents the scale and impact of deprivation and demonstrates the futility

of espousing simplistic explanations of social problems or adopting simplistic policy solutions.

Two of these research programmes will be briefly recorded here, since each brings new evidence to bear upon the problem of constancy of development. An exceptionally sophisticated methodology was employed by Quinton and Rutter (1984), whose research programme falls into two parts.

The *retrospective* study was undertaken to examine the extent to which serious current family and parenting problems are associated with similar adversities in the parents' childhoods and the extent to which they arise anew in each generation through social hardship unassociated with previous disadvantages. The in-care group consisted of a consecutive series of 48 white families living in one inner London borough who had children admitted into residential care on two or more occasions during a continuous eight-month period. A comparison group of 47 was randomly drawn from families with a child in the same age group, living in the same area and who had not used residential facilities.

The mothers with children in care presented a picture of striking emotional and social problems, in contrast to those (also relatively disadvantaged) whose children were not admitted to institutions. So far as social background variables are concerned the two groups of mothers did not differ significantly, but 49 per cent of the 'problem' mothers had a parent with psychiatric, drink or criminal difficulties, compared with 32 per cent in the comparison group. However, of all the background factors, it was discordant and aggressive family relationships that most clearly differentiated the parental backgrounds of these groups of mothers. Rates of early adversities and problems and teenage problems were greater in the in-care sample than in the contrast group, and these were found to relate to current disadvantages and the criteria for selection of these mothers into the study. The links were, however, insufficient to explain the association between childhood adversities and parenting breakdown. Lack of marital support appeared as a key factor in the continuity of family problems, probably because it helps to perpetuate earlier psychological difficulties and hinders the development of parenting skills and satisfactory relationships with children.

This study left indeterminate the extent to which the continuities in the in-care sample were due to chance rather than to a persistent lack of resources or to structural or personal factors leading to deviant mate selection. Accordingly, a *prospective* study was undertaken of subjects aged 21 and 27 years in 1978 for whom there was a great deal of information recorded by Jack Tizard and colleagues when they had been as children in residential care. Over 100 adults, previously resident in one of two children's homes, were traced and compared with a sample of similar age who had never been in care, who had lived their childhood in inner London and whose behaviour at school had been assessed (in connection with another study) on the Rutter questionnaire. As might be expected, there were formidable problems in tracing these samples.

The records examined left no doubt as to the severity of the personal problems in the backgrounds of the institutional group: 70 per cent had a deviant parent; 73 per cent had a home with marital discord or separation; 56 per cent had been neglected, abused or abandoned; and 76 per cent had been reared in poor circumstances of poverty.

Although the institutions had been run on child-centred lines, and most of the residents had the company of siblings, their recollections as adults of their childhood relationships were on the whole negative. Few remembered important attachments; not that their experiences had been harsh, primitive or restrictive, but rather that their lives had lacked personal meaning or affection. Parental visits, which varied in frequency, were remembered positively but without strong feelings of attachment.

The controls for the prospective study were drawn up from somewhat less-deprived families than those in the retrospective study, and compared with the residential sample there was a very great difference in the nature of family relationships, with strikingly low rates of psychiatric disorder, criminality, separation of parents or harsh discipline.

The residential sample were significantly more likely than their controls to be in semi- or unskilled employment or living on social security. Nearly one-third of the women and two-fifths of the men had currently handicapping psychiatric disorders, the great majority of which consisted of long-standing personality problems, whereas of the controls only 5 per cent had current difficulties, none of which was rated as a personality problem. On the other hand, 40 per cent of the ex-care women were currently *without* difficulties, as were 34 per cent of the men.

A detailed study was made of the parenting behaviour of the two groups. Results showed that despite the fact that *all* of the ex-care women had experienced institutional rearing for part of their childhood and most had also experienced poor parenting, as many as 31 per cent showed good parenting, a rating made for just less than half of the comparison group, over 50 per cent of whom showed some problems in parenting, although far fewer showed severe problems.

Overall, the evidence runs counter both to the view that early experiences irrevocably change personality development and also to the suggestion that any single process is involved. However, some continuities may be perceived: adverse experiences may affect behaviour or attitudes or opportunities – each of these may foster continuities or discontinuities through the *selection* of environments or through their *production*. The complex interplay between environment and behaviour increases the risk of adverse (or happy) chains of circumstances.

The second project to be described concerns a type of intervention. One way of breaking a cycle of disadvantage is by removing children from deleterious environments and placing them in homes that are likely to promote normal intellectual and social development.

There is a vast and expanding literature in which the characteristics of adopted children are compared with those of their adoptive and true parents. In turn, these findings are contrasted with the relationship between parent–child characteristics in normal families. Most of these investigations, however, have not collected information on adoptees as adults, although there are some recent exceptions. The study of individuals towards the end of the major developmental sequence is of seminal importance, granted what is now beginning to be known about the interplay of biological and social factors across the years of childhood.

Late adoption has for a long time been seen as second best, often to be avoided; partly because parents usually prefer to receive infants, partly because such children are often hard to place by virtue of background problems and partly because there has been a strongly held belief in the critical significance for later development of early rearing practices that may have been less than ideal. For good reasons, therefore, there are comparatively few studies of late-adopted children. Triseliotis and Russell (1984) report on a sample of 44 late adoptees interviewed in early adulthood and also a group of 40 young adults who had been reared in institutions after being taken into care.

The authors faced formidable problems, of which the most difficult was the assembly of a sample of adopted 'hard to place' children born in the 1950s. At that time late adoption was rare and was actually discouraged as unlikely to be successful. The further problem of tracing these children as adults was so considerable that only a little under half of those who met the criteria for inclusion could be found and interviewed. The ex-institutional adults were somewhat more easily traced, although only 59 per cent were located and interviewed. Sample loss is, of course, always selective, and raises the problem of unknown biases. Although those 'lost' did not differ in their early records from those 'found', the authors point out that:

it is certainly *possible* that our two sub-samples diverged earlier in life, and we have no way of knowing whether the 'lost' sample did better, worse or the same as the sample retained. It is also essential to avoid simplistic comparisons between the outcome for the adopted and residential samples. Rather they are to be seen as reflecting the life histories of two groups, who have some similarities but also some important differences in background.

The late adoptees were settled into their adoptive homes between ages 2 and 8, with a mean age of 3½. They had been in care for an average of two-and-a-half years before final placement, preceded by three or four moves between institutions or foster homes. Not surprisingly, some 40 per cent displayed moderate-to-severe emotional and behavioural problems before adoption. The delay in adoption occurred mostly because of questions connected with the natural parents' social or emotional conditions or with the child's physical or psychological state. In effect, there were many doubts at the time as to whether these 'high-risk' children should be adopted at all.

Detailed findings are clearly presented. The main results, supplemented by sympathetic inclusion of some verbatim responses by the young adults, indicated that the adopted sample demonstrated definite discontinuities with the material, social and personal circumstances of their natural families. They were mainly much more likely to resemble their adoptive families. However, it is of interest that social mobility from the adopting parents has been high in both directions; only 14 of the 44 remained in the same social class as their adopted father. Eight were one class higher, seven were two classes higher and two were three classes higher; eight were one social class lower, and five between two and four classes lower.

As might be expected, the outcome for those who had been institutionally reared was on average less satisfactory than for those who had been adopted. Nevertheless, only a minority displayed serious personal pathologies, others had escaped the cycle of disadvantage and many had good educational achievements. The discussion of the factors in the different patterns of rearing which appear to have influenced the diverging lifestyles of the two groups should be of great value to social workers and policy makers.

This study provided further evidence that many children may become achieving, emotionally secure adults despite an unfortunate early start in life. It may be concluded that the quality of the social relationships experienced during the major rearing period (perhaps from 5 to 15 years) is likely to have a critical bearing upon outcome in later life.

Other studies in this programme yield congruent results. So here again the constancy notion has to be modified, and modified in a situation where social pressures *not* to change are likely to be at their most potent.

Discussion

The theme can now be restated. Changes in ordinal position and relative level are common. In most situations these are likely to arise as much for genetic/maturational reasons as from sensitivities to minor environmental variations (or changes in motivation). Where major environmental shifts occur, whether by accident or design, average individual responses may be considerable. Increasing age is associated with some stabilization of characteristics and probably attenuates the potential for change, especially in normal circumstances. There may be several reasons for this (e.g. factors intrinsic to the aging process, social pressure, forced or chosen life paths, external or self-labelling, or all in combination). But such attenuation does not necessarily imply an end to responsiveness, even at relatively late ages, especially among the disadvantaged.

Three qualifications must nonetheless be offered: 1. the definition of constancy employed obviously affects the interpretation of empirical data. A narrow definition is preferred here, simply because a wide one inevitably reflects the likelihood of so many different life paths for individuals that it really begs the question; 2. there is no reason to suppose that the development of each human trait is equally constant or variable. In general terms, however, all early psychological characteristics (e.g. temperament, intelligence) are poor predictors of later status; furthermore, the longer the period, the less accurate the prediction. These findings are partly a reflection of the fact that in most reported studies somewhat different qualities have been measured at various ages, a situation ameliorated when similar scales have been used from early childhood to maturity. They also reflect the complex dynamics of personal, transactional relations between biological and social trajectories; 3. some individuals or groups show little change (e.g. the severely subnormal, the organically impaired mildly subnormal and autistics). But there are normal individuals, too, who exhibit consistency rather than variability, and we have little information on why this should be so, other than guessing, as a fall-back interpretation, that genetic factors may be primarily responsible.

From qualifications we can turn to the implications of this evidence, of which three may be outlined. First, evolution seems to have shaped us in such a way that we possess a degree of constancy in development but also a potential for change in changing circumstances. This plasticity is, of course, not limitless. Research has illuminated two types of change: breakdown under stress (not discussed in this article) and recovery from adversity after environmental improvement. As yet we are fairly ignorant of the processes whereby desirable constancies in development are promoted and maintained, and equally so about the factors we call vulnerability and resilience. These represent major challenges for research.

The second implication is that even among the grossly disadvantaged there is a natural escape rate, although in general the inverse care law operates: those most in need of help are least likely to receive it, seek it or, if accepted, to benefit from it. The question of creating a more just society will continue to command attention. It is clear that the concepts of deprivation or disadvantage are not absolute but relative. There have been considerable general improvements, but only too obviously these have not ironed out unacceptable inequalities. The Warsaw study's findings are sobering in this respect. In that city for 30 years inequalities in housing and schooling have been largely overcome and inequalities in income greatly reduced. Among school children, however, the same correlates with parental occupation have been demonstrated as in the West, suggesting a perseveration of parental attitudes and the presence of differential genetic influences (Firkowska *et al.* 1978).

The view that genetic factors strongly influence human characteristics is one which often, for ideological reasons, many people have been reluctant to accept. This should not be so, for it is well known that a given genotype may have a variety of phenotypical expressions, depending on the life context of the individual. Jensen, for example, not renowned for his emphasis on environmental influences, has stated that with an assumed heritability of 0.7–0.8 for intelligence, environmental variation would permit IQ differences of 45 points (Jensen 1981). Scarr (1981) has suggested that an enlightened social policy ought to maximize the heritability in all groups. Populations with low heritabilities are those with the greatest environmental inequalities.

The third implication is that for those whose level of functioning has been markedly depressed by social conditions, interventions can be successful. But there are many pitfalls, especially when intervention does not involve a complete and permanent ecological change. The American nationwide Head Start programme is a case in point. This was mounted on a wave of enthusiasm in the expectation that early compensatory interventions would break the cycle of poverty and semi-literacy. On our own model, however, we were able in 1967, before any results were available to us, to predict that this programme would 'stand or fall, not on what it achieves in the preschool years, but on whether these diversions in development are subsequently reinforced' (Clarke 1968). Numerous studies have subsequently documented the 'wash-out' effect of substantial IQ increases accruing to children who had experienced preschool programmes of varying duration, although in some of high quality there are modest remaining effects on later achievement and adjustment (see Clarke (1984) for a summary and discussion). Zigler, who was himself deeply involved in the Head Start programme, has stated his position as follows: 'in retrospect it is hard to believe that so much confidence could have been placed in one isolated year of intervention in one "magic period" in a child's life' (Zigler and Valentine 1979, p.13). 'It is now my view that such tokenistic programs probably are worse than no programs at all. The danger...is not so much that they damage children as that they give the appearance that something useful is being done, and thus become the substitute for more meaningful efforts' (p.365). Ramey (1982), in his commentary upon the findings of the Consortium Longitudinal Studies (Lazar and Darlington 1982), comments on the poor outcome at follow-up, noting 'that these results obtained in spite of the efforts of some of our leading scientists and educators, testifies to the difficult and complex set of conditions associated with lower socio-economic status in this country' (p.149). The burden of the argument advanced in this paper is, of course, that preschool intervention that is not buttressed by further and ongoing environmental improvement will never solve the personal and social problems of the disadvantaged.

We end on a more subjective note, and express views which we believe Jack Tizard might have shared. Currently humanity's first concern must be physical survival from the warring dogmatisms which are globally pervasive. Granted survival, its other priority must be to create conditions which allow and promote the fullest development of human potential; probably the majority of the world's population underfunctions in attainment, personality development and intelligence. The studies sampled indicate the varying possibilities for change as well as the constraints upon change which are built in to the human system. However, just as we believe that WHO's slogan ' Health for All by the Year 2000' is unrealistic (although noble in intent), so, too, must one emphasize the formidable problems, economic, political and familial, which bar the way to a betterment of the human condition. Perhaps a more widespread recognition that this can already be achieved in some individual cases, or in particular groups, may help to undermine the fatalistic notion of a necessary constancy in human development, and represent one of many changes in outlook which the late twentieth century demands.

Summary

Neither genetic programmes nor social influences necessarily unfold in a constant way, and their interactions are complex. The role of chance events adds a further and sometimes potent uncertainty in prediction equations. Both constancies and changes of ordinal position and/or level occur for most characteristics in normal circumstances but, following significant ecological improvement, personal changes among the disadvantaged can be much larger. Recent research emphasizes the inadequacy of considering either genetic or environmental effects during one period of development outside the context of preceding and subsequent influences. It is to long-term consistent influences that importance must be ascribed.

References

Bandura, A. (1982) 'The psychology of chance encounters and life paths.' *American Psychologist 37*, 747–755.

Binet, A. (1920) *Les Idées Modernes sur les Enfants.* Paris: Bibliotheque de Philosophie Scientifique.

Block, J. (1971) *Lives Through Time.* Berkeley, CA: Bancroft Books.

Block, J. (1980) 'From infancy to adulthood: a clarification.' *Child Development 51*, 622–623.

Bloom, B.S. (1964) *Stability and Change in Human Characteristics.* New York: Wiley.

Bowers, K.S. (1977) 'There's more to Iago than meets the eye: a clinical account of personal consistency.' In D. Magnusson and N.S. Endler (eds) *Personality at the Crossroads: Current Issues in Interactional Psychology.* Hillsdale, NJ: Erlbaum.

Bowlby, J., Ainsworth, M.D., Boston, M. and Rosenbluth, D. (1956) 'The effects of mother–child separation: a follow-up.' *British Journal of Medical Psychology 29*, 211–247.

Brim, O.G. and Kagan, J. (1980) *Constancy and Change in Human Development.* Cambridge, MA: Harvard Educational Press.

Brown, M. (1983) 'Despite the Welfare State.' *SSRC Newsletter 48*, March, 9–11.

Brown, M. and Madge, N.J. (1982) *Despite the Welfare State.* London: Heinemann.

Clarke, A.D.B. (1968) 'Learning and human development – the 42nd Maudsley Lecture.' *British Journal of Psychiatry 114*, 161–177.

Clarke, A.D.B. (1977) 'Presidential address: predicting human development: problems, evidence, implications.' *Bulletin of the British Psychological Society 31*, 249–258.

Clarke, A.D.B. and Clarke, A.M. (1954) 'Cognitive changes in the feebleminded.' *British Journal of Psychology 45*, 173–179.

Clarke, A.D.B., Clarke, A.M. and Reiman, S. (1958) 'Cognitive and social changes in the feebleminded–three further studies.' *British Journal of Psychology* 49, 144–157.

Clarke, A.M. (1982) Developmental discontinuities: an approach to assessing their nature. In L.A. Bond and J.M. Joffe (eds) *Facilitating Infant and Early Childhood Development*. Hanover, NH: University Press of New England.

Clarke, A.M. (1984) 'Early experience and cognitive development.' *Review of Research in Education*.

Clarke, A.M. and Clarke, A.D.B. (1976) *Early Experience: Myth and Evidence*. London: Open Books; New York: The Free Press.

Dennis, W. (1973) *Children of the Crèche*. New York: Appleton-Century-Crofts.

Epstein, S. (1983) 'The stability of confusion: a reply to Mischel and Peake.' *Psychological Review 90*, 179–184.

Firkowska, A., Ostrowska, A., Sokolowska, M., Stein, Z., Susser, M. and Wald, I. (1978) 'Cognitive development and social policy.' *Science 200*, 1357–1362.

Freud, S. (1949) *An Outline of Psycho-analysis* (translation by J. Strachey). London: Hogarth Press.

Giuganino, B.M. and Hindley, C. (1982) 'Stability of individual differences in personality characteristics from 3 to 15 years.' *Personalitiy and Individual Differences 3*, 287–301.

Hindley, C. and Owen, C.F. (1979) 'Analysis of individual patterns of DQ and IQ curves from 6 months to 17 years.' *British Journal of Psychology 70*, 273–293.

Jensen, A.R. (1977) 'Cumulative deficit in IQ of blacks in the rural South.' *Developmental Psychology 13*, 184–191.

Jensen, A.R. (1981) 'Raising the IQ: the Ramey and Haskins study.' *Intelligence 5*, 29–40.

Kadushin, A. (1970) *Adopting Older Children*. New York: Columbia University Press.

Kagan, J (1980) 'Four questions in psychological development.' *International Journal of Behavioural Development 3*, 231–241.

Kagan, J. and Moss, H.A. (1962) *Birth to Maturity*. New York: Wiley.

Koluchová, J. (1972) 'Severe deprivation in twins: a case study.' *Journal of Child Psychology and Psychiatry 13*, 107–114.

Koluchová, J. (1976) 'A report on the further development of twins after severe and prolonged deprivation.' In A.M. Clarke and A.D.B. Clarke (eds) *Early Experience: Myth and Evidence*. London: Open Books.

Lazar, I. and Darlington, R. (1982) 'Lasting effects of early education: a report from the Consortium for Longitudinal Studies.' *Monographs of the Society for Research in Child Development 47*, Nos 2–3.

Lewis, H. (1954) *Deprived Children*. London: Oxford University Press.

MacFarlane, J.W. (1964) 'Perspectives on personality consistency and change from the Guidance Study.' *Vita Humana 7*, 115–126.

Mischel, W. (1968) *Personality and Assessment*. New York: Wiley.

Mischel, W. (1977) 'On the future of personality measurement.' *American Psychologist 32*, 246–254.

Plomin, R. (1983) 'Developmental behavior genetics.' *Child Development 54*, 253–259.

Quinton, D. and Rutter, M. (1984) *Childhood Experience and Parenting Behaviour.* London: Heinemann, in press.

Ramey, C. (1982) 'Commentary on "Lasting effects of early education: a report from the Consortium for Longitudinal Studies" (Lazar, I. and Darlington, R.).' *Monographs of the Society for Research in Child Development 47*, Nos 2–3.

Scarr, S. (1981) *Race, Social Class and Individual Differences in IQ.* Hillsdale, NJ: Erlbaum.

Scarr, S., Caparulo, B.K., Ferdman, B.M., Tower, R.B. and Caplan, J. (1983) 'Developmental status and school achievements of minority and non-minority children from birth to 18 years in a British Midlands town.' *British Journal of Developmental Psychology 1*, 31–48.

Shapiro, M.B. (1951) 'An experimental approach to diagnostic testing.' *Journal of Mental Science 97*, 748–764.

Spearman, C. (1904) '"General intelligence": objectively determined and measured.' *American Journal Psychology 115*, 201–292.

Svendsen, D. (1982) 'Changes in IQ, environmental and individual factors: a follow-up study of EMR children.' *Journal of Child Psychology and Psychiatry 23.* 69–74.

Svendsen, D. (1983) Factors related to changes in IQ: a follow-up study of former slow learners. *Journal of Child Psychology and Psychiatry 24*, 405–413.

Tew, B.J. and Laurence, K.M. (1983) 'The relationship between spina bifida children's intelligence test scores on school entry and at school leaving: a preliminary report.' *Child Care Hearlth and Development 9*, 13–17.

Thomas, A. (1981) 'Current trends in developmental theory.' *American Journal of Orthopsychiatry 51*, 580–609.

Thomas, A. and Chess, S. (1957) 'An approach to the study of sources of individual differences in child behavior.' *Journal of Clinical and Experimental Psychopathology and Quarterly Review of Psychiatry and Neurology 18*, 347–357.

Thomas, A. and Chess, S. (1976) 'Evolution of behavior disorders into adolescence.' *American Journal of Psychiatry 133*, 539–542.

Thomas, A. and Chess, S. (1977) *Temperament and Development.* New York: Brunner/Mazel.

Triseliotis, J. and Russell, J. (1984) *Hard to Place: the Outcome of Late Adoptions and Residential Care.* London: Heinemann, in press.

Watson, J.B. (1928) *Psychological Care of Infant and Young Child.* New York: Norton.

Wedge, P. and Essen, J. (1982) *Children in Adversity.* London: Pan Books.

Wilson, R.S. (1983) 'The Louisville Twin Study: developmental synchronies in behavior.' *Child Development 54*, 298–316.

Yule, W., Gold, D.R. and Busch, C. (1982) 'Long-term predictive validity of the WPPSI: an 11-year follow-up study.' *Personality and Individual Differences 3,* 65–71.

Zigler, E. and Valentine, J. (1979) (eds) *Project Head Start: A Legacy of the War on Poverty.* New York: The Free Press.

CHAPTER 7

The Adult Outcome of Early Behavioural Abnormalities

Commentary

During the 12 years when we worked in an institution for the learning disabled (then termed 'mental defectives'), it was one of our greatest pleasures to design and execute programmes of rehabilitation for a wide variety of residents. In many cases we were able to restore young people to lead normal lives in society; with others we were only partially successful. Thus, we realized that there were constraints on what could be done. This article addressed the problem of early behavioural abnormalities and of constancies across time. These are presented in the order of the difficulty with which their problems diminish or disappear, with or without special intervention. There are, of course, variations in severity within each category. We believe that the order we have used remains unchanged. What is new, however, relates to our Note at the end of the chapter. There were several reports at the Seattle Congress of the International Association for the Scientific Study of Intellectual Disability (2000) concerning the successful replication of the Lovaas research on the good effects with autistic children of intensive behavioural intervention. Apart from this approach we invite our readers to be sceptical about 'miracle' cures of severely afflicted individuals which appear in the media or even in scientific journals, while recognizing that partial amelioration can occur in individual cases.

The Adult Outcome of Early Behavioural Abnormalities*

A.M. Clarke and A.D.B. Clarke

Greater constancies across time are to be expected in seriously deviant conditions compared with less abnormal development. Selective reviews are offered on adult outcomes of severe mental retardation, autism, conduct disorders, mild retardation and adjustment disorders of childhood. In the first category, a highly dependent life path is inevitable. For autism there is a small 'escape rate'. With conduct disorders, around half have a very poor outcome. An important prospective study of mild retardation, supported by other findings, indicated that two-thirds of those who were administratively classified as retarded in childhood were, as young adults, no longer in need of special services. Finally, adjustment disorders of childhood only rarely show continuities into adult life. Each category is heterogeneous in aetiology, and multifactorial influences commonly operate in individual cases. The presence of an organic component appears to narrow the range of reaction between constitution and environment. It seems probable that, with increasingly common social and familial disruptions, conduct disorders, mild retardation and adjustment problems will become increasingly prevalent, whereas biomedical advances are likely to reduce the incidence of severe retardation.

Introduction

Major advances in understanding human development have occurred during the last two or three decades (Clarke and Clarke 1986b). The topic of this article suggests that two of these should be specifically mentioned. First, the idea that there was a necessary constancy in development has given way to an awareness that there are both constancies and changes during the life path. These may differ for different psychological processes, some being more constant or more variable than others. There are two interacting trajectories during the whole life span, the biological trajectory and the social trajectory. Neither are likely to develop in a linear fashion, hence their interactions are very complex. Sometimes changes represent little more than fluctuations, but quite

* This article first appeared in 1988 in the *International Journal of Behavioural Development 11*, 1, pp.3–19. Reprinted by permission of Professor R.K. Silbereisen, Editor of the *International Journal of Behavioral Development*, the Psychology Press and the International Society for the Study of Behavioural Development.

often reflect long-term trends. They do not arise primarily from errors of measurement, although the extent of these can usually be established. Rather they reside in the nature of development itself (Clarke and Clarke 1984).

The second major advance in our understanding must also be noted: from the work of Chess and Thomas since the mid-1950s (reviewed by Chess and Thomas 1984), and from research by Bell (1968), Sameroff and Chandler (1975) and Sameroff (1975), it has become increasingly clear that the individual is not a passive recipient of environmental influences, but reaches out to the environment and receives feedback which tends to modify behaviour. The difficult child is disliked and is thereby reinforced in this behaviour: the bright child seeks and receives more adult attention, while the backward unintelligent child becomes increasingly dispirited by failure experiences. These examples of the transactional model underline the need to be aware that to some extent individuals are agents in their own development, unwittingly but sometimes powerfully. One would expect that these processes would be at their most potent at the extremes of temperament and intellect, simply because the extreme child is likely to have a larger impact upon the surroundings, for good or ill, thus not only altering that environment, but in so doing altering himself. Specifically, greater constancies in development would seem to be more likely where abnormal development already exists, for whatever reason. It would of course be a reasonable hypothesis that organically produced deviance would result in greater constancies than would occur in socially influenced abnormality (Clarke and Clarke 1984, 1986a).

In the space available very brief accounts will be offered of some major early deviant conditions, the nature of these, what is known concerning their aetiologies, and finally their outcome at adulthood. They will be arranged in order of outcome from exceedingly poor to good. The criteria employed for the latter will relate both to adult independence and to freedom from the necessity of treatment or containment. Finally, in an overview, the implications of the summarized data will be examined.

Severe mental retardation

Mental retardation is usually defined in terms of an IQ below 70 in association with problems of social adaptation (Grossman 1983). The more severe retardation (sometimes subdivided into moderate, severe and profound impairment) is taken to describe those below about IQ 50. There are a very large number of causes, ranging from genetic (e.g. chromosomal aberrations, the action of recessive or dominant genes) to infective agents (e.g. rubella in early pregnancy, or meningitis in childhood), to toxins (e.g. alcohol, mercury, lead) or complications of the birth process itself. The end-point of these pathologies involves CNS damage or malformation. Even here, however, transactional processes are likely to operate. It would be over-simple to believe that the Down's child functions at a low level simply because of the physical and mental effects of the 47th chromosome; born into a parental, and later wider, environment of disappointment or even outright rejection, such influences are liable to modify even these powerful biological effects. There are obvious methodological problems in comparing the rejected subnormal child with the accepted and stimulated, but differing outcomes are commonly reported. Nevertheless, under varying social conditions such children show either a greater constancy in development, or in some cases a deteriorating condition associated with premature aging (Clarke, Clarke and Berg 1985).

Research in the 1950s by such persons as Tizard, O'Connor and the present authors accepted that severely retarded children or adults gave a picture of marked psychological, and often physical, impairment. Yet the application of skilled training techniques could transform their functioning in limited areas such as perceptual-motor skills. Particular areas of function could sometimes be substantially increased, with both retention of learning and some transfer. More recently this early work has been replicated by Gold (e.g. 1973, 1978) and the use of prosthetic devices, whether by internalized slogans ('Try another way' aiming to combat the rigidity typical of these persons) or by micro-electronic technology (e.g. Lovett 1985), has extended the possibilities of amelioration.

At the same time, better medical care has increased the life span of such persons, while there are some indications of a decreasing incidence of severe retardation. Taken together, overall prevalence is probably roughly in balance.

There is a clear correlation between social adaptation and IQ below 50. Those persons close to this rather arbitrary borderline may with support achieve a degree of independence. For example, they may travel on their own to sheltered workshops or youth clubs. At the other end of the scale, the more profoundly retarded may fail to achieve speech, may be grossly impaired physically as well as mentally and may die young. Thus the category of severe mental retardation is a wide one. Although functioning at different levels, all members have in common an incapacity to lead independent lives. On this criterion the prognosis is very poor. However, the evolution of behaviour modification techniques has done much to overcome inappropriate behaviour, as well as inducing desirable characteristics. The influence of these methods has been pervasive, and has done much to assist the management of these individuals and to improve the quality of their lives. In only a minority of cases, if identified very early, is there any chance of effective biomedical treatment (e.g.

the dietary treatment of phenylketonuria, surgery for hydrocephalus, thyroxin extract for hypothyroidism). An overview of research in this area has been provided by Clarke and Clarke (1987).

Autism

Much research on this serious condition has been undertaken since Kanner (1943) published his account of 11 children with an apparently identifiable syndrome common to them all and capable of differentiation from other psychiatric disorders. The most important features are impairment of language, impairment in the ability to form social relationships, an insistence on sameness, and an early age of onset, before 30 months. Despite the prevalence of cognitive and affective problems in autistic persons, it appears valid to differentiate the syndrome from mental retardation and childhood schizophrenia (Rutter 1978). Causes of autism are not as yet well understood, and indeed remain the subject of controversy. It seems probable that these may be multifactorial, and also that different constellations may lead to the same end-point. For example, autistic features have been identified in cases of lead poisoning and untreated phenylketonuria. There seems to be little doubt that genetic factors are often involved; thus Folstein and Rutter (1977) studied 11 pairs of MZ twins, and ten pairs of DZ twins, in a group of which at least one twin showed the syndrome of infantile autism. There was a 36 per cent pair-wise concordance rate for autism in MZ twins, with 0 per cent for the DZs. For cognitive abnormalities, MZ concordance was 82 per cent, compared with DZ at 10 per cent. In 12 out of 17 pairs discordant for autism, the autistic twin's condition was associated with a biological hazard likely to result in brain damage. Similarly, Lobascher, Kingerlee and Gabbay (1970) suggested that 56 per cent of their sample exhibited unequivocal evidence of organic cerebral disease. A recent study of concordance in twins is reported by Ritvo, Freeman, Mason-Brothers, Mo and Ritvo (1985).

A long-term study of the outcome in adolescence (Rutter 1981) showed a large number of differences between autistic children and their controls, selected from the clientele of the same hospital. One quarter had developed epileptic fits during adolescence, with the strong implication that the autistic syndrome had arisen as a result of organic brain dysfunction. Rutter, Greenfield and Lockyer (1967) have pointed to the preponderance of males, an excess of first borns and of professional backgrounds among parents.

In terms of intellectual and social competence, the later outcome was poor, with very few entering paid employment and about half incapable of leading an independent existence (Rutter et al. 1967). Poor outcome was associated with low IQ, degree of language impairment and total symptom score in early childhood (Rutter 1981).

Very little progress has been made in biomedical forms of treatment, so that at present education and social training provide the best means of remediation. Rutter and Bartak (1973) followed up children in three special units with widely differing educational philosophies. Holding constant IQ and certain other less powerful predictors of academic achievement, they were able to show a significant effect of a highly structured learning environment and concluded that large amounts of specific teaching in a well-controlled classroom are likely to bring the greatest benefits in terms of scholastic attainment and co-operative behaviour in a free play situation. However, there was a marked tendency for children with higher initial IQs to benefit most, and there was no consistent tendency for an improvement in scholastic ability to be associated with social or behavioural improvement. Further, the gains made at school did not transfer to the home situation, and there was no difference between the units on parental measures of behaviour or social responsiveness.

A carefully planned home intervention study was therefore undertaken in which individually constructed programmes based on behavioural techniques were used and the parents were the principal therapists (Howlin 1980; Rutter 1981, 1985). Sixteen boys aged 3 to 11 years, without overt neurological or sensory impairment and a non-verbal IQ of 60 or above were compared with a short-term matched control group who were receiving no consistent form of treatment. Results after six months showed that the programme was effective in causing parents to modify their behaviour towards their autistic children, and in reducing the level of disturbed behaviour. There was also a significant increase in the children's communication. However, long-term follow-up, while favouring the treatment group on behavioural indices, showed a much less favourable outcome in terms of language use. Initial language capacity rather than the non-verbal IQ was related to outcome, and although the children's ability to use language to communicate did not diminish, they failed to make gains in level. In other words the treatment programme appeared to have been useful in modifying their performance but had not affected their competence.[1]

Conduct disorder

This is defined as 'a repetitive and persistent pattern of conduct in which either the basic rights of others or major age-appropriate societal norms or rules are violated. The conduct is more serious than the ordinary mischiefs and pranks of children and adolescents' (*Diagnostic and Statistical Manual of Mental Diseases,*

1980). It will be seen that the major element is a persistent violation of societies' rules, and the overlap with the category of delinquency, *particularly recidivism*, is substantial. We offer no apology in a brief section for equating the two for the following reasons:

1. Studies of hidden or self-reported delinquency invariably reveal that although a large number of male juveniles (perhaps all of them) commit at least one indictable offence during their childhood years, those who are caught and convicted on several occasions have committed more and *more serious* offences, either than those who walk free, or than one-time offenders (Gibbons 1970; West and Farrington 1973).

2. More controversially, Robins and Ratcliff (1980) offer what seems to the authors very persuasive evidence that there exists a single syndrome made up of a broad variety of antisocial behaviours arising in childhood and continuing into adulthood. The evidence adduced for this view came from three samples with which Robins has been concerned: (a) a 30-year follow-up of children referred to a child guidance clinic; (b) a follow-up of a sample of inner-city black men aged 30 to 35, with IQs above 85, by means of interview and record searches; (c) a follow-up of Vietnam veterans.

Lack of any recorded antisocial activity in childhood virtually precluded delinquency later, while a wide variety of early misconduct were precursors of adult problems, although in only about half the cases. In other words, the overall *level* of childhood deviant behaviour was a better predictor of the level of adult deviance than was any particular childhood behaviour. There was, for example, no evidence that violent offenders were more or less pathological than property offenders, rather a record of violence was associated with the total number of arrests.

Concerning the aetiology of conduct disorders, it has been argued from adoption studies that there is a genetic predisposition for adult criminality (Hutchings and Mednick 1974), but according to Shields's (1973) careful review, while twin studies of adults show some greater concordance of MZ over DZ pairs, the situation is very different in juvenile delinquency where there was similar MZ/DZ concordance, as would be expected were environmental influences the predominant factor.

One study which has explored these in great depth is that of West and Farrington (1973, 1977) and West (1982) which shows a strong degree of concordance in adult outcome with that by Robins and her associates. The effects of adverse family backgrounds, often coupled with below-average intellectual competence, were observable by teachers in primary schools whose ratings of 'troublesomeness' of children aged 8–10 are significant predictors of future delinquency. West and Farrington's prospective longitudinal study (1973, 1977) is invaluable because it avoids many of the sampling biases which may be found in studies based on clinics or remand homes, and also because it was a planned, prospective longitudinal research.

These investigators chose a crowded working-class area of London in which there were no private schools and where most people did not own their homes; the vast majority were English. They studied all the boys aged 8–9 who were attending six typical primary schools and 12 boys from a school for the educationally subnormal, a total of 411, and then followed them through adolescence and into adult life in order to determine who would become delinquent. Detailed ratings of home backgrounds were made by social workers, and numerous tests were given to the boys.

As noted, the factor which best predicted future delinquency was a measure of 'troublesomeness' derived from observations by teachers and classmates at primary school. The 411 boys were then divided into three categories, and of the 92 categorized as most troublesome 44.6 per cent became juvenile delinquents, compared with only 3.5 per cent of the 143 boys in the 'least troublesome' category (West 1982). The author comments that this is somewhat depressing because it implies that deviant behaviour observable at an early age is likely to persist and take a delinquent form as boys grow older. It also seems somewhat mysterious since there is no logical reason why untidiness, poor concentration and similar features at 10 should foreshadow the sort of activities, such as stealing or breaking into shops, which are the typical offences of adolescent juvenile delinquents. Moreover, it is unlikely that the teachers' adverse opinions, operating as self-fulfilling prophecies, were the most important causal link in the chain, although this may have been significant in some cases.

West is clear about the limits of prediction on the basis of five adverse background factors: low family income, large family size, unsatisfactory child-rearing practices, parental criminality and low IQ in the child. From these it would have been possible to identify a minority of boys who were at risk of becoming delinquents, but it would not be possible to make a confident assertion about the outcome for any given individual. Although the group of 63 boys who had a constellation of several adversities produced as many as 31 juvenile delinquents, they also produced 32 who were to have clean records. Moreover, a majority of the juvenile delinquents, 53 in number, did not belong to the high-risk group as defined by the variables studied in this project.

Could it be that one important factor in the causal sequence by which some children become convicted in adolescence while others do not is the kind of secondary school which they attend? Although West found little evidence to support the view that senior schools differentially affected the outcome for pupils in terms of delinquency, other research bearing upon the problem indicates the likelihood that schools as institutions and individual teachers within them can be important factors in ameliorating antisocial tendencies, or conversely exacerbating them. (See Reynolds 1976; Rutter et al. 1979; Galloway, Ball, Blomfield and Seyd 1982). Rutter and Giller (1983) outline evidence for other protective factors which may tip the balance in individual cases.

Turning now to intervention, West (1982) writes 'Most young adult offenders have begun as juvenile delinquents.' In his study 68 per cent of the men convicted for offences committed between the 19th and 25th birthdays had been previously convicted. There is general agreement that there are no easy solutions to the problems of treatment and prevention, not surprising in view of the multifactorial nature of the causes which involve a personal predisposition, adverse family influences, the wider social context including the peer group, and also opportunity. West maintains that the question now being asked is whether research has anything at all of practical value to contribute to policy on prevention, treatment and control of delinquency. He offers a summary of the methodologically sound investigations which include either random allocation to treatment and control groups, or carefully matched controls, and both short-term and long-term follow-ups. The relatively few systematic evaluations of important projects have on the whole failed to demonstrate a significant decrease in arrests or convictions, although there are exceptions, particularly with programmes including an element of systematic behaviour modification such as that of Seidman, Rappoport and Davidson (1980). Successful treatment of delinquents by means of counselling has not been statistically validated, and in this connection the long-term outcome of the Cambridge Somerville project (McCord 1978) stands as a monument to the careful planning of a community treatment project designed to prevent delinquency and its failure to fulfil its promise.

Mild mental retardation

As noted under severe retardation, the criteria involve both low IQ and problems of social adaptation, whether already existing or envisaged in the individual child or adult. In practice, mild cases are seldom identified before the age of school entry, and indeed sometimes not at all. Here the distinction must be made between true and administrative prevalence, the latter normally being far smaller than the former. There is clear evidence that many children with IQs between 50 and 70 (the conventional range for these conditions) are never labelled as such. They are likely to be drawn from less deprived circumstances and/or to show less difficult behaviour.

This brings us to a consideration of causes. First, there is no doubt that a proportion of the administratively identified individuals owe their condition to the same range of aetiologies as do the severe. However, by definition the effects have been less damaging; these persons usually comprise about 30 per cent of the whole mildly retarded group. The remainder appear to owe their condition to polygenic inheritance interacting with social adversity, sometimes of extreme degree. There has in the past been some controversy concerning these causes, some arguing for a wholly environmental and some for a wholly genetic explanation. The truth lies between these; there is no doubt that social factors play a part, and often a very significant part, in aetiology but they are not the only factor (Clarke and Clarke 1986a).

An important prospective study in Aberdeen, initiated by the late Herbert Birch, has thrown much light on mild retardation in a number of reports over the last 17 years. All children in the city born between 1952 and 1954 were carefully assessed in 1962. Those administratively classified and with IQs less than 70 comprised 9.4 per 1000; all those administratively classified, 12.6 per 1000; and all administratively classified plus those having IQs below 70, 27.4 per 1000. From this it is clear that there were many labelled cases with IQs above 70, and that many children with IQs below 70 were not labelled at all. Hence different criteria yield different estimates. Nevertheless, at the age of 22, two-thirds of the administratively classified were not receiving any special mental retardation services, and of these, 89 per cent of the males were in full-time employment (Richardson and Koller 1985; and for a summary, see Clarke and Clarke 1985, pp.443–4).

There is unanimity in the literature that administrative prevalence declines steeply after school age, during the last few years of which intellectual demands upon the child may be at their greatest. Thereafter, some individuals become 'camouflaged' in an undemanding lifestyle. Others slowly learn what society demands of its members; yet others exhibit delayed intellectual maturation as a recovery from severe early adversity (Clarke, Clarke and Reiman 1958; Svendsen 1982). Those whose condition is the result of an organic pathology, however, show a considerable constancy in development and their prognosis is relatively poor. The remainder, if removed from conditions of adversity, tend to merge into the duller, unskilled section of the population. Numerous prospective follow-up studies underline this difference; however, current social problems, including unemployment in developed countries, may have already altered this otherwise reasonably hopeful picture. Certainly, at all levels of retardation, there is a heightened prevalence of emotional instability, and personality problems as much as intellectual retardation are often the reasons for administrative action.

It has been argued that, since relatively spontaneous improvements occur in many of the mildly retarded, greater assistance might accelerate and increase such changes. To effect these, long-term intervention would be needed.

Adjustment disorders of childhood

Adjustment disorders have been defined in DSM-III as 'a maladaptive reaction to an identifiable psycho-social stressor, that occurs within three months after the onset of the stressor. The maladaptive nature of the reaction is indicated by either impairment in social or occupational functioning or symptoms that are in excess of a normal and expected reaction to the stressor. It is assumed that the disturbance will eventually remit after the stressor ceases or, if the stressor persists, when a new level of adaptation is achieved' (*Diagnostic and Statistical Manual of Mental Disorders* 1980, p.299). The final section of this statement represents a succinct summary of research findings in this area.

As with other abnormal conditions, adjustment disorders may arise from a variety of different, and sometimes overlapping, causes. There are a number of obvious variables: the family context, especially the quality of parenting; the degree of match or mismatch between parents, and between parents and child; the qualities of individual vulnerability and resilience during or following stress, to which we have drawn attention from time to time since 1959; the enhanced probability of disorder in those with organic brain dysfunction (e.g. Rutter and Sandberg 1985); the doubled risk of emotional and conduct dis-orders in inner London compared with the Isle of Wight (Rutter *et al.* 1975). Identifying six risk factors, these authors showed that the possession of one yielded no greater risk than occurred in controls. Two had a multiplicative effect resulting in a fourfold increase in risk, while four factors produced a tenfold increase.

Whether the disorder is situation-specific or pervasive is obviously relevant to outcome. Isolated transient emotional or conduct disorders are very common in normal children. What is important is the developmental inappropriateness of the problems (Rutter and Sandberg 1985, p.213).

The work of Chess and Thomas (1984) has already been mentioned. Commencing in 1956, they initiated the New York Longitudinal Study, a prospective programme of intensive assessment and follow-up from infancy to early adulthood. As the authors note (Chess and Thomas 1984, p.9), it 'represents the one study with prospective longitudinal data starting in early infancy and antedating in all cases the onset of behaviour disorder, with a substantial sample size and no loss of subjects over time'. As such it provides the main data set for this part of our article.

The sample consisted of 133 middle- to upper-middle-class subjects, gathered through personal contact during pregnancy or shortly after birth, with parents who were willing to co-operate in a long-term study of normal child development. Only one parent refused to participate. There was an advantage in using a socioculturally homogeneous group, allowing this powerful variable to be held roughly constant. An important incentive, both in joining the study and remaining within it, lay in the free availability to parents of highly qualified and experienced staff over many years. It is a tribute to this, and to the personal relationships built up, that sample attrition did not occur.

Adjustment disorders represent a wide range of very common behavioural problems which, as the authors note, in many cases represent age-specific behaviours which, though troublesome, are not suggestive of pathological deviation. Sometimes the issue is a simple one involving inappropriateness of the routines employed by parents. Suggestions of alternative ways of handling the child can be effective. When problems do not resolve, psychiatric evaluation and sometimes treatment are necessary (Chess and Thomas 1984, p.34).

In childhood, some 40 cases out of the total of 133 children were identified as exhibiting adjustment disorders. Of the former, 25 were mild cases, ten moderate and five were severely disturbed. Onset occurred modally between 3 and 5 years. By adolescence 24 out of 40 had recovered and two had improved, with no significant predictive differences arising from the early classification in mild, moderate or severe.

The adjustment of three children was unchanged by adolescence, ten were mildly or moderately worse and one was markedly worse. By early adulthood, 29 cases had recovered, with additionally five showing improvement. In the vast majority, those who had shown recovery in adolescence maintained this into early adult life. Those, however, who neither recovered nor improved by adolescence tended to grow worse with the years.

Twelve new cases appeared during adolescence, of whom half had recovered, and two had improved by early adulthood, that is, over a rather short period.

Not only were qualitative evaluations available, but sophisticated statistical techniques were also employed. These confirmed and elaborated the clinical findings. Age 3 ratings were used as predictors in multiple regression analyses. Maternal attitudes as a set of attributes always showed a significant relationship with adult adjustment. Adjustment at 3 years was almost always a significant predictor; temperament, however, was not so. Using these main dimensions, the multiple correlations with adult adjustment ranged from 0.42 to 0.46, close to what one of the present authors described as 'nature's favourite correlation coefficient', that is, the expected relation over lengthy periods for behavioural characteristics (Clarke 1978). These figures account for between 17 and 21 per cent of common variance, suggesting some continuities but considerable change over time. However, using the set correlation method, the 11 variables representing childhood adjustment, difficult-easy temperament, childhood environment and presence of a clinical diagnosis together accounted for 0.429 of the adult attribute variance. Unbiased estimates reduced this to 0.341, an estimate (34%) of the communality between child and adult sets of data.

> This is a relatively high figure 'considering the 15 year age span involved, and the tremendous physical and psychological changes and social expectations in the transitions from childhood to adolescence to early adulthood. At the same time this leaves over 60% of the variance unaccounted for…an interactionist viewpoint would predict that quantitative group measures could not capture the many special features of the child's behaviour and the environmental influences which would affect the sequences of psychological development differently in different youngsters' (Chess and Thomas 1984, p.99).

In summary, this important study shows a considerable (but not total) discontinuity between childhood and early adulthood adjustment disorders. The discontinuity is doubtless enhanced by the skilled professional advice available to parents, advice which the authors regarded as moderately or highly successful in about half the cases. The writings of Chess and Thomas emphasize the 'goodness of fit' model, and the transactional consequences on both children and their parents when either match or mis-match occur. Chess and Thomas (1984, pp.20–23) define 'Goodness of fit' between parents and children as follows:

> When the organism's capacities, motivations and style of behaving and the demands and expectations of the environment are in accord, goodness of fit results…(potentiating)…optimal positive development. Should there be dissonance…there is poorness of fit which leads to maladaptive functioning and distorted development.

Although the sample was exclusively middle class, there is evidence that the findings have much in common with those of other studies. Where social values and parental practices differ markedly, however, one would expect different frequencies and indeed different types of disorder. It would nevertheless be our expectation that the general principles arising from the New York Longitudinal Study would have considerable general application.

The classic 30-year retrospective follow-up study by Robins (1966) of a child guidance clinic sample is entirely consistent with the description noted above. Emotional disorders, such as abnormal anxiety or depression, were in the majority of cases self-limiting, unlike the poor outcome for those exhibiting antisocial disorders. Or again, the Isle of Wight study (Rutter, Tizard and Whitmore 1970) showed that in a total population of 10–11-year-olds with disorder, more than half were better some four or five years later.

A study by von Knorring, Andersson and Magnusson (1987) adds further information to this area of research, for it provided data on a large, representative sample, prospectively from 10–24 years, and retrospectively from 0–9 years. In reviewing relevant literature, these authors note the higher incidence of childhood disorders in cities, compared with towns and rural areas, and a higher incidence in boys than girls which, however, is reversed during adolescence. Conduct disorders may, however, be dealt with in other ways than clinically, but the authors underline the poor prognosis for these, with good outcomes for children with emotional disorders.

The criteria for inclusion in the von Knorring *et al.* (1987) sample were different from those of the Chess and Thomas research, for they depended on the rather tough criterion of psychiatric referral during childhood through to early adulthood.

The findings, however, endorse other work; only three out of 28 children exhibiting anxiety and emotional disorders before 9 years were still in psychiatric care in early adulthood, while a quarter of a large group with later onset, 10–14 years, and almost half with an onset between 15–19, were still in psychiatric care between 20–24. Males who had attended special classes were at particular risk for disorder.

Discussion

For reasons of space this review has had to be selective. The precursors of schizophrenia, or the hyperkinetic syndrome, for example, have not been considered. Moreover, each condition outlined would justify an article, or indeed a book, on its own. In spite of omissions, and brief summaries of complex issues, the principles which emerge from the present evaluation seem to be well supported. For those readers who require a more detailed acquaintance with the literature, the book edited by Mednick and Baert (1981) is highly recommended. This covers a very large number of carefully conducted European prospective longitudinal studies, presented as an empirical basis for the primary prevention of psychosocial disorders.

Within each of the categories of abnormality described in this article there are common factors which justify their compartmentalization. It must be recognized, however, that there is a heterogeneity of aetiology within each; as an extreme example let us recall that there are some 200 or more different causes of severe retardation. Many paths lead to Rome, and outcome, too, can be varied, sometimes minimally and sometimes greatly, depending upon the particular condition. It is also obvious that in an individual child or adult two or more conditions may coexist; for example, a mildly retarded individual with epilepsy and a conduct disorder.

The role of genetic and constitutional factors is often misunderstood. These do not normally dictate a precise outcome, but determine a range of reaction within which the phenotype may be formed, depending on genetic–environment interactions. This range may be narrowed where substantial CNS impairment exists (as in severe retardation where genetic aetiologies are common) or wide where psychosocial causes are primarily involved (as in many adjustment disorders in children). There are also transactions; as noted, to some extent the characteristics of individuals affect their environments, and in so doing through feedback mechanisms modify or reinforce their own development.

A favourite slogan at one time was that 'there are no problem children, only problem parents', an attractive over-simplification. While there are, indeed, problem parents (e.g. uncaring, or psychopathic) there are also problem children (e.g. autistic, or temperamentally extreme). Above all there are problem interactions and transactions. Such poorness of fit can set off a chain of events through development. Most transactions, for a variety of reasons (e.g. maturation in the child, changing social environment) are incomplete, and are likely, except in temperamentally extreme children, to attenuate over time. Not only are genetic factors often involved, their programmes unfolding in a non-linear fashion, but equally the child's environment inevitably changes as age increases. To regard these interactions as complex is an understatement.

On many occasions (e.g. Clarke and Clarke 1976) we have described human development as potentially somewhat open-ended, taking into account both the theoretical motion of ranges of reaction, and empirical studies on changes during development in individuals exposed to changing ecologies. How far do these views fit abnormal early development and its outcome? In cases of severe retardation, not at all, using our criteria of adult independence and freedom from the necessity of treatment or containment. In autism, however, there is a small but significant 'escape rate'. This seems to be considerably greater in mild retardation, administratively defined, but the prognosis for conduct disorders is generally regarded as poor, although only about half the cases in Robins and Ratcliff's study showed continuity. Adjustment disorders in childhood do not in general lead to continuities, except in extreme cases, so here the outcome for these very common, and sometimes at the time, serious problems, is good.

Throughout we have commented on psychological treatment, indicating that there can be positive though limited improvements in severe retardation and autism. For conduct disorders, which certainly arise in the context of severe stressors, the situation seems poor, unless a drastic change in ecology can be achieved. Mild retardation in many cases improves more or less spontaneously, but active educational and directive counselling techniques can help. Counselling of parents and children with adjustment disorders is also often effective.

In the future, more information is needed on the processes initiated in pathological situations, and on why certain children are highly resistant to stress, while others have a low threshold for stress reactions (e.g. Clarke and Clarke 1959; Garmezy and Tellegen 1984). In a wider context, social and familial disruptions, which appear to be increasingly common, are likely to augment the incidence of conduct disorders, mild retardation and adjustment problems of childhood. Psychosocial causes require social and educational solutions which societies will underestimate or ignore at their peril. On the other hand, biomedical advances are probably already reducing the incidence of the pathologies leading to severe mental retardation.

Note

1   Lovaas (1987) reports the results of intensive behavioural treatment for 19 autistic children below the age of 4 years, who received more than 40 hours of professional one-to-one treatment per week, with parental participation to ensure that every waking hour was accounted for. Compared with two control groups these children made and retained very large gains in IQ and scholastic attainment, 47 per cent achieving normal intellectual and educational functioning, in contrast to 2 per cent of the control group subjects. In common with other researches it was found that mental age and degree of language abnormality significantly predicted outcome from pre-intervention measures. Results of this study appear to be so important that, despite the apparent cost, replication would seem mandatory.

References

Bell, R.Q. (1968) 'A reinterpretation of the direction of effects in studies of socialization.' *Psychological Review 75*, 81–95.

Chess, S. and Thomas, A. (1984) *Origins and Evolution of Behavior Disorders: From Infancy to Adult Life.* New York: Brunner/Mazel.

Clarke, A.D.B. (1978) 'Presidential address: Predicting human development: problems, evidence, implications.' *Bulletin of the British Psychological Society 31*, 249–258.

Clarke, A.D.B. and Clarke, A.M. (1959) 'Recovery from the effects of deprivation.' *Acta Psychologica 16*, 137–144.

Clarke, A.D.B. and Clarke, A.M. (1984) 'Constancy and change in the growth of human characteristics.' *Journal of Child Psychology and Psychiatry 25*, 191–210.

Clarke, A.D.B. and Clarke, A.M. (1986a) 'Etiology update and review: II. Psychosocial factors: correlates or causes?' In J. Wortis (ed) *Mental Retardation and Developmental Disabilities 14*, 36–49. New York: Elsevier.

Clarke, A.D.B. and Clarke, A.M. (1987) 'Research on mental handicap, 1957–1987: a selective review.' *Journal of Mental Deficiency Research*, in press.

Clarke, A.D.B., Clarke, A.M. and Reiman, S. (1958) 'Cognitive and social changes in the feebleminded: three further studies.' *British Journal of Psychology 49*, 144–157.

Clarke, A.M. and Clarke, A.D.B. (1976) *Early Experience: Myth and Evidence.* London: Open Books.

Clarke, A.M. and Clarke, A.D.B. (1985) 'Lifespan development and psychosocial intervention.' In A.M. Clarke, A.D.B. Clarke and J.M. Berg (eds) *Mental Deficiency: The Changing Outlook* (4th edn). London: Methuen.

Clarke, A.M. and Clarke, A.D.B. (1986b) 'Thirty years of child psychology: a selective review.' *Journal of Child Psychology and Psychiatry 27*, 719–759.

Clarke, A.M., Clarke, A.D.B. and Berg, J.M. (1985) (eds) *Mental Deficiency: The Changing Outlook* (4th edn). London: Methuen.

Diagnostic and Statistical Manual of Mental Diseases (3rd edn) (DSM-III) (1980). Washington, DC: American Psychiatric Association.

Folstein, S. and Rutter, M. (1977) 'Infantile autism: a genetic study of 21 twin pairs.' *Journal of Child Psychology and Psychiatry 18*, 297–321.

Galloway, D., Ball, T., Blomfield, D. and Seyd, R. (1982) *Schools and Disruptive Pupils.* London and New York: Longman.

Garmezy, N. and Tellegen, A. (1984) 'Studies of stress-resistant children: methods, variables and preliminary findings.' In F. Morrison, C. Lord and D. Keating (eds) *Applied Developmental Psychology 1*, 231–287. New York: Academic Press.

Gibbons, D.C. (1970) *Delinquent Behaviour.* Englewood Cliffs, NJ: Prentice-Hall.

Gold, M.W. (1973) 'Research on vocational habilitation of the retarded: the present, the future.' In N.R. Ellis (ed), *International Review of Research in Mental Retardation*, Vol. 6, 97–147. New York: Academic Press.

Gold, M.W. (1978) *Try Another Way.* Training manual, National Institute of Mental Retardation, Austin: Marc Gold and Assoc.

Grossman, H.J. (1983) *Classification in Mental Retardation.* Washington, DC: American Association on Mental Deficiency.

Howlin, P. (1980) 'The home treatment of autistic children.' In L.A. Hersov and M. Berger (eds) *Language and Language Disorders in Childhood.* Oxford: Pergamon, 115–145.

Hutchings, B. and Mednick, S.A. (1974) 'Registered criminality in the adoptive and biological parents of registered male adoptees.' In S.A. Mednick, F. Schulsinger and B. Bell (eds) *Early Detection and Prevention of Behaviour Disorders.* Amsterdam: New Holland Publishing Co.; New York: American Elsevier.

Kanner, L. (1943) 'Autistic disturbances of affective contact.' *The Nervous Child 2,* 217–250.

Lobascher, M.E., Kingerlee, P.E. and Gabbay, S.S. (1970) 'Childhood autism: an investigation of aetiological factors in twenty-five cases.' *British Journal of Psychiatry 117,* 525–529.

Lovaas, O.I. (1987) 'Behavioral treatment and normal educational and intellectual functioning in young autistic children.' *Journal of Consulting and Clinical Psychology 55,* 3–9.

Lovett, S. (1985) 'Microelectronic and computer-based technology.' In A.M. Clarke, A.D.B. Clarke and J.M. Berg (eds) *Mental Deficiency: The Changing Outlook* (4th edn). London: Methuen, 549–583.

Mednick, S.A. and Baert, A.E. (eds) (1981) *Prospective Longitudinal Research: An Empirical Basis for the Primary Prevention of Psychosocial Disorders.* Oxford: Oxford University Press on behalf of the WHO Regional Office for Europe.

McCord, J. (1978) 'A thirty-year follow-up of treatment effects.' *American Psychologist 33,* 284–291.

Reynolds, D. (1976) 'The delinquent school.' In P. Woods (ed) *The Process of Schooling.* London: Routledge and Kegan Paul, 1–12.

Richardson, S.A. and Koller, H. (1985) 'Epidemiology.' In A.M. Clarke, A.D.B. Clarke and J.M. Berg (eds) *Mental Deficiency: The Changing Outlook* (4th edn). London: Methuen, 356–400.

Ritvo, E.R., Freeman, B.J., Mason-Brothers, A., Mo, A., Ritvo, A. M. (1985) 'Concordance for the syndrome of autism in 40 pairs of afflicted twins.' *American Journal of Psychiatry 142,* 74–77.

Robins, L. (1966) *Deviant Children Grown Up.* Baltimore: Williams & Wilkins.

Robins, L.N. and Ratcliff, K.S. (1980) 'Childhood conduct disorders and later arrest.' In L.N. Robins, P.J. Clayton and J.K. Wing (eds) *The Social Consequences of Psychiatric Illness.* New York: Brunner/Mazel.

Rutter, M. (1978) 'Diagnosis and definition.' In M. Rutter and E. Schopler (eds) *Autism: A Reappraisal of Concepts and Treatment.* New York: Plenum.

Rutter, M. (1981) 'Longitudinal studies of autistic children (United Kingdom).' In S.A. Menwick and A.E. Baert (eds) *Prospective Longitudinal Research: An Empirical*

Basis for the Primary Prevention of Psychosocial Disorders. Oxford: Oxford University Press for WHO Regional Office for Europe, 267–269.

Rutter, M. (1985) 'Psychopathology and development: links between childhood and adult life.' In M. Rutter and L. Hersov (eds) *Child and Adolescent Psychiatry: Modern Approaches* (2nd edn). Oxford: Blackwell Scientific Publications, 720–739.

Rutter, M. and Bartak, L. (1973) 'Special educational treatment of autistic children: a comparative study. II. Follow-up findings and implications for services.' *Journal of Child Psychology and Psychiatry 14*, 241–270.

Rutter, M. and Giller, H. (1983) *Juvenile Delinquency: Trends and Perspectives.* Harmondsworth: Penguin Books.

Rutter, M., Greenfield, D. and Lockyer, L. (1967) 'A five to fifteen year follow-up study of infantile psychosis. II. Social and behavioural outcome.' *British Journal of Psychiatry 113*, 1169–1182.

Rutter, M., Maughan, B., Mortimore, P., Ouston, J. and Smith, A. (1979) *Fifteen Thousand Hours: Secondary Schools and their Effects on Pupils.* London: Open Books.

Rutter, M. and Sandberg, S. (1985) 'Epidemiology of child psychiatric disorder.' *Child Psychiatry and Human Development 15*, 209–233.

Rutter, M., Tizard, J., and Whitmore, K. (1970) *Education, Health and Behaviour.* London: Longman.

Rutter, M., Yule, B., Quinton, D., Rowlands, O., Yule, W. and Berger, M. (1975) 'Attainment and adjustment in two geographical areas: III. Some factors accounting for area differences.' *British Journal of Psychiatry 126*, 520–533.

Sameroff, A.J. (1975) 'Early influences on development: Fact or fancy.' *Merrill-Palmer Quarterly 21*, 267–294.

Sameroff, A.J. and Chandler, M.J. (1975) 'Reproductive risk and the continuum of caretaking casualty.' In F.D. Horowitz, M. Hetherington, S. Scarr-Salapatek and G. Siegel (eds) *Review of Child Development Research 4*, Chicago: University of Chicago Press, 187–244.

Seidman, E., Rappoport, F. and Davidson, W.S. (1980) 'Adolescents in legal jeopardy: initial success and replication of an alternative to the criminal justice system.' In R.R.Ross and P. Gendreaux (eds) *Effective Correctional Treatment.* Toronto: Butterworths.

Shields, J. (1973) 'Heredity and psychological abnormality.' In H.J. Eysenck (ed) *Handbook of Abnormal Psychology* (2nd edn). London: Pitman Medical, 540–603.

Svendsen, D. (1982) 'Changes in IQ, environmental and individual factors: a follow-up study of former slow learners.' *Journal of Child Psychology and Psychiatry 24*, 405–413.

Von Knorring, A-L., Andersson, O. and Magnusson, D. (1987) 'Psychiatric care and course of psychiatric disorders from childhood to early adulthood in a representative sample.' *Journal of Child Psychology and Psychiatry 28*, 329–341.

West, D.J. (1982) Delinquency: *Its Roots, Careers and Prospects.* London: Heinemann.

West, D.J. and Farrington, D.P. (1973) *Who Becomes Delinquent?* London: Heinemann.

West, D.J. and Farrington, D.P. (1977) *The Delinquent Way of Life.* London: Heinemann.

CHAPTER 8

Varied Destinies
A Study of Unfulfilled Predictions

Commentary

Prediction is the hallmark of scientific method, yet to be aware of the complex interplay between the many influences in human development requires a principle of individual developmental uncertainty. Rather than considering predictive successes, in this chapter in honour of Professor Barbara Tizard we aimed to exemplify the extent of unfulfilled predictions. Especially in the area of psychopathology, a study of those who avoided their expected destiny may assist in the understanding of the particular condition and offer clues to its remediation.

In indicating predictive failures we consider in turn studies of personality development, the supposed long-term significance of early attachment, the varied outcome of childhood sexual abuse and finally we look again at intelligence. Under normal circumstances for this latter, only a minority show sequential changes, these defying the otherwise broadly accurate IQ predictions. For those, however, who have experienced rescue from malevolent conditions, the situation is entirely different as shown, for example, by Sir Michael Rutter's team which continues to study the outcome for rescued Romanian orphans brought to this country (Chapter 20) as well as in other early adoption studies (e.g. Chapters 4, 18 and 19).

Of course, it might well be argued that, in spite of the hugely complex nature of human development, behavioural prediction is surprisingly good. Yet one must remind oneself that in long-term studies one is dealing with individual probabilities, not certainties, and that, for good or ill, a substantial minority may escape their apparent destinies.

Varied Destinies: A Study of Unfulfilled Predictions[*]

Alan Clarke and Ann Clarke

For well over four decades we have enjoyed Barbara Tizard's friendship and admired her as a scientist. During this period she has exercised her creative, critical and analytic ability in several areas of psychology, has been a devoted wife and mother and latterly, as a widow, took over responsibility for the Thomas Coram Research Unit founded by Jack Tizard. It is a pleasure and privilege to offer a chapter for this book, the contents of which reflect her wide range of interests and important contributions to psychology and social policy.

The establishment of cause–effect relations and their accurate prediction has been the hallmark of the scientific method, nowhere more obvious than in the physical sciences where it originated. Yet Heisenberg in 1927, after making vital contributions to quantum mechanics, stated his Uncertainty Principle which was to have a major effect on scientific thinking. Gleick (1992) summarizes Heisenberg's narrow definition: 'a particle cannot have both a definite place and a definite momentum,' adding that the implications seemed to cover a broader territory than the atom and its interior (p.429). Thus entered into science an element of unpredictability which challenged earlier views, more recently augmented by chaos theory.

Behavioural science by its very nature has to live with a good deal of uncertainty. Psychologists tend to get excited about correlations as low as 0.50 between childhood and adult characteristics, even though this accounts for only 25 per cent of common variance. Immediate reliability on tests or other assessments of 0.90 or a little above is very acceptable, but test–retest reliability virtually never approximates to 1.00. This failure to maintain precise rank order arises from personal fluctuations which may be important in screening programmes, but are of relatively little significance in developmental predictions. Such fluctuations can be cancelled out by repeated assessment over fairly short periods, yielding greater predictive power than from a single 'snapshot'. But if in a longitudinal study only before and after measures are available, such transitory variations may indicate a trend where none exists, or indeed conceal a 'true' change, depending on the direction of the two 'errors'. These latter are usually thought somehow to reside in the test as opposed to the individual.

[*]   This chapter is reprinted by kind permission of Taylor and Francis, originally appearing in B. Bernstein and J. Brannen (eds) (1996) *Children, Research and Policy*, pp.47–62.

However, true test error can occur, sometimes dramatically, where, within a test, different standard deviations are found for different ages, or where there are differences between different assessment devices.

In complex systems (and this includes individual development) alteration in one or more variables can affect the whole and thus reflect, or impinge on, the life path. This view becomes obvious when, even from an armchair viewpoint, we consider our description of fundamental parameters of development (Clarke 1982). First, the biological trajectory may wax or wane at different periods and may differ for different processes. The adolescent growth spurt is one example, and the growing heritability for IQ in adolescence is another (Wilson 1985). Second, there is a psychosocial trajectory which, too, develops and changes for the individual, whether in the micro-, meso- or macro-environment. Third, there are interactional/transactional processes. To varying extents individuals both affect and reflect environmental influences (Scarr and McCartney 1983) in feed-forward and feedback processes. In some sense they unwittingly play a causal role in their own development. Finally, chance encounters (Bandura 1982) or chance events can sometimes alter the direction of the life path. Consideration of these interacting complexities suggests a degree of unpredictability for the individual, a principle of developmental uncertainty.

In determining whether predictions are likely to be strongly or only partially fulfilled, account must be taken of the process involved; thus, much higher correlations have been found for indices of IQ than for any single personality variable. Furthermore, much will depend on the time span over which forecasts are made: the longer the time period, the less accurate in all but the most deviant conditions. Above all, it is important to note whether broad or narrow predictions are required. Dividing a population into top and bottom 50 per cent will lead to fewer changes in category compared with splitting the distribution into ten bands.

Two or three variables taken together (and sometimes suitably weighted) can often yield important long-term predictions of particular characteristics, or life-path outcomes. The next step might be to add further measures in the hope of increasing predictive power. In such circumstances a law of diminishing returns operates; multiple correlations are likely to increase but only by small amounts. This reflects the web of related measures, such that the additional variables, correlated with the first two or three, overlap in their predictive power.

Predictions may be based on some sort of a constancy model: that is, with respect to age peers, people change little as they develop. Alternatively, a knowledge of the natural history of a particular condition may suggest an actuarial prediction (e.g. the decline in relative ability of Down's Syndrome children with increasing age). Or again, predictions may rely on knowledge of the common effects of particular events (e.g. divorce), or on the expected outcome of interventions.

We argue that the study of those who defy predictions is of interest in its own right but, may also have a general bearing on our understanding of the dynamics of development. For abnormal conditions, in particular, those who escape their expected destiny may yield evidence on prevention. It is quite common to show that some severe adolescent problem yields a very bad adult prognosis, perhaps affecting 80 per cent. The 20 per cent whose adult outcome differed are sometimes brushed aside in discussion, and occasionally circular arguments (e.g. 'the original diagnosis must have been wrong') explain them away. In line with the principle of developmental uncertainty, we indicate that there is nearly always an 'escape' rate from abnormal conditions.

This chapter addresses the question of failures in predicting individual development. Depending both on the particular characteristic, as well as the time span involved, failures of precise prediction may be nearly as common as successes but, owing to the less positive emphasis, are less likely to be discussed directly. Within the constraints of space we outline some recent research findings in just four areas: personality development, early attachment, child sexual abuse and intelligence. Within each, we sample a few of the studies which illuminate the problem of predictive error.

The extent of predictive failures

Personality development

In *Lives Through Time* Block (1971) used a Q-sort method to describe each of 150 subjects in the earlier Oakland and Berkeley Guidance Studies, at the ages of about 15, 18 and 33. Correlating individuals' scores with similar later ones, average correlations of 0.75 (15–18) and 0.55 (18–33) were obtained. Note the lower correlations for the longer period, a customary finding. A wide range of individual correlations was obtained, ranging from considerable constancy at one extreme to complete inconstancy at the other (i.e. no prediction from the early scores). Thus both constancies and changes were exhibited. Before taking these findings at face value, two points need to be made: 1. the original scores, taken years before the analysis, had imperfect reliability; and 2. the later Q-sort would also show imperfect reliability. Taken together, some of the changes would have arisen from these 'errors'. Not surprisingly, these data have been open to different interpretations (Block 1980; Clarke and Clarke 1984). While Block argues for continuities, Macfarlane (1964), who had conducted the Berkeley Study, commented with surprise that 'Many of our most mature and competent adults had severely troubled and confusing childhoods and adolescences. Many of our highly successful children and adolescents have failed to achieve their predicted potential...but we were not always wrong! We did have several small groups whose adult status fulfilled theoretical expectations', that is, that personality does not alter and is therefore predictable.

A further *caveat* must be advanced. It may well be that while global personality assessments show both constancies in some, and changes in others, over time, perhaps some dimensions show greater continuities, but are obscured in overall evaluations. This would probably be the view of Kagan who has identified early shyness as showing strong continuities. Nevertheless, Kagan and Snidman (1991) and Kagan (1992) indicate that even with high heritability, a very substantial minority show phenotypic changes over time. Some who were unusually inhibited as infants were no longer so later, while others who had been sociable and fearless had later become shy with adults and children (Kagan 1992, p.994). Such changes were presumably the result of intervening experiences. However, the majority of very inhibited children may be at risk of a very introverted adulthood.

A notable addition to the literature on this problem has been provided by Kerr *et al.* (1994) who carried out on a Swedish longitudinal sample a 'conceptual replication' of Kagan's work. Among questions raised were whether extremes of inhibition showed greater stability over time than non-extremes, and whether there are gender differences in stability. We have ourselves (1988) suggested that extremes are likely to have a different developmental history than others.

Data on a large sample consisted of mothers' ratings over a 16-year period, and psychologists' ratings over the first 6 years of life. The former was concerned with perceived shyness towards strangers, and the latter with inhibited behaviour in the testing situation. On the question of temporal stability for the whole group, the findings reflected the two principles to which we have drawn attention over several decades. Correlations increase with increasing age, and the longer the time gap between assessments, the lower the correlation (i.e. the greater the likelihood of change in individual ordinal position). In the context of the present theme, the greatest interest is in whether there are differences in stability between those at the extremes of the distribution versus those in the non-extreme group. For the first six years, stability data supported Kagan's findings. However, 'behaviour did change in the long run... For most of our subjects the early causes of extremely inhibited or uninhibited behaviour were not long-lasting' (p.144). Although ratings were more stable for children in the extreme groups, stability into adolescence was only found for inhibited females. Here the authors speculate that culturally shared notions of gender-appropriate behaviour influence the stability of inhibition. This, then, is a study that emphasizes for many of the sample a relative long-term unpredictability of a personality characteristic. We must be aware, however, that overt behaviour may cover up internal inhibitions, and that self-awareness of our own personality may lead to compensatory overt behaviour (Chess and Thomas 1984). For a useful overview, see Plomin and Dunn (1986).

Using information from the Berkeley Guidance Study, Caspi, Elder and Bem (1988) followed up a group of late childhood shy children at ages 30 and 40. Very significant associations were found, especially for men, with delayed marriage, delayed fatherhood, as well as entry to a stable career. The authors indicate the likelihood that childhood shyness leads to avoidance of novel situations, particularly at life transitions, and point to the reciprocal person/environment dynamics which can maintain behaviour. Although the differences between adult outcomes of shy and non-shy children are often striking, the data make clear that predictions from late childhood are imperfect, with overlaps between these groups. It would be important to know the mechanisms for individual predictive failure. This study is very important in view of the late childhood baseline, a time when in many cases shyness would have become habitual, and also in the very lengthy follow-up to early middle age.

There is a vast literature on prediction from child or adolescent abnormal personality, with some hundreds of longitudinal studies (see, for example, Mednick and Baert 1981). Here we examine just two. Rodgers (1990) used a 36-year follow-up of a national birth cohort to study the associations between childhood behaviour and personality with affective disorder. The adult criterion was the Present State Examination. The author regards the accuracy of prediction as unimpressive (p.411), but in a few instances the prognosis was especially poor, notably for bed-wetting frequently at age 6, frequent truanting at age 15 and speech problems at the same age. Even the identification of groups with multiple risk factors failed to yield a high number of cases.

Another study which repays close reading has been reported by Esser, Schmidt and Woerner (1990). In a rather brief longitudinal account of a large cohort of children between the ages of 8 and 13, around 16 per cent at age 8 exhibited moderate or severe psychiatric disorders. The same percentage was found at age 13, but the distribution of diagnoses at this later age had changed substantially, with a remarkable increase in conduct disorders, with similar rates for girls as for boys. For us the most interesting finding was the fairly common switch from no disorders at age 8 to disorders at age 13, and from disorders at age 8 to no disorders at age 13. Specifically, one half of the disordered

8-year-olds were similarly rated at 13, while half were not. Adverse family situations and learning disabilities were associated with new conduct disorders,
but more accurate prediction for emotional disorders were the number of life
events and adverse family situations. At one extreme, three-quarters of those
with conduct disorders at age 8 were persistently disordered at age 13, but, at
the other, early neurotic disorders were likely to remit. Such findings are amply
supported by previous work.

Early attachment

This area of research owes its origin to John Bowlby (1951). His views on the
importance for mental health of a warm, permanent relationship with the
mother were later extended and developed, with strong influences from animal research, especially that of Lorenz. Ainsworth and Wittig (1969)
extensively elaborated the significance of attachment and created the Strange
Situation test. One prediction from these contributions is that children who
have not experienced an appropriate early attachment should find difficulty in
developing bonds with their own children.

Fonagy, Steele and Steele (1991), Fonagy et al. (1994) and Steele, Steele
and Fonagy (1995) have reported fascinating material on the intergenerational
transmission of attachment behaviour. During first pregnancies mothers and
fathers-to-be were asked to describe their own childhood relations with their
parents, and were classified as secure/insecure via the Adult Attachment Interview. After the birth of their babies the children were assessed at 12 and 18
months, enabling them to be classified as secure or insecure in the Strange Situation. Maternal perceptions of their own childhood attachment predicted
subsequent infant–mother secure/insecure attachment patterns 75 per cent of
the time. Thus a high level of prediction was confirmed. Not only do the
authors discuss their successful predictions, but also consider the 25 per cent
'error', examining cases where prenatally reported early attachment security
coincided with insecurely attached children, as well as prenatally reported
attachment insecurity related to securely attached offspring. Various speculative explanations, including some environmental circumstances, were offered.
Such findings illustrate our view that a single criterion (in this case early
attachment) is unlikely to provide a wholly satisfactory account of complex
behaviour, even when predictively powerful. Although Steele, Steele and
Fonagy (1995) discuss temperament briefly, this factor may well be of importance in the Strange Situation, especially at extremes of temperament. This
characteristic, with its substantial genetic influence, may well be one of the

mediating variables between parents and offspring (see also Benoit and Parker 1994; Fox, Kimmerley and Schafer 1991; and Goldsmith and Alansky 1987).

Fonagy's work is particularly useful in the present context of prediction, suggesting that early attachment may have long-lasting effects. However, it is an open question whether early security/insecurity is a direct causal influence on adult outcome, or whether it is a marker for ongoing influences throughout childhood and adolescence. If temperament is, indeed, one of several media-tors, its ongoing continuity in some cases may reflect indirectly from early attachment. In a notable review, Rutter (1995) believes that 'we are very far from having reached an understanding of the development of relationships or of the ways in which distortions in relationships play a role in psychopathology...attachment is not the whole of relationships' (p.566).

Another review concerning insecure attachment has been produced by van IJzendoorn, Juffer and Duyvesteyn (1995). They conducted a meta-analysis of attachment studies on children aged between 12 and 24 months. Among other things, they found that interventions are more effective in changing parental insensitivity than in altering children's attachment inse-curity. This is reminiscent of the findings of Chess and Thomas (1984) who argued that 'goodness of fit' between parents and young children could be more easily achieved via small change in parents' characteristic behaviour towards them. Van IJzendoorn, Juffer and Duyvesteyn believe that later mea-sures of attachment are more difficult to interpret. Most subjects in attachment studies are very young.

What emerges very strongly from work on late adoption (e.g. Clarke and Clarke 1976; Tizard 1977) and from studies of isolated children, discovered late and subsequently habilitated (Skuse 1984), is that delayed attachments occur and can be maintained. This is just one example of the move away from the notion of critical (rather than sensitive) periods of development.

Childhood sexual abuse

By now there is a vast literature on this problem, and no one can underestimate its seriousness. There is a widespread belief that adverse psychological conse-quences are inevitable. Such a view is understandable in the light of both the incidents themselves and the probable type of family context in which many of them occur. But since most of the studies have been retrospective on the basis of clinic samples, it is likely that there may have been a reporting bias; those seriously affected may not be wholly representative of all cases of childhood sexual abuse.

Some recent and powerful evidence on this problem has been produced by Mullen *et al.* (1993, 1994). A postal questionnaire was sent to 2250 randomly selected New Zealand women. Information was sought on a range of sociodemographic and family factors, as well as screening for the subjects' experience of sexual and physical abuse during childhood and adulthood. Included was the 28-item General Health Questionnaire, as well as other measures. Two groups were selected for interview, 298 who reported childhood sexual abuse and an equivalent number who had not so reported. Very detailed information was recorded. As might be expected, a history of child sexual abuse was associated with increased psychiatric problems in later life. While the focus was on mental health difficulties, 'it should not be overlooked that many victims gave no account of significant psychiatric difficulties in adult life' (Mullen *et al.* 1993, p.728). In other words, they had escaped the usual prediction. Furthermore, the authors go on to state that 'The overlap between the possible effects of sexual abuse and the effects of the matrix of social disadvantage...were so considerable as to raise doubts about how often, in practice, it operates as an independent causal element.'

The authors' second contribution amplifies the picture in detailing risk factors for the ill effects of such abuse. It is of interest that only 53.8 per cent of the women attributed long-term effects directly to abuse. Fear of men, lack of trust, damage to self-esteem and self-confidence, as well as sexual problems were among the difficulties they described. Much of the adult *sequelae* may arise from these factors and may be second-order effects (Mullen *et al.* 1994, p.45) and therefore potentially preventable.

Turning to the other half of the problem, there is a widespread belief that perpetrators of child sexual abuse have themselves inevitably been abused as children. If this were so, then very precise predictions might be made. Again, there may have been a reporting bias for such beliefs. An important three-year Scottish study by Waterhouse, Dobash and Carnie (1994) indicates, among other things, that the conventional view is simplistic and to an extent incorrect.

The first part of this research involved quantitative analyses of the records of 501 cases of child sexual abuse, drawn from social work, criminal justice and health service files. One of the problems was the uneven amount of information available on the abusers, so that for a particular question there might be either full data recorded (e.g. employment/unemployment) or particular information for some but not for others. Thus, for the central question here, we find that in only 201 out of 501 was there an indication as to whether the abusers had suffered some form of sexual or physical abuse as children. Only 23 per cent were so recorded; this leaves a question mark over the remainder where nothing specifically relevant was noted, perhaps through lack of investigation, or through lack of perceived importance, or because it had not occurred.

The second part of the study is more revealing about our chosen theme. It used one- to two-hour skilled, in-depth interviews with 53 abusers, mainly in prison, a reasonably representative sample of this population. Again, a large amount of important information emerged. Here we note only that almost half described their childhoods as 'unhappy'. Offences were either classified as 'familial' (48 per cent) or 'extra-familial' (52 per cent). The childhood backgrounds of the latter were generally quite different from those abusing within the family. They were more likely to have grown up in disrupted families in which significant parental violence towards them was noted, or where a parental mental health problem existed. They were more likely to have experienced prolonged separations or to have grown up in institutions. They were much more likely to have suffered sexually abusive behaviour as children than were the familial offenders. However, of the total sample of abusers interviewed (53) only 22 (41 per cent) reported early sexual abuse, while 31 did not. As noted, these former tended to come from more disrupted families than those who had not so suffered.

The findings of this study confirm, yet again, that for complex behaviour, the search for single causes is unlikely to be successful. In this, as in other fields, there exists a web of interrelated factors which indicate probabilities of varying strengths, not certainties.

Intelligence

Much of the classic longitudinal work on IQ has shown that variability in development was as impressive as constancy, and that both were involved in any large sample reared under normal conditions (Clarke and Clarke 1984).

However, it has never been possible in any of the numerous attempts to show environmental correlates of IQ change in the normal population. Thus, these must have been due to individual fluctuations, or to different tests used at different ages, or in a minority to sequential increments or decrements. More recent research, using the Wechsler Intelligence Scale for Children-Revised (WISC-R) has, unlike the earlier work, tended to emphasize constancy over time. Thus, Yule, Gold and Busch (1982) followed a normal sample of Isle of Wight children, assessed on the Wechsler Preschool and Primary Scale of Intelligence (WPPSI) at 5½ and retested 11 years later at 16½ on the WISC-R. Results correlated a high 0.86. However, 10 per cent of the children changed by more than 13 points from their original score and our rough calculations suggest that around 30 per cent would have altered by more than half a standard deviation either way, our arbitrary standard of significance. Another example has been provided by Tew and Laurence (1983) reporting a 0.92 correlation between IQs at age 5 and age 16 for spina bifida children. Nevertheless, almost 30 per cent varied by more than 10 points and 16 per cent by more than a standard deviation over this 11-year period.

A further example comes from research reported by Moffitt et al. (1993). Using a New Zealand sample of 794 children, assessed at ages 7, 9, 11 and 13 on the WISC-R, these authors suggest that overall IQ change is either negligible in amount, unreliably measured or both. However, a good deal of intra-individual variability occurred. Thus 107 children (13.5 per cent of the sample) showed changes which via cluster analysis could be grouped into six reliable patterns. There were no significant correlates of changes. While this variability was marked, the amount of cumulative and sequential change averaged only 5.3 IQ points across the seven years. Only one of the six patterns showed a monotonic trajectory, that of IQ increment, applying to only 3 per cent of the sample. 'In general, then, patterns of IQ change appear to conform to recovery curves and seem to reflect level-maintaining or even level-seeking phenomena...IQ appears to be elastic rather than plastic' (p.496). These findings surprised the authors, being for them unfulfilled predictions.

While these three examples tend to emphasize that only in a minority do sustained, sequential changes take place within relatively constant environments, we wish to underline 'relatively'. Quite significant alterations in children's circumstances do not influence IQ, although they may well impinge on other characteristics. However, where children are rescued from dire circumstances, the situation is entirely different, for gross environmental deprivation may have very marked detrimental effects which in certain better circumstances may be reversed (Clarke and Clarke 1992).

The predictive value of infant tests has until recently been largely written off (including by ourselves) on the grounds of very low correlation with later IQ due, it has been assumed, to the total lack of correspondence between the content of early and later measures. In addition, growth is so fast in the first year of life that fluctuant abilities may predominate. During the last decade, however, there has been increasing interest in the predictive power of infant information-processing, including response to novelty, habituation and other aspects of perception. Correlations as high as 0.61 have been reported (Slater et al. 1989) between length of fixation to a novel stimulus at the age of 6 months and the WISC at 8 years, although the majority of predictive in-dices fell well short of this value. (See also Slater 1995 for an overview.)

McCall and Carriger (1993), in their meta-analysis, gave a raw median correlation of 0.45 between habituation and recognition memory assessments in the first year of life and IQ measured at between 1 and 8 years of age. It must be remembered that any sizeable correlation is surprising when we consider the low reliabilities reported for the early measures. There is a degree of controversy surrounding these results. A troubling finding is an association between sample size and predictive correlation. These authors report a −0.60 correlation on the basis of a collation of data assembled by Bornstein and Sigman (1986), and in their own meta-analysis −0.56 for all samples, −0.79 for habituation samples and −0.46 for recognition. It has been suggested that extreme scores, particularly for at-risk infants, might account, at least in part, for the results.

Laucht, Esser and Schmidt (1994) studied a sample of 226 3-month-old infants recorded as 'at risk', using habituation-dishabituation methods of assessment. Cognitive development was assessed at the age of 2 and 4½. There was a significant prediction of outcome, as expected, but correlations from the more conventional infant tests such as the Bayley were higher. Many have claimed the superiority of early information-processing over the latter. The authors also found that early biological and social factors better predicted later IQ. Laucht, Esser and Schmidt attribute the many recently reported higher correlations between the new infant tests and later IQ to small sample sizes, leading to differential publication of high versus low correlations, a suggestion also considered by McCall and Carriger (1993). The debate will continue.

In conclusion, recent work suggests that, under normal circumstances and using individual Wechsler tests, relatively accurate broad prediction of adolescent IQs may be made around age 5. Such predictions become more precise with increasing age. It might be added that educational measures are more variable, and we would remind readers that the IQ was originally designed to predict educational ability.

Discussion and conclusions

We have already noted three possible assumptions upon which predictions may be based: 1. a constancy model; 2. a knowledge of the natural history of particular conditions; and 3. an awareness of the common effects of particular events or interventions. In the areas we have sampled, such assumptions are to varying extents imperfect; internal and external influences are at work and changing throughout the life span. In successive reviews over the last four decades we have pointed to growing evidence for this conclusion. Nor are we alone in holding this view. Yet, as Kagan (1992, p.993) points out:

the indefinite preservation of a young child's salient qualities, whether intellectual ability or a secure attachment, remains an ascendant assumption in
developmental work… There is an inconsistency between the contemporary
commitment to the importance of the local context which changes, and a
belief in the capacity of early encounters to create immutable structures which
will be preserved.

Prediction of individual development will continue to be seen as necessary and
useful, but there needs to be a greater awareness of the likelihood of false
positives and false negatives. Obviously some abnormal conditions such as
severe mental retardation or autism imply accurate and gloomy prognoses for,
for example, independent living. Even here, however, we should be aware that
for some handicapped persons, a wide range of outcomes is possible. For
example, Carr (1994) found a 60-point IQ range in Down's Syndrome adults.

In a wide-ranging yet succinct review of 'Pathways from childhood to
adult life', Rutter (1989) drew attention to personal life transitions where psychological changes are likely, and where a reinforced pathway may continue,
or a new one may be established. He goes on to write 'Not only will behaviour
be shaped by the biological substrate, genetically or non-genetically determined, as well as by psychosocial influences, but equally the past and present
are likely to have effects. Most crucially they are not independent of one
another' (p.146). Rutter also refers to the unduly simplified question of
whether a person's behaviour is the result of past or present experiences.

It is of interest that in what must have been one of his last contributions,
Bowlby (1988) had developed a life-span point of view, rejecting the idea of
an early and necessary predetermination of development and emphasizing
ongoing interactions throughout life. Such reformulations must have occurred
through his awareness of increasing evidence against his earlier views.

It might well be argued that in view of the complexity of human development, the degree of accurate prediction so often achieved for behavioural
measures is surprisingly good. Reverting to the simple model proposed at the
outset, four parameters were suggested: biological and social trajectories, both
of which may be non-linear across time, interactional/transactional processes
in which individuals may play some part in influencing their own development
and, finally, chance encounters or events which can sometimes divert the predicted life path. While one or two writers have discussed the latter (Bandura
1982; Lewis 1990), there appears to be a dearth of empirical studies on the
role of chance. However, some researchers have made it clear that chance has
played a part in the lives of members of their samples. For example, Rutter,
Quinton and Liddle (1983) have indicated that for those seriously at risk for

pathology (having been taken into care from disastrous backgrounds and then reared in children's homes), chance events such as a relationship with a stable partner may divert the individual from a predictably undesirable outcome.

We have argued (Clarke and Clarke 1988) that greater continuities across time are to be expected in seriously deviant conditions compared with less abnormal development, pointing to the sometimes heterogeneous aetiologies for particular syndromes, with multifactorial influences combining in individual cases. The presence of an organic component appears greatly to narrow the range of reaction between constitution and environment, and we warned that increasing social and family disruption may increase the prevalence of conduct disorders, adjustment disorders and school failure.

In all of these, however, there will be a minority who escape the prediction. There is excellent documentation of 'spontaneous' recovery and escape from disadvantage, without any formal interventions (e.g. Kolvin *et al.* 1990; Pilling 1990). The factors associated with such unfulfilled predictions include, in broad terms, individual attractiveness, problem-solving ability, an internal locus of control, networks of social support, schools where children are valued and learning is encouraged, a peer group which is prosocial and a capacity for purposeful planning. Conversely, factors likely to militate against escape from disadvantage are individual irritability, low IQ, low emotional security, few emotional ties and chaotic family (Clarke and Clarke 1992). We should add to these a gender effect in withstanding stress, boys being more vulnerable than girls up to puberty, and vice versa thereafter. In evaluating predictions, we must once again note the relevance of length of follow-up. In a study of the background of a New Zealand sample of multiple-problem adolescents, reared in seriously disadvantaged environments, 87 per cent had by age 15 developed at least one behavioural or mental health problem (Ferguson, Horwood and Lynskey 1994). So 13 per cent had not. However, reviewing the literature, the authors go on to indicate that 'with the passage of time young people with serious problem behaviours grow out of these problems, or at least modify the ways in which problem behaviours are expressed'. Having left 'their original family environments they may be exposed to further life and socialization experiences which may overwrite their social learning processes accumulated during childhood' (p.1137). This is a rather optimistic view.

While we have suggested factors promoting escape from disadvantage, what about the unfulfilled predictions for children reared in ordinary circumstances? Here there are a number of sometimes interacting factors. First, imperfect test reliability which usually represents individual fluctuations or the 'unreliability' of persons. Second, the use of non-comparable assessments at different ages; third, the length of time over which predictions are made.

Fourth, the changing internal or external influences leading in some cases to sequential cumulative alterations, sometimes affecting and sometimes reflecting the life path.

In an earlier publication (1992, p.154) we summarized our orientation as follows:

> We see development as a series of linkages in which characteristics in each period have a probability of linking with those in another particular period. But such probabilities are not certainties, and deflections for good or ill are possible, but always within limits imposed by genetic, constitutional and social trajectories.

From time to time we have urged that development is *potentially somewhat* open-ended. We have italicized two words, the first to indicate that all too often people can get locked into a life path from which they have neither the need, nor the desire, nor even the ability or temperament, to escape. The second reiterates that there are clear constraints to change, whether from genetic 'ceilings', from aging effects or from social pressures. Radical departures from predicted outcomes are for most people unusual. But the imperfections of precise prediction are increasingly obvious. Perhaps the last word could come from a Russian writer of the 1920s, Zamyatin (quoted by Stone 1993): 'Man is like a novel: one does not know until the very last page how it will end.'

References

Ainsworth, M.D.S. and Wittig, B. (1969) 'Attachment and exploratory behaviour of one-year-olds in a strange situation.' In B.M. Foss (ed) *Determinants of Infant Behaviour 4*, 113–116.

Bandura, A. (1982) 'The psychology of chance encounters and life paths.' *American Psychologist 37*, 141–155.

Benoit, D. and Parker, K.C.H. (1994) 'Stability and transmission of attachment across three generations.' *Child Development 65*, 1444–1456.

Block, J. (1971) *Lives Through Time*. Berkeley, CA: Bancroft Books.

Block, J. (1980) 'From infancy to adulthood: a clarification.' *Child Development 51*, 622–623.

Bornstein, M.H. and Sigman. M.D. (1986) 'Continuity in mental development from infancy.' *Child Development 57*, 251–274.

Bowlby, J. (1951) *Maternal Care and Mental Health*. Geneva: World Health Organization.

Bowlby, J. (1988) 'Developmental psychiatry comes of age.' *American Journal of Psychiatry 145*, 1–10.

Carr, J. (1994) 'Long-term outcome for people with Down's Syndrome.' *Journal of Child Psychology and Psychiatry 35*, 425–439.

Caspi, A., Elder, G.H. and Bem, D.J. (1988) 'Moving away from the world: life course patterns of shy children.' *Developmental Quarterly 24*, 824–831.

Chess, S. and Thomas, A. (1984) *Origins and Evolution of Behavior Disorders*. New York: Brunner/Mazel.

Clarke, A.D.B. and Clarke, A.M. (1984) 'Constancy and change in the growth of human characteristics.' *Journal of Child Psychology and Psychiatry 25*, 191–210.

Clarke, A.M. (1982) 'Developmental discontinuities: an approach to assessing their nature.' In L.A. Bond and J.M. Joffe (eds) *Facilitating Infant and Early Childhood Development* 58–77. Hanover: New England University Press.

Clarke, A.M. and Clarke, A.D.B. (1976) (eds) *Early Experience: Myth and Evidence*. London: Open Books.

Clarke, A.M. and Clarke, A.D.B. (1988) 'The adult outcome of early behavioural abnormalities.' *International Journal of Behavioural Development 11*, 3–19.

Clarke, A.M. and Clarke, A.D.B. (1992) 'How modifiable is the human life path?' *International Review of Research in Mental Retardation 18*, 137–157.

Esser, G., Schmidt, M.H. and Woerner, W. (1990) 'Epidemiology and course of psychiatric disorder in school age children – results of a longitudinal study.' *Journal of Child Psychology and Psychiatry 31*, 243–263.

Ferguson, D.M., Horwood, L.J. and Lynskey, M. (1994) 'The childhoods of multiple problem adolescents: a 15-year longitudinal study.' *Journal of Child Psychology and Psychiatry 35*, 1123–1140.

Fonagy, P., Steele, H. and Steele, M. (1991) 'Maternal representations of attachment predict the organization of infant–mother attachment at one year of age.' *Child Development 62*, 891–905.

Fonagy, P., Steele, M., Steele, H., Higgitt, A. and Target, M. (1994) 'The Emanuel Miller Memorial Lecture, 1992. The theory and practice of resilience.' *Journal of Child Psychology and Psychiatry 35*, 231–257.

Fox, N. A., Kimmerley, N.L. and Schafer, W.D. (1991) 'Attachment to mother/attachment to lather: a meta-analysis.' *Child Development 62*, 210–225.

Gleick, J. (1992) *Genius: the Life and Science of Richard Feynman*. New Yor:. Pantheon Books.

Goldsmith, H.H. and Alansky, J.A. (1987) 'Maternal and infant temperamental predictors of attachment: a meta-analytic review.' *Journal of Consulting and Clinical Psychology 55*, 805–816.

Kagan, J. (1992) 'Yesterday's premises, tomorrow's promises.' *Developmental Psychology 28*, 990–997.

Kagan, J. and Snidman, N. (1991) 'Temperamental factors in human development.' *American Psychologist 46*, 856–862.

Kerr, M., Lambert, W.W., Stattin, H. and Klackenberg-Larsson, I. (1994) 'Stability of inhibition in a Swedish longitudinal sample.' *Child Development 65*, 138–146.

Kolvin, I., Miller, F.J.W., Scott, D. McL., Gatzanis, S.R.M. and Fleeting, M. (1990) *Continuities of Deprivation?: The Newcastle Thousand Family Study.* Aldershot: Gower House.

Laucht, M., Esser, G. and Schmidt, M. (1994) 'Contrasting infant predictors of later cognitive functioning.' *Journal of Child Psychology and Psychiatry 35,* 649–662.

Lewis, M. (1990) 'Development, time and catastrophe: an alternate view of discontinuity.' *Life-span Development and Behavior 10,* 325–350.

Macfarlane, J.W. (1964) 'Perspectives on personality consistency and change from the Guidance Study.' *Vita Humana 7,* 115–126.

McCall, R.E. and Carriger, M.S. (1993) 'A meta-analysis of infant habituation and recognition performance as predictors of later IQ.' *Child Development 64,* 57–79.

Mednick, S.A. and Baert, A.E. (eds) (1981) *Prospective Longitudinal Research: an Empirical Basis for the Primary Prevention of Psychosocial Disorders.* Oxford: Oxford University Press on behalf of the WHO Regional Office for Europe.

Moffitt, T.E., Caspi, A., Harkness, H.R. and Silva, P.A. (1993) 'The natural history of change in intellectual performance: who changes? How much? Is it meaningful?' *Journal of Child Psychology and Psychiatry 34,* 455–506.

Mullen, P.E., Martin, J.L., Andersen, J.C., Romans, S.E. and Herbison, G.P. (1993) 'Childhood sexual abuse and mental health in adult life.' *British Journal of Psychiatry 163,* 271–332.

Mullen, P.E., Martin, J.L., Andersen, J.C., Romans, S.E. and Herbison, G.P. (1994) 'The effect of child sexual abuse on social, interpersonal and sexual function in adult life.' *British Journal of Psychiatry 165,* 35–47.

Pilling, D. (1990) *Escape from Disadvantage.* London: Falmer Press.

Pilomin, R. and Dunn, J. (eds) (1986) *The Study of Temperament: Changes, Continuities and Challenges.* New York: Erlbaum.

Rodgers. B. (1990) 'Behaviour and personality in childhood as predictors of adult psychiatric disorder.' *Journal of Child Psychology and Psychiatry 31,* 393–414.

Rutter, M. (1989) 'Pathways from childhood to adult life.' *Journal of Child Psychology and Psychiatry 30,* 23–51.

Rutter, M. (1995) 'Clinical implications of attachment concepts.' *Journal of Child Psychology and Psychiatry 36,* 549–571.

Rutter. M., Quinton, D. and Liddle. C. (1983) 'Parenting in two generations: looking backwards and looking forwards.' In N. Madge (ed) *Families at Risk.* London: Heinemann Educational.

Scarr, S. and McCartney, K. (1983) 'How people make their own environments: a theory of genotype-environment effects.' *Child Development 54,* 424–435.

Skuse, D. (1984) 'Extreme deprivation in childhood. II. Theoretical issues and a comparative review.' *Journal of Child Psychology and Psychiatry 25,* 543–572.

Slater, A. (1995) 'Individual differences in infancy and later IQ.' *Journal of Child Psychology and Psychiatry 36,* 69–112.

Slater, A., Cooper, R., Rose, D. and Morison, V. (1989) 'Prediction of cognitive performance from infancy to early childhood.' *Human Development 32*, 158–166.

Steele, H., Steele, M. and Fonagy, P. (1995) 'Associations among attachment classifications of mothers, fathers and their infants.' *Child Development 67*, 541–555.

Stone, M.H. (1993) 'Long-term outcome in personality disorders.' *British Journal of Psychiatry 162*, 299–313.

Tew, B.J. and Laurence, K.M. (1983) 'The relationship between spina bifida children's intelligence test scores on school entry and at school leaving: a preliminary report.' *Child Care: Health and Development 9*, 13–17.

Tizard, B. (1977) *Adoption: A Second Chance.* London: Open Books.

Van IJzendoorn, M.H., Juffer, F. and Duyvesteyn, M.G. (1995) 'Breaking the intergenerational cycle of insecure attachment: a review of the effects of attachment-based interventions on maternal sensitivity and infant security.' *Journal of Child Psychology and Psychiatry 36*, 225–248.

Vizard, E., Monk, E. and Misch, P. (1995) 'Child and adolescent sex abuse perpetrators: a review of the research literature.' *Journal of Child Psychology and Psychiatry 36*, 731–756.

Waterhouse, L., Dobash, R.P. and Carnie, J. (1994) *Child Sexual Abuse.* Edinburgh: The Scottish Office Central Research Unit.

Wilson, R.S (1985) 'The Louisville Twin Study: developmental synchronies in behaviour.' *Child Development 54*, 298–316.

Yule, W., Gold, D.R. and Busch, C. (1982) 'Long-term predictive validity of the WPPSI: an 11-year follow-up study.' *Personality and Individual Differences 3*, 65–71.

PART II

Research Problems…
and Solutions

CHAPTER 9

Regression to the Mean
A Confused Concept

Commentary

Groups selected on the basis of extreme test scores (either very high or very low) tend, on later reassessment, to score on average closer to the population mean. This is an accurate, descriptive statement. However, as a catch-phrase, 'regression to the mean', sometimes termed 'statistical regression', has taken on a pseudo-explanatory role, which has fooled many, including ourselves. Such statements as changes 'can occur on purely statistical grounds' and that these are of 'no psychological significance' can be found from time to time in the literature.

Our early work inevitably posed the question whether the resilience we had noted could be enhanced by formal early educational programmes which might break cycles of deprivation. Hence we began to analyse early interventions (e.g. Head Start, in the USA). If improvement appeared after such programmes, how far did they reflect an expected regression and nothing more? Indeed, one or two comments on our own work had suggested that our results had arisen from this factor, easily countered by pointing to controls and to clear evidence that differing social histories of those who showed considerable regression versus those who did not were involved (see Chapters 2 and 3). In this article we indicate that regression is primarily behavioural (and not a statistical ghost) and we identify two types of factors involved.

Regression to the Mean: A Confused Concept[*]

A.D.B. Clarke, Ann M. Clarke and R.I. Brown

It is suggested that psychologists, like other people, are not entirely immune from the tendency to 'blind themselves with science'. Statistics in particular provide a convenient *mystique* and thus an encouragement to use catch-phrases in describing events we do not fully understand. One typical example is the phrase 'regression to the mean', often used to explain changes in extreme test score and usually regarded as a wholly statistical problem without psychological implications. This paper, however, by reference to physical and psychological data, attempts to indicate its primarily behavioural bases and to show why groups chosen for study on the basis of extreme test score will tend to regress towards the mean of the general population, while regression of extreme scores in groups not so selected will be towards the mean of their own specific population. There appear to be two main factors at work. 1. The effects of fleeting, inconstant personal alterations in response to the test (the so-called 'errors of measurement' which are more complex than they sound). 2. The essentially non-linear nature of most individual physical or psychological growth. To say without further qualification that test scores have changed 'because of regression' gives no greater information than to state that they have changed because they have changed.

Statement of the problem

The concept of regression towards the mean,[1] which in psychology is intimately linked with the problem of errors of measurement, arises from the following established facts. 1. The correlation between test and immediate retest, which theoretically should be perfect, in practice never reaches unity. 2. The tendency of extreme scores at both ends of the normal distribution to move towards the mean of the distribution on retest. 3. The fact that test–retest correlations tend progressively to diminish with time. Below the age of 20, this diminution is in the order of 0.04 per year, excluding children under 5 years of age, where it is larger (see Eysenck 1953; Thorndike 1933, 1940).

It is the purpose of this article to present in some detail factors to account for these observed findings.

---

[*] This article first appeared in 1960 in the *British Journal of Psychology 51*, 2, pp.105–117. Reprinted by permission of the British Psychological Society.

Introduction

One has only to read *Psychological Abstracts* to become painfully aware that, like others, we psychologists are not entirely immune from the tendency to blind ourselves with science. Statistics in particular provide a convenient *mystique* and thus an encouragement to use catch-phrases in describing events we do not fully understand. One typical example is the phrase 'regression to the mean': a tendency for extreme scores to move towards the average on retest is often tersely described and explained in these terms, with the implication that such changes are statistical, involve only errors of measurement, are of no psychological significance and merit little further discussion. It is of course true that it cannot be considered apart from statistics, but after all, statistics represent measures of behaviour, and it is to behaviour primarily that we must look for explanations of regression. In this paper, therefore, we attempt to comment on the concept, to show that considerable confusion has existed and to indicate its behavioural bases. Our suggestions, it must be admitted, have emerged only slowly and painfully from the background of our own – and we suspect other people's – confusion. It is not suggested, however, that the principles we have advanced are novel, although we have not seen them presented in detail elsewhere, and it seems likely that they will be unfamiliar to many psychologists.

Present use of the concept

The following are examples taken from the literature.

1. McNemar (1940) cites 54 children, between IQ 140 and 149, who on retest a week later lost an average of 5 points which he attributed to regression resulting from 'errors of measurement' from Binet, Form L to Binet, Form M.

2. The same writer (McNemar 1940) indicates that, 'unless variability increases from test 1 to test 2, the correlation between initial IQ and gains *must* be negative since in practice r_{12} will never reach unity'. This seems to be a sophisticated way of saying that unless people move away from the mean on test 2, they will move towards it. He adds, however, that 'this of course does not explain the negative correlation…'.

3. Terman's group of gifted children, chosen on the basis of an initial IQ of 140 or above, showed an average decrease on later testing due, in McNemar's opinion, solely to regression.

4. Eysenck (1953) shares this view about the Terman study, stating that: 'as a whole the group was still highly superior intellectually, the boys having dropped slightly in IQ and the girls having dropped somewhat more, a regression effect towards the mean which might have been expected on purely statistical grounds...'. The literal-minded might perhaps be forgiven if he interpreted this as indicating that pure statistics might possess an anti-feminist bias.

5. Discussing this same problem, Miles (in Carmichael 1954) states that detailed analysis of various factors failed to reveal the causes of the score decrement. The score decrease in the boys was attributed to 'a difference in the tests used or to simple regression; for the girls the larger decrement was attributed to these factors or to a change in developmental rate and age of intellectual maturation. A sex difference in social motivation might also have been involved'. A similar differential decrement occurred on achievement test quotients... 'Here again test standardization and regression factors were probably involved.'

6. The same writer (Miles 1954) discusses various follow-up reports concerning late adolescent or young adult mental status of gifted children after 6–16 years from their first selection. Over 80 per cent maintained their position while all the remainder were in high centiles, and 'none regressed to the mean'.

7. Cronbach (1949) states that: 'A person's earned score on a test is his true score, plus or minus some chance error. The *true score* is the average we would get if we tested him over and over, ironing out the unpredictable variations. Of course "good luck" makes the raw score higher than the true score, and "bad luck" makes the raw score lower. Then if we find a person with a very high score, more likely than not, part of that score is due to good luck. If we test him again, we can expect him to slip towards his true score since chance rarely favours the same person continually. The general rule for regression is: scores above average will more often decline than increase on retesting; scores below average will tend to increase on retesting. When a person is found to have an IQ of 150, then his "true" IQ is likely to be a few points lower. *How far scores shift on retesting depends on the reliability coefficient.*' [Our italics.]

8. Vernon (1951) commenting on Schmidt's (1946) rightly criticized study of IQ gains in defective children, states that: 'The correlation

between tests applied to a representative group four-and-a-half to seven-and-a-half years apart would hardly exceed 0.60, and might be lower. *Hence, due to regression effects alone,* we would expect an apparent rise in average IQ of 19 points, that is from 52 to 71. The statistically untrained person finds this very difficult to grasp, but it is really quite simple. If a representative group was tested (with accurately standardized tests) at 12 and 16 years, there would be as many children with IQs below 70 on the second as on the first occasion. But they would not all be the same children. *Owing to imperfect correlation* some of those scoring above 70 at 12 fall below 70 at 16, and vice versa. If, therefore, we pick out only those below 70 at 12 years [as Miss Schmidt has done] they inevitably show an average rise by 16; this rise has no psychological significance at all since we are neglecting the above 70s who show a fall in the same period...' [Our italics.]

9. Clarke, Clarke and Reiman (1958) state that 'Statistical regression towards the mean is another concept frequently used to account for IQ changes; where this concerns errors of measurement on the same or different tests, or where different tests have a low initial correlation when given within a day or two of each other, then this is entirely correct. In such cases, regression of extreme scores is inevitable and of no psychological significance.' As will be seen later, errors of measurement are primarily behavioural and therefore it is incorrect to state (as in this and example 8.) that they are of no psychological significance.

These quotations give one little help in understanding what regression really is; instead, if some of the statements are taken literally (particularly those emphasized by our italics), the impression may be gained that often the statistical cart has been put before the behavioural horse, and that in the test situation the person and his score are puppets manipulated by the strings of *r*. A similar point has been made by Burt in an unpublished Note on the Concept of Regression which he kindly sent us. He writes that some authors discuss regression 'as though regression itself was a physical cause'.

In summary, then, the following points emerge from the literature.

1. Changes in test score 'due to regression' are the result of errors of measurement (usually undefined) and are psychologically meaningless.

2. Such changes are thought of as being primarily of a statistical nature.

3. The greater the distance from the universe mean, the greater will be the regression.

4. Regression changes can be exceedingly large: see Vernon's (1951) view that 19 points of the increments claimed by Schmidt could be accounted for by regression.

5. Time between test and retest seems to be considered relevant to the amount of regression; thus in example 8. we find 'The correlation...over four and a half years...would hardly exceed 0.60... Hence due to regression effects alone...'

The problem of regression to the mean is one aspect of the larger problem of test reliability, and it is appropriate, therefore, to recapitulate briefly some points made elsewhere (Clarke *et al.* 1958). Two quite distinct aspects are involved: 1. the tendency for the test to measure the same quality in the same way on different occasions; and 2. the tendency for the quality measured to remain the same at different points in time. The first is best measured by immediate or almost immediate retest,[2] which will tend on the average to give a maximal estimate of 'errors of measurement', and the second by retesting at varying time intervals. In general it is found that the longer the time interval the greater the tendency to individual change and hence the lower the correlation coefficient. Eysenck (1953), for example, calculated from Thorndike's (1933, 1940) data that the fall-off in correlation tended to be linear, averaging 0.04 per year; since there is no reason to suppose that errors of measurement are cumulative, this must be due to other factors.

The only article known to the writers which approaches a satisfactory description of regression is that by McNemar (1940), although the explanatory bases remain unstated. He gives examples from the fields of mental and physical measurement and indicates for instance that, if a number of 8-year-old children are selected for unusual height and are then measured again at the age of 16, their mean height will then be nearer the universe mean than eight years earlier. If, however, a number of children of Swedish extraction were similarly measured and re-measured, at both ages their mean height will be half a standard deviation above the universe mean (presumably for genetic reasons) and regression of extreme scores will be towards their own mean rather than the general American mean. In other words, McNemar believes that *if a group of persons with extreme scores is selected on the basis of extreme first score, then regression will be towards the universe mean, but if a group of persons with extreme scores is selected on factors other than initial score, then the regression of extremes within the extreme group will be towards its own mean rather than towards the universe mean.* He admits that regression here is a descriptive rather than an explanatory concept, but although he comes near to stating the explanation, he leaves the argument at this point. McNemar's view sounds almost magical but the present paper attempts to show its essential correctness and to seek explanations. These will involve two factors, namely errors of measurement (and all that this signifies) and irregularity of growth processes.

Suggested explanations

Errors of measurement

This concept in psychology is usually taken to cover relatively temporary factors which interfere in some way with the operation of a hypothetical 'true' intelligence (or other quality) in the test situation. The empirical basis for this assumption is the lack of a perfect correlation, already referred to, which theoretically should exist between test and immediate retest. The following remarks, therefore, are entirely confined to a consideration of the causes underlying the failure of *immediate* test–retest correlations to reach unity.

The phrase 'chance' is often used in connection with errors of measurement; sometimes 'chance errors' are regarded as synonymous with the latter. It is our contention that' chance' like 'regression to the mean' is something of a catch-phrase,[3] used to explain anomalies in the test situation and to dismiss unexpected facts which may 'spoil' results. Furthermore, it is felt that this much-used concept requires frequent and detailed examination, and in this connection the late Sir Alexander Fleming made an important statement when he said: 'Never neglect any appearance or happening which seems to be out of the ordinary; more often than not it is a false alarm but it *may* be an important truth…'

It is our submission that 'errors of measurement' may involve two groups of factors, which may separately or together influence a test score, and further, that it will depend upon the nature of the test which of the two groups is the more influential.

Factor I includes such effects as alterations in mood, fatigue, boredom, illness, emotional disturbance (most of which may tend to produce errors in logical thinking), changes in motivation, misunderstanding of the instructions, practice, learning or test sophistication, failure on the part of the tester to establish rapport, to score correctly or to give the test correctly.

Factor II involves 'chance' in the narrow sense of the concept, the deliberate 'taking a chance' or guess-work by the subject.

The first group of variables may affect any test situation; the second, however, will clearly operate in some circumstances more than in others. On the whole, intelligence tests are constructed of two types of problem, the 'open' and the 'closed' (or forced choice). The 'open' type includes, for example, Wechsler's comprehension, arithmetic and vocabulary tests, where the subject is required to give an entirely individual and independent answer to an open question. The '*closed*' type includes Raven's Progressive Matrices, the Mill Hill Vocabulary (Set A, Synonyms) and a number of paper and pencil group intelligence tests, where the subject is required to *select* from a limited number of responses the one which is the most appropriate. One would expect a subject to get on the average one in six correct on the Mill Hill Vocabulary (Set A) simply by spinning a coin, whereas one would not expect him to get any right on the Wechsler Vocabulary by pure guess-work. Putting it another way, a Chinese peasant, for example, with no knowledge of English whatever, would be likely to score a certain number of correct responses on the former Vocabulary test, but none on the latter. Norms, of course, take this into account.

We come now to consider how these two factors operate in the test situation and to account for the observed fact of regression of extreme scores arising from the so-called 'errors of measurement'.

Factor I. These variables tend to have effects which are normally distributed around a person's 'true' score. Clearly, however, they cannot be so distributed at the extremes of a distribution, particularly if the test has an absolute 'floor' and an absolute 'ceiling' (e.g. the Progressive Matrices). Figure. 9.1 suggests the effects of Factor I at the extremes.

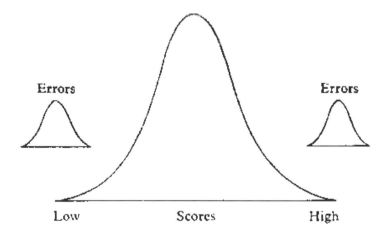

Figure 9.1: At extremes 'errors' can only move towards the distribution centre ('floor' and 'ceiling' effects)

Obviously, if a person has a near-zero or near-top score on initial test, then on retest Factor I errors cannot take him below zero or above the top score respectively, but can only appreciably alter his position in the inwards direction; and the greater the distance from the mean, the greater will be this effect on the average. For example, a score of 5 out of 60 has only four below it but the whole distribution above it so that Factor I variables have on the average a greater chance of increasing than decreasing the score.

Factor II. 'Taking a chance' or guessing are far less important sources of error (i.e. of departure from 'true' score) than the many aspects subsumed under Factor I, and little need be said about them. Nevertheless, like Factor I, they will tend to have effects which are normally distributed so that Figure 9.1 again applies. In addition (a) they operate almost exclusively in closed tests such as Wechsler's Picture Arrangement and others already mentioned; (b) the more difficult the test item the more likely is guess-work to be used; and (c) as a corollary, the less intelligent the subject, the more likely is guess-work to be used.

The effects of Factors I and II can be summarized as follows: in tests where these play any part in successes and failures (and for Factor I this is true of most) regression of extreme scores is likely on immediate retest, solely because of errors of measurement which, providing that the test is properly standardized, are due in the main to short-term personal fluctuations. It should not, however, be inferred that regression is a simple phenomenon, since it would appear to result from the interaction of many variables. For example, practice effects are found to be greater in persons of high than low intelligence. In the former egression will occur, while in the latter, regression will result, the amount of egression from this source being greater than regression. On the other hand, since the items on most mental tests become progressively more difficult, it tends to be harder for an individual to obtain higher than lower scores; therefore, on these grounds alone, it is rather more likely that he will obtain his original score or less. It should, however, be noted that this will result in regression only for top scores since for low scores egression will occur. Furthermore, in tests which have an absolute 'floor' and 'ceiling', regression will tend to occur in persons of both high and low intelligence. The matter is further complicated by the fact that when any extreme group is selected on the basis of first test extremes, those with high IQs have sometimes gained their scores due in part to favourable Factor I and II effects, while those of low IQ have sometimes gained their scores partly due to unfavourable effects which on retest will result in regression.[4]

Finally let us note that these effects are always behavioural primarily and statistical only secondarily; the phrase 'errors of measurement' tends to divert us from this fact because it wrongly concentrates upon the measurement rather than on the quality measured. There has been little interest in such errors because psychologists have been much more concerned with intra-individual constancy than with inconstant factors. Sir Cyril Burt (1955 and personal communication) also stresses implicitly the behavioural basis of errors of measurement.

> The word "error" tends to suggest an antithesis between a "true" measurement and a measurement that includes a superadded "error-factor". It seems…that the real antithesis is between what is *relevant* to your purpose at the time and what is irrelevant. Thus my own definition of an error of measurement would be "that part of the measurement that is attributable to factors irrelevant to the quality or quantity I want to estimate".

Growth as a non-linear process

We come now finally to a consideration of the progressively diminishing test–retest correlation with time. This diminution has been repeatedly demonstrated in the age range 5–20, and of course in infancy also. So far as the normal adult population is concerned, too little is known for any precise conclusions to be reached, but it is most unlikely that the correlation will diminish as rapidly once the peak of intellectual growth has been reached.

Factors affecting long-term test–retest correlations we believe to be twofold:

1. Recovery from severe emotional disturbances which disrupt the activity of potential intelligence. This cause of IQ variability has been discussed by many writers and attention was drawn to it by Vernon (1955). In addition, gross deterioration precipitated by organic or functional disease such as senile dementia or schizophrenia is also relevant.

2. Non-linearity of growth processes which includes variation in the age when mental growth ceases.

The first factor probably operates to a rather limited extent in the general population although it is of great importance to clinical psychologists. Attention will therefore be concentrated on growth as a non-linear process.

Physical measurement

In general, individual growth of all kinds tends to be non-linear with time. As Dearborn and Rothney (1941) demonstrate: 'Growth, both mental and physical, seems to be characterized not infrequently by cycles…' The assumptions underlying the measurement of mental growth are somewhat controversial (e.g. the problem of possible inequality of units of measurement at different points in a scale, as well as the problem of an absolute zero). So we will begin by considering physical growth and revert to McNemar's argument. As we have seen, McNemar believes that the essential factor for distinguishing regression towards the universe mean from regression of the mean of the specific population lies in whether or not initial selection of subjects was on the basis of first extreme score. We argue further that errors of measurement are unlikely to be large, are probably fairly uniform throughout the ranges of physical measurement, and are therefore unlikely to affect differentially the extremes of the distributions. Thus regression of physical measurements either to the universe mean, or indeed to the mean of a specific population, is *unlikely to be due to errors of measurement but to more intrinsic factors.* (Nevertheless, physical measurements are by no means so precise and error-free as many would believe [see Thompson in Carmichael 1954] although in general they are more accurate than mental measurements.)

The explanation appears to be quite simple and to depend on the non-linearity of growth with time. It is usually assumed that genetic factors allow a broad range of possibilities of development and the specific course of growth or point reached in an individual will, within his genetic framework, depend on environmental factors (e.g. nutrition). For example, it is unlikely that the genetics of height have altered during the last half century but there has in fact been a significant increase in mean national height. Probably under good conditions, most reach somewhere to their upper limits of potential and under bad, their lower limits. Putting it a different way, there seems to exist within persons a tendency which (a) makes extreme deviation from their own 'personal mean' a matter of low probability, and (b) the maintenance of extreme deviation for any lengthy period during growth even more improbable. The only exception to these rules is the period at which, for anyone, growth ceases; and here our 'musical chairs' or 'roundabout' theory may be helpful. A person may for some years have been fluctuating around a given extreme (with respect to others of his age group), or indeed gradually reaching it. When growth ceases, he may be on the apogee of his fluctuation and rather like the 'odd man out' in a game of musical chairs, or a seat on a roundabout when it happens to have stopped at the peak of the sine curve it describes, be left as a rather more extreme deviant than in the past he normally has been.

We can now turn to examples which will make this clear. Figure 9.2 shows (a) the average weight curve for young babies, together with the curve for one particular baby, and (b) an average and an individual height curve for one child, which illustrate in its simplest form the general principle running through this discussion.

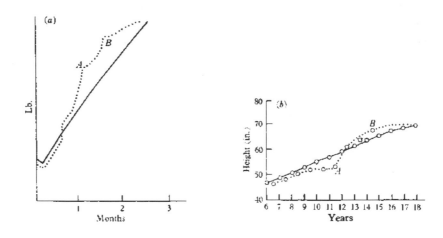

Figure 9.2 (a) Average weight increase for young babies (continuous line) and the weight increase of one baby (dotted line). (b) After Thorpe (1946). The growth in height of one subject (dotted line) compared with the average (continuous line)

The baby and the child happen to show what for them are two extreme deviations at points *A* and *B*. But for every point of extreme deviation, there are many more of less extreme deviation. This illustrates McNemar's essential correctness in stating that a group selected on the basis of extreme test score will regress towards the population mean subsequently. A group of babies selected as being heavy, or children tall, for their age, would include a number who at the particular time of selection were at their points *A* or *B*. And as a group, they, like the examples in Figure 9.2, would be more likely to be less extreme later or indeed earlier. But this regression is in no sense due to errors of measurement but simply because of irregularity of the growth process.

Similarly, McNemar's tall 8-year-old children were, at the time of selection, extreme deviants (for their age group) from the population mean. Later, because of non-linearity of growth, they would tend to be relatively less extreme. The 8-year-old Swedish children, on the other hand (selected for being Swedish), would show regression of their own extreme deviants in height, but at 16 would maintain their average deviant position with respect to the general population. Both are due to inconstancy of growth increments within their respective genetic potentialities.

The same general principles are clearly at work in the two individual curves shown in Figure 9.3. Once again, extreme deviation from the population mean does not occur very often and is never maintained for long.

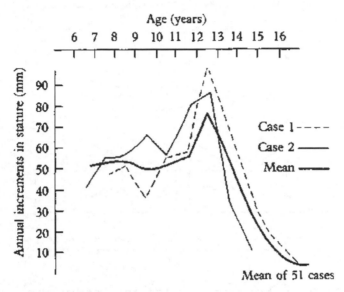

Figure 9.3 After Dearborn and Rothney (1941). This shows annual increments in height of two girls compared with the mean of 51 subjects, chosen at random from a larger study

Mental measurement

We are now in a position to turn to mental tests. In spite of the special problems of mental measurement, mental growth curves do not seem essentially very different from physical growth curves and, once again, exhibit variations in rate of development in individual cases. Figure 9.4 shows a variety of mental growth curves taken from various sources and samples. It will be seen that precisely the same points discussed in detail with reference to height and weight seem to apply to cognitive growth. It should be noted, however, that the analogy between physical and mental growth, though a very useful and instructive one, fails to hold at two points. The first, already mentioned, is that with physical measurements the errors are smaller and probably uniform throughout the particular range, but the second is also important, that 'with mental measurement the mere fact of having been tested affects the (later) result...' (Sir Cyril Burt, personal communication). No doubt factors such as these account for the rather greater variability of mental test results than of physical measurement.

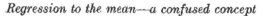

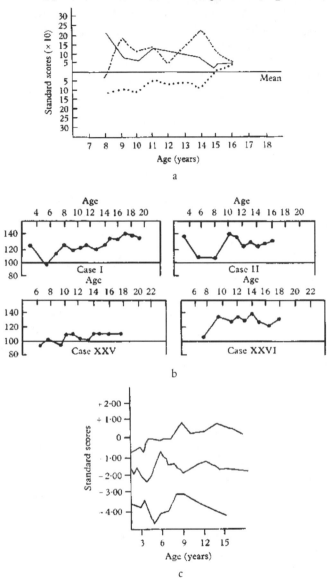

Figure 9.4 (a) After Dearborn and Rothney (1941). This shows the earlier cognitive history of three subjects who happened to have reached the same point, 0.5 sigmas, above the mean of 256 girls at age 16. (b) After Hilden (1949). This shows IQ changes in 4 out of 30 cases studied. These fluctuations are probably exaggerated owing to variability of standard deviation on the Stanford–Binet; Hilden, however, also discusses the results in terms of standard scores. (c) After Honzik, Macfarlane and Allen (1948). This shows longitudinal data on three cases, and illustrates the usual finding of greater variability of IQ in the earlier years

We have seen that Factors I and II errors will lead to regression of extreme scores and that such changes represent fleeting, inconstant personal fluctuations. As noted earlier, regressions of this sort can best be assessed by immediate retest, and on any well standardized test (e.g. WAIS, etc.) they are unlikely to be large. But do we possess any way of establishing over and above this whether trends towards the mean are due to growth changes as opposed to Factors I and II effects? The following criteria do in fact aid this distinction, although of course there is no reason why genuine test score increment or decrement may not be superimposed on change arising from errors of measurement.

1.   Selection of a group on the basis of initial extreme mental test score will result in 'chance' regression towards the population mean. The maximal amount of such regression can be determined by immediate retest.

2.   If an extreme group is studied initially, and there is subsequently a wastage of subjects for reasons of less extreme initial test scores, then the group will show a greater than usual regression of its mean towards the population average due to errors of measurement.

3.   If a test has an immediate retest correlation of 0.9 or above, on a given population, then regression due to errors of measurement must be small. Such errors tend to be non-cumulative, and if as time passes greater changes occur, they must be due to something other than these.

4.   If changes occur which are linked with obviously meaningful external factors, are long term in trend and are more or less maintained, this will militate against explanations in terms of errors of measurement which have neither constancy nor permanent cognitive significance.

5.   If initially equated groups regress to significantly different extents, then something other than errors of measurement is involved.

In summary, in this section we have tried to show that because of variations in physical and mental growth rates, there exists a tendency to regression of extreme deviants. Such regression is primarily organismic and only secondarily statistical, and is certainly neither physically nor psychologically meaningless.

Conclusions

The explanations advanced in this paper to account for regression have been essentially twofold: 'errors of measurement' (Factors I and II), the extent of which can on the average be determined by immediate retest, and 'non-linearity of the growth processes'. This latter, of course, needs further explanation, which is beyond the scope of this article; most authorities would, however, agree that it is a compound of intrinsic and extrinsic factors. It is the task of experimental method to investigate the factors relevant to regression in a particular population, and methodologically this is a straightforward procedure. In conclusion, to say that 'test scores have changed because of regression' gives no greater information than to say that they have changed because they have changed. The phrase 'regression to the mean' is thus meaningless unless it is qualified by 'errors of measurement' or by 'non-linearity of growth processes', and these themselves need further qualification in a particular case if they, too, are not to become mere catch-phrases.

It may have been noted that the principles we have advanced are precisely similar to those thought to describe the data '*of biological regression*' between generations. But in both cases, when considering the total population, *egression* from the mean usually balances regression, and in both, a law of central tendency, i.e. of the improbability of reaching and maintaining an extreme position with respect to the population average, seems (for a variety of reasons) to be involved.

The writers wish to thank Dr Max Hamilton, who originally suggested that this paper should be written and who later made valuable criticisms, and Dr J.F. MacMahon, Dr G.W. Granger and Mr J.P.N. Phillips, all of whom made useful comments. We are particularly indebted to Sir Cyril Burt for his detailed suggestions and constructive criticisms.

Notes

1   No attempt is made here to deal with '*biological regression*', that is, regressive changes between *generations*; in this paper we are only concerned with intra-individual or intra-group changes. Nor do we aim to discuss regression coefficients and the prediction of a given variable value from its known relationship with another.

2   Thorndike (1933, 1940) believes that 0.9 is the most likely coefficient for immediate retest correlation but there is of course some variation, depending on sample, test and tester, around this value.

3   'Non-homoscedasticity' is yet another catch-phrase frequently invoked to account for IQ variability. 'Because of the fan-shaped test–retest scattergram', it is said, 'high IQs tend to alter more than low IQs.'

Obviously the fan-shaped distribution here is an effect not a cause of change, which must be sought in other factors.

4   On second testing, favourable Factors I and II effects influence low IQ group averages more than unfavourable, and, at the top end of the distribution, unfavourable Factor effects have greater influence than favourable. This can be demonstrated in the following manner. If there were equal numbers of persons with different IQs forming a rectangular distribution, and we were to select on first test all those with IQs between, say, 120 and 130, some would have obtained their score by favourable and others by unfavourable Factors I and II effects. Yet others would have obtained it because it was their 'true' score (i.e. score minus Factor effects). Now, for the sake of argument, suppose the maximum range of Factors I and II effects were 10 points, in any one direction, then it would be possible for a person of real IQ 110 or 140 to fall in the 120–130 range. Since Factors I and II effects tend to be normally distributed around any point in a distribution (except at the 'floor' or 'ceiling', as already mentioned) we can state that, in our example, X per cent of those obtaining a score of 110 and X per cent of those obtaining a score of 140 will fall in the 120–130 range. If these persons were retested it would be unlikely that the same Factor effects would again favour or hinder them to the same extent and they would thus tend to approximate to their 'true' scores. The number of persons in our rectangular distribution with real IQs of 110 and 140 would be identical, therefore both groups would be equally represented in our selected sample. Thus on retest, though individuals would probably change their scores, the average score would remain approximately the same (assuming no practice effects).

Now let us consider the case of normal, as opposed to rectangular, distribution of intelligence. The same criteria will apply; a similar percentage, with 'true' scores of 110 and 140 being affected by favourable and unfavourable Factor effects respectively. Due, however, to the distribution of intelligence, more persons score 110 than 140. Therefore X per cent of the former represents a greater number of people than X per cent of the latter. Thus, if we retest persons in our respective range of which more obtained that score by favourable than unfavourable Factor effects, we must expect a lowering in average IQ (regression). A similar argument is relevant to the lower end of distribution.

References

Burt, C. (1955) 'Test reliability estimated by analysis of variance.' *British Journal of Statistical Psychology 8*, 103–118.

Carmichael, L. (ed) (1954) *Manual of Child Psychology*. London: Chapman and Hall.

Clarke, A.D.B., Clarke, A.M. and Reiman, S. (1958) 'Cognitive and social changes in the feebleminded – three further studies.' *British Journal of Psychology 49*, 144–157.

Cronbach, L.J. (1949) *Essentials of Psychological Testing.* New York: Harper.

Dearborn, W.F. and Rothney, J.W.M. (1941) *Predicting the Child's Development.* Cambridge, Mass: Sci.-Art.

Eysenck, H.J. (1953) *Uses and Abuses of Psychology.* Harmondsworth: Penguin.

Hilden, A.H. (1949) 'A longitudinal study of intellectual development.' *Journal of Psychology 28,* 187–214.

Honzik, M.P., MacFarlane, J.W. and Allen, C. (1948) 'The stability of mental test performance between two and eighteen years.' *Journal of Experimental Education 17,* 309–324.

McNemar, Q. (1940) 'A critical examination of the University of Iowa studies of environmental influence upon the IQ.' *Psychological Bulletin 37,* 63–92.

Miles, C.C. (1954) 'Gifted children.' In L. Carmichael (ed) *Manual of Child Psychology.* London: Chapman and Hall.

Schmidt, B.G. (1946) 'Changes in personal, social and intellectual behaviour of children originally classified as feebleminded.' *Psychological Monographs 60.*

Thompson, H. (1954) Physical Growth. In L. Carmichael (ed) *Manual of Child Psychology.* London: Chapman and Hall.

Thorndike, R.L. (1933) 'The effect of the interval between test and retest on the constancy of the IQ.' *Journal of Educational Psychology 24,* 543–549.

Thorndike, R.L. (1940) '"Constancy" of the IQ.' *Psychological Bulletin 37,* 167–186.

Thorpe, L.P. (1946) *Child Psychology and Development.* New York: Ronald Press.

Vernon, P.E. (1951) 'Recent investigations of intelligence and its measurement.' *Eugenics Review 43,* 125–137.

Vernon, P.E. (1955) 'The psychology of intelligence and *g*.' *Bulletin of the British Psychological Society 26,* 1–14.

CHAPTER 10

Sleeper Effects in Development
Fact or Artifact?

Commentary on Chapters 10 and 11

One of the important changes underlying President Johnson's War on Poverty was the launching of Project Head Start, a nationwide programme of pre-school education. This aimed to give poor, socially deprived (mainly black) young children an educational boost *before* they entered formal school at 6 years of age. These crash courses still continue and provide relief to parents and a decent meal at midday. With the theory that intelligence (equated with IQ) underlies achievement, a prime goal was to boost IQ to such an extent that the pupils would enter school with a confident repertoire and succeed in their studies. This for the individual was a one-shot inoculation against the effects of social deprivation. By 1969, however, the outcomes were sufficiently discouraging to prompt A.R. Jensen to publish his notorious article in the *Harvard Educational Review*, 'How much can we boost IQ and scholastic achievement?' His explanation for intervention's limited effects was that poverty and deprivation were the results of the inferior genetic constitutions of the poor.

One concept which was loosely used to explain away the disappointing outcome of Head Start was the notion of 'sleeper effects'. This suggested that there would be a much delayed response to intervention, preceded by a long period during which no effects would be visible. Then, as we indicate later, the effects would appear like a submarine breaking surface.

In the 1970s a self-appointed group of eminent researchers (of whom Seitz was a member, see Chapter 11) formed a Consortium for Longitudinal Studies. This aimed to evaluate the outcomes of high-quality preschool inter-ventions. On follow-up in adolescence, although the earlier very significant effects on IQ had washed out, there were important reductions in special class placement, and to a lesser extent retention in grade. Among the more remark-able of the Consortium findings it seemed that neither type nor duration of the programmes, presence or absence of language goals, training or non-training

189

of teachers produced differential results. It did not seem to matter what was done, nor when it was done nor for how long within the broad limits of high quality (non-Head Start) university-based programmes. As long as something good was done, a chain of events was set in motion. Nevertheless, gains were modest. Later evidence suggested that this chain involved parents as well as children in continuing interaction and hence a continuing intervention. A number of authors, noting the early 'washout' of programme effects, believed that a later reversal takes place reinstating the claims of intervention success.

Victoria Seitz produced a critique of the first paper on sleeper effects, to which our reply is to be found in Chapter 11. She would have been aware of our trenchant criticisms of Head Start programmes, and as a member of the Consortium would have been keen to establish the benefits of high quality, non-Head Start programmes. For whatever reason, her article seemed to suggest we were anti-intervention in general. There was no problem in refuting her views and continuing to argue that Head Start was no panacea for the problems of social deprivation. Seitz's critique, however, was useful in enabling us to take our argument much further forward, and to continue to state our case that really successful intervention is difficult to achieve unless there has been a long duration improvement in the child's ecology.

Have our articles laid to rest the sleeper effects catch-phrase? No, it remains alive and well and these two papers remain of current relevance. For example, Golombok (2002) has studied the effects of adoption by lesbian couples. So far as school-age adopted children are concerned there was no evidence of confusion about gender identity compared with children raised by heterosexual couples. However, it was argued that sleeper effects might exist, such that children reared by lesbian mothers might experience difficulties in emotional well-being and in intimate relationships when they grew up. But a group followed to adulthood did not differ from their counterparts in terms of quality of family relationships, psychological adjustment or quality of peer relationships. Moreover, the majority identified as heterosexual in adulthood (p.1408). So the possibility of sleeper effects was not confirmed. Our articles' main use is to warn against the seemingly explanatory, attractive phrases which may describe something unusual but fail to identify causes, immediate antecedents and thus lack explanatory power.

Sleeper Effects in Development: Fact or Artifact?*

A.D.B. Clarke and Ann M. Clarke

The evolution of the concept of 'sleeper effects' is traced from the work of J. Kagan and H.A. Moss (1962) to the present time. The phenomenon was originally inferred, without cross-validation, in the domain of personality, from correlations with early events which were stronger late in development than earlier. More recently it has been extended to account for long-term attainment differences associated with the presence or absence of preschool intervention. It seems possible that the original evidence may have capitalized upon chance fluctuations of few among many correlations. What is more certain, however, is that as currently used the term is imprecise, usually unjustified, and irrelevant to the supposed later effects of brief early intervention.

There are a number of concepts in psychology and psychiatry which are purely descriptive yet are often used loosely as if they possessed explanatory power. One such concept is the 'sleeper effect,' the notion that behavioural variables intrinsic or extrinsic to the individual may have consequences, the manifestations of which are delayed. For example, in his posthumous book Freud (1949) stated that 'It seems that neuroses are only acquired during early childhood (up to the age of 6), even though the symptoms may not make their appearance until much later...' (p.51). Such notions provide tempting biological analogies. The long-delayed effects of carcinogenic agents, including exposure to ionizing radiations, the incubation period for some common illnesses, the action of 'slow' viruses, are obvious examples. This article will review evidence for the existence of 'sleeper effects' as potentially important factors in child development, and will indicate that the concept is normally employed with such imprecision or lack of justification as to have become of little value.

Modern origins of the term

The term 'sleeper effect' appears to have first been used in a still very influential book by Kagan and Moss (1962), the criterion being the demonstration of a:

> stronger relation between a variable measured early and measured late in development than between similar variables measured contemporaneously or

---

*   This article first appeared in 1981 in *Developmental Review 1*, pp.344–360.

more contiguously in time. We have called this set of circumstances the 'sleeper effect'...[it]...is purely descriptive, for such an effect could occur for a variety of reasons. (p.278)

The essential feature of a 'sleeper effect' is that behavioural correlations between very early events and pre-adolescent or adolescent ratings substantially (or significantly) exceed correlations between the same early events and ratings more proximate in time for children *growing up in fairly constant environments*. Thus the family has not changed, the neighbourhood has not changed, yet an orderly pattern of increasing correlations with adult status so often found in longitudinal studies of development is not demonstrated.

The concept of 'sleeper effects' arose at a period in time when the *zeitgeist* in developmental psychology was firmly rooted in the idea of the critically formative role of early experience. In March 1964 *Child Development* contained a report by Kagan entitled 'American longitudinal research on psychological development', the result of a survey conducted in 1962 and commissioned by the Social Sciences Research Council of the USA. The author writes that:

> The Committee on Socialization and Social Structure of the Social Sciences Research Council (USA) initiated the survey of some of these programs in order to assess information available at these institutions. This survey was not exhaustive and the *criteria for selection were determined in part, by its interest in the effect of early socialization experiences and the child's behavior during pre-adolescent and adolescent years.* (p.3, present authors' italics)

Kagan himself has radically altered his position during the intervening period and in two of his recent books (Kagan 1979; Lomax, Kagan and Rosenkrantz 1978) 'sleeper effects' are not mentioned at all. Other psychologists and psychiatrists, however, appear to have remained conceptually in this critical period. The main data on which Kagan based his concept are summarized in Tables 10.1 and 10.2. Several personality variables rated in infancy showed higher individual correlations with adult dependence on a love object than did this variable during the intervening period. However, we must note that the high correlations apply in three cases to males and only in one instance to females and are selected from a very wide range of behavioural ratings across time. We also note that no cognitive dimension is mentioned as showing 'sleeper effects'; it would indeed have been remarkable if this had occurred, in view of the often replicated longitudinal studies which show an orderly progression of increasing correlations with adult status across time.

In addition, two aspects of maternal behaviour in the child's infancy related much more strongly to adult achievement behaviour and withdrawal

Table 10.1 Evidence for 'sleeper effects': the relation between selected child and adult behaviour

		Adult dependence on a love object	
Child behaviour	Age	Males	Females
Fear of harm	0–3	0.69****	0.01
	3–6	0.20	0.29
Irrational fears	6–10	0.18	0.06
	10–14	0.12	0.60***
Avoidance of danger	6–10	0.21	0.31
	10–14	0.23	0.54**
Passivity	0–3	0.47**	0.26
	3–6	0.16	0.20
	6–10	0.25	0.33
	10–14	0.26	0.23
Childhood hyperkinesis	3–6	−0.61****	−0.03
	6–10	−0.19	−0.16
	10–14	0.02	0.07

Source. Data extracted from *Birth to Maturity* by J. Kagan and H.A. Moss (1962), Appendix 5: Table 2, p.57; Appendix 6; and pp.278–279. Reprinted by permission of J. Kagan and John Wiley and Sons, Inc.
**$P<.05$ (2 tails).
***$P<.01$ (2 tails).
****$p<.001$ (2 tails).

Table 10.2 Evidence for 'sleeper effects'; relationship between maternal behaviour and female children's behaviour at adulthood

	Adult achievement behaviour	
	Age range	Correlations
Maternal critical attitude toward daughters	0–3	0.59***
	3–6	0.18
	6–10	0.22
	Adult withdrawal from stress	
Maternal protection of a daughter	0–3	0.52***
	3–6	−0.01
	6–10	−0.14

Source. Data from *Birth to Maturity* by J. Kagan and H.A. Moss (1962), pp.278–279. Reprinted by permission of J. Kagan and John Wiley and Sons, Inc.
***$p<.01$.

from stress, respectively, than in the intervening period between ages 3 and 10 (see Table 10.2).

The main evidence for 'sleeper effects' offered by Kagan and Moss is to be found in the detailed Appendices to their book. There are also around 65 correlations quoted in the main-text tables between ages 0–3 and adult behaviour. Of these, only one was significant for males and two for females.

The first and most obvious explanation for the phenomenon is that, because the data are based on ratings rather than formal tests, they are spurious or unreliable in some way; moreover, the numbers were not large (36 males and 35 females) and in the case of childhood hyperkinesis considerably less, 25 and 25, respectively. Kagan and Moss, however, argue persuasively that the ratings were reasonably reliable. Kagan himself was well aware of the importance of cross-validation (Kagan and Moss 1959), and it is therefore remarkable that the major findings were not later cross-validated with some of the many other children in the Fels longitudinal study, or indeed with the findings of other authors engaged in longitudinal studies.

We know of another report, published contemporaneously by Bronson (1962) which, if not offering cross-validation, at least makes the same point as Kagan using somewhat similar evidence. In his discussion of the theoretical significance of critical periods, Bronson made the following methodological point concerning the evaluation of the long-term significance of early experience:

> Conclusive documentation of the 'critical period' quality of these early developmental phases is difficult since the relative irreversibility of orientations acquired during these stages can be directly established only by cases where marked changes have occurred in the character of the early environment. The present strategy therefore is to study a corollary hypothesis. If the principle of maturationally determined critical periods is correct, then these stages, when the organism is initially and maximally involved in the channelling of newly matured motivational systems, will constitute the most sensitive ages for the prediction of later characteristics. Predictions made from observations of the child before the appropriate period of the most salient learning, will fail to reflect important motivational determinants; predictions made at a later stage will be obscured by the child's involvement in a new developmental task. (p.128)

Bronson worked in connection with the Berkeley Growth Study and wrote:

> This paper focuses upon two fundamental aspects of personality hypothesized to be significantly determined by events in the first three years: the extent of involvement with other people, and the development of an

orientation of independence and competence in coping with problems presented by the environment. The longitudinal data presented here relate the former characteristic to developments during the first year of life and the latter to influences effective in the third year. These findings are in general accord with the emergence of critical developmental stages described in contemporary clinical theory. (p.127)

The author took his criterion age as 9–10½ years. Adjective ratings were made by examiners following sessions spent in the administration of the Stanford–Binet Intelligence Test. The adjectives focused on two aspects of behaviour: the child's orientation toward the examiner; and his approach to the intellectual problems presented by her. In a footnote Bronson indicated that:

> While many of these later ratings were done by the person making the pre-school judgments, the finding (below) of marked sex difference in the continuity of personality characteristic over this age span argues against the presence of any significant halo effects in these later ratings. (p.129)

Table 10.3 Early responsiveness and mid-childhood correlates		
	Involvement with people (9–10½ years)	
	Boys	Girls
Responsiveness to persons (10–15 months)	0.73*** (n=24)	−0.33 (n=20)
Responsiveness to persons (2–3 years)	0.24 (n=23)	0.02 (n=21)
	Competitive orientation (9–10½ years)	
Responsiveness to toys (10–15 months)	0.04 (n=24)	0.09 (n=20)
Responsiveness to toys (2–3 years)	0.45** (n=23)	0.11 (n=21)
Responsiveness to persons (10–15 months)	0.18 (n=24)	−0.05 (n=20)

Source. Data extracted from 'Critical periods in human development' by G. Bronson. *British Journal of Medical Psychology*, 1962, 35, 127–133.
**$p<.05$.
***$p<.01$.

The data are given in Table 10.3. Once again, and perhaps significantly, the 'sleeper effect' shows up for male subjects but not for females, and this time, so far as can be judged from the record, there was no selection of correlations. Furthermore, for boys and girls, responsiveness to toys at the age of 2½ does appear to correlate at the .05 level with later IQ. The number of subjects was 24 boys and 22 girls.

Each of these studies shows intriguing evidence for the presence of 'sleeper effects' in the domain of personality development but in one case the *n* was rather small and it is a pity that the characteristics were dissimilar across the studies so that one cannot really be accepted as cross-validation for the other.

Finally, in this section some indication should be given of the mechanisms which Kagan and Moss inferred as lying behind their 'sleeper effects'. For the child's early versus adult behaviour, it is possible that the data for early life were more adequate than for the school years, and the lower correlations between characteristics at these ages and later behaviour might thus be due to methodological inadequacies. Such an interpretation is not, they believed, persuasive in the light of other findings over the particular age periods. More probable is an interpretation based on the view that such characteristics as passivity, fear of harm, or hyper-kinesis:

> are subject to restrictive ego controls when the child enters school. These…are not easily detected in the everyday behavior of the school age child, and we do not know what derivative responses to code in order to assess this disposition. Prior to school entrance, these responses are less disguised in form and can be assessed with more accuracy. (Kagan and Moss 1962, p.197)

It is interesting to note the implication that the effects are possibly present but under control or disguise because the child learns to inhibit their overt expression. A covert existence of such characteristics during the school years could be expressed in derived forms later in adolescence and adulthood.

For 'sleeper effects' from early maternal behaviour, the explanation is more complex. It depends on the view 'that the reciprocal nature of the mother–child interaction changes with time' (p.279), a 6-year-old being more likely to produce a major alteration in maternal behaviour than a 2-year-old. Early maternal behaviour is less contaminated by this feedback system and is thus more likely to express her fundamental needs. Basic early attitudes are felt to exercise a more lasting effect upon the child's developing behaviour, even though they are superseded by modifications later. There is an implicit assumption here that 'early' means 'permanent' (Clarke and Clarke 1976).

Kagan and Moss were properly tentative about their 'sleeper effects' and their marked association with males for childhood behaviour and with females for maternal correlates. They point out the possibility that their ratings for later childhood may have been less sensitive than those for earlier childhood, although they believe this unlikely because of the many correlations between concurrent child behaviour and concurrent maternal attitudes at the later periods. Moreover, they indicate a second possibility, namely, that their maternal variables may have been measuring qualitatively different responses, and therefore possessed different meaning at different periods.

The Kagan and Moss study was conducted very carefully, with checks on the reliability of ratings and blind assessment of adult characteristics. The authors were clearly intrigued about their 'sleeper effect' concept but advanced it fairly in the light of the findings, and with a full expression of alternative possibilities. It seems strange therefore that others should have adopted one of these interpretations (albeit their favoured one) without looking for confirmatory evidence in the form of replication. Lacking this, and in the light of Kagan's own change of orientation as well as other work, with hindsight one speculates whether the significant early correlations with adult characteristics may not have arisen from capitalization upon chance fluctuations of variables, selected from a larger number. As will be indicated, however, there are also other possibilities.

Recent usage

Interest in continuities and stability of behaviour during the 1960s was not only a reflection of the work of Kagan and Moss, but was further reinforced by Bloom's (1964) equally influential book. The term 'sleeper effect' was congruent with the view that early life was the formative period, and it rapidly entered the language system of developmental scientists. The mid-1960s and onwards was the era when intervention became a humane concern of most thinking social scientists. But hopes of breaking the cycle of disadvantage by rather brief early intervention were soon to be dashed. Numerous commentators with very different theoretical orientations made this clear (e.g. Bronfenbrenner 1974; Clarke and Clarke 1974, 1976, 1977; Jensen 1969). Among several writers, Scarr and Weinberg (1978) put the position well:

> In its baldest form, naive environmentalism has led us in to an intervention fallacy. By assuming that all of the variance in behavior was environmentally determined, we have blithely promised a world of change that we have not delivered, at great cost to the participants, the public, and ourselves. (p.690)

Alternative explanations have, however, also been advanced. Apart from the unlikely possibility that severe environmental deprivation (which in some cases may be cumulative) could be prevented by intervention in the early years *only*, it is also probable that its effects may be exceedingly difficult to shift within the context of their origin (Clarke 1981). It is, however, not surprising that those who had very open and proper vested interests in early intervention should continue to search for masked influences of programmes, adding to the IQ as the main evaluation instrument, and adopting appropriate educational criteria.

The 'sleeper effect' concept received renewed interest and a further boost as a result of a Symposium held at the 1977 meeting of the American Association for the Advancement of Science. Here some influential researchers reported the results of a large number of studies claiming a solid, long-term benefit in children who had earlier experienced preschool programmes. Until this time it had increasingly been accepted that gains from such brief interventions 'washed out' within a year or two of primary schooling. Some of these investigators believed that 'sleeper effects' had operated, with delayed benefits to the ex-preschool children. The Symposium was published the following year (Brown 1978a).

Several points must be noted before further evidence is outlined. First, the majority of studies from 1977 and onwards report differences in scores between experimental and control (or contrast) groups unlike the original work of Kagan and Moss (1962) who inferred 'sleeper effects' from changing correlations across time within the same sample. Second, while IQ differences remained a prime focus of concern in evaluating the outcome of intervention, additionally, as indicated above, such factors as scholastic achievement, parent and child attitudes, grade retention, and allocation to special classes are now taken into account. Third, whereas Kagan and Moss were comparing analogous behaviour at different points of development these later researchers, mainly using studies which were not planned with long-term evaluation in mind, often either lacked a data base for later analogous behaviour, or such a base was inappropriate (e.g., one cannot measure educational failure before education is commenced).

It will be obvious that the concept proposed by Kagan and Moss to account for possible discontinuities in the personality domain has been substantially altered to account for results in terms of educational achievement and current aspirations.

The views expressed in the AAAS Symposium were later to be further expounded and elaborated by 12 research groups, the work of which had been central to the discussion. These came together as the *Consortium on*

Developmental Continuity (Lazar, Hubbell, Murray, Rosche and Royce 1977) later renamed more neutrally as the *Consortium for Longitudinal Studies* (Lazar and Darlington 1978). This is a self-appointed group of distinguished researchers into preschool intervention who have in common a very open and proper interest in establishing long-term gains from early intervention. Thus in the first report, Lazar *et al.* (1977) give four reasons for following up children who had been the subjects of preschool intervention. Among these was the concern of members about 'the building band-wagon of professionals who were denying the importance of early experience or continuity of experience in later life...' (p.5).

The Consortium authors made valiant attempts to analyse the long-term outcome from these unusually well-designed and therefore, as they point out, atypical programmes, most of which were initiated prior to the establishment of Project Head Start, and to show that while significant differences between experimental and control children did not persist in the long term (had such differences faded then reappeared, then one might have begun to talk about 'sleeper effects' in the original sense), nevertheless on such factors as allocation or otherwise to special education very significant differences were evident. It is, however, important to note that the authors nowhere use the term 'sleeper effects'; others have not been so careful. One of the several problems in interpreting these findings is the lack of knowledge on what happened to the families between programme termination and later follow-up. The second and longer (1978) report is commendably and rightly cautious, although sticking to the main conclusions. A recent summary is to be found in Darlington, Royce, Snipper, Murray, and Lazar (1980). There are, however, several alternative explanations, which do not carry the assumption of early changes in children lying dormant for years before becoming effective.

The following are some examples of recent uses of the term.

Meier (1978) writing an introduction to Brown's book refers to a forthcoming report documenting:

> many of the unparalleled successes of Head Start during its first decade. They include mention of the emergence of a 'sleeper effect' wherein significant differences are found at older ages although none were found earlier...the 'washout effect' seems to be reversed or at least attenuated with the passage of time. (p.2)

Seitz, Apfel and Efron (1978) refer to their programme, and to grade 5 performance where their Follow Through female group continued to be superior to their controls on a number of measures: 'there is thus some evidence for a sleeper effect for these girls' (p.99) which nevertheless disappeared by seventh grade. Referring to the same study, Brown (1978b) also draws attention to 'sleeper effects'.

Hainline and Feig (1978) in their discussion of a study by Hetherington (1972) use the term in its original sense. They regard it as 'one of the first to suggest that the effects of father absence in girls may show a "sleeper effect", appearing in adolescence when interactions with males and sexual activities increase' (p.37). Hetherington herself does not use the term but indicates that there are few effects of paternal absence on the development of girls in the pre-school or elementary school years, and believes that these only appear at puberty as the result of changed social interactions. However, it should be noted that Hainline and Feig failed to replicate Hetherington's results.

Stipek, Valentine and Zigler (1979) state that:

> The re-evaluation of the Developmental Continuity Consortium has shown that early intervention does have 'sleeper effects' on two indices of school performance: grade retention and use of special education classes. (p.482)

Bronfenbrenner (1979) provides a final example, endorsing the notion of 'sleeper effects' in connection with Elder's (1974, 1979) and Elder and Rockwell's (1978) work on children of the depression. He indicates that Elder and his colleagues appear to have shown that the adolescent and adult effects of relatively severe reduction in family income differed not only according to initial social status, but also according to the age of the children at the time of the crisis. For middle-class adolescent children the changes in family lifestyle appear to have had a later beneficial effect, whereas the authors maintain that similar events occurring during the 'formative years'. although not apparent during the early school years, exerted a debilitating effect much later. The critical factor was 'the transition from the protective environment of the elementary school to the achievement pressures of adolescence' (p.285). Bronfenbrenner goes on to propose a more general hypothesis (No. 48):

> Developmental effects are not likely to be manifested until the person moves from his present primary setting into another, potential primary setting, that is, from a setting that has instigated and currently maintains the person's present level and direction of functioning to another setting requiring the person to take initiative to find new sources of stimulation and support... Sleeper effects of earlier primary settings are most likely to be observed after primary transitions have taken place, since these are usually separated in time by months or years...the enduring developmental effects of a setting cannot be effectively assessed within that same setting...as long as a person remains in the same primary setting, one cannot know with any assurance whether that setting is having a beneficial or baneful influence on the person's growth; the

behavior observed may be merely adaptive and not reflect any genuine developmental change. (p.266)

The use of the term appears acceptable in this context.

The criteria for 'sleeper effects' and possible explanations

As Bronson (1962) has indicated, conclusive documentation of the 'critical period' quality of early developmental phases is difficult since the relative irreversibility of orientations can be directly established only by cases where there have been marked changes in the environment. Thus, lacking this, the essential criteria for 'sleeper effects' in the Kagan and Moss and Bronson tradition involve a limited or non-existent effect of an environmental influence early in life, followed by a stronger relationship later with the early measured variable. Conversely, this narrow concept cannot be applied under the following circumstances:

1. where there is a complete lack of an earlier relevant data base

2. where a relevant data base would be impossible (e.g., school failure at age 4) either for initial or interim measurement

3. where, although there is available a relevant data base, either no attempt has been made to measure effects during an intervening period before the later measurement, or there was an absence of opportunities for their expression.

A relatively common example of the latter is partial acquisition of a foreign language which appears to have been lost until a further much later exposure reveals that the system lay dormant or 'slept'. However, at any point during this intervening period, the skill could equally have been manifest. It seems clear that in cases 1. and 2. the use of the term 'sleeper effect' is totally unjustified, but in 3. some might feel that the term specifies a range of common behavioural processes, not necessarily related to age or stage of development. But, in this sense, any behavioural characteristic not being currently elicited can be conceived of as 'sleeping'. This is a much wider concept than that originally proposed by Kagan and Moss (1962), and appears to be so all-embracing as to account for a substantial proportion of all potential behaviour.

There are in fact three, non-mutually exclusive, explanations for the phenomena reported, over and above the 'sleeping' model:

1. *The intervening variable model* suggests that something happened to the parents, correlated with early intervention or personal circumstances, which had an ongoing or later effect upon the children. Early maternal

characteristics, for example, may themselves be correlated with later events which in turn are associated (perhaps causally) with later child behaviour. Thus in a recent British early intervention study, Armstrong and Brown (1979) show that while differing programmes produce no difference in later educational outcome, changes in parental attitude do not 'wash out' in the same way. They believe that this influence may be something that will emerge at a later date. The intervening variable model has been most cogently commented upon by White[1] who writes that:

> a sleeper effect might show up…via potentiation of parental advocacy. Schools generally reserve judgments about children in the early grades…while beginning serious teaching of children near the middle school years. It is possible that parental involvement in preschools might pay off at this time.

Elsewhere he notes 'what sleeps may be some kind of mobilisation of parental knowledge…[which]…in the later years of school enables them to negotiate more effectively with regard to the status and treatment of their offspring in school'. In these examples, of course, it is the *parental* motivational system which is thought to be the active agent.

With this conclusion we heartily concur, but with the proviso that it can actually be shown that the intervention programme is likely to have affected parents of treated children. In some studies, of which that of Seitz *et al.* (1978) is an example, there is evidence that parents whose children were differentially exposed to Follow Through versus non-Follow Through were on average of somewhat higher educational status, but quite importantly had also enrolled their children more than twice as often in Head Start than the comparison group (p.87), thereby presumably indicating higher aspirations. Here there is no reason to invoke any assumption of differential parental gain, since the evidence suggests that important parental attitudes toward education existed in advance of the children's intervention programme. In this case one would endorse White's formulation,[1] merely adding that parental motivation probably never slept.

Evidence for this view is to be found in *Lasting Effects After Preschool* (Lazar and Darlington 1978). Programme and control children were not different in IQ before intervention; at age 6 the former scored significantly higher and maintained this superiority for at least three years. At the latest adolescent follow-up, however, the significance of these differences had disappeared, although on average a difference in favour of the programme children remained. The difference between groups was, however, significant for math achievement tests but not for reading although there was a suggestive trend.

The major difference was in assignment to special education classes and retention in grade. These effects remained when the sex, ethnic background, early
IQ, type of programme, length of intervention, number of hours per year of
instruction, presence or absence of language goals, degree of parental involvement, location of programme (centre versus home), training or non-training of
teachers, were controlled in the analyses. Is it really likely that these variables
were differentially unimportant if the programmes themselves were directly
responsible for long-term effects on the children? As the authors themselves
point out, it seems probable that non-cognitive aspects of development were
affected. Of the four areas explored, two yielded strong results: the mothers of
preschool children had much higher vocational aspirations than the children
had for themselves. Second, the children were much more likely to mention
achievement-related reasons for feeling proud of themselves. Whether these
programmes *directly* affected any of the children's later accomplishments seems
doubtful; in view of the evidence the intervening variable appears adequate in
accounting for such effects as could be demonstrated.

Miller,[2] a member of the Consortium, did not find 'sleeper effects,' but has
indicated that, for example, one programme group that was low on IQ and
achievement immediately after preschool was the highest in these areas at the
end of first grade. She believed that unmeasured programme effects after preschool mediated these later performances, another example of the intervening
variable model.

2. *The random fluctuation model* accepts that in developmental studies it is
difficult over long intervals to fail to obtain some examples of 'nature's favourite correlation coefficient, about 0.35' (Clarke 1978, p.252). If this were a
'true' correlation, random changes or sample changes may from time to time
increase or decrease it, altering its significance. The smaller the sample size, the
more likely are such fluctuations to be important.

Seitz, Apfel and Rosenbaum[3] in a later follow-up of work reported by
Seitz *et al.* (1978) compared Follow Through and non-Follow Through boys
for, among other things, General Information, finding non-significant differences in the third grade, significant differences in the sixth grade, and
non-significant differences in the eighth grade. Variations in the scores of the
comparison group appear to be responsible for the changes from
non-significance to significance and back again. Had the follow-up been terminated after sixth grade, a 'sleeper effect' might have been assumed. A rather
similar finding for Cohort 2 girls emerged in respect of PPVT IQs; the Follow
Through sample scored significantly higher only in the fifth grade.

Earlier, however, others as well as Seitz herself had been persuaded that
'sleeper effects' were present in her findings. Thus Brown (1978b) referring to

the Head Start and Follow Through results in the Seitz programme stated that 'when these children were given continuing attention as they developed, there was no "fade out" of intellectual gains for those who were ahead at the end of the programme. In fact there appeared to be "sleeper effects" which showed up several years after the end of the program' (p.170).

A 'sleeper effect' may in some instances reflect no more than random fluctuation in either experimental or control groups (or both) as one measure or another moves into or out of phase with an earlier one. However, where several entirely different factors show similar changes at the same time, such a model is unlikely to be applicable; we know of no such finding.

3. *The insensitive measurement model* suggests the possibility that the 'sleeping' of a characteristic may merely indicate that the wrong type of measurement was used at one time but not at another; Kagan and Moss considered this possibility. White[1] exemplified it very well: 'Our measurement instruments for evaluation are so limited and crude that it is conceivable that indices available at ages 4 or 5 might not detect effects while more complex and richer instruments available later would do so. One imagines that a sleeper effect might emerge as a measurement artifact.'

Palmer[4] writes that:

> While I am cognizant of the fact that biologists are comfortable with the concept of 'sleeper effects' as it is related to late maturing responses and an interaction between heredity and environment, I believe as scientists the burden of proof is on us to show that the so-called 'sleeper effect' is a phenomenon other than (due to) faulty or inadequate measurements. If a treatment is given at time 1 and there are no effects at time 2, but they are manifest at time 3, the burden of proof is upon the investigator to show that a specific measurement, for example, IQ is capturing the same cognitive characteristics of the child at time 2 and 3. It is more parsimonious to assume that the effects at time 3 were not measured at time 2.

Conclusions

Research workers like Kagan and Moss (1962) were entitled to advance hypotheses to account for their findings. They did so by inventing or reinventing the 'sleeper effect' concept to describe some strange fluctuations in correlation coefficients for a number of measures of early development in their sample. Others, however, did not await the cross-validation of these findings but swooped upon an exciting notion, perhaps with origins in biology, reified it, generalized it, and gave it common currency. This process appears to be something of a hazard in the behavioural sciences, with ideas such as maternal deprivation, critical periods and regression to the mean all having been used with abandon and imprecision both in research and clinical practice.

It seems possible – or even probable – that the few very early moderate correlations with adult characteristics in the Kagan and Moss study arose from chance fluctuations in rather small samples, ranging from 25 to 36 for each sex. The book itself records hundreds of correlations, and it is not entirely clear whether those mentioned in connection with 'sleeper effects' have been selected from a much larger number than the 17 usually recorded in most of the tables. If this were so, then the whole basis for the origins of the modern concept might be dubious.

The nationwide US Head Start programme, initiated in the mid-1960s, 'was designed to improve children's intellectual skills, to foster their social and emotional development, to help meet their health and nutritional needs, and to involve parents and the larger community in these purposes' (Darlington *et al.* 1980, p.202). This was a period of humane optimism about the development of society and of individuals. No doubt much concurrent good arises from these programmes, but the hope of breaking the cycle of disadvantage via brief preschool interventions with family and community support was, however, all too rapidly dissipated, and ultimately it was realized that only a total ecological change might be effective for the families or children of the most seriously deprived. Small wonder then that any suggestion that Head Start had delayed consequences, and that 'washout' might be mitigated by the later expression of submerged effects, was temptingly attractive to those whose hopes had been dashed. As White[1] has put it, the Consortium results have been used politically and 'there has been too much "selling" of imperfect data on behalf of children, and…some of that selling has backfired'. Like ourselves, he believes the findings have raised an empirical possibility, worthy of pursuit, and considers that attempts to validate them on other samples could be undertaken without too much difficulty. This we would strongly support. It is of course obvious that political usage of results has no necessary bearing upon their validity, but it is clear that *interpretations* may be strongly affected one way or the other by extraneous factors.

Where research workers within and without the Consortium followed up ex-preschool pupils and found differences between them and their control or contrast groups, they had to explain to themselves and others how this linked with the well-attested findings on the 'washout' of Head Start effects within a few years of programme termination. The 'sleeper effect' concept existed ready-made, and there appeared to be no consideration of alternative possibilities at the time of the AAAS 1977 conference. Yet the basis for establishing such effects was mostly lacking; the criteria used by many of its symposium members were neither measured nor measurable earlier. At the same time the concept was often stretched to accommodate the persistence of a given advantage thought to be derived from intervention compared with the lower status of the contrast children on the same single-shot measure.

Where a comparable assessment existed in adolescence, Consortium data (IQ) showed the same 'washout' of the significance of differences as all previous studies. Furthermore, there was no significant effect on reading (of course unmeasurable at age 6 school entry). There was an effect on math, which may well have been there from the start had they measured it annually, and very significant effects on allocation to special education and grade retention (again unmeasurable at school entry). So there is *no* justification for the term 'sleeper effect' being used correctly or reasonably in connection with later effects of preschool programmes. There are a number of possible alternative reasons for such findings.

It would be an unusual social or educational research worker who would not readily assert that important environmental events may initiate new and sometimes progressive cycles. But the term 'sleeper effect' seems to us inappropriate to cover such relatively common phenomena. Furthermore, as already indicated, in considering the effects of intervention, it is very important to establish that parental influences existing in advance of the initiation of a programme are not confused with the effects of that intervention. Moreover, effects of programmes on parental motivation should not be confused with direct influences of the programme on their children.

In all the examples quoted, 'sleeper effects' are assumed to have arisen from learning in its broadest sense. Yet nothing we know about cognitive learning has suggested that its effects start by being concealed, remain somnolent, and then appear much later. If indeed this does happen, then our knowledge needs some revision. If such effects are there all the time, but are unmeasured, or insensitively measured, or have no opportunity for expression, then they are somnolent only in the sense that any aspect of current behaviour being unused at a particular time might also be regarded as 'sleeping'. In this event most potential behaviour is somnolent most of the time, and such a wide concept seems of little use.

That children's test scores or behavioural measures can wax and wane during development, and that there is an easy confusion between cause and effect across time, is hardly news. Thus we incline to the view that all cases of narrowly defined 'sleeper effects' involve intervening, random fluctuation and insensitive measurement variables. In addition, the term is sometimes used without any apparent justification whatever. We share, however, Kagan's opinion[5] that open-mindedness on the existence or otherwise of 'sleeper effects' is the most appropriate stance. In the meanwhile, the term should be put on ice, until the necessary prospective research has been undertaken.

Notes

1 White, S.H. (1979) Personal communication, 7 November.

2 Miller, L.B. (1979) Personal communication, 4 December.

3 Seitz, V., Apfel, N.H. and Rosenbaum, L.K. (1978) *Projects Head Start and Follow Through: A Longitudinal Evaluation of Adolescents.* Paper presented at the NICHD Conference on Prevention of Retarded Development in Psychosocially Disadvantaged Children, University of Wisconsin, 25 July.

4 Palmer, F.H. (1979) Personal communication, 21 December.

5 Kagan, J. (1979) Personal communication, 8 August.

References

Armstrong, G. and Brown, F. (1979) *Five Years On.* University of Oxford: Oxford Department of Social and Administrative Studies.

Bloom, B. (1964) *Stability and Change in Human Characteristics.* New York: Wiley.

Bronfenbrenner, U. (1974) *A Report on Longitudinal Evaluations of Pre-school Programs. Vol. 2. Is Early Intervention Effective?* Washington, DC: DHEW Publication No. (OHD) 74-25.

Bronfenbrenner, U. (1979) *The Ecology of Hutman Development.* Cambridge, Mass: Harvard University Press.

Bronson, G. (1962) 'Critical periods in human development.' *British Journal of Medical Psychology 35*, 127–133.

Brown, B. (ed) (1978a) *Found: Long-term Gains from Early Intervention.* American Association for the Advancement of Science, Boulder, Colo: Westview Press.

Brown, B. (1978b) 'Long-term gains from early intervention: An overview of current research.' In B. Brown (ed) *Found: Long-term Gains from Early Intervention.* American Association for the Advancement of Science, Boulder, Colo: Westview Press.

Clarke, A.D.B. (1978) 'Presidential address: Predicting human development: Problems, evidence, implications.' *Bulletin of the British Psychological Society 31*, 249–258.

Clarke, A.D.B. and Clarke, A.M. (1977) 'Centennial Guest Editorial: Prospects for prevention and amelioration of mental retardation.' *American Journal of Mental Deficiency 81*, 523–533.

Clarke, A.M. (1981) 'Developmental discontinuities: An approach to assessing their nature.' In L.A. Bond and J.M. Joffe (eds) *Facilitating Infant and Early Child Development.* Hanover, N.H: University Press of New England.

Clarke, A.M. and Clarke, A.D.B. (eds) (1974) *Mental Deficiency: The Changing Outlook* (3rd ed). New York: The Free Press.

Clarke, A.M. and Clarke, A.D.B. (eds) (1976) *Early Experience: Myth and Evidence.* New York: The Free Press.

Darlington, R.B., Royce, J.M., Snipper, A.S., Murray, H.W. and Lazar, I. (1980) 'Preschool programs and later school competence of children from low-income families.' *Science, 208* 202–204.

Elder, G.H., Jr (1974) *Children of the Great Depression.* Chicago: University of Chicago Press.

Elder, G.H., Jr (1979) 'Historical change in life pattern and personality.' In P. Baltes and O. Brim (eds) *Life Span Development and Behavior* (Vol. 2). New York: Academic Press.

Elder, G.H., Jr and Rockwell, R.C. (1978) 'Economic depression and post-war opportunity: A study of life patterns in hell.' In R.A. Simmons (ed) *Research in Community and Mental Health.* Greenwich, Conn: JAI Press.

Freud, S. (1949) [*An Outline of Psychoanalysis.*] (J. Strachey, trans.) London: Hogarth Press.

Golombok, S. (2002) 'Adoption by lesbian couples.' *British Medical Journal 324,* 1407–1408.

Hainline, L. and Feig, E. (1978) 'The correlates of childhood father absence in college-aged women.' *Child Development 49,* 37–42.

Hetherington, E.M. 'Effects of father absence on personality development in adolescent daughters.' *Developmental Psychology 7,* 313–326.

Jensen, A.R. (1969) 'How much can we boost IQ and scholastic achievement?' *Harvard Educational Review 39,* 1–123.

Kagan, J. (1964) 'American longitudinal research on psychological development.' *Child Development 35,* 1–32.

Kagan, J. (1979) *The Growth of the Child.* Hassocks, Sussex: Harvester Press.

Kagan, J. and Moss, H.A. (1959) 'Parental correlates of child's IQ and height: A cross-validation of the Berkeley Growth Study results.' *Child Development 30,* 325–332.

Kagan, J. and Moss, H.A. (1962) *Birth to Maturity.* New York: Wiley.

Lazar, I. and Darlington, R. (1978) *Lasting Effects After Preschool.* Washington, DC: DHEW Publication No. (OHDS) 79-30178.

Lazar, I., Hubbell, V.R., Murray. H., Rosche, M. and Royce, J. (1979) *The Persistence of Preschool Effects: A Long-term Follow-up of Fourteen Experiments.* Washington, DC: The Consortium on Developmental Continuity, Education Commission of the States. DHEW Publication No. (OHDS) 78-30130.

Lomax, E.M.R., Kagan, J. and Rosenkrantz, B.G. (1978) *Science and Patterns of Child Care.* San Francisco: Freeman.

Meier, J.H. (1978) 'Introduction'. In B. Brown (ed) *Found: Long-term Gains from Early Intervention.* American Association for the Advancement of Science, Boulder, Colo: Westview Press.

Scarr, S. and Weinberg, R.A. (1978) 'The influence of "family background" on intellectual attainment.' *American Sociological Review 43*, 674–692.

Seitz, V., Apfel, N.H. and Efron, C. (1978) 'Long-term effects of early intervention.' In B. Brown (ed) *Found: Long-term Gains from Early Intervention.* American Association for the Advancement of Science, Boulder, Colo: Westview Press.

Stipek, D.J., Valentine, J. and Zigler, E. (1979) 'Project Head Start: A critique of theory and practice.' In E. Zigler and J. Valentine (eds) *Project Head Start: A Legacy of the War on Poverty.* New York: The Free Press.

CHAPTER 11

Intervention and Sleeper Effects
A Reply to Victoria Seitz

Commentary

See Commentary at the beginning of Chapter 10.

Invention and Sleeper Effects:
A Reply to Victoria Seitz [*]

Ann M. Clarke and A.D.B. Clarke

Victoria Seitz (1981) has misperceived and misunderstood our position
(Clarke and Clarke 1981). For example, our argument endorsed a
transactional and not a main-effect model, nor was our aim to argue that early
intervention has no important later consequences, nor did we dispute Consortium findings (Lazar and Darlington 1978). In fact, agreements with Seitz
greatly exceed disagreements. Our scepticism about whether a behavioural
treatment can have long-range effects without also having earlier ones
remains. Long-term changes appear to result from ongoing long-term
processes.

Science advances not only by the discovery of new facts, but also by the
cut-and-thrust of critical debate leading to reformulation of theoretical positions. While we welcome, and benefit from, hard-hitting evaluations of our
work, the criticisms advanced by Victoria Seitz (1981) appear largely based on
misperception and misunderstanding of our position. In some cases they echo
points made in our article (Clarke and Clarke 1981) almost as if we had not

---

[*]   This article first appeared in 1982 in *Developmental Review 2*, pp.76–86.

made them. In the interest of clarity we first summarize very briefly our earlier argument, and then turn to the major points offered by Seitz.

The sleeper effect *concept* apparently originated in the work of Freud. In modern developmental literature the *term* was first used by Kagan and Moss (1962) to describe changing values of correlation across time, such that there occurred a stronger relation between a variable measured early and measured late in development than between similar variables measured contemporaneously or more contiguously in time. We showed how more recent usage had altered from examining correlations to assessing the effects of intervention. While it had been widely accepted that early intervention effects 'washed out', reports over the last few years began to suggest that later in development, the subjects of some high-quality preschool programmes showed a significant benefit. The sleeper effect concept existed ready-made as describing both 'washout' and later improvement. Somehow effects became somnolent only to reawaken years later. We wish, however, to remind readers that the recently reported effects of some early childhood intervention programmes are most regularly and strikingly apparent in terms of a reduction in allocation to special classes and grade retention, to a far greater extent than occurs on more objective measures of cognitive ability, such as standardized achievement and IQ tests (Lazar and Darlington 1978).

Over and above the 'sleeping model' we suggested three additional explanatory possibilities: 1. the intervening variable model in which, for example, 'what sleeps may be knowledge...[which]...in the later years of school enables...[the parents] to negotiate more effectively with regard to the status and treatment of their offspring in school'; 2. random fluctuation of correlation coefficients at different points in time around a 'true' value; and 3. insensitive measurement, suggesting that the sleeping of a characteristic may indicate that the wrong type of measurement was used at one time but not at another. These are obviously not mutually exclusive, and we certainly found them more compelling than the 'sleeping' model. However, in the penultimate sentence of our paper we stated that we share Kagan's current position in accepting that open-mindedness on the existence or otherwise of sleeper effects is the most appropriate stance. This hardly suggests the dogmatism which Seitz apparently perceives in our review. We also believe that the use made by Hovland, Lumsdaine and Sheffield (1949) of the term is a specific example of a general category of behavioural characteristics which we suggested is too wide to be useful in the developmental context. All potential behaviour, unused at any one point in time, is in a sense 'sleeping'.

The critique

Our main object, as stated, was to 'indicate that the concept is normally applied with such imprecision or lack of justification as to have become of little value'. Seitz, however, infers a different purpose: 'The Clarkes' real intention in objecting to sleeper effects is evidently to argue that early childhood intervention programmes have no important later consequences.' This is clearly not the case since we did not dispute the findings of the Consortium, but offered some speculations on the *processes* which may underlie the demonstrated *outcomes*. We could of course add to these in light of the complex evidence from various sources, but to do so would be less relevant to our purpose which was to suggest the likelihood that the preschool programmes initiated, at least in some cases, a cycle of effects on parents and children which was ongoing. Such an interpretation would accord with our position stated in one of our books (1976), on the same page from which Seitz offers another quotation:

> The effects of social learning through modelling, identification with selected adults and peers and feedback from the environment operate on the maturing organism in ways as yet little understood. The child, of course, is not a passive receptor of stimulation but rather is an increasingly dynamic being, who to some extent *causes* his own learning experiences... There is thus the possibility that early experience may produce particular effects which, acting upon later environments, result in reinforcing feedback, thus prolonging early learning effects. The disturbed institutional child, placed in foster care, may elicit from the foster mother antagonistic responses which strengthen the child's instability. The resulting correlation between early and later behaviour is, as implied, likely to reflect indirect rather than direct causality, and here the child may become the unwitting agent of his own later difficulties. The unsophisticated observer may attribute these to early adversity; in a sense he would be both right and wrong in so doing. All this underlines the prime importance of considering what follows particular early experience which may prolong what would otherwise be transitory effects, good or bad. (p.13)

In a lecture in early 1977, reprinted later (Clarke and Clarke 1979), we stated that the child 'plays some part in causing his own development in his transactions with the environment. This is one of the ways in which early experiences *may* be perpetuated, albeit indirectly rather than directly. So there is indeed the possibility that early experience may produce particular effects which, acting upon later environments, result in reinforcing feedback, thus prolonging or perpetuating such effects' (p.144).

That we fully accept intervention as sometimes having 'important later consequences' is also clearly implied in the very paper with which Seitz's review is concerned. 'It would be an unusual social or educational research worker,' we wrote, 'who would not readily assert that important environmental events may initiate new and sometimes progressive cycles.' Nor did we challenge the stated results of the Consortium (Lazar and Darlington 1978) but quoted with approval the view of Sheldon White on parents as mediators of the later effects of intervention (the intervening variable model) as well as that of Francis Palmer on the possibility that the sleeping of a characteristic may merely indicate that the wrong type of measurement was used at one time but not at another (the insensitive measurement model). The large differences in assignment to special education and the less strong findings on retention in grade reported by the Consortium, remained when almost all possible early causal factors (e.g. type or duration of programme, presence or absence of language goals, training or non-training of teachers) were controlled in the analyses. In this remarkable situation, where it apparently did not matter what was done nor when it was done within the broad limits of a high-quality pre-school programme, then one must surely invoke ongoing familial changes, especially in the mothers, as the authors themselves indicate. We are thus probably dealing not only with early intervention but also with longer-term, continuing effects within the family and the school.

We now turn to a further serious misconception. After rightly implying the error in following an earlier model of intervention which suggested that a single-shot inoculation would provide immunity from later adversity, Seitz believes that we have proffered an equally fallacious suntan model. 'They view intervention as if children were being passively exposed to a treatment that enhanced their cognitive abilities. Upon discontinuation of the programme, however, as if they were returning from the sunny climes to the winter of their everyday inadequate environments, the Clarkes expect the children's cognitive skills to fade forever.' There are two points here; first, the alleged passivity of the child exposed to intervention. The quotations from our work already offered in the paragraphs above are quite sufficient to refute this charge. Second, while it is perfectly true that IQ differences between experimental and control children, even in the high-quality programmes of the Consortium, do indeed fade, our paper indicated a transactional model which accounted for long-term effects of intervention which Seitz also echoes. To use her metaphor, the sun continues to shine (perhaps a little wanly) within the family and within the school. She goes on to suggest that we have dismissed these studies 'by leveling methodological criticisms against a handful...and ignoring the rest'. On the contrary, we did not dismiss the results; rather we cast doubt on sleeper effects as being responsible and explored alternative possibilities.

Seitz writes that what she calls 'delayed change' may be negative as well as positive. Agreed; we said this in the first of the quotations (Clarke and Clarke 1976, p.13) in the present paper. It is for this reason that we have frequently urged prolonged intervention and have also considered the often satisfactory outcome of total ecological change by late adoption. It might also be recorded that for most who work in the developmental field, intervention problems are conceived only in terms of desired effects/non-effects. We should add to this the possibility of negative or damaging side effects, one example of which is provided by McCord's (1978) 30-year follow-up of the Cambridge –Somerville intervention programme designed to reduce the incidence of delinquency in a disadvantaged population.

Turning now to Seitz's section on 'Explaining Delayed Treatment Effects,' we note two models proposed by her, the Dormant Change and Transactional Models. In the former, she has two arguments, both of which were considered in our paper. Thus, referring to Freud's views we wrote 'Such notions provide tempting biological analogies. The long-delayed effects of carcinogenic agents, including exposure to ionizing radiations, the incubation period for some common illnesses, the action of "slow" viruses, are obvious examples.' In justifying the Dormant Change Model, Seitz echoes these points, but succumbs to the temptation noted above: 'One of the best examples of a case where an effect appears to be dormant is provided by mutagenic radiation. Changes in genetic material may lie undetected until an affected child is conceived... Certain forms of immunization...also change organisms in a manner not readily detected until or unless certain environments are later encountered...' Quite so, but it would require a further article to delineate the perils of 'tempting biological analogies' which have sometimes misled developmental scientists. Let us, however, offer one example. There is a clear indication that fetal growth passes through certain critical periods. This concept from embryology was extrapolated to early animal development and then to human behavioural development. Writing in 1962, Harlow and Harlow stated that their experiments with rhesus monkeys 'indicate that there is a critical period somewhere between the third and sixth month of life, during which social deprivation, particularly deprivation of the company of its peers, irreversibly blights the animal's capacity for social adjustment' (p.138). Commenting on the effects of late intervention after one year of social isolation, however, Novak and Harlow (1975) reversed their former view: 'The present study offers a compelling argument against the critical period interpretation since a one year incarceration period, spanning nearly the entire infancy of the subjects, should be sufficiently long to produce permanent deficits if the critical period theory were applicable' (p.463). A later report (Novak 1979) indicated that: 'The ability of isolation-reared monkeys to acquire sophisticated patterns of behaviour is inconsistent, in principle, with typical critical period hypotheses, which assert that such patterns require the appropriate stimulation early in life for their subsequent expression' (p.60).

Seitz continues by citing Bronfenbrenner's (1979) argument that 'the enduring developmental effects of a setting cannot be effectively assessed within that same setting' (p.266). Again the echo of our paper (the same quotation) comes from Seitz. She goes on to cast some doubt on the Dormant Change Model and is now apparently on our side, writing that 'it would not be surprising if it were later shown that all changes are transactional in nature, with events setting into motion probabilistic sequences of other events'. This is elegantly stated, and of course we agree because this was one of the explicit themes of our paper. Our theme has gone unrecognized by Seitz, however, for while she believes we have understood the value of transactional models, we are thought to have adopted a simple model in conceptualizing intervention and its effects. We have already indicated that we do not, as she says, 'object to findings...that appear to reflect effects of mediating variables such as changed parental attitudes'. We reiterate that this was one of our main arguments, so once again a man of straw has been set up and knocked down.

Perhaps the most impressive and well-controlled study included in Consortium data, to which Seitz refers, is by Schweinhart and Weikart (1980). Their interpretation of their findings is well put and fits the transactional model we have adopted. They write:

> As data accumulate, it is clear that we are viewing a complex network of causes and effects. The preschool intervention has been successful over the years because its effects became the causes of other effects as well... Preschool education leads to increased commitment to schooling and increased cognitive ability at school entry (the latter after the effect of cognitive ability prior to preschool has been taken into account). Family socioeconomic status, even though restricted to impoverished families and unrelated to cognitive ability within this sample, is still an antecedent of school achievement. Cognitive ability at school entry is indeed a gateway to better school performance, with a higher cognitive ability at school entry leading to greater commitment to schooling, higher school achievement and fewer years spent receiving special education services. Commitment to schooling and fewer years in special education combined in leading to fewer delinquent offenses, while achievement led to more delinquent offenses. (p.64)

Intervention effects on this model never became dormant; the triggering effect of a high-quality programme sets in motion ongoing consequences. These are not sleeper effects, nor does Seitz's new term 'delayed treatment effects' adequately describe them. Rather they are effects of intervention, some direct and others indirect.

Seitz has in fact misunderstood our position on the relative importance of IQ as a measure of the efficacy of programmes. We have long been concerned about what appeared to be a narrow focus upon IQ differences as the only appropriate indication of effects between treated and control children in intervention experiments, although we also believe they should continue to be used in these contexts. They provide important contrasts as outcome measures both in relation to achievement tests and also to the more subjective assessments by teachers which commonly lead to grade retention or placement in special classes, thus yielding the positive effects of at least some intervention projects. Schweinhart and Weikart (1981) found that at follow-up their preschool intervention group did not differ from randomly allocated controls in terms of IQ but did differ in terms of achievement measures; they comment as follows:

> The disappearance of IQ gains has been taken to mean that the effects of compensatory preschool education are temporary at best. Yet, as IQ gains disappeared in the Perry Project, we found persistent and cumulative preschool effects on teacher ratings, grade placement, and academic achievement.

> School achievement, particularly at eighth grade, cannot be affected directly by preschool experience – a mediating variable is logically necessary. It might be expected that IQ would be this mediating variable; apparently it is not.

> The environment of poverty, when it occurs, usually persists throughout childhood and seems to provide little opportunity to experience the domain measured by intelligence tests at any age... Yet intelligence theoretically refers to one's ability to adapt, cope with, and learn from one's environment, even when it is an environment of poverty. Our present intelligence tests simply do not have the scope of our theoretical definitions of intelligence. Until they do, it seems a dangerous expedient to equate the concept of intelligence with IQ.

> It is reasonable to state that intelligence encompasses both the IQ tests and adaptive functioning in one's actual environment. Using this definition, we can make the parsimonious assumption that quality preschool education positively affects intelligence. Its effect on IQ, however, is not supported by the post-preschool environment of poverty, so that effect withers away with time.

> At the same time, preschool may positively affect adaptive functioning in the actual school environment. This improved adaptive functioning creates a

more positive social dynamic and thereby supports and maintains itself. Children who attended preschool actually do function better in school, are perceived and treated as functioning better, therefore continue to function better, and so on. All of the preschool benefits found in this study – achievement, IQ, classroom behavior, grade placement – may be taken as evidence of improved functioning in the school environment. We offer this interpretation not as a final answer, but as a line of thought worthy of pursuit. (p.123)

The authors further attribute the anomalous disparity between IQ and achievement test measures to motivational differences between the two groups which had their origins in the preschool period (p.124). We have selected this experiment for particular attention because of its sophisticated design, important and interesting results, and thought-provoking interpretation, although we appreciate the authors' concern that their results may not generalize to other settings.

We are unsure how to interpret Seitz's introduction into her argument of the cross-lagged panel analyses in relation to intelligence and achievement. We wrote that 'The essential feature of a "sleeper effect" is that behavioural correlations between very early events and pre-adolescent or adolescent ratings substantially (or significantly) exceed correlations between the same early events and ratings more proximate in time for children *growing up in fairly constant environments.*' Crano, Kenny and Campbell (1972), whom she quotes, were by contrast interested in a very cautiously stated attempt to determine the direction of causality across time between 'intelligence' and achievement. They used a large battery of tests on a very large sample including both suburban and 'core' children (the latter being pupils in schools eligible for comprehensive programmes of aid, p. 266). Their stated objective was to discover whether, using the time-precedence notion of causality, intelligence caused achievement or conversely achievement caused intelligence, carefully pointing out that their model did not obviate the possibility of some reciprocal causation operating as a feedback loop. In fact among suburban children on the global measures, intelligence in grade 4 correlated with grade 6 achievement, $r = .7329$, while achievement in grade 4 predicted grade 6 intelligence, $r = .7049$ ($t(3991) = 3.479$, $p<.001$, two tailed). For the core children the corresponding correlations were .6086 and .6180, respectively ($t(1498) = -.521$, $p>.05$, that is, not significant). The predominant causal sequence for all subjects was in the direction of intelligence causing later achievement. Dividing the total sample into core and suburban subunits, however, revealed that this sequence only held within the suburban sample; if any relationship existed in the core sample, it was opposite to that of the suburban group (pp.270 and 271). More detailed analyses led the authors to suggest that among less advantaged children achievement appears to cause intelligence.

We were unaware of this important paper when we wrote (1975) shortly after its publication:

> Much has been outlined with respect to intelligence, but this has in the text sometimes been linked with attainment. We offer no apologies, and here we follow Vernon in accepting that an IQ test is just as much an attainment test as is a measure of reading. Unlike the latter, however, it taps a much wider range of cognitive skills. The view is also shared with Vernon that the IQ does not by itself 'cause' scholastic attainments, and indeed we consider there may well be two-way interactions between them. Test results may never be used as direct indications of biological potential. Here there is an open conflict with the views of the late Sir Cyril Burt. (p.199)

It seems that the opinions we expressed are similar to those advanced by Crano *et al.*, whose evidence in conjunction with other researchers has in fact led us in recent years to modify somewhat our position as stated above. In any case we do not perceive a relationship between these lines of argument and the 'sleeper effect'; the biosocial causes of individual differences in intelligence and attainment are as yet not precisely understood, and are certainly beyond the scope of this debate.

Seitz is correct in amending our definition of sleeper effects: 'the notion that behavioural variables intrinsic or extrinsic to the individual may have consequences the manifestations of which are delayed'. She would delete the adjective 'behavioural' and this we accept.

We believe that Seitz is also correct in introducing the problem of low statistical power in samples with small N's such that 'an effect can appear and disappear like a star twinkling in the heavens...[yet]...the effect itself, like the star is real'. Nevertheless, there are, in addition, random fluctuations around 'true' values which may mislead. Where significance levels for 'real' effects in small samples are doubtful, replication in similar or extended populations will greatly enhance the probability that possible random fluctuations are not present.

Conclusions

We have throughout sought to emphasize that our objection to the term 'sleeper effect' in a developmental context is that it does not convey any sense of active ongoing biological and social interactions which include dynamic social transactions, often of a reciprocal nature. For the same reasons we are not altogether happy with the suggested introduction of the alternative term 'delayed effects' – why not just the neutral term 'treatment effects'?

It is evident that, on balance, our agreements with Seitz greatly outweigh our disagreements. She seems to have misunderstood our position, and the present paper has been chiefly concerned with documenting our rebuttal of what appear to be insubstantial criticisms. We have wondered how such misunderstandings could have arisen and whether our consistent and prolonged attack on the 'single inoculation' model of intervention may be at the root of the problem, misperceived as an attack on intervention in general. In the final chapter of our book (1976) on early experience we wrote:

> It would be more than unfortunate if this book played any part in a reaction against the new humanism, on the mistaken grounds that 'it doesn't matter what happens early in life'. Thus while the evidence does suggest that no mother of a very young child should feel bound to remain at home (provided satisfactory alternative caretaking arrangements can be made) equally no mother should feel that her responsibilities diminish after her child becomes older. Nor does the evidence condone bad institutions, or 'problem families' or refugee camps, simply because their unfortunate effects can, in many cases, be reversed. Nor would we wish to see nursery schools either opened or closed as a result of this debate. That such schools fail to show long-term effects is no argument against their existence, both for the present benefit to the child and also to his mother. There is absolutely no implication that infancy and early childhood are unimportant, only that their long-term role is by itself very limited. (p.272)

The later data of Lazar and Darlington (1978) would, as indicated, demand some modification in the penultimate (but not the ultimate) sentence.

The recent evidence for some long-term effects is not inconsistent with our continuing belief, despite Epstein's (1974) evidence, that the early years of rapid maturation do not represent a critical (or even exceptionally sensitive) period for learning, particularly cognitive learning. That young children can be successfully taught cognitive skills which enable them to achieve significantly higher scores on intelligence tests is not in doubt and may occur for a variety of reasons, some of which have recently been described by Jensen (1981). In most circumstances these effects appear to fade which is hardly surprising in view of the qualitative changes which occur in cognitive abilities as the underlying biological programme develops in interaction with the social and educational environment within which children happen to find themselves. For a somewhat different yet concordant explanation of why effects are likely to fade, the reader is invited to consider Piaget's brief and elegant exposition of his theory and its implications (Piaget 1970). We are also of the opinion that successful intervention is exceedingly difficult to achieve within the ecological context of the social processes which give rise to mild retardation and scholastic maladjustment. The somewhat different outcomes of differing strategies should assist further clarification of the extent to which helping programmes can facilitate development across the years of schooling, and counteract the effects of cumulative deficit (Jensen 1974, 1977, 1981), while new research endeavours may yield further important insights into the processes through which the development of abilities and attainments are stabilized, accelerated or decelerated.

References

Bronfenbrenner, U. (1979) *The Ecology of Human Development*. Cambridge, Mass: Harvard University Press.

Clarke, A.D.B. and Clarke, A.M. (1981) '"Sleeper effects" in development: Fact or artifact?' *Developmental Review 1*, 344–360.

Clarke, A.M. and Clarke, A.D.B. (eds) (1975) *Mental Deficiency: The Changing Outlook* (3rd edn). New York: The Free Press.

Clarke, A.M. and Clarke, A.D.B. (eds) (1976) *Early Experience: Myth and Evidence*. New York: The Free Press.

Clarke, A.M. and Clarke, A.D.B. (1979) 'Early experience: Its limited effect upon later development.' In D. Shaffer and J.F. Dunn (eds) *The First Year of Life: Psychological and Medical Implications of Early Experience*. New York: Wiley.

Crano, W.D., Kenny, D.A. and Campbell, D.T. (1972)' Does intelligence cause achievement?' *Journal of Educational Psychology 63*, 258–275.

Epstein, H. (1974) 'Phrenoblysis: Special brain and mind growth periods. I. Human brain and skull development. II. Human mental development.' *Developmental Psychobiology 7*, 207–216 and 217–224.

Harlow, H.F. and Harlow, M.K. (1962) 'Social deprivation in monkeys.' *Scientific American 207*, November, 136–146.

Hovland, C.I., Lumsdaine, A.A. and Sheffield, F.D. (1949) *Experiments on Mass Communication*. Princeton, NJ: Princeton University Press.

Jensen, A.R. (1974) 'Cumulative deficit: A testable hypothesis?' *Developmental Psychology 10*, 996–1019.

Jensen, A.R. (1977) 'Cumulative deficit in IQ of blacks in the rural South.' *Developmental Psychology 13*, 184–191.

Jensen, A.R. (1981) 'Raising the IQ: The Ramey and Haskins study.' *Intelligence 5*, 29–40.

Kagan, J. and Moss, H.A. (1962) *Birth to Maturity*. New York: Wiley.

Lazar, I. and Darlington, R. (1978) *Lasting Effects After Preschool*. Washington, DC: DHEW Publication No. (OHDS) 79-30178.

McCord, J. (1978) 'A thirty-year follow-up of treatment effects.' *American Psychologist 33*, March, 284–289.

Novak, M.A. (1979) 'Social recovery of monkeys isolated for the first year of life. II. Long-term assessment.' *Developmental Psychology 15*, 50–61.

Novak, M.A. and Harlow, H.F. (1975) 'Social recovery of monkeys isolated for the first year of life. I. Rehabilitation and therapy.' *Developmental Psychology 11*, 453–465.

Piaget, J. (1970) 'Piaget's theory.' In P.H. Mussen (ed) *Carmichael's Manual of Child Psychology (Vol. 1)* (3rd edn). New York: Wiley.

Schweinhart, L.J. and Weikart, D.P. (1980) *Young Children Grow Up: The Effects of the Perry Preschool Program on Youths through Age 15*. Ypsilanti, Mich: High/Scope Press.

Schweinhart. L.J. and Weikart, D.P. (1981) 'Perry preschool effects nine years later: What do they mean?' In M.J. Begab, H.C. Haywood and H.L. Garber (eds) *Psychosocial Influences in Retarded Performance (Vol. 1)*. Baltimore, Md: Univesity Park Press.

Seitz, V. (1981) 'Intervention and sleeper effects: A reply to Clarke and Clarke.' *Developmental Review 1*, 361–373.

CHAPTER 12

Some Research Problems...
and Solutions

Commentary

This brief chapter from *Early Experience and the Life Path* (2000) is reprinted here by permission of Jessica Kingsley Publishers. It was written primarily to indicate, to those unfamiliar with research methods, the complexities of studying the human life path, and the necessary safeguards to be employed in interpreting and generalising the results.

The chapter is mainly concerned with longitudinal (outcome) studies, whether prospective (follow-forward) or retrospective (trace-back). Six subsections explore this theme, and the stability or otherwise of environmental influences.

Some Research Problems...and Solutions[*]

A.M. Clarke and A.D.B. Clarke

Signpost: Longitudinal methods, their advantages and difficulties

In this chapter it is the writers' aim to draw attention to four basic problems in longitudinal research. These are 1. the probable difference in outcome in retrospective versus prospective research on the same problem; 2. the potentially distorting influence of sample loss on follow-up results; 3. the limits to

---

[*]   This article first appeared in A.M. Clarke and A.D.B. Clake (eds) (2000) Early Experience and the Life Path. London: Jessica Kingsley Publishers, pp.23–28.

generalization and the possibility of sample specificity; 4. environmental continuities versus change, as well as the crucial role of the latter in evaluating the effects or otherwise of early experience.

Longitudinal methods

1. Retrospective

The *retrospective* (follow-back) approach can be relatively rapid, and therefore cheaper than the prospective (follow-forward) method. Starting as it does with a clearly delineated group, retrospective studies will often have available earlier records, sometimes supplemented by interviews, giving a picture of the individual's or group's past life path. Since these are often concerned with unusual samples (e.g. criminals, psychiatric patients), and since to attain the label of 'unusual', some lapse of time is to be expected, continuities in personal histories are common, and often strong. For example, in such individuals one bad period can be followed by, and lead to, further bad periods *ad infinitum*, hence the likelihood of continuity. One problem with the retrospective method is that, while continuities may be apparent, there is no way of knowing how many had similar experiences yet failed to develop in the way characteristic of the identified group.

2. Prospective

The *prospective* method is lengthy, expensive and often deals with a more heterogeneous population than does the retrospective. Outcome is likely to be much more varied than those in retrospective samples who almost by definition form relatively homogeneous groups. Sample loss can be a major problem, possibly biasing the overall results since this is usually a selective attrition. For example, if one follows up a socially deprived population and, many years after first identification, a minority is untraceable, it is likely that the 'lost' members will to some extent have escaped the consequences of their early life. This means that the remaining 'captive', non-mobile members are likely to have done less well than the 'lost'. Overall results will thus give a gloomier picture than would be justified for the original, total group. On the other hand, if a preschool programme loses its less promising members, the average for the remainder will be higher. Empirical examples have been provided in a summary article by Wolke *et al.* (1995). It is very important to document drop-outs, write these authors, in following up pre-term children:

mothers with low educational attainments and those with infants with serious developmental delay or disability are most likely to drop out of surveillance programmes…parents who have not come to terms with their child's developmental deficits may tend to avoid situations where these difficulties are highlighted… It is worrying that more poorly educated mothers and their very pre-term infants who would benefit most from early intervention are most difficult to keep in follow-up studies. (p.443)

Without tracing such drop-outs who do badly, a better overall picture obtains for the rest and this may be wrongly generalized to *all* very pre-term infants.

Most researchers try to cope with the problem of sample loss by checking that early assessments for those lost were on average no different from those retained. This is like saying that everyone is equal at the start of a race, and will therefore remain equal at the finish. The lesson here is to avoid sample loss by every means and this depends on resources, both human and financial.

3. The problem of measurement

There is also the *problem of measurement*. Whether in physics, biology or psychology, all measurement involves error, even though in some sciences the error may be infinitesimal or very small. Because of daily personal fluctuations which may be completely insignificant in the long term, measurement errors can be significant in the behavioural sciences. Supposing an individual under-functions (for example, for emotional reasons, or from fatigue in some baseline assessment) yet later functions normally, a spurious increment may be noted. So, more than two (and preferably many more) measures across time are necessary to detect trends. These personal fluctuations tend to cancel each other out in repeated measurements. And then there is the problem of deciding at the outset of a prospective longitudinal study which measures are to be used later, remembering that cost may be important.

To recapitulate, it is to be expected that retrospective and prospective studies will not yield exactly the same answers to the same research question. The starting point for a retrospective study is often a homogeneous population traced backwards over somewhat similar life paths. For a prospective study, divergent life paths over time are common when followed onwards from baseline, especially if the latter is assessed very early in life when development is rapid and fluctuant.

Often researchers have been concerned with single factors with predeterministic potential. There is always the possibility that each may reflect wider influences than the factor itself. For example, a record of separation between parent and child, especially if often repeated, may occur in the context of some disastrous situation, and a correlation between the particular factor, in this case separation, may if taken on its own, mask a constellation of other diversities.

4. The range of data presented

It may be important in presenting data to include the ranges of scores as well as means and standard deviations; for a fine example see O'Connor *et al.* (1999a), who, best of all, include a scattergram thus enabling readers, if they so wish, to carry out further analyses using all the basic information.

5. Independent assessment

Whenever possible, ratings or other measures should be assessed by independent researchers *blind* to the hypothesis and to other assessments. It is well known that expectancies can both affect data collection or its interpretation.

6. Clinic samples and limits to generalization

Much research in developmental psychiatry and some in developmental psychology has arisen, as earlier noted, in the study of clinic samples. But not all disordered individuals find their way to clinics. Are those who do not less affected than those who do? Or is it sometimes a matter of chance whether referral or self-referral takes place? It seems a reasonable guess that, by and large, the more seriously disordered persons will be found in the retrospective clinic samples, and if so, generalization to non-clinic individuals may be overly pessimistic. This likelihood is certainly supported in studies of the outcome for those who in childhood had suffered sexual abuse. A pessimistic picture is presented in a notable review of what must have been mainly clinic samples (Stevenson 1999) compared with a less gloomy situation for a substantial number of children reflected in a study of a random sample of the general population reporting in adulthood a history of sexual abuse and its effects or non-effects (Mullen *et al.* 1993, 1994).

Case studies and research on groups

Valuable lessons may be derived from following up individual severely deprived children after rescue. Here again there may be selective reportage of those who benefited versus those who made unsuccessful adaptations. The findings, however, would be replicated, although in a minor key, in investigations of the outcome for less severely deprived children moved to a better situation. If dramatic recovery are the findings in the former case, less dramatic findings, but in the same direction, are to be expected in the latter, less damaged children. So there is a probable congruence between the two forms of study.

Environmental continuities versus change

In attempting to identify the role of early experience in later development, there are a number of additional problems which need to be outlined. Under ordinary circumstances children experience some continuities of care. For example, 'good' care in early life tends to be followed by the same qualities later; so, too, with 'bad' care, 'average' care or 'inconsistent' care. Hence any early effects are likely to be reinforced subsequently. This being so, one would expect, if anything, enhanced correlations between early and later (even adult) characteristics. A note of caution must, however, be issued. Early characteristics are usually very different from later; for example, intelligence as measured at age two has little obviously in common with intelligence at adolescence. While the former may possess seeds of the latter, many intellectual processes are undeveloped or unformed at the early age. Moreover, genetic programmes do not necessarily follow straight paths (see Wilson 1985), so in essence it may be very difficult to interpret links which exist. And if such links are not very strong, this would be expected from the foregoing. Perhaps broader early and later assessments might show more interpretable information.

A second approach will be less equivocal. One needs to study before and after effects on development when some sharp change in the child's circumstances occurs. Here are two examples: suppose that the child has 'good' early experiences until age 3. These are followed by prolonged adversity. Do the former provide protection against the effects of the latter? Now suppose that a child has 'bad' early experiences followed by a strong, positive intervention. Does the latter overcome the effects of the former? This approach provides the toughest test of the permanence, or otherwise, of the effects of early experience. In practice, there is a great deal more information on the changes from 'adverse' to 'good' than vice versa.

Summary

Retrospective and prospective studies of children under ordinary circumstances will identify the strength of links between early and later characteristics. Since retrospective investigations tend to relate to homogeneous 'unusual' groups, these links will be stronger than is found in prospective data where wider ranges of outcome are usually involved. For many individuals, behavioural characteristics tend to alter differentially under natural conditions, in spite of social and educational pressures, than tend to keep children on a self-fulfilling prophetic path. Such qualities in turn may affect and reflect the social context for good or ill. Additionally, in addressing the longitudinal method, some attention was paid to generalizing from clinic samples to wider populations. This is part of the common problem of recognizing the possibility of sample specificity in research findings. Finally, sample loss in prospective studies is a major hazard in long-term research.

References

Mullen, P.E., Martin, J.L., Anderson, J.C., Romans, S.E. and Herbison, G.P. (1993) 'Childhood and sexual abuse and mental health in adult life.' *British Journal of Psychiatry 163*, 271–332.

Mullen, P.E., Martin, J.L., Anderson, J.C., Romans, S.E. and Herbison, G.P. (1994) 'The effect of child sexual abuse on social, interpersonal and sexual function in adult life.' *British Journal of Psychiatry 165*, 35–47.

O'Connor, T.G. and the English Romanian Adoptees Study Team (1999a) 'The effects of global severe privation on cognitive competence?' *Child Development 71*, 376–390.

Stevenson, J. (1999) 'The treatment of the long-term sequence of child abuse?' *Journal of Child Psychiatry and Psychology 40*, 89–111.

Wilson, R.S. (1985) 'The Louisville Twin Study: Developmental synchronies in behaviour.' *Child Development 58*, 295–316.

Wolke, D., Söhne, B., Ohrt, B. and Riegel, K. (1995) 'Follow-up of preterm children: Important to document the drop-outs.' *Lancet 345*, 447.

PART III

Intelligence

CHAPTER 13

Polygenic and Environmental Interactions

Commentary

When we were writing the first chapter of our 1976 book, *Early Experience: Myth and Evidence*, we found it prudent to start by indicating what the book was *not* about. We were not then concerned primarily with the major problem of whether and to what extent the physical and social environment influences the development of personal attributes such as intelligence and social adjustment. Had this been our aim, a large number of, often excellently documented, empirical studies would have been included, some of which emphasize the importance of genetic and constitutional variables.

In this present chapter we present a summary of evidence, up to 1985, on *polygenic* and environmental variables. The chapter appeared in our textbook on mental retardation which also presented the (rather extensive) information on *single* gene effects, such as those that determine eye or skin colour, which are also very important in understanding the aetiology of many human abnormalities. Most human characteristics such as stature, intelligence, sociability, extraversion are thought to be due, partly at least, to the effects of many genes, thus the word *polygenic* inheritance. These are thought to interact in the womb and later with the physical and psychological environment. There remains, however, considerable controversy as to the relative importance of either. In a situation in which there is a very similar environment, heredity will be shown to be the more important; where there are very different environments affecting, for example, separated identical twins, the environmental effect (if present) will be clear. Even so, most studies show heredity as very important. As indicated, environmental effects are most obvious when serious adversities depress normal development, and are equally clear when such children are rescued and placed in a superior context, allowing the most obvious expression of resilience, a process (or processes) which itself has a significance genetic component (see Chapter 21).

Polygenic and Environmental Interactions[*]
Ann M. Clarke

Introduction

To argue that anything as complex as human behaviour has multifactorial origins demanding a systems analysis is today almost a statement of the obvious. This does not, however, mean that a search for significant main effects in populations is unwarranted, provided that these can be shown in replicated studies across place and time.

In the various reviews we have offered in successive editions of this text we have consistently argued for both nature and nurture in combination as factors determining individual differences in intelligence, and although our thinking has matured over the years, taking account of new, often very sophisticated research findings, our attitude was well expressed by Zigler (1968):

> Not only do I insist that we take the biological integrity of the organism seriously, but it is also my considered opinion that our nation has more to fear from unbridled environmentalists than…from those who point to such integrity as one factor in the determination of development.

In 1969 an article was published in the *Harvard Educational Review* which raised a storm not only in the USA but throughout the English-speaking world and beyond. Arthur Jensen, addressing himself to the problem of 'How much can we boost IQ and scholastic achievement?', concluded that intelligence as measured in standardized tests is highly heritable, a composite value for it being given as 0.77 'which becomes 0.81 after correction for unreliability (assuming an average test reliability of 0.95)'. He further suggested that prenatal influences might well contribute the largest environmental influence, and discussed evidence which persuaded him that social class and racial variations in intelligence could not be accounted for by differences in the social environment but must be attributed partially to genetic differences. Jensen offered this as a

---

[*]   This chapter first appeared in A.M. Clarke, A.D.B. Clarke and J.M. Berg (eds). (1985) *Mental Deficiency: The Changing Outlook*. 4th Edn. London: Methuen. New York: The Free Press. p.267–290.

major reason for the failure of the Head Start programme significantly to improve the learning abilities of children at risk of retardation on entry into school. A very large number of these children were black, and the implication was apparently clear: their IQs and scholastic attainment could not be substantially boosted. In a country such as the USA, with a strong egalitarian tradition, having painfully gone through the process of desegregating their education establishments, and believing they were in the process of building a great society, Jensen's conclusions resulted in a furious response particularly from those concerned with the education of disadvantaged children. 'Jensenism' became a term of abuse, and some investigators started to look very critically at the quality of the empirical evidence on which his conclusions were based. In this connection the extensively cited researches of the late Sir Cyril Burt were (belatedly) pronounced fraudulent to an extent not as yet fully established (Clarke and Clarke 1980; Gillie 1976; Hearnshaw 1979). Kamin (1974), whose excavations into the researches underpinning the genetic contribution to variation in intelligence have been explosively influential, felt able to offer a perhaps incautiously extreme conclusion.

While maintaining that 'to assert that there is no genetic determination of IQ would be a strong and scientifically meaningless statement' he did, however, conclude that 'there exist no data which should lead a prudent man to accept the hypothesis that IQ scores are in any degree heritable'. Further, although apparently making a distinction between IQ scores and intelligence, Kamin felt able to end his book with a long quotation from Watson (1930) which included the statement:

> Give me a dozen healthy infants, well-formed, and my own specified world to bring them up in and I'll guarantee to take anyone at random and train him to become any type of specialist I might select – doctor, lawyer, artist, merchant-chief and, yes, even beggar-man and thief, regardless of his talents, penchants, tendencies, abilities, vocations, and race of his ancestors.

Since 1974 a large number of important studies bearing directly upon the nature–nurture issue have been published which, taken together with earlier work, point to the following conclusions with respect to intelligence test scores:

1. In the words of R.S. Wilson (1983) 'that there is a strong developmental thrust in the growth of intelligence that continues through adolescence, and is guided by an intrinsic template or ground plan. The template is rooted in genetic processes that operate all through childhood and adolescence'. This may be conceived as a biological trajectory which both underlies normal

maturational processes from conception to maturity and also to an unknown extent accounts for individual differences.

2. No current investigator in the field of behavioural genetics denies the importance of the environment, and many are working hard to discover which environmental variations are helpful in potentiating development and which are disruptive. However, the precise effects of environmental events or by what processes they operate remain little understood except in environments of fairly severe disadvantage.

3. The environment can be shown to have deleterious effects where circumstances are exceptionally disadvantageous.

4. Removal of children from disadvantaged environments to favourable circumstances generally results in improvement in cognitive functioning.

5. As yet no early period in development has been identified which can be considered critical in the sense that the demonstrated effects of social disadvantage are irreversible, provided there is total ecological change.

Some scholars argue with Hebb (1949) that in normal circumstances nature and nurture are interlocked to such an extent in the development of intelligence and individual differences that to seek to establish which might be more important is scientifically meaningless. We disagree with this view, and suggest that research which might illuminate the nature and degree of the range of reaction to different environments is important not only in its own right but also for its general social implications. It must, however, be emphasized that, granted an assumption of a genotype interacting with various environments, it is useful to think in terms of a range of reaction within which the phenotype will be formed. It should come as no surprise, therefore, that heritability indices vary from study to study; the h^2 statistic is only characteristic of a given population, not a fixed value for a given trait (Vandenberg 1971). Among the factors which will affect the expression of heritability are age (Scarr and Weinberg 1983; Wilson 1983), race and probably type of test, those with a predominantly verbal content being more likely to be influenced by the social environment than non-verbal and numerical tests.

A review of recent literature on polygenic factors will of necessity be brief, since so large and specialized a topic, mostly based on studies of non-retarded individuals, would be inappropriate in a book of this kind. Investigations of the heritability of IQ are based on a fairly simple, but very clear model of how genetic factors might work. For excellent expositions the reader is referred to Plomin *et al.* (1980) and to Jensen (1981), who also discuss elaborations of the model. It should be borne in mind that while there are biological patterns of inheritance originating with Mendel's work over a century ago which are capable of making precise predictions such as are discussed in other parts of this book, a parallel environmental model is not as yet available, leading to occasional difficulties in interpretation and agreement among researchers. Furthermore, in the real world allowance has to be made for the fact that many of the conditions underlying predictions for the polygenic model do not apply precisely.

Genetic factors relating to individual differences in the general population

Were we to assume *perfect* reliability of measurement, *no* effect of environmental variables, before, during or after birth, no dominance or epistasis, random mating, *and* a representative sample of a population, the polygenic model would predict that the correlation among different classes of kinship would depend upon the number of genes the relatives had in common, thus:

MZ twins	1.0
DZ twins	0.5
Siblings	0.5
Single-parent–offspring	0.5
Mid-parent–offspring	0.7071
Grand-parent–grandchild	0.25
Uncle, aunt–niece, nephew	0.25
Half-siblings	0.25
First cousins	0.125
Unrelated persons	0.00

In all cases, of course, the correlations should be the same whether the biological relatives are reared together or apart, since in this hypothetical (and totally unlikely) model the environment is assumed to have no effect whatever.

Erlenmeyer-Kimling and Jarvik (1963) were the first researchers systematically to collate data to test the hypothesis that there would be a relationship between degree of biological kinship and IQ. They presented median correlations based on 52 studies (30,000 correlational pairings) and found that the hypothesis was substantiated, although some of the kinship categories in those far-off days yielded no or few studies, and the extensive kinship data published by Burt had yet to be declared fraudulent and were therefore included. Moreover, studies demonstrating mid-parent–offspring correlations and single-parent–offspring correlations were treated as equivalent although the predicted correlations differ (0.7071 and 0.50 respectively; see McAskie and Clarke 1976). As might be expected, the correlations within each category of kinship varied, presumably reflecting differences in testing procedures and the nature of the samples. For a very detached review of Erlenmeyer-Kimling and Jarvik's work the reader is referred to Kamin (1974), who makes a number of substantial criticisms.

More recently Bouchard and McGue (1981) have performed, in the light of Kamin's attack, the difficult and exacting task of updating the material, providing a comprehensive contemporary summary of the world literature on IQ correlation between relatives. Recent studies are included, according to strict and explicit criteria, and some of the original ones deleted (among them Burt's) which did not meet important methodological requirements. The 111 studies, including 59 reported in the 17 years subsequent to the Erlenmeyer-Kimling and Jarvik summary, yielded 526 familial correlations based upon 113,942 pairings. In general the pattern of average correlations is consistent with the pattern predicted on the basis of polygenic inheritance. Although the overall trend in the data was strong, the individual data points were heterogeneous, as they were in the original collation. Bouchard and McGue attempted to discover the basis for the variations in outcome of studies, without any great success. Furthermore, there were clear indications of environmental effects, in addition to the genetic influences on IQ to an extent unascertainable from this particular meta-analysis.

Two factors which are likely to have affected some of the correlations, and hence the heterogeneity are: 1. the socioeconomic status (SES) range (correlated with IQ) within each sample; and 2. where children are concerned, the age at testing. Reed and Rich (1982) illustrate the former point with reference to the data collected by Reed and Reed (1965) which included several thousand persons whose IQs had been determined when they were schoolchildren and later collated, making possible kinship correlations on an exceptionally large and representative sample of the US population. From this source 1029 pairs of parents with one or more offspring were identified, all tested when they were in their teens. Correlations and regression coefficients are presented for each offspring's IQ on the mid-parental average IQ and a demonstration made of the effect of truncation on each statistic. Thus, the mid-parent–offspring correlation for the whole sample was 0.531; for a subsample where the mid-parent IQ was one standard deviation above the mean (IQ 114 and above, n=259) it was 0.218; for the middle range (IQ 74 to 114, n=1664) it was 0.327, and for the low IQ range (IQ 74 and below, n=106) the correlation was 0.419. The authors argue, correctly we believe, that a correlation as low as 0.08 between 559 gifted parents and 1027 offspring in Terman's study of the gifted, included in McAskie and Clarke's (1976) analysis, would be explained by truncation rather than by a lack of transmission of favourable genetic and environmental factors.

The effect of age on certain kinship correlations for IQ is illustrated by Wilson's (1983) study, which also highlights the related issue of heritability being to some extent age dependent. In a well-designed longitudinal study of a very large sample of MZ and DZ twins and their younger singleton siblings it has been shown that on age-appropriate tests of development very young MZ twins are not substantially different in concordance from DZ twins, but around the age of 18 months significantly greater concordance for MZ than DZ emerges, and heritability is seen to increase. By contrast DZ correlations reached a high point at 36 months, then progressively declined to an intermediate level by school age, ultimately reaching the level predicted by the polygenic model at 15 years of age, at which point in time the singleton/DZ twin correlations converged. (The WISC or WISC-R was used at ages 7, 8, 9 and 15.)

These factors are likely to have affected some of the individual correlations collated by Bouchard and McGue, but the paper is recommended for its careful and fair-minded weighing of evidence. The detailed findings are not incorporated into this chapter; instead, a few of the average correlations (in each case representing several studies and, with the exception of monozygotic twins reared apart, large samples) are presented. These are as follows: monozygotic twins reared together, 0.86; monozygotic twins reared apart, 0.72; dizygotic twins reared together, 0.60; siblings reared together, 0.47; siblings reared apart, 0.24; cousins, 0.15; adopting mid-parent–offspring, 0.24; biological mid-parent–mid-offspring, reared together, 0.72.

Among the important new data included in this review are two adoption studies by Scarr and Weinberg (1976, 1978, 1983), which deserve special albeit brief attention. The Transracial Adoption Study provided a very large amount of data on 101 white families who generally had children of their own but decided to adopt predominantly black or interracial infants. The hypothesis to be tested was that these children would perform as well on IQ and school achievement tests as white adoptees by virtue of being reared 'in the culture of the tests and the schools'. This was found to be the case, the interracial adoptees scoring above the national average, although below their adopted siblings.

The Adolescent Adoption Study was designed to assess the cumulative impact of differences among family environments at the end of the childrearing period. A total of 104 adoptive white families and 120 biological families, representing a wide range of parental occupations and educational status, was studied. In the case of the adopting families a criterion for inclusion was that there were at least two unrelated children adopted in early infancy in each. Once again a wealth of data was obtained concerning this large sample of families, ranging from working to upper-middle class, of particular importance since the adoptees were between 16 and 22 years, as were the offspring in the biological families. Furthermore, comparisons could be made across the two studies.

It was evident in both that parent–offspring correlations were higher for the biologically related than socially related, the results showing significant heritability for IQ. The adopted children's IQ scores were more closely correlated with the educational levels of their natural mothers than with the IQs of their adoptive mothers and fathers. The results of these large-scale new studies replicate the findings of earlier workers (Burks 1928; Leahy 1935) while providing evidence for changes in the pattern of sibling correlations as age increases. The young siblings in the transracial study were quite similar, whether genetically related or not; however, there was a zero correlation among the adolescent adopted siblings, strikingly different from the equivalent correlation in the biological families. The authors' interpretation of these results is that younger children are more influenced by differences among their family environments than older adolescents, who are freer to choose their own niches.

Many of the research articles published by Scarr and her colleagues, covering much wider territory than the two adoption studies, have been assembled in an important book, *Race, Social Class and Individual Differences in IQ* (Scarr 1981), together with critical evaluations by others. Here Scarr states (p.458):

> Going straight to the heart of the matter, I think that most evidence points to 'heritability' of about 0.4 to 0.7 in the US white population and 0.2 to 0.5 in the black, given that 'heritability' here means the proportion of genetic variance among individuals sampled in twin and family studies, which as I have repeatedly noted, are not representative of bad environments. If one could

include people with really poor environments, the proportion of environmental variance might rise; on the other hand, the genetic variance might also be increased. It is hard to predict whether or not the proportions of variance would change, and in which direction.

It is important to note here the small effects of environmental differences on IQ scores among the people in our white family samples. This suggests that within the range of 'humane environments', from an SES level of working to upper middle class, there is little evidence for differential environmental effects within the whole group. The average level of these environments is such that the black and white children reared by these families perform intellectually somewhat above the population average, even though they have average biological parents. Thus, the environments sampled in family studies are better than average at fostering intellectual development. But why are the relatively poor families rearing black and white *adopted* children whose IQ scores are nearly as high as those in professional families? It must be that all of these seeming environmental differences that predict so well to outcome differences among biological children are not primarily environmental differences, but indices of genetic differences among the parents and their biological offspring.

This statement serves as a summary of a consensus view on genetic factors influencing the development of intelligence and individual differences across a broad range of environments within an advanced society; implies a range of reaction within which the phenotype will be formed; and indicates certain limitations in our knowledge concerning those born and reared in disadvantaged environments. Before moving on to a discussion of the effects of depriving social conditions, a brief review will be presented of a few studies concerning the relatives of individuals identified as having low IQs or being administratively dealt with as handicapped.

Genetic factors in the families of contrasting types of subnormal persons

Much of this book is concerned with advances in our understanding of the effects of specific and in some cases identifiable single genes, and chromosomal abnormalities and the consequences of severe traumata or noxious substances before, during and after birth, each of which is likely to cause fairly severe (rather than mild) retardation. The results of numerous prevalence studies are in broad agreement that these catastrophes are fairly evenly distributed across social classes (see, for example, Birch *et al.* 1970) and account for a small proportion of pupils with learning problems, or mildly retarded children and adults with IQs not greatly below 70–75. More often than not these mentally handicapped persons have IQs below 50, although it should always be remembered that there can be no single point in the distribution of IQ which will yield clearly dichotomous populations. We have already seen that behavioural geneticists agree about the importance of the environment interacting with the genetic template as it becomes activated over time, and that in severely disadvantaged environments development may be considerably retarded. One of the predictions which follows from the polygenic model is that of intergenerational regression towards the mean, which will, however, be attenuated with assortative mating which in many human populations is rather high, correlations among mates averaging 0.4 to 0.6. By the same token there should be substantial regression among the siblings of a person retarded by reason of polygenic inheritance.

It should, therefore, be possible to identify by means of kinship data two populations among the mentally retarded, those whose retardation appeared to arise from a specifically identifiable (biomedical) cause and those whose retardation is the result in part at least of polygenic inheritance, representing the lowest end of the normal distribution of intelligence. A distinction between 'pathological' and 'subcultural' types of mental deficiency was made by Lewis (1933) and explored by Penrose (1939) and Fraser Roberts (1952) whose studies contrasted the siblings of children with very low IQs and those who were backward or mentally retarded with IQs above 50. The hypothesis stated that the siblings of severely retarded children (that is, persons with a presumed pathological condition) should be of approximately normal intelligence, while the siblings of the normal variants in intelligence, assumed to be extreme deviants in the same way as the intellectually brilliant, should 1. not be of average intelligence, but 2. on the whole be more intelligent than the identified person. Despite the handicap of poor intelligence tests and (in the case of Fraser Roberts) an attempt to fit the data within predetermined IQ limits (which was not altogether successful) the hypothesis, was, broadly speaking, confirmed, or at least not disconfirmed.

The ever-vigilant Kamin (1974) strongly criticized Jensen's (1969) reporting of the Roberts study, and in addition made a number of criticisms of his own which served to cast doubt upon the validity of the findings and their interpretation. It is thus important that the study has been replicated in a manner which takes account of most of the criticisms.

Johnson *et al.* (1976) used data reported by Reed and Reed (1965) in order to determine whether siblings and parents of persons of varying degrees of retardation differ systematically from each other. Reed and Reed traced the ancestors and descendants of 289 persons who were residents in an American colony for the mentally retarded some time between 1911 and 1918, resulting in information on 82,217 persons. The original probands were classified on the basis of contemporary clinical notes and other examinations into: 1. a primarily genetic category which included diagnosed genetic anomalies and children of consanguineous marriages; 2. probably genetic (cultural-familial); 3. environmental, i.e. the result of perinatal trauma or early illness severe enough to account for their retardation; and 4., the largest category of all, 123 probands with no definite physical anomalies, no evidence of early trauma and no familial history of mental defect.

For Johnson et al.'s purposes it was obviously necessary for an original proband to have an IQ score and also at least one sibling, which criteria eliminated 47 of them, leaving 242 probands who could be used for their analysis. These were divided into six categories of IQ (1–19, 20–29, 30–39, 40–49, 50–59 and 60–79, only one person being above 69 in the last category) and the number of dead, mentally retarded or normal (or of unknown ability) siblings recorded, the total being 1499. There was a highly significant relationship between the IQ level of the proband and the percentage of retarded siblings and their mean IQs. The mean IQ of the 106 retarded siblings of probands who themselves had IQ scores was 45.32. Siblings of probands in the 0–39 range were below this mean in 35 cases, above in 12. Siblings of probands in the 40+ range were below the mean eight times, above 51 times. A comparison of those siblings above and below the mean, by probands' ability levels, yielded a highly significant chi-square value while analysis of variance of the IQs of siblings in the six proband ability groups yielded a highly significant F value. Retarded persons lower in ability were less likely to have retarded siblings than probands of higher ability. However, if they did, these were less likely to be of lower ability than the retarded siblings of the more intelligent probands.

Parental occupational level significantly differentiated between the low- and high-ability retarded persons, as did their IQ scores (when available). Parents of the higher-level retarded persons were more likely themselves to be retarded than those of lower levels. Despite the statistical confirmation of the original hypothesis, the authors point out that the overlap between relatives of high- and low-level retarded persons was substantial, and that the 'clinical' and 'familial' groups are not as distinct as has sometimes been suggested.

Obtaining a statistically significant trend from these data is surely all that would have been possible, granted the nature of the original diagnostic system and proportion of probands of unknown origin. Moreover, it should again be emphasized that boundaries in nature are very seldom as distinct as the classifications we seek to impose on phenomena. Thus, in the unlikely event of obtaining new data conforming in every respect to agreed methodological criteria, there is every reason to suppose that categories would overlap. If such classification is to be maximally useful, it must seek minimal misclassification. Dichotomies, in particular, often polarize what are effectively adjacent and insignificantly different points on continua. Because of the complexity of aetiology and its environmental interactions, it is probable that subdividing criteria still further will better reflect reality than a simple dichotomous assessment.

It may well be that a tripartite classification into pathological, subcultural (polygenic factors interacting with social environmental adversity) and normal variants without social adversity would do less injustice if applied to new data. Even so, anomalies would remain; Birch *et al.* (1970), in their careful clinical and epidemiological study of a total child population, point to the probable amplifying effects on pathological retardation of poor social circumstances and the ameliorating effects of good conditions on a similar degree of central nervous system damage. An individual might descend into, or move out of, a psychometric or administrative classification of retardation as a result.

We have indicated that there is a considerable difference between administrative and 'IQ' prevalence. Thus in the Birch *et al.* study the administrative prevalence of subnormality was 1.26 per cent during childhood. The association of mild retardation with lower social class was amply confirmed, and related to a combination of large families, drawn from areas of poor housing where crowding was frequent. However, another group comprising 1.48 per cent of the population was identified psychometrically as having IQs below 75. It is our surmise that such children may have been drawn from less adverse conditions, therefore exhibiting fewer behavioural problems and thus no special need for identification; it seems more likely that their low IQs primarily reflected the operation of normal polygenic variation arising from parentage which was itself below average intellectually.

While we believe a tripartite classification of causes may be more helpful than a dichotomous one, it is also obvious that in individual cases a combination of influences is likely to be responsible for a given level of functioning.

Environmental disadvantage

It would be unwise to accept low heritability estimates as the sole, or even the most important, evidence for the effects of the physical and/or social environment in the absence of *direct* indicators. In a book addressed to problems of mental retardation, particular attention should be paid to studies showing the effects of environmental disadvantage, provided they are not readily amenable to alternative interpretations in terms of genetic covariates, or open to methodological criticism. It has been surprisingly difficult to identify many studies which meet these criteria; however, the following summaries should suffice to indicate the potential power of adverse environments upon development.

The first are case studies which demonstrate the devastating effects of severely depriving environments in producing mental retardation, and also the potentiality in some children at least for its reversal.

Kingsley Davis (1947) contrasted two children, both of whom suffered exceptionally abnormal rearing situations until the age of 6 and whose later outcome after rescue differed, one showing but little, and the other substantial improvement. Both were illegitimate children who had been kept in isolation; both were rachitic upon discovery, having been malnourished and sheltered from sunlight; both were unable to talk, in one case owing to total neglect, and in the other because she had been locked in an attic with her deaf-mute mother. This latter child, given the pseudonym Isabelle, had the advantage of an active rehabilitation programme undertaken by Mason (1942). Her wild, fearful behaviour improved and she rapidly learned to speak; her IQ trebled in a year and a half. At the age of 14 she had passed sixth grade in a public school and was apparently progressing normally.

More recently a very fully documented account has been given of severely deprived twin boys born in Czechoslovakia in 1960 (Koluchová 1972, 1976). Their mother died shortly after their birth, and they were placed in a children's home for a year. They then proceeded to the home of an aunt who kept them for six months. When they were 18 months old their father, a simple inarticulate man, married a psychopathic woman who had no feelings for young children yet took them into the home. They had reached the age of 7 before it was discovered that for most of the intervening period the boys had been kept isolated in a cellar, and had been cruelly treated and malnourished.

Experts who examined them found that they were severely rachitic and mentally handicapped. They could barely speak, they could hardly walk, were terrified of ordinary household objects and quite unable to recognize the meaning of pictures. It is not surprising that they were very emotionally disturbed. The twins were admitted to hospital for medical treatment after which they were placed in a children's home. Their physical and mental condition improved; they learned to walk, run, jump, ride a scooter and gradually to show less fear of strangers. During this time Dr Koluchová, a psychologist, was active in the supervision of the rehabilitation programme. The boys were placed in a school for the mentally retarded and simultaneously were fostered (and later adopted) by two unmarried sisters who had previously undertaken the care of children from deprived homes. They have provided the long-term security, stimulation and love which has ensured an entirely normal and happy outcome for the twins, who are now 24. Their progress in the school for the subnormal was rapid and they began to outstrip their classmates. In spite of the risk involved they were placed in a normal school where, of course, they were at first a long way behind their age peers in attainment.

With special coaching they were later able to skip a class at school while still leaving time for hobbies such as sport and piano playing. They loved reading and showed signs of technical talent, which is now helping them in the first stages of their careers. They are entirely normal socially and emotionally, and above average in intellectual competence. It is important to note, however, that when they were first discovered a number of experts considered that, in view of their terrible condition and the extraordinary way they had been treated, they had been damaged beyond hope of recovery.

Their IQs, which were about 40 when first discovered, rose to 80 and 72 (WISC Full Scale) at the age of 8 years 4 months; 95 and 93 at the age of 11; 100 and 101 at 14 and were said at the age of 20 to be in the range of 115 (Koluchová 1981, personal communication). Both are in further technical education, specializing in electronics; their social and emotional development as young adults is described as excellent.

Another case of early severe adversity has been reported by Angela Roberts, lately of Manchester University (Clarke 1982). She had spent a period in Bogota, Colombia, associated with a missionary orphanage which catered for a small group of abandoned illegitimate babies, or infants given up because their parents could not cope. The illegitimate were usually the babies of young teenage servants and were sometimes literally foundlings. One little boy, Adam, was abandoned at 4 months and first received into a reformatory for girls. Our colleague visited him there and described the conditions as appalling. His main diet was a watery vegetable soup and porridge, and he remained in a bleak, bare, windowless room in perpetual darkness, unless the door was open. On admission to the mission orphanage Adam, aged 16 months, weighed only 5.809 kg. He had the physical signs of nutritional marasmus, his head was infested, he had scabies, a fungal rash and numerous sores. Emotionally he was completely withdrawn; he could not sit, crawl or walk. His development appeared similar to that of a 3-month-old infant. A local doctor diagnosed him as an extremely malnourished, mentally retarded spastic. By the age of 23 months his weight was 10.433 kg, he could sit up from a prone position, could stand holding furniture, could imitate two words together and could feed himself with a spoon. A month later he could stand without support for a few seconds, and could walk around his cot holding on with one hand. At 26 months, ten months after admission, he weighed 11.794 kg, took his first independent steps, had improved emotionally and in other ways, and at 32 months was adopted by a North American family. There were, of course, problems; Adam was doubly incontinent and frequently bit his sister. However, by the age of 5 he was essentially average both mentally and physically. At the age of 8 years 8 months Adam was found to have a Full Scale WISC IQ of 113. His adopted sister from the same orphanage, who had also been clinically diagnosed as malnourished but had not experienced the same degree of deprivation, has at the age of 8 years 5 months an IQ of 102. Both children are doing well at school and neither has a serious emotional problem.

A further two cases of extreme early deprivation have been reported by Skuse (1984a). The sisters had been reared in infancy and early childhood by a microcephalic, mentally retarded and psychiatrically disturbed mother. Social services had asked a physician to visit when the children were aged 3.6 and 2.4 years respectively. He reported that they took no notice of anyone or anything except to scamper up and sniff strangers, grunting and snuffling like animals. Later a health visitor found them tied to the bed with leashes, partly because the mother insisted on keeping the flat spotlessly clean, and partly because she feared they might fall off the balcony.

The two children commenced playgroup attendance, the elder making tremendous strides and the younger little progress, her behaviour being decidedly odd. In her case, head circumference was below the third percentile, and she had a flattened occiput. There was partial bilateral syndactyly of the second and third toes and they lacked distal phalanges.

Nine months later assessments were carried out at 4 years 11 months and 3 years 9 months, respectively. The elder was well grown and lively, but still had practically no comprehensible language. Her social skills were at the 2½-year level. The younger was described as miserable, withdrawn and as smelling and mouthing objects. She avoided eye contact and rocked persistently when alone. Pica was a great problem, she slept poorly, wandering at night in search of food and showing no fear of the dark. By now the children had been taken into care in a children's home because of persistent maltreatment.

The elder girl made rapid progress in this institution and was ready to start school full time at 6 years. By then her social skills were only 9–15 months below age norms; physically she was at the 50th percentile. The younger child began to attend a special school for retarded children at age 5, but at 7½ her behaviour caused her to be sent to an autistic unit. Incidentally, an albino, severely retarded, autistic half-brother has been traced.

The elder girl has demonstrated a consistent trend towards recovery in virtually all aspects of cognitive functioning, emotional adjustment and social relationships. There remain some articulatory difficulties and relative social disinhibition but she is regarded as having excellent potential for normal development. She has been happy in her children's home for some nine years and continues to attend school.

The author suggests that the younger child is the subject of congenital vulnerability and supports our contention that grossly deprived children without such constraints have a good prognosis after removal from adversity. A second and equally useful paper (Skuse 1984b) reviews the whole field of severe deprivation in early childhood, offering a detailed analysis of six studies in an endeavour to elucidate what unusual experiences during childhood are sufficient and necessary for normal development. He also assesses the extent to which critical periods of development exist, and suggests what minimal compensatory influences are necessary to alleviate psychological handicaps arising from early adversity. He concludes that, in the absence of genetic or congenital anomalies, or a history of gross malnourishment, victims of such deprivation have an excellent prognosis, although some subtle deficits in social adjustment may persist. Most human characteristics, with the possible exception of language, are virtually resistant to obliteration even by the most dire early environments.

Case-histories such as these and others of a similar kind illustrate in a tragic but dramatic way the effect of physical and social deprivation on developing humans, together with later recovery granted special help and complete removal from the depriving circumstances. As we have critically evaluated Skeels's (1966) classic study elsewhere, we will therefore omit it here. The 'experimental group' provides case studies of the advantageous effects of late adoption for children who appeared to be subnormal in infancy.

The second category of studies concerns an important phenomenon known as cumulative deficit, and in this connection two research papers have been chosen for presentation here because of the involvement of A.R. Jensen, a hereditarian not known for his sympathy with environmental hypotheses. Cumulative deficit is intended to explain the increasing decrement in IQ relative to population norms as a function of age in groups considered environmentally deprived. According to the hypothesis the decrement is a result of the cumulative effects of environmental disadvantages on mental development.

Jensen (1974) provides a critical review of the literature, faulting the cross-sectional and longitudinal methods used by many of those investigating the tendency for some disadvantaged children to decrease in IQ across the years of schooling, a phenomenon first noticed by Gordon (1923) in England who recorded that among children brought up on canal boats, leading a nomadic existence with little or no schooling, the mean Binet IQ of the youngest child in the family was 90, of the second youngest 77, of the third youngest 73 and of the oldest 60.

To overcome the many methodological criticisms raised in connection with many of the published researches, Jensen proposed as the unit of measurement differences in standardized test scores between older and younger siblings, the older being expected to have lower scores. He found a small but significant decrement in verbal but not non-verbal IQ among black but not white schoolchildren in California, and concluded that cumulative deficit was not a problem in that state.

But in a large sample of black and white children in rural Georgia there was a substantial linear decrement in blacks between ages 5 and 16, of 1.62 verbal IQ points *per year* and 1.19 points of non-verbal. The overall IQ decreased 1.42 points per year, cumulatively 14 to 16 points over the whole time range. There was no similar effect in white children living in the same area. Jensen (1977) concluded that his findings demanded an environmental interpretation, at least in part. The loss in relative status which Jensen demonstrated among children from a particularly disadvantaged community could occur in certain families within a community, as suggested by Heber *et al.* (1968) who studied 586 children of 88 mothers from the same slum area, 40 of whom had IQs of 80 and above, while the remaining 48 had IQs of below 80. Cross-sectional testing within these families showed a marked disparity between the groups. Children from families with the more intelligent mothers showed a normal pattern of average IQs between 90 and 95; children of retarded mothers declined to an average of below 65 at age 14. The possibility of some genetic input into this sorry state of affairs does not, in the light of Jensen's more recent work, invalidate the conclusion that certain children are at risk for mental retardation by virtue of exceptionally disadvantaged environments.

Finally we present a study which amplifies the results of the few authentic researches concerning separated identical twins (Juel-Nielsen 1965; Newman *et al.* 1937; Shields 1962), despite the lack of immediate connection with mental retardation.

Schiff *et al.* (1978) employed an entirely novel method which could usefully be followed by others. They searched the files of six public adoption agencies in France to find children of two lower-class parents adopted early into upper-middle-class homes who also had a sibling or half-sibling reared by the biological mothers. There are some problems with the presentation of the data, which inspire caution in interpreting the findings. However, 32 adopted children were located, born to mothers and fathers who were unskilled workers; only 20 biological half-siblings were found, reared by their own mothers.

The 20 home-reared children of varying ages were reported as having average IQs of 94.5 and the 32 adoptees 110.6, while on another test the scores were 95.4 and 106.9, respectively. In terms of school attainment the authors state that the two groups were typical of their rearing environments. Certainly the home-reared children were very much more likely than their adopted siblings to have presented educational problems. Only four out of 32 adopted children had repeated a grade or been in a special class, whereas 13 out of 20 home-reared siblings had. A fuller version of this research project has been published (Schiff *et al.* 1982) giving a table of IQ scores for the 20 children reared by their natural mothers. WISC IQ data for 18 children and scores provided by the school on the remaining two reveal that three children were borderline retarded with IQs of 69, 71 and 78; the remainder lay between 86 and 111, seven having IQs over 100. Only six of the adopted children had WISC IQs below 100, the lowest being 81. It is pertinent to add that no child was offered for adoption who had been 'organically deficient at birth' (Schiff *et al.* 1982, p.182). However, SES-matched controls selected from the classmates of the adoptees had significantly higher average IQs (see also Dumaret 1985).

An extension of this project has been undertaken by one of Schiff's collaborators, Dumaret (1985). She made a detailed study of all the progeny of 28 mothers, one of whose children was adopted. These subjects were divided into three groups:

1. Children abandoned before the age of 1 month and placed for adoption before 7 months in a privileged social environment.

2. Children remaining with the mother or another member of the family and raised in a disadvantaged social environment.

3. Children abandoned, left or taken away from the family and raised in foster homes or children's homes.

The results – increases in IQ and diminution of scholastic failures for the adopted children, by contrast with the home- or institution-reared – show that the social environment has important effects. Adoption played a dynamic role, permitting these children to develop their intellectual resources thanks to a favourable social, cultural and familial environment. The difference between groups 1. and 2. was similar to the average difference between the corresponding social groups in the general population. The children reared in institutions appeared to be at a particular disadvantage, many being mentally retarded. Even in the case of those with IQs of 100 or above, educational problems were normal occurrences. The author's interpretation is that 'the effects of long-term emotional deprivation are superimposed on the effects of the social environment; the fate of these children is the combined result of these two effects'.

It is important to emphasize that Schiff et al.'s demonstration of an environmental effect on IQ and achievement differences between half-siblings reared in different social contexts does nothing to invalidate studies showing high heritability for intelligence. Rather, it adds to the limited evidence indicating in a direct way the effects of differing social environments, which are also indicated by adoptive studies and studies of identical twins reared together or apart, referred to earlier in this chapter. As McNemar (1938) commented in connection with Newman et al.'s sample of 19 pairs of monozygotic twins reared apart:

> it appears that the only evidence which approaches decisiveness is that for separated twins, and this rests ultimately upon the fact that four pairs reared in really different environments were undoubtedly different in intelligence. This fact can neither be ignored by the naturite nor deemed crucial by the nurturite.

The long-term outcomes of psychosocial intervention in early life designed to prevent mental retardation in children born into families 'at risk' have been examined elsewhere and will not be discussed here. Suffice it to say that there is no evidence that intervention confined to the preschool period among children who remain in their deprived families results in the maintenance of IQ increments through adolescence. Nevertheless, some gain in educational status from atypical programmes has been demonstrated. Jensen (1981), in a commentary on attempts to raise the IQ of disadvantaged children, has expressed the position as follows:

> Even with heritability in the range of 0.70 to 0.80, the magnitude of environmental effects can be considerable. With a standard deviation of 7.5 IQ points, for example, and assuming that existing environmental effects on IQ are normally distributed (for which there is good evidence), the total range of environmental influences would be about six σ, or 45 IQ points. Intervention that produces IQ changes within that range is not in the least incompatible with present estimates of the broad heritability of IQ.

> The real problem, however, has been in bringing the environmental influences on IQ under experimental control. Even though evidence on the genetic analysis of IQ leaves considerable latitude for nongenetic influences, psychologists have not yet discovered more than a fraction of the nongenetic factors that contribute to IQ variance or how they can be experimentally harnessed to raise IQ markedly and permanently. Although it may come as a surprise to many psychologists, at present, we know more about the genetics

of IQ than we know about environmental influences on IQ, except for extreme deprivations and traumas that are too rare to contribute importantly to the IQ variance of the general population. My hunch is that the nongenetic variance in IQ is the result of such a myriad of microenvironmental events as to make it extremely difficult, if not impossible, to bring more than a small fraction of these influences under experimental control. The results of all such attempts to date would seem to be consistent with this interpretation.

Similarly Plomin and DeFries (1980) commented:

> In fact, we know of no specific environmental influences nor combinations of them that account for as much as 10 per cent of the variance in IQ. For example, the longitudinal Collaborative Perinatal Project (Broman, Nichols and Kennedy 1975) reported correlations between prenatal/neonatal factors and 4-year-old IQ scores for over 26,000 children. Even at 4 years of age, all the prenatal and neonatal measures combined explain less than 4 per cent of the variance in IQ scores. Another example is the relationship between IQ and birth order/family size (Zajonc and Marcus 1975). Earlier born children and children in smaller families tend to have higher IQs on the average. However, birth order and family size account for less than 2 per cent of the variance of IQ in a population. (Grotevant, Scarr and Weinberg 1977)

With this perhaps slightly pessimistic statement in mind we turn now to a consideration of two environmental variables, each of which has been promoted in the context of a wide audience of professionals and the general public as depressing intellectual functioning and contributing to mental handicap.

Two potential hazards: malnutrition and exposure to lead

The first serious studies of malnutrition in relation to brain growth and mental development began in the 1960s. As many writers have indicated, unravelling the specific effects of malnutrition is exceedingly difficult for it exists in a web of other adversities which in combination are associated with backwardness and failure to thrive. Hence if it is found that children's development, and indeed their subsequent adult status, are below cultural norms, any one or more of these adversities could be either causally related or mere correlates. A masterly review of some of the problems has recently been provided by Richardson (1984) who draws attention to the climate of opinion which stimulated research in this field. First, 'the conceptual model underlying most of the research was that malnutrition caused damage to the central nervous system which was then reflected in intellectual impairment, and further that the brain's vulnerability was related to the speed of growth of the brain'. It had been shown by Dobbing (1964) that the main growth spurt occurred in the last trimester of pregnancy and during the first two years of postnatal life (Dobbing and Sands 1973). Richardson notes that this model, which focused on physical development, may have led to scant attention being paid to correlated social environmental factors and their effects. Moreover, he indicates that this theory was reinforced by the long-held belief, challenged by Clarke and Clarke (1976), that early development exercises a critically important influence on later development. He argues that because of the inadequacies of the experimental controls in many studies, the association between malnutrition and retarded intellectual development either could be a spurious one, or could represent one of many factors which together might be responsible.

Richardson summarizes and critically evaluates a wide range of evidence from many parts of the world, emphasizing the methodological problems connected with empirical research with humans in this field, concluding that it is 'still an open question of what forms of malnutrition under what conditions have long-term effects on impairing intellect and at present there is no clear evidence that such effects exist'.

The more recent research shows that malnutrition must be considered among an array of social and biological variables over time which influence intellectual development and, further, there is evidence that the effects of malnutrition can be overcome by later favourable experiences. It is now clear that primary prevention of malnutrition cannot be achieved by shipments of food but must attend to the social and economic needs of those who are impoverished.

Commenting on Richardson's chapter, an additional point has been made by Sartorius (1984), who regards research on the effects of malnutrition on mental development as unjustifiably in the centre of many research agendas. Malnutrition is a consequence of many factors and is thoroughly undesirable, regardless of its effects on mental development.

In a commentary upon Richardson's evaluation of the effects of malnutrition, Yule (1984) 'was struck by the parallels in conceptual and methodological problems facing research into supposed effects of malnutrition with that into the supposed effects of lead on development'. Both sets of researches began with a reasonable but simple hypothesis. A lot of malnutrition or lead ingestion is clearly harmful; can a bit less do a bit less harm? The issues surrounding this question are, as indicated, much more complex than perhaps they sound. For example, the alleged central nervous system impairment is difficult to test, social factors are difficult to measure and to control, and:

sloppy concepts of 'subclinical' effects obscured the issues. Pressure groups and politicians quickly took 'sides' making rational discussion even more difficult... Some of the studies underline the basic resilience of human infants. Others underline the wide individual differences which are the essence of our humanness. All point to the complex interactions between children and their effective social environments.

Rutter (1980) has provided a careful and comprehensive account of research into raised lead levels as it relates to cognitive and social-behavioural functioning, which stresses the methodological problems often overlooked or ignored by researchers in this area. These include biased samples, problems in reliably determining the body lead burden, difficulties in the assessment of psychological and behavioural impairment, inadequate statistical control for the possible confounding effects of other variables (particularly genetic factors and social disadvantage), and small sample sizes. He concluded that clinic-type studies of children with high lead levels provide good evidence that blood lead levels persistently raised above 60 µg/100 ml are probably associated with an average reduction of some 3 to 4 IQ points, even in asymptomatic children. The more difficult issue is how far there may be cognitive impairment with blood lead levels in the 20 to 40 µg/100 ml range. Rutter cautiously concluded that, although the findings are somewhat contradictory, the evidence suggests that persistently raised blood lead levels in the range above 40 µg/100 ml may cause cognitive impairment (a reduction of 1 to 5 IQ points on average) and less certainly may increase the risk of behavioural difficulties.

The use of shed deciduous teeth to examine the body lead burden appears to be a more reliable method than blood levels, a method pioneered by Needleman and colleagues (1972, 1974, 1979), who showed that children with high levels of dentine lead scored significantly below children with low dentine lead on the WISC-R, and that lead level was correlated with teachers' ratings of classroom behaviour.

Yule (1984) reported that his own pilot study tended to parallel Needleman's results, but that studies by Winneke and colleagues in Germany and by Smith in England both indicated that when social factors were statistically controlled the effect was statistically non-significant (see Smith 1983; Winneke 1983). Two important additional points were made by Yule. First, that where the data are reported it is generally noted that the relationship between lead and IQ is stronger in working-class than in middle-class groups; in one of his most recent studies in a predominantly middle-class area no relationship could be found with either IQ or teachers' behaviour ratings. Second, Yule argues that an overall average difference of only 2 to 5 IQ points has considerable implications for the prevalence of mild handicap, since a significant increase in children with IQs below 70 would be expected.

Conclusions

Recent twin and adoption studies have confirmed earlier findings of the high heritability of intelligence in a wide range of environments which, however, usually exclude disadvantaged minority groups. It is, furthermore, increasingly evident that the genetic programme unfolds over time. If it is conceded that a proportion of the between-family variance is accounted for by genetic–environmental interaction within families, then it must follow that children with relatively poor heredity for intelligence may have the additional disadvantage of being reared in suboptimal environments. If the social environment is important, a proposition accepted by all behaviour geneticists, then these children must rely on chance events or the chance effects of intergenerational regression to the mean as a way out of the cycle of disadvantage, unless they are provided with superior rearing environments. In some areas of extreme disadvantage cumulative deficit may occur.

Consideration of the evidence leads to the likelihood of complex multifactorial origins of mental retardation in an unknown, albeit probably relatively small, proportion of an advanced nation's population. The demonstration of genetic factors as an important determinant in individual differences in IQ in the general population leads to the assumption that on occasion these will be the major cause of mild mental retardation in children reared in circumstances which cannot be considered disadvantageous, while many who might in other environmental contexts become victims are, in fact, protected.

Some genetic contributions in families subject to social disadvantage place a group of children at risk during the developmental period. The risk becomes exacerbated if there is in addition a lack of consistent intellectual stimulation, parental cruelty or chronic neglect, chaotic social relationships, poor nutrition, exposure to pollution, infections and irregular attendance at school, or combinations of some of these.

No planned intervention study to date has succeeded in substantially and permanently raising the IQ and scholastic achievement of children at risk for mental retardation. There are as yet no satisfactory research findings concerning outcomes for children of this kind were they to be adopted into advantaged homes. However, case studies exist, some reviewed in this chapter, of children who had exhibited mental retardation following exceptional environmental adversity, attaining normal development upon removal.

The study by Schiff *et al.* (1978, 1982), although not of children identified as being at risk for retardation, is at least suggestive of what might happen if the 'myriad of microenvironmental events' so eloquently expressed by Jensen (1981) were positive rather than negative. It will, however, be recalled that the lower-class social environment in which the children were reared was not sufficient to render them mentally retarded, although many had been retained in grade (repeating a school year) or received special educational provision.

Nor is it likely that adoption into high-status families offers a viable solution to the problem of so-called 'subcultural subnormality' in a free society. Consideration of life-span development of mildly retarded persons, who have been administratively identified as in need of special services as children, suggests that the outcome for them as adults is not seriously disadvantageous compared with peers who have never been identified. It should, perhaps, also be borne in mind that in any society, perhaps particularly those which increasingly rely on complex cognitive skills, there will always be those whose individual qualities appear less adequate than others'. Until a more humane social organization evolves, these persons may experience discrimination. Although schools cannot compensate for society, it seems likely to this author that some educational establishments are already protecting pupils from the worst consequences of social disadvantage, and that others could be enabled to do more. There is increasing evidence, some of it summarized by Rutter (1983), that teachers, preferably working in partnership with parents, can offer children at risk for developmental retardation substantial support both cognitively and socially. Perhaps compensatory education across the years of schooling need not necessarily fail.

References

Birch, H.G., Richardson, S.A., Baird, D., Horobin, G. and Illsley, R. (1970) *Mental Subnormality in the Community: A Clinical and Epidemiologic Study.* Baltimore, Md: Williams & Wilkins.

Bouchard Jr, T.J. and McGue, M. (1981) 'Familial studies of intelligence: a review.' *Science, 212,* 1055–1059.

Broman, S.H., Nichols, P.L. and Kennedy, W.A. (1975) *Preschool IQ: Prenatal and Early Developmental Correlates.* Hillsdale, NJ: Lawrence Erlbaum.

Burks, B. (1928) 'The relative influence of nature and nurture upon mental development: a comparative study of foster parent/foster child resemblance and true parent/true child resemblance.' *Yearbook of the National Society of the Study of Education,* part 1, 27, 219–316.

Clarke, A.M. (1982) 'Developmental discontinuities: an approach to assessing their nature.' In L.A. Bond and J.M. Joffe (eds) *Facilitating Infant and Early Child Development*. Hanover, NH: University Press of New England, 58–77.

Clarke, A.M. and Clarke, A.D.B. (eds) (1976) *Early Experience: Myth and Evidence*. London: Open Books; New York: The Free Press.

Clarke, A.M. and Clarke, A.D.B. (1980) 'Comments on Professor Hearnshaw's "Balance Sheet on Burt".' In H. Beloff (ed), *A Balance Sheet on Burt: Supplement to the Bulletin of the BPS 33*, 17–19.

Davis, K. (1947) 'Final note on a case of extreme isolation.' *American Journal of Sociology 52*, 432–437.

Dobbing, J. (1964) 'The influence of early nutrition on the development and myelination of the brain.' *Proceedings of the Royal Society 159*, 503–509.

Dobbing, J. and Sands, J. (1973) 'Quantitative growth and development of the human brain.' *Archives of Disease in Childhood 48*, 757–767.

Dumaret, A. (1985) 'IQ, scholastic performance and behaviour of sibs raised in contrasting environments.' *Journal of Child Psychology and Psychiatry 26*, 553–580.

Erlenmeyer-Kimling, L. and Jarvik, L.F. (1963) 'Genetics and intelligence: a review.' *Science 142*, 1477–1479.

Gillie, O. (1976) 'Crucial data faked by eminent psychologist.' *Sunday Times*, London, 24 October.

Gordon, H. (1923) *Mental and Scholastic Tests among Retarded Children* (Education Pamphlet 44, Board of Education, London). London: HMSO.

Grotevant, H.D., Scarr, S. and Weinberg, R.A. (1977) 'Intellectual development in family constellations with adopted and natural children: a test of the Zajonc and Marcus model.' *Child Development 48*, 1699–1703.

Hearnshaw, L.S. (1979) *Cyril Burt: Psychologist*. London: Hodder and Stoughton.

Hebb, D.O. (1949) Organization of Behaviour, New York, Wiley.

Heber, R., Dever, R. and Conry, J. (1968) 'The influence of environmental and genetic variables on intellectual development.' in H.J. Prehm, L.A. Hamerlynck and J.E. Crosson (eds) *Behavioral Research in Mental Retardation*. Eugene, Oreg: University of Oregon, 1–22.

Jensen, A.R. (1969) 'How much can we boost IQ and scholastic achievement?' *Harvard Educational Review 39*, 1–123.

Jensen, A.R. (1974) 'Cumulative deficit: a testable hypothesis?' *Developmental Psychology 10*, 996–1019.

Jensen, A.R. (1977) 'Cumulative deficit in IQ of blacks in the rural south.' *Developmental Psychology 13*, 184–191.

Jensen, A.R. (1981) 'Raising the IQ: the Ramey and Haskins Study.' *Intelligence 5*, 29–40.

Johnson, C.A., Ahern, F.M. and Johnson, R.C. (1976) 'Level of functioning of siblings and parents of probands of varying degrees of retardation.' *Behaviour Genetics 6*, 473–477.

Juel-Nielsen, N. (1965) 'Individual and environment: a psychiatric-psychological investigation of monozygotic twins reared apart.' *Acta Psychiatrica Scandinavica 30*, 325–332.

Kamin, L.J. (1974) *The Science and Politics of IQ.* Hillsdale, NJ: Lawrence Erlbaum.

Koluchová, J. (1972) 'Severe deprivation in twins: a case study.' *Journal of Child Psychology and Psychiatry 13*, 107–114.

Koluchová, J. (1976) 'A report on the further development of twins after severe and prolonged deprivation.' In A.M. Clarke and A.D.B. Clarke (eds) *Early Experience: Myth and Evidence.* London: Open Books; New York: The Free Press, 56–66.

Leahy, A.M. (1935) 'Nature–nurture and intelligence.' *Genetic Psychology Monographs 17*, 241–305.

Lewis, E.O. (1933) 'Types of mental deficiency and their social significance.' *Journal of Mental Science 79*, 298–304.

Mason, M. (1942) 'Learning to speak after six and one half years of silence.' *Journal of Speech Disorder 7*, 295–304.

McAskie, M. and Clarke, A.M. (1976) 'Parent–offspring resemblances in intelligence: theories and evidence.' *British Journal of Psychology 67*, 243–273.

McNemar, Q. (1938) 'Newman, Freeman and Holzinger's Twins: a study of heredity and environment.' *Psychological Bulletin 35*, 237–249.

Needleman, H.L., Davidson, I., Sewell, E.M. and Shapiro, I.M. (1974) 'Subclinical lead exposure in Philadelphia schoolchildren: identification by dentine lead analysis.' *New England Journal of Medicine 290*, 245–248.

Needleman, H.L., Gunnoe, C., Leviton, A., Reed, R., Peresie, H., Maher, C. and Barrett, P. (1979) 'Deficits in psychologic and classroom performance of children with elevated dentine lead levels.' *New England Journal of Medicine 300*, 689 695.

Needleman, H.L., Tuncay, O.C. and Shapiro, I.M. (1972) 'Lead levels in deciduous teeth of urban and suburban American children.' *Nature 235*, 111–112.

Newman, H.H., Freeman, F.M. and Holzinger, K.J. (1937) *Twins: A Study of Heredity and Environment.* Chicago: University of Chicago Press.

Penrose, L.S. (1939) 'Intelligence test scores of mentally defective patients and their relatives.' *British Journal of Psychology 30*, 1–18.

Plomin, R. and Defries, J.C. (1980) 'Genetics and intelligence: recent data.' *Intelligence 4*, 15–24.

Plomin, R., Defries, J.C. and McClearn, G.E. (1980) *Behavioral Genetics: A Primer.* San Francisco: Freeman.

Reed, E.W. and Reed, S.C. (1965) *Mental Retardation: A Family Study.* Philadelphia and London: Saunders.

Reed, S.C. and Rich, S.S. (1982) 'Parent/offspring correlations and regression for IQ.' *Behaviour Genetics 12*, 535–542.

Richardson, S.A. (1984) 'The consequences of malnutrition for intellectual development.' In J. Dobbing, A.D.B. Clarke, J. Corbett, J. Hogg and R.O. Robinson (eds) *Scientific Studies in Mental Retardation.* London: Macmillan.

Roberts, J.A. Fraser (1952) 'The genetics of mental deficiency.' *Eugenics Review 44,* 71–83.

Rutter, M. (1980) 'Raised lead levels and impaired cognitive behavioural functioning: a review of the evidence.' *Developmental Medicine and Child Neurology 22,* Suppl. 42.

Rutter, M. (1983) 'School effects on pupil progress: research findings and policy implications.' *Child Development 54,* 1–29.

Sartorius, N. (1984) 'Critique of "The consequences of malnutrition for intellectual development" by S.A. Richardson.' In J. Dobbing, A.D.B. Clarke, J. Corbett, J. Hogg and R.O. Robinson (eds) *Scientific Studies in Mental Retardation.* London: Macmillan.

Scarr, S. (1981) *Race, Social Class and Individual Differences in IQ.* Hillsdale, NJ: Lawrence Erlbaum.

Scarr, S. and Weinberg, R.A. (1976) 'IQ test performance of black children adopted by white families.' *American Psychologist 31,* 726–739.

Scarr, S. and Weinberg, R.A. (1978) 'The influence of "family background" on intellectual attainment.' *American Sociological Review 43,* 674–692.

Scarr, S. and Weinberg, R.A. (1983) 'The Minnesota Adoption Studies: genetic differences and malleability.' *Child Development 54,* 260–267.

Schiff, M., Duyme, M., Dumaret, A., Stewart, J., Tomkiewicz, S. and Feingold, J. (1978) 'Intellectual status of working-class children adopted early into upper-middle-class families.' *Science 200,* 1503–1504.

Schiff, M., Duyme, M., Dumaret, A. and Tomkiewicz, S. (1982) 'How much *could* we boost scholastic achievement and IQ scores? A direct answer from a French adoption study.' *Cognition 12,* 165–196.

Shields, J. (1962) *Monozygotic Twins Brought Up Apart and Brought Up Together.* London: Oxford University Press.

Skeels, H.M. (1966) 'Adult status of children with contrasting early life experiences.' *Monographs of the Society for Research in Child Development 31,* 3, no. 105.

Skuse, D. (1984a) 'Extreme deprivation in early childhood: I. Diverse outcomes for three siblings from an extraordinary family.' *Journal of Child Psychology and Psychiatry 25,* 523–541.

Skuse, D. (1984b) 'Extreme deprivation in early childhood: II. Theoretical issues and a comparative review.' *Journal of Child Psychology and Psychiatry 25,* 543–572.

Smith, M. (1983) 'Lead, intelligence and behaviour', paper presented to Association for Child Psychology and Psychiatry, London, January.

Vandenberg, S. (1971) 'What do we know today about the inheritance of intelligence and how do we know it?' In R.C. Cancro (ed) *Intelligence*. New York: Grune & Stratton, 182–218.

Watson, J.B. (1930) *Behaviorism*. Chicago: University of Chicago Press.

Wilson, R.S. (1983) 'The Louisville Twin Study: developmental synchronies in behavior.' *Child Development 54*, 298–316.

Winneke, G. (1983) 'Neurobehavioural and neuropsychological effects of lead.' In M. Rutter and R. Russell Jones (eds) *Lead versus Health: Sources and Effects of Low Level Lead Exposure*. Chichester: Wiley.

Yule, W. (1984) 'Critique of "Exposure to lead as an environmental factor in mental retardation" by H.A. Waldron.' In J. Dobbing, A.D.B. Clarke, J. Corbett, J. Hogg and R.O. Robinson (eds) *Scientific Studies in Mental Retardation*. London: Macmillan.

Zajonc, R.B. and Marcus, G.B. (1975) 'Birth order and intellectual development.' *Psychological Review 82*, 74–88.

Zigler, E. (1968) 'The nature–nurture issue reconsidered.' In H.C. Haywood (ed) *Social-Cultural Aspects of Mental Retardation*. New York: Appleton-Century-Crofts, 81–106.

CHAPTER 14

Parent–Offspring Resemblances in Intelligence
Theories and Evidence

Commentary

This article presents a facet of the very extensive literature on the hereditary and environmental basis of IQ test results. Parent–offspring correlations have been studied over several decades, as part of the large and complex question of heritability, but this paper represented the first attempt to collate all studies which included data on the natural parent–offspring resemblances in intelligence. Criteria for inclusion were that intelligence tests were given to both parents and offspring, reasonably appropriate statistical analysis carried out and that the populations were not grossly abnormal. Seventeen studies between 1928 and 1974 were included; seven were rejected, including that by Cyril Burt (1961) which demonstrated so many anomalies that there was no possibility of using the data in conjunction with the others. Detailed investigation of this and other research articles on the same topic led us seriously to question its validity (see Chapter 15).

One of the strengths of this analysis was its indication that very different statistical methods and very different research data were relevant to conclusions. For example, the degree of assortative mating (like marries like) or mid-parent IQ versus single parent IQ materially affected the findings. So the type of sample studied was hugely relevant to outcome. This diversity and heterogeneity of population made it impossible to conclude with any confidence that one particular investigation was more representative of hypothetical 'general population' than another. Thus the question was raised whether such a concept has any useful meaning with respect to genetic and environmental components in IQ variation. The discussion concerns the problems encountered in the analysis.

Readers uncomfortable with statistical analysis as used in this most technical chapter may wish to read the introduction and the first two paragraphs of the Discussion to get a flavour of the field. Alternatively, they may wish to skip this contribution and move on to the more exciting 'Burt Affair'.

Parent–Offspring Resemblances in Intelligence: Theories and Evidence[*]

Michael MacAskie and Ann M. Clarke

A review of data on parent–offspring resemblances in intelligence is presented in the context of correlation, regression and variance predictions from the polygenic model and an environmental model. Consideration was given to reliability, test equivalence and long-term stability of IQ scores. Results indicate that much of the difference among offspring IQ scores is not directly attributable to parental IQ, and that some is due to other between-family variables. The magnitude of single-parent–offspring correlations was related to the degree of assortative mating present in samples. Evidence on whether parent–offspring resemblances in IQ are transmitted genetically or environmentally is on the whole lacking. A single study provides evidence for some degree of genetic transmission, but it is argued that the present polygenic model is inadequate.

The problem of the contribution of heredity and environment to differences in intelligence is obviously not reducible to a single question. It is made up of a number of issues (e.g. wide and narrow heritability),[1] each of which may be investigated in a variety of ways. Thus a proper understanding of such a broad topic cannot be achieved in a single study of one aspect; an integration of evidence from numerous sources is required. However, the value of such an integration will depend crucially upon the soundness of each component contributing to it.

Several wide surveys have been published (e.g. Erlenmeyer-Kimling and Jarvik 1963; Eysenck 1973; Herrnstein 1973; Jencks 1973; Jensen 1969), but if any of these reviewers' assessments prove correct (which they might), it will certainly not be due to the care with which they have handled the evidence.

[*] This article first appeared in 1976 in the *British Journal of Psychology* 67, 2, pp.243–273.

Even Jencks's most sophisticated attempt failed to match an elaborate mathematical analysis with a commensurate attention to the nature of the data.

This article is concerned with a detailed consideration of a small portion of the evidence: studies of parent–offspring resemblances in intelligence. Even within this narrow area, there are a number of ways of looking at the data. First, the notion of resemblances can be interpreted as meaning either resemblance in actual performance or resemblance in relative level of performance with respect to an age group. For intelligence, the former requires a direct comparison between the performance of parents and offspring at the same age on the same test. Most studies use the latter method, the comparison being based on measures derived from performances on different sets of items at different ages. Unfortunately, psychological theories underlying test construction are inadequate to treat resemblance in type as meaningful. For example, the vagaries of item construction have led to the inclusion of different types of problem for young children and adults, despite the use of similar item analysis procedures. In these circumstances comparison is valid only to the extent that performance at one point in time relates significantly to performance at another. Thus the questions of correlations among tests and the predictive validity of IQ scores must be considered.

Second, resemblances can be analysed by different statistical methods. Direct predictions can be made by regression equations and the extent to which such predictions are in error may be assessed by correlations. A correlation coefficient, of course, gives only an average error value and reveals nothing about the way in which errors are distributed. To determine this another kind of analysis may be needed. Whichever method is used, theoretical predictions can be made both for single-parent–offspring resemblance and for mid-parent–offspring resemblance. In addition, total population forecasts can be made.

In the following discussion of theoretical predictions, the assumption is made initially that differences in intelligence are due entirely to genetic factors or entirely to the environment. The fact that such positions are rarely, if ever, adopted does not vitiate the utility of considering their potential outcome.

Genetic predictions

The genetic predictions which have been made concerning parent–offspring resemblances have been entirely based on a simple additive polygenic model. On the whole the correlational predictions from this model are well understood; those for regression have occasioned some confusion, while those for variances have scarcely been contemplated. The failure to consider the latter predictions which are both easy to make and to test, represents a major fault in assessing adequately the predictions of the polygenic model. In view of psychologists' keen attention to sampling problems in other contexts, this appears to be a strange inconsistency.

Correlation predictions

The correlational predictions are well known, mathematically correct and require no explication. With random mating the single-parent–offspring correlation is 0.5 and the mid-parent-offspring correlation is 0.7071. Despite this disparity, the two have been confused: thus, Erlenmeyer-Kimling and Jarvik (1963) include both single-parent– and mid-parent–offspring correlations in the same line of their well-known graph.

Assortative mating will increase both of these, with the single-parent correlation becoming closer to the mid-parent correlation as the degree of assortative mating increases. A problem in considering the effects of assortative mating on correlations (and on variance) is that they are cumulative over a number of generations (see Stanton 1946). This is particularly pertinent to the genetics of intelligence where assortative mating is probably higher than for other characteristics.

Dominance will reduce the correlations, but since there is neither adequate empirical evidence, nor any theoretical reason, for assuming a particular degree of dominance, no meaningful predictions can be made. This lack of specificity has, however, been put to good use in accounting for anomalies in obtained results.

Regression predictions

The predictions concerning regression are somewhat less well understood than those concerning correlations. First, the relationship between correlation and regression does not seem to be fully appreciated, and second, single-parent and mid-parent relationships have again been confused (see Eckland 1967; Eysenck 1973; Herrnstein 1973; Jensen 1973, for examples). The confusion may have been helped by the lack of separate linguistic forms for referring to a parent taken singly and parents taken in pairs: the phrase 'relationship between parents and children' is totally ambiguous.

With random mating, single-parent–offspring regression will be 0.5 (i.e. regression to the mean), decreasing to zero as assortative mating increases to 100 per cent. *There is no regression from mid-parent IQ on the polygenic model.* The fact that the mid-parent-offspring correlation is less than unity (e.g. 0.7071) does not entail regression to the mean. Regression, in the usual sense of the word, is normally equal to 1 minus the regression coefficient from the regression equation. To deduce a regression coefficient from a correlation coefficient one must take into account the relative variance of the two variables [$y = r$ $(\sigma y/\sigma x)x$] and it happens that the variance ratio effect exactly cancels the correlational effect for mid-parent–child regression (e. g. when $r = 0.7071$, $\sigma x = 0.7071\ \sigma y$, since mid-parent variance = half parent variance, and parent variance = offspring variance).

Variance predictions

Predictions can be made both about the pattern of variance of offspring IQ across different levels of parental IQ and also the total variance of the offspring compared with the total variance of the parents.

For mid-parent–offspring IQ the pattern prediction is dramatic. The variability of the progeny will be maximal when the mid-parent IQ is average and will be minimal (= 0) when the mid-parent IQ is extreme (high or low). Pairs of extreme parents will, of course, both be entirely isozygous[2] for high or low genes, a condition which can only lead to zero variance in the progeny. With random mating the single-parent–child variance will also decrease towards the extremes though to only half the maximum value (instead of zero as in the mid-parent case). With progressively greater degrees of assortative mating the single-parent pattern will increasingly resemble the mid-parent pattern.

The total variance of parents and offspring will be the same under random mating, but with assortative mating this will increase from generation to generation. The shape of the distribution will also change from normal to bimodal under assortative mating.

Environmental predictions

Before environmental predictions can be made an environmental model must be found, and this is not easy since most psychologists have been too canny to be explicit on the matter. However, implicit in studies of environmental effects there appears to be a simple additive vector model. It thus seems reasonable to see what the predictions of such a model might be for parent–offspring resemblances. This model of how the environment might operate is not one to which the authors subscribe. It is specific to two-parent families, and may not generalize to either single-parent or multiple-rearing conditions. The formulation was forced upon us by the total absence of any model, coupled with numerous vague and often potentially contradictory statements in the literature concerning parental environmental effects. It may, however, have value in indicating the direction in which reformulation may be necessary.

Correlational predictions

If one were to assume that the environment produced by parental intelligence is the only relevant variable, that the effective contribution of each parent is equal to half his or her intelligence, and the contribution of both is the simple sum of the two, then, with random mating, the single-parent–offspring correlation would be 0.7071, and the mid-parent–offspring correlation, unity. Assortative mating would, of course, increase the former. These rather high correlations can easily be reduced to fit results by denying that parental intelligence is the only environmental variable, and attributing decreases to other factors incompletely correlated with parent intelligence.

Perhaps more realistically, the model can be adapted to make differential predictions concerning parent and/or offspring sex. Thus an 'exposure' model would predict mother–offspring correlations higher than father–offspring, assuming that mothers spend more time with children; an 'identification' model would predict mother–daughter or father–son correlations higher than mother–son or father–daughter. Neither of these patterns can be predicted on a sex-linked genetic hypothesis.

Differential predictions could also be made in relation to the period in which the environment is presumed to operate, *provided changes of environment are involved*. Since no study reported in this review concerns such changes, there is little point in considering the predictions.

However, it may be pertinent to observe that if an environmental variable operates cumulatively over time, correlations with it will not necessarily increase with age. Thus Jensen's (1974a) rejection of a cumulative environmental effect on the basis of failure of correlations to increase is invalid, since the particular context considered involved no change.

The same point applies to Bloom's (1964) conclusion that the first few years of life are environmentally critical since the longitudinal correlations change little thereafter. Furthermore, by contrast, genetic models can predict correlational changes with age, for while the genetic material is implanted at conception, it can become effective at any age, as in the case of hereditary diseases of late onset.

Regression predictions

Assuming parent intelligence as the only environmental variable, and that mating is random, single-parent–offspring regression half way to the mean would be predicted (the same amount, as with the genetic model). On an environmental model regression will decrease as assortative mating increases, and increase to the extent that the other variables, which determine the offspring's intelligence, are not entirely correlated with parent IQ.

The question of mid-parent–offspring regression is of particular interest since it has been fallaciously assumed that such an effect could only be accounted for by genetic influences. It has already been stated that the polygenic model predicts no regression from mid-parent; this fact is, however, frequently overlooked. Eysenck (1973) provides one example: in his collation of confusions about regression there is a genetic prediction using a formula in which the regression produced is actually determined by *what is not inherited*: Child IQ = Population mean + Heritability × (Mid-parent IQ – Population mean). In this case regression = 1 – Heritability. 'Heritability' is not equivalent to a genetic explanation, but merely states the extent of a genetic contribution. A total genetic explanation requires Heritability = 1; anything less than unity entails an environmental (including error) component. It is this *latter* factor which produces regression in the formula.

On the implausible assumption that parent intelligence is the only relevant environmental variable, the prediction concerning mid-parent–offspring regression is the same as that for the 'polygenic' model: none. Mid-parent–child regression, if it occurs, thus constitutes evidence against both models.

Variance predictions

The major issue concerning the variance pattern, in view of the somewhat surprising genetic predictions, is the distribution for different levels of mid-parent IQ. Any differences concerning single-parent–offspring patterns will be diluted versions of the mid-parent contrasts.

If parent IQ were the only relevant variable, then the offspring variance for different levels of mid-parent would be uniformly zero. If not, then the pattern of variance will depend on the distribution of other environmental variables with respect to mid-parental level. In the absence of any specifically expected non-regularities in the relative distribution of these, it may perhaps be supposed that they are evenly distributed. This 'in ignorance' model would then predict uniformity of distribution of offspring variance at each mid-parental level, whereas the polygenic model does not.

The implications of an additive environmental model for total population variance are theoretically interesting. Starting with the unlikely assumptions of random mating, exclusive influence of parent intelligence and equal parental contribution (amounting in deviation terms to half each parent's deviation from the mean) we find that the offspring population variance will be halved each generation. (Child variance will equal mid-parent variance, since child IQ = mid-parent IQ, and, with random mating, mid-parent variance will be half the single-parent variance.) Assortative mating will reduce the effect, but only if this were perfect could the variance remain constant across generations. Variance reduction will also be less if environmental variables other than parent intelligence are operative.

There are only two ways to avoid an intergenerational variance reduction: either by postulating egression or by adding a variance-producing moderator variable. The first alternative would mean that the offspring IQ would exceed mid-parent IQ for bright parents and fail to reach it in the case of dull parents. Since empirically this is not the case, the second alternative becomes mandatory.

By a moderator variable we mean one which alters the effect of another without itself having any direct influence, and which also varies independently of the variable it modifies. The genetic model has, of course, such a 'variable' in the random segregation of parental genes. On this model only half of the total child variance is directly attributable to parental phenotype (predicted mid-parent–child correlation = 0.7071), the other half being due to the chance or capricious combination of genes. If a moderator were identifiable it would be correlated with outcome in the same way as an ordinary variable. The difference is that a moderator's effect depends in some way upon the values of the moderated variable. With a simple multiplicative relationship between the two, the contribution of the moderator variable would fall to zero when the variance of the moderated variable were also zero. By contrast the proportional contribution to variance of an independent variable would increase as the moderated variable variance decreased.

If moderator variables have to be introduced to maintain variance, their presence will also affect correlations, since the moderator variance contribution will constitute an error in the context of assessing the effect of the moderated variable.

Combining genetic and environmental models

Most psychologists are agreed that intellectual differences are not solely the product of either heredity or of environment, but of both. There would also appear to be substantial agreement that these two factors do not combine in a simple additive way: some kind of interaction is involved, though no one has as yet expressed precisely the nature of this interaction. It is for want of any properly formulated alternative that we have little choice but to consider the possibility of predictions based on an additive model in which only the proportions may vary. It is, of course, entirely possible that a collective judgement based on all these unspecified ways of interacting might in the end be additive.

The latitude present within each of the very simple models already outlined was sufficient to make it impossible to arrive at very much in the way of firm predictions. Plausible 'adjustments' of one kind or another could easily be made within either model. With these various latitudes now occurring in combination, perhaps the most precise prediction to be made is that the possibilities for 'adjustment' now become even greater.

Even on the assumption of an additive combination of genetic and environmental factors, few predictions are possible concerning the effect of different proportions of each; an obvious exception is the case of foster studies. When the problems arising from errors of measurement (as yet to be discussed) are added to these uncertainties, resolutions are even more difficult. In the circumstances one can do little other than suggest whether results fit better or worse one or other model.

For correlations, the restrictions resulting from the introduction of moderator variables make the environmental predictions very similar to their genetic counterparts in most cases. Clear distinctions only occur for the sex-related

Table 14.1 Test reliabilities		
Test	*Reliability coefficients*	*Average*
Alpha	0.94, 0.95, 0.90, 0.87, 0.91, 0.92, 0.98	0.93
Binet	0.83, 0.91, 0.91–0.97, 0.95–0.98	0.93
Cattell	0.80, 0.70s, 0.95	0.82
Otis	0.81, 0.96, 0.95, 0.87, 0.88, 0.93, 0.79	0.88
Raven's Matrices	0.79, 0.88, 0.79, 0.85, 0.83–0.93, 0.85	0.85
Wechsler/WAIS	0.97, 0.94	0.96

correlations. Regression is also non-discriminatory which leaves the neglected area of variance in which the clearest differential predictions can be made.

Test errors and their effects

The various theoretical predictions are based on the assumption that perfect measurement is involved. Now even if one accepts the definition of intelligence as that which is measured by intelligence tests and thus avoids all the problems of relating these measures to external criteria, this still leaves a number of 'internal' problems in interpreting test scores, namely: reliability, standardization, test equivalence and longitudinal stability.

Confronted with studies straddling an age span of 1–60+, conducted from the 1920s to the 1970s and employing a variety of intelligence tests, standardized in different places, and by no means self-evidently comparable, the possibility of test error as a major component in the variety of reported findings was apparent. It had been hoped that a careful analysis of these problems as they might pertain to studies of family resemblances would be available, so that a simple summary statement could be made here. Unfortunately our search proved fruitless, and we were thus forced to collect together data from a variety of sources in order to make at least some assessment of the order of magnitude of these potential errors.

Test unreliability

Table 14.1, which should be regarded as no more than a slight improvement on guessing, simply gives the reliability coefficients we have seen reported on the various tests involved in this article. It includes a mixture of split-half, test–retest and equivalent-forms reliability coefficients obtained on an assortment of samples and even involving different versions of the same test.

It seems not unreasonable to assume that test unreliability will operate largely as a random error, entailing a reduction in parent–offspring correlations of something between 4 and 18 per cent depending upon the test involved. It is possible that the quoted reliability figures are slight underestimates, involving as they do additional ' errors' of delay and/or equivalence. For this reason correction for attenuation due to test unreliability is regarded as a dubious procedure. Since the errors here are probably small, and there is little evidence of consistent differences with respect to reliability from test to test, it seems unlikely that this factor will vary much among studies.

Test-standardization errors

Test-standardization errors in the form of gross differences in means and SDs *between* parents and offspring test scores will, of course, produce errors in regression and population variance predictions but correlation would be unaffected. Errors *within* each group (parents or offspring) will produce an unsystematic effect similar to test unreliability. In almost all studies both parents and offspring are each composed of groups of different ages and thus liable to such within-group effects if the means and SDs at each age are not the same.

For children aged 5–18 years, the 1937 Stanford-Binet standardization data (McNemar 1942) show that the SDs vary 1.3 points, on average, about the mean of SDs and the means vary 1.2 points. Crude calculations using these average errors reveal that they would only reduce correlations by ½ per cent. It is unclear whether the above are normative errors or sampling errors. Dearborn and Rothney (1941) have shown that sampling differences occur between tests, but the extent to which they occur within tests can only be a matter of speculation; however, even mean and SD disparities of 10 points produce only an 8 per cent error.

For adults, cross-sectional samples (which are the appropriate ones in this context) reveal appreciable changes in mean IQ according to age. The typical adult sample in parent–offspring studies has an average age of between 40 and 45 years and a range of about 40 years. A crude estimate based on the data of Wechsler (1958), Doppelt and Wallace (1955) and Schaie and Strother (1968) suggests that the average disparity within such a range will be about 10 points. For SD changes with age we estimate an average disparity of about 3 points, based solely on the *graphs* of Foulds and Raven (1948). Combined, these errors would produce a 5–6 per cent reduction in correlations when age corrections have not been applied.

Alström (1961) and Cattell and Willson (1938) provide comparisons of age-corrected and uncorrected correlations; for the former the differences are 6, 13 and 4 per cent, and for the latter 23 per cent. The effect of using two tests with disparate means on the children in Outhit's (1933) study was looked at, but here the rather small predicted errors (2.8, 2.4, 1.6 per cent) did not fully materialize (2, 0.7, 0.15 per cent).

Test equivalence

No less than six different intelligence scales have been used in the studies included in this review; furthermore, various forms of a single scale may occur not only across studies, but also within them, e.g. the 1916 and 1937 Binet (Forms L and M). Obviously an important issue is to what extent these various tests are measuring the same thing.

The prediction of changes in parent–offspring correlation resulting from errors due to lack of test equivalence depends upon the error model adopted. Assumptions have to be made on two issues: first, the location of the errors, and second, whether they will operate randomly or systematically across generations. On the first issue (location), any lack of correlation between two scales

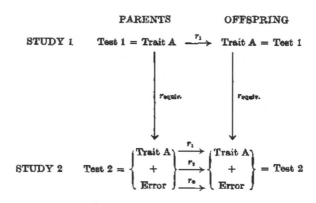

Figure 14.1 Diagram showing the operation of a test equivalence error across two studies.

Table 14.2 Inter-test correlations					
	Binet	Cattell	Otis	Raven's PM	Wechsler (WAIS and WISC)
Alpha	0.73, 0.8–0.9 Av = 0.81	—	—	—	0.74
Binet		0.56–0.85 Av = 0.71	0.63, 0.51 Av = 0.57	0.71, 0.86, 0.62 0.54, 0.68 Av = 0.68	0.83, 0.91, 0.62, 0.93 0.89, 0.82, 0.76, 0.77 Av = 0.82
Cattell			0.73	—	0.84
Otis				—	0.67
Raven's PM					0.91, 0.62, 0.85, 0.75 0.55, 0.72 Av = 0.73

could be interpreted either as error in only one of them (i.e. Scale 1 measures Trait A and Scale 2 measures Trait A plus error) or as error in both (i.e. Scale 1 measures Trait A plus error; Scale 2 measures Trait A plus error). Where there is error in only one scale, a change of scale must involve a change of error variance and thus a change in correlation is expected. However, where there is error in both scales, a change of scale simply involves substituting one error for another, which, given error equality, produces no change in correlation.

On the second issue, a problem arises when different tests appear in two or more studies. In the simplest case shown in Figure 14.1, Study 1 uses Test 1 for parents and offspring, while Study 2 uses Test 2 for both.

Here, the error arising from the lack of equivalence of Test 1 and Test 2 might either be random across parents and offspring, or constitute a trait showing a definite relationship (r_e). In the former case it functions as an intergenerational error further reducing the correlation, and in the latter it constitutes a confounded variable which, if $r_e > r_1$, would increase the correlation.

In view of these indeterminancies, precise predictions cannot be made and one can only specify the upper limits of such errors from test equivalence data. Table 14.2 shows our collection of test intercorrelation data which once more, hopefully, represents an improvement on guessing.

The upper limit for errors resulting from imperfect test equivalence would be a reduction of $(1 - r_{equiv.}) \times 100$ per cent in the parent–offspring correlations. With the overall average $r_{equiv.}$ from the Table (0.73) this would amount to a 27 per cent correlation reduction. Test equivalence, or rather lack of it, thus constitutes a potentially large source of error.

Relevant evidence on the actual magnitude of these errors is both scant and in varying degrees indirect but fairly encouraging. Skodak and Skeels's (1949) study shows an 8 per cent disparity between the 1916 and 1937 Binet correlations (estimating the reliability loss in this study is not possible since testing was done in a single session with items common to both tests being taken only once). Conrad and Jones (1940) and Outhit (1933) used the Army Alpha for adults and older children and the Binet for younger children, thus providing a same/different comparison confounded (adversely) with age. The disparities (for single-parent–offspring correlation) are 0 and 6 per cent respectively (7 per cent mid-parent). Indirect evidence from longitudinal studies of child IQ involving test switches between Binet and Wechsler variants, and in one case the Terman Group Test, produced no test change effect (Honzik et al. 1938; Kangas and Bradway 1971; Pinneau 1961; Skodak and Skeels 1949). Unfortunately we have no evidence at all on this matter for the

Cattell and Otis tests nor for Raven's Matrices. However, the Otis and Army Alpha appear fairly similar, which is not surprising in view of their historical connection.

Longitudinal stability

Earlier we commented that in the absence of an adequate intelligence test theory scores obtained at different ages could not meaningfully be compared directly, but only to the extent that one was predictive of the other. This issue is thus effectively a special case of test equivalence and contains the same kind of error prediction indeterminacies, i.e. one can only estimate the maximum possible disparities. Direct evidence for estimating these is mostly lacking for the age differences between parents and offspring to be found in the studies. Hence, we attempted to make rather crude extrapolations from the longitudinal data provided by: Bayley (1949, 1957), Bradway and Thompson (1962), Ebert and Simmons (1943), Hirsch (1930), Honzik (1972), Honzik *et al.* (1938), Kangas and Bradway (1971), Sontag *et al.* (1958).

Our somewhat *ad hoc* procedure consisted of grouping the data into age bands (e.g. early, middle and late childhood) and combining the results in each age band using weighted z scores. The data were then plotted graphically (see Figure 14.2), spacing the age bands at equal intervals along the age scale and carrying out linear extrapolation, weighting the projection according to the ns at each point in the one case where this was applicable. Clearly the validity of our extrapolation depends upon the appropriateness of our age scaling. The reasonable uniformity of the slopes of the different plots (each representing a different starting age) suggest that the procedure was not radically in error.

Since the average age of most parents in the studies falls between the middle and late adult bands, we have computed the longitudinal correlations to this point from each of the earlier bands (see Table 14.3). Given our estimates of longitudinal instability, it would be possible for parent–offspring correlations to increase or decrease by as much as 18–61 per cent, depending on the age disparity involved.

Test errors in combination

If parents and offspring were entirely homogenous with respect to age, and were given the same test, then only errors of reliability would operate. If one assumes that these are randomly distributed, they would reduce parent–offspring correlations by about 5–10 per cent. Regression would be increased proportionately, and overall variance trends masked to this extent.

Since almost without exception the studies include parents and offspring who vary around a mean age, standardization errors will also operate, again presumably randomly, and to the extent of about 5–10 per cent. Combining the two, an expected reduction in correlation of between 10 and 20 per cent should be envisaged.

However when one considers the less than perfect equivalence of tests, and the facts concerning long-term changes of test score, the added uncertainty concerning the error model means that one can do little more than estimate the upper and lower limits of their effects on correlation.

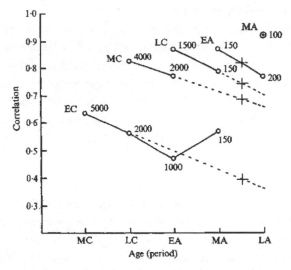

Figure 14.2 Graphs showing longitudinal correlations for IQ scores from different age bands together with projections. Numbers beside points denote the number of entries in the correlation. EC, early childhood (3–5 years); MC, middle childhood (6–9 years); LC, late childhood (10–14 years); EA, early adulthood (15–21 years); MA, middle adulthood (22–42 years); LA, late adulthood (43+ years). Points marked + are used for estimates in Table 14.3

Table 14.3 Estimated longitudinal correlations to middle/late adulthood (40–45 years)	
From early childhood (3–5 years)	0.39
From middle childhood (6–9 years)	0.69
From late childhood (10–14 years)	0.74
From early adulthood (15–21 years)	0.82

Test equivalence errors were placed as potentially ranging from 0 to about 30 per cent. Since the assessment of test equivalence involves test unreliability already, there is no need to add this again to the maximum estimate, but it does need adding to the minimum, making the range from 5 to 30 per cent. Combining this with standardization errors gives a range between 10 and 40 per cent for studies involving a change of test.

Longitudinal errors were placed between 0 and 60 per cent but the latter figure was for prediction from early childhood. An upper region of 20–30 per cent is most applicable for most studies. Again longitudinal errors already include unreliability, hence their effect, when combined with standardization errors, could be between 10 and 40 per cent.

Combining the effects of equivalence and standardization errors involves unreliability twice, for which allowance must be made. Furthermore, while it is reasonable simply to add small errors, this obviously should not be done for larger ones: each error must be applied to what the preceding errors have left. Our estimate, based on the speculations enumerated above, is that all test errors in combination may affect parent–offspring correlations minimally to the extent of 10 per cent and maximally 65 per cent.

The studies

An attempt has been made to produce a comprehensive collection of studies which include data on natural parent–offspring resemblances in intelligence. Those included all meet the following criteria: that intelligence tests were given to both parents and offspring, reasonably appropriate analyses carried out, and the population sampled not grossly abnormal. For each paper a brief outline is provided, giving some detail concerning the size and nature of the sample, the country or origin where outside the USA, the tests used, and such corrections carried out by individual authors as feature in the data we have used. Statistical data relating to these investigations are collated in Table 14.4. The studies are presented in rank order of size of single-parent–offspring correlation, both in the outlines and in Table 14.4.

Cattell and Willson (1938)

Sample. 101 English families, initially those of a test standardization sample willing to co-operate, resulting in a skew to high IQ. To compensate, parents of schoolchildren in classes for the dull and two guidance clinics were approached. Markedly bimodal distribution of parents. Range – corrected correlations used.

Tests. Cattell Scales 0 to III, designed to have an unusual SD of 27. Age corrections applied to older scores.

Outhit (1933)

Sample. 51 families of four or more offspring, most American born, all native English speakers, literate. Excluded: mentally ill, alcoholics, epileptics, TB, VD and unwillingness to co-operate. Biased to high SES.

Tests. Parents and offspring over 12, Army Alpha. Offspring below 12, 1916 Binet. Several growth limits for the Army Alpha were tried: the first yielded appreciably higher IQs of offspring than parents. Age 14 years and 10 months was chosen, giving same average of parents and offspring, to fit Outhit's assumption of no difference (pp. 21 and 22). Total data on age and IQ included; reanalysed by us; minor discrepancies; only our figures included.

Leahy (1935)

Sample. Control group for a foster study, 194 families, of North European, non-Jewish extraction, in urban communities of over 10,000. Markedly skewed to high SES. Only one child per family tested.

Tests. Parents, Otis Intermediate A. Offspring, 1916 Binet. Supplementary data give a mid-parent–offspring correlation for natural children of some foster parents.

Conrad and Jones (1940). An extension to a study published by Jones in 1928.

Sample. 269 families, representative of rural New England population. All families native-born, English speakers, literate, with two or more offspring. Original sample shows negative skew in distribution of parents' test scores.

Tests. Parents and offspring over 10, Army Alpha. Offspring age 3½ – 13, 1916 Binet. Between ages 10 and 14, 44 offspring were tested on both and a composite score used. Results converted to sigma scores, based on data from 1215 people aged 10–65 tested in the same community.

Alström (1961)

Sample. 50 families selected from a sample of twin pairs, resident in Greater Stockholm, Sweden, first identified at induction to military service, and willing to co-operate. Offspring: 26 monozygotic, 24 dizygotic pairs, plus 82 siblings, virtually all adult. Parents said to be a representative sample of Swedish population.

Test. Swedish Wechsler (excludes: Digit Symbol, Block Design and Object Assembly). Corrections made to scores over age 37. Means and SDs appear based on uncorrected scores, but correlations on corrected scores. Mid-parent–offspring correlation: personal communication by Professor Alström. In calculating parent–offspring correlations, mid-twin IQ was used, each pair one entry only.

Burks (1928)

Sample. Control group for a foster study; 105 families representing wide geographical area; all English speaking; markedly skewed to high SES. Only one child per family was tested.

Test. Slightly shortened 1916 Binet (both parents and offspring). Considered age-correcting scores but decided against.

Higgins et al. (1962)

Sample. Part of a cohort numbering 82,217 collected as follows: the grandparents of 289 residents in a colony for the mentally retarded sometime between 1911 and 1918 were traced. Information on descendants and their spouses, sometimes through seven generations, was obtained. Of these only 2.7 per cent were mentally retarded, so intellectual normality is assumed. This study reports on those families for whom IQ values were available for both parents and one or more of their offspring (1016 mothers, 1016 fathers and 2039 offspring).

Tests. Taken from various records, mostly school. Group tests of the Kuhlmann or Otis type, also some unspecified individual tests. Mean age of parents at test, 14.2; offspring, 8.65.

Kagan and Moss (1959)

Sample. 99 children from the Fels longitudinal study (n=140), tested regularly from age 2½ to 11. Approximately 50 per cent of fathers and 27 per cent mothers were college graduates: high SES.

Tests. Mothers, Otis A; fathers, Otis B. Offspring, 1937 Binet, Forms L and M alternatively. 'Smoothed IQs': average of three scores around each age reported.

Gibson (1970)

Sample. Scientists below the age of 35, employed by Cambridge University, England (n=157, mean IQ 126.5). Of these 76 had fathers who were tested, 71 per cent were from the two highest social classes.

Test. Fathers and scientist sons: WAIS. Since this study is based on *offspring* of known high academic achievement, the correlation is eliminated from most analyses.

Waller (1971). See under Higgins *et al.* for description of original population and tests.

This sample. 173 male offspring aged 24 or older, and 131 fathers. Mean age of fathers at test: 15.9; sons 13.38. Degree of overlap, if any, between this sample and that used by Higgins *et al.* is unknown.

Polansky et al. (1969)

Sample. Young children in day-care centre with low IQ mothers.

Tests. Mothers, WAIS. Offspring, Binet.

McCall (1970)

Sample. Parent–offspring pairs selected from the Fels longitudinal study (see Kagan and Moss for sample and tests). 35 pairs in which parents and offspring were tested at the same age in childhood.

Guttman (1974)

Sample. 100 Israeli families in middle-class neighbourhoods. Of 200 parents, 131 were doctors, lawyers or teachers, mostly from Eastern Europe.

Test. Raven's Progressive Matrices (individual, 35 min). Age range of sample taking the same test was 8–61; all scores age-corrected, but procedure seems dubious. Correlations calculated on scores: no IQ conversions.

Skodak and Skeels (1949)

Sample. Part of a sample of 100 children from below average social background placed in adoptive homes under the age of 6 months. In 63 cases the natural mother's IQ was known.

Tests. Mothers, 1916 Binet. Offspring, 1916 Binet at mean ages 2, 3, 7 and 13 (approx). Also 1937 Binet at 13. Since all data are included in the original paper, we reanalysed parent–offspring correlations.

Oden (personal communication)

Sample. Part of the Terman gifted group (n=1528) selected in childhood as having IQs above 135. As is well known, in later life, regression to the mean had occurred (McNemar 1947). The correlation reported is on 559 gifted subjects tested as children, and 1027 offspring.

Tests. Parents, 1916 Binet. Offspring, 1937 Binet, Form L.

Snygg (1938)

Sample. Canadian cohort of 312 young children of low social background placed in foster homes (79 per cent in first year of life, 90 per cent before two).

Tests. Mothers, 1916 Binet. Offspring, Kuhlmann–Binet and 1916 Binet.

Freeman et al. (1928)

Sample. Part of a large study of foster children. In 28 families a comparison was made of foster parents' IQ with their own and foster children. Only mid-parent–offspring correlation reported.

Tests. Parents, Otis Higher Form. Offspring, 1916 Binet.

Jones (1928). See Conrad and Jones.

A number of studies which did not meet the criteria for selection were excluded:

Adams and Neel (1967) – offspring were the result of incestuous relationships.

Brandon (1957) – various tests used, including social maturity; and fathers' IQs were estimated.

Burt (1943, 1955, 1961) – the 1955 study used estimates of parental IQ. The 1961 study is probably the most widely quoted statement on parent–offspring regression, and claims to develop the 1943 data. However, careful inspection reveals a grossly inadequate description of the material and how it was collected. References to further details in other papers proved empty, and the trail through a number of publications led nowhere. Despite some cautious phrases, including one on the relative unreliability of the adult IQ assessment, the 1943 paper proclaims a mean IQ of 153.2 for his higher professional group, which exceeds that of the Terman gifted group, at a time when Terman could not find a test suitable for such exceptional adults. By 1961 the mean IQ of the higher professional group had miraculously shrunk to 139.7, but, surprisingly, the range for the offspring underwent no change during the same period. Several authors have recently attested to the unsatisfactory nature of Burt's work (Clarke and Clarke 1974; Jensen 1974b; Kamin 1973). The latter has concluded that 'the numbers left behind by Professor Burt are simply not worthy of serious scientific attention'.

Eaves (1973) – this analysis of the Reed and Reed (1965) data was excluded for using analysis of variance which is inappropriate to the question of parent–offspring resemblances.

Halperin (1945) – some IQs were estimated, and all the data categorized for computing the correlation.

Honzik (1957) – parents' IQs were estimated from education.

Penrose (1933) – some IQs were estimated and the correlation based on categorized data.

Willoughby (1928) – a curious psychometric cocktail of subtests from various sources was used, hardly to be regarded as a standardized intelligence test.

Data analysis

In analysing the data, we have been concerned to look at all the variables which might separately, or in combination, be relevant to the question of parent–offspring resemblance, regardless of their potential significance to a genetic or an environmental model as at present conceived. In doing so we have borne in mind the possibility that neither model is adequate, and that the empirical results available have been hard obtained, thus deserving of study in the hope that new hypotheses might emerge. An attempt has been made to carry out a relatively systematic analysis of the data dealing in turn with the correlational, regression and variance findings, looking for both consistencies and anomalies in the results.

There were a number of statistical problems in handling the data. The two basic sampling problems require different treatments when combining the results of different studies. The within-study sampling problem, i.e. the extent to which the data from a study is representative of the sampling procedure used within it, depends upon the n in the study and is dealt with by using weighted z scores:

$$z_{av} = [\Sigma z(n-3)]/[\Sigma(n-3)].$$

Table 14.4: Summary data on studies of natural parent–offspring resemblance

Author and date	Correlations — Single parent-offspring	Correlations — Mid-parent-offspring	Correlations — Assort. mating	ns — Families	ns — Offspring	ns — Parents	Mean IQ — Offspring	Mean IQ — Parents	s.d. — Offspring	s.d. — Parents	Average age — Parents	Average age — Offspring	Tests — Parents	Tests — Offspring	Additional information
Cattell & Willson (1938)	0·60	—	0·71	101	101	—	106	109	32*	29*	Adult	12	Army Alpha	Cattell	* s.d. for test: 27
Outhit (1933)	0·62	0·67	0·74	51	257	—	107*	107*	19	17	42	12	1916 Binet, Army Alpha	1916 Binet, Army Alpha	* Means made equal
Leahy (1935)	0·51	0·60	0·41	194	194	—	—	110	—	15	Adult	9	Otis Intermed.	1916 Binet	
Conrad & Jones (1940)	0·49	—	0·52	269	508E	—	-0·09*	0·15*	1·01*	1·00*	41	8 and 16	Army Alpha	Kuhlmann–Binet	* Sigma scores
Alström (1961)	0·49	0·56	0·47	50	132	—	99	106	14	13	56	28	Wechsler (Swedish)	Wechsler (Swedish)	
Burks (1928)	0·45	0·52	0·55	105	105	—	111	115	19	15	8	8	1916 Binet (lopped)	1916 Binet (lopped)	
Higgins et al. (1962)	0·44	—	0·33	1016	2039	—	102	103E	15	16E	14	9	Various 'Otis type'	Various 'Otis type'	
Kagan & Moss (1959)	0·43 Av.	—	—	>59	99	—	Above av.	Above av.	—	—	Adult	3-10	Otis	1937 Binet (smoothed) possibly some 1916s	
Gibson (1970)	0·37	—	—	76	76	—	123	131	11	6E	48M	16M	Raven's P.M.	Raven's P.M.	
Waller (1971)	0·36	—	—	131	173	—	89	103	16E	16E	16	13	Various 'Otis type'	Various 'Otis type'	
Pojansky et al. (1969)	0·35	—	—	65	65	—	76M	94M	—	—	Adult	Adult	WAIS	WAIS	
McCall (1970)	0·32 Av.	—	—	35	35	—	—	—	—	—	3-11	3-11	1916 and 1937 Binet (smoothed)	1937 Binet (smoothed)	
Guttman (1974)	0·28	0·41	0·26	100	208	—	110E	110+E	11	10E	Adult	Adult	Raven's P.M.	Raven's P.M.	
Skodak & Skeels (1949)	0·27 Av.	—	—	63	63	—	86	113 Av.	16E	14 Av.	Adult	2-14	1916 Binet (mostly)	1916 and 1937 Binet	
Oden (person. comm.)	0·08	—	—	559	1027	—	183	133	15	18	Child	Child	1937 Binet	1937 Binet (mostly)	
Snygg (1938)	0·05 Av.	—	—	312	312	—	78	95	11E	10E	2-14	1-5+	1916 Binet	1916 Binet	
Freeman et al. (1928)	—	0·35	—	28	28	—	—	—	—	—	Adult	10E	Otis Higher	1916 Binet	
Leahy (1935) additional	—	0·36	—	20	20	—	—	—	—	—	Adult	—	Otis Intermed.	1916 Binet	
Jones (1928)	—	0·59	0·60	105	—	—	—	—	—	—	—	—	Army Alpha	1916 Binet, Army Alpha	

Notes: M, median; E, estimate; Av., average for same group at different ages.

However, errors due to different sampling procedures between different studies are unaffected by n and best dealt with by taking unweighted z scores. With such a procedure the problem arises as to what n to use for significance testing. To test for non-significance we have treated every study as having the n of the largest study, and testing for significance have used the smallest n, thus in each case making a conservative estimate.

The appropriate n for each study also presents problems because the same individuals may appear more than once in the correlation calculation. Again we have used maximum or minimum values according to which was the least favourable for the hypothesis being tested; the maximum value being the number of entries. Where the proper minimum value could not be established, we have used the number of families since the minimum cannot be less than this.

For direct comparisons, all the various correlations should have been corrected or not to the same degree, but unfortunately almost every study seems to have gone its own way in this respect. Since the majority of correlations were not age-corrected, we have taken non-age-corrected values where available. None of the correlations include corrections for attenuation. We considered carrying out range corrections since the SDs varied from study to study, but were unable to establish the appropriate SDs for every test. For example it was impossible to adjust Burks's correlation derived from non-age corrected 'lopped' Binet IQs.

Readers should be warned that some of the figures quoted in various tables and used in our analyses have been derived from published data, but do not always correspond exactly with those their authors chose to present, or those cited by others. In some cases our reanalysis of the published raw data yielded marginally different figures; in others it was possible to calculate from the data given results which were not pertinent to the original authors' argument, but which were needed for our purpose.

Results

Single-parent–offspring correlations

Casual inspection of the column of single-parent–offspring correlations in Table 14.4 reveals a range from 0.80 to 0.05 (subgroups from two studies, Snygg and Gibson, are reported with small *negative* correlations). Needless to relate, no theoretical model predicts such diversity, hence a major consideration in our analyses was attempting to account for it.

Sex of parent and offspring

Four studies report separate correlations for father–son, father–daughter, mother–son and mother–daughter (Conrad and Jones, Guttman, Kagan and Moss, Outhit). Despite large numbers of entries, comparisons yielded nothing approaching significance. Similarly, no difference was obtained when comparing father–offspring with mother–offspring correlations (Alström, Burks, Cattell and Willson, Conrad and Jones, Guttman, Higgins *et al.*, Kagan and Moss, Leahy, Outhit), this time with even larger *n*s. Thus, all such distinctions have been ignored, where separate correlations were given they were collapsed, and studies giving only single-sex parent–offspring correlations treated as equivalent.

Dominance by superior versus inferior parent

Two authors examined a possible differential relationship between offspring IQ and either the more or less intelligent of each pair of parents. The results were essentially negative: for Jones the correlation with the superior parent was 0.57 and for inferior 0.55; Outhit reports 0.57 and 0.62 respectively.

Age: parents tested as children versus parents tested as adults

Excluding foster studies and deviant IQ group studies (to be discussed), there were three investigations in which the parents were tested as children (Higgins *et al.*, McCall, Waller) and eight in which the parents were tested as adults (Alström, Burks, Cattell and Willson, Conrad and Jones, Guttman, Kagan and Moss, Leahy and Outhit). The former group produced lower correlations than the latter as a group: weighted $r = 0.43$ and 0.52 respectively, $p < 0.01$; unweighted $r = 0.37$ and 0.52 respectively, $p < 0.08$. *Since only three studies involved the parents as children (two from the same sample and possibly overlapping) and since the unweighted significance is low, we are disinclined to accept this evidence as more than suggestive.*

Age of offspring at testing and within-study test changes

Two studies are commonly cited as showing an increasing parent–offspring correlation as the age of the latter increases: Honzik (1957) and Skodak and Skeels (1949). The former used estimates of parental IQ from education; since this procedure probably involves more 'error' than 'effect', the evidence must be regarded as weak. In the latter study (of fostered children) there does appear to be a rising correlation in early childhood. However, inspection of Figure

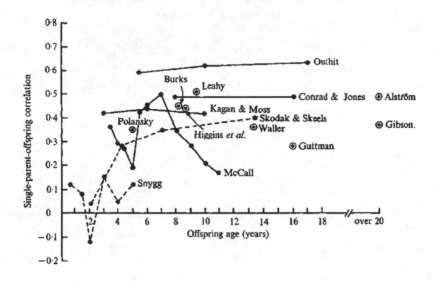

Figure 14.3 Graphs showing single-parent–offspring correlations by offspring age.
- - - denotes studies of fostered children.

14.3 makes it apparent that neither other longitudinal studies (Kagan and Moss, McCall, Snygg) nor cross-sectional studies (Conrad and Jones, Outhit) show a similar trend. Nor is there any evidence for an increase in parent–offspring correlation beyond the age of 4 across the studies. However, it remains possible that there is an age trend from birth to about 4 years.

It should be noted that both Outhit and Conrad and Jones used a different test for younger children than for both older offspring and adults. Here we have, therefore, a change of test *added* to the age change, yet with no significant effect. Although in about half the studies involving young children, different tests were used for parents and offspring, above the age of 14 (offspring) the same test was used in all cases for both, again without apparent effect. It is difficult to avoid the conclusion that, on the whole, above the age of 4, neither age nor the type of test used systematically affects the parent–offspring correlation, and to note that the studies by Outhit and Conrad and Jones, using virtually the same procedures with respect to tests and age, yield substantially different results.

			Parent IQ		Offspring IQ		
Study	r	Parent dev from 100	Mean	SD	Mean	SD	n of offspring
Oden	0.08	+52	152	15	133	18	1027
Gibson	0.37	+23	123	11	131	6	76
Snygg	0.13	−22	78	11E	95	10E	312
Polansky et al.	0.35	−22	78M	—	94M	—	65
Skodak and Skeels	0.38	−14	86	16	106	15	63

Table 14.5 Single-parent–offspring correlations for deviant IQ groups

Notes: Gibson, means computed from table of cases used in correlation; Snygg, SDs estimated from SE of mean; Polansky et al. Medians only given; Skodak and Skeels, IQ data as given at age 13 (1916 Binet). E, estimate; M, median.

Fostering and non-fostering studies

If there is any environmental contribution to offspring intelligence, a diminished natural parent-child correlation would be expected in foster studies. There are only two such reports in the sample (Skodak and Skeels, Snygg). In addition to the problem of few studies, there are two further complications: first Snygg's involves fairly young children, and second the mothers in both groups are on average of low IQ.

Only the most stringent comparison between foster and non-foster studies (in the latter case excluding Oden and Gibson as deviant groups) failed to reach an acceptable level of significance on a one-tailed test: $p < 0.07$. This particular comparison involved taking correlations with offspring above age 4 only, using unweighted averages, with minimum n, and range-correcting Snygg's correlation from 0.13 to 0.28, a dubious procedure based on SD estimates which may well have been too low. All other comparisons yielded differences significant beyond the 0.02 level.

Thus, taken as a group, the correlations in these two studies appear to be lower than others, but this ignores the obvious disparity between the two (see

Figure 14.3). It is curious that Snygg, with an individually tested sample of 312 offspring and their mothers, is so rarely cited.

Deviant IQ groups

Five of the studies concern parent groups which deviate about one SD or more from 100. Table five gives the relevant details.

The average correlation of this group is significantly lower than the average of less deviant groups (p <0.001). Two of the five studies have already been discussed as involving fostered children. Other complications arise: 1. with the exception of Gibson and Skodak and Skeels, a number of young children are included; 2. Oden's correlation is based on parents tested as children; 3. the added unreliability of assessing high IQ; and 4. Gibson, certainly, and possibly Snygg have low SDs.

The Terman–Oden correlation has not previously been published, and was made available through the kindness of Dr Oden, who wrote: 'The number of Binet-tested parents in the chart is limited to those for whom offspring Binet IQs were also available in 1955... The correlation between parent and child test scores was not published in *The Gifted Group at Mid-life* (vol. V of the series) because the restricted range made it impossible to get a high r. The obtained r is significant only because of the large ns.'

Assortative mating

Inspection of the columns in Table 14.4 giving single-parent–offspring and parent–parent correlations indicates that there is considerable variation in the latter, and that the two are related. Table 14.6 presents the available data in rank order of assortative mating. Even on a simple product-moment correlation, the relationship between single-parent–offspring r and assortative mating is significant: $r = 0.85$, p <0.01.

An attempt was made to remove the effect of assortative mating from the single-parent–offspring correlations using the partial correlation procedure. This involves considering the parents as separate but correlated variables. The results are included in Table 14.6. In view of the ensuing considerable reduction in the variability of correlations, it seems reasonable to conclude that a powerful source of difference between the separate studies is the degree of assortative mating. It will, however, also be noted that, with one exception, all the correlations are reduced well below that expected by either a genetic or an environmental model (as at present conceived), granted random mating, and assuming that parent IQ related variables are of major importance.

Table 14.6 Assortative mating and single-parent–offspring correlations			
Study	Assortative mating	Single-parent–offspring	Single-parent–offspring (partial)
Outhit	0.74	0.62	0.31
Cattell and Willson	0.71	0.80	0.55
Burks	0.55	0.45	0.27
Conrad and Jones	0.52	0.49	0.32
Alström	0.47	0.49	0.34
Higgins et al.	0.33	0.44	0.35
Guttman	0.26	0.28	0.22

Mid-parent–offspring correlations

It will be recalled that the genetic model predicts a mid-parent–offspring correlation of 0.7071 and the simple parent IQ related environmental model a correlation of 1.0. Column 2 of Table 14.4 gives the published mid-parent correlations for nine studies. They vary from one exceeding 0.7 (estimated from Cattell and Willson) to 0.35 (Freeman et al.). The majority fall a long way short of those predicted, and indicate a large source of variance in parent–offspring correlations unaccounted for by mid-parent IQ. Average weighted mid-parent–offspring correlation: 0.57; unweighted, 0.51.

Correlation and family variance contribution

Two statistical techniques have been used in the investigation of parent–offspring resemblance: correlation and analysis of variance. Strictly speaking, only the former can provide valid data; the latter, buttressed by a genetic model, has been used for this purpose (Eaves 1973). If the model were correct, the two techniques should provide equivalent results; however, there is reason to suppose that there are important disparities.

The total variance in a set of families consists of within-family variance, between-family variance related to mid-parent IQ and between-family variance unrelated to this. A mid-parent–offspring correlation coefficient only incorporates the between-family IQ related variance as the effect, leaving the rest as error. However, analysis of offspring variance by family groups includes both IQ related and unrelated between-family variance as effects. Thus, the latter is wider than the former. Data were available from two studies in which a direct comparison could be made: Outhit's published results and Alström's unpublished data, which he kindly sent us.

In each case, we have analysed the data to establish whether a significant degree of between-family variance unrelated to mid-parent IQ was present, using a covariance procedure. This removed the between-family correlated variance from the total, making it possible to test whether the remaining between-family variance significantly exceeded that within families. The results are shown in Table 14.7 below:

Table 7. Evidence for between-family effects unrelated to parent IQ (decimals removed)

Outhit: mid-parent–offspring correlation 0·665

	Analysis of variance				Analysis of covariance			
	S.S.	d.f.	Var. est.	F	S.S.	d.f.	Var. est.	F
Between-families	48 442	50	969	—	16 805	50	336	—
Within-families	23 100	206	112	8·64	23 100	205	113	2·98
Total	71 542	256	279	—	39 904	255	156	$P < 0.001$

Alström: mid-parent–offspring correlation 0·599

	Analysis of variance				Analysis of covariance			
	S.S.	d.f.	Var. est.	F	S.S.	d.f.	Var. est.	F
Between-families	8 714	34	256	—	4 659	34	137	—
Within-families	6 322	85	74	3·45	6 322	84	75	1·82
Total	15 036	119	126	—	10 981	118	93	$P < 0.025$

It appears that in both studies there is a significant amount of between-family variance unrelated to mid-parent IQ. From this, one must conclude: (a) that analysis of variance should not be used as a substitute for correlation to determine the degree of parent–child resemblance, but does provide a useful complement, and (b) that there are variables other than parental IQ associated with families, influencing offspring IQ. Test error, of course, does not account for this result since it features in both within - and between - family variance.

Regression

There are two ways of assessing parent–offspring regression which are, theoretically, equivalent. The first involves a comparison of the average deviation of the parents from the test *standardization mean* with the average deviation of the offspring from the same mean. The second uses the parent's deviation from the *parent group mean* and the offspring's deviation from the *offspring group mean*. However, in practice, there are a number of factors which may produce disparities between these two estimates.

The first method will obviously reflect standardization errors, while the second method will not. Secular trends, reflected in intergenerational gains or losses, will operate in the same way as standardization errors, but in this case the choice of method will depend upon one's purpose. Finally, since effects have been found which are unrelated to natural parent intelligence, the way in which these are distributed may modify regression. The possibility must be entertained that the selection procedures used to obtain parent–offspring samples may operate in such a way that they are not truly representative of the total population with respect to these variables. An obvious example is afforded by foster studies.

Group mean regression

(a) *Single-parent–offspring regression.* The amount of regression found in each study is shown in Table 14.8 expressed as a percentage, and in the main calculated from correlation and SD data; deviant IQ groups are dealt with separately. The unweighted average is 52 per cent, and the results predictably reflect the same influences as the single-parent–offspring correlations: regression decreases as assortative mating increases, and is higher in 'deviant' groups (see Table 14.9).

(b) *Mid-parent–offspring regression.* Neither the genetic nor the particular environmental model outlined predicts any regression from mid-parent IQ. It was possible to calculate the regression which actually occurs in the case of five studies: Outhit, 38 per cent; Alström, 37 per cent; Burks, 53 per cent; Jones, 27 per cent; average 39 per cent. Thus, regression from mid-parent IQ appears to be substantial.

(c) *Regression from deviant groups.* A summary of the evidence is given in Table 14.9. There are three studies involving low IQ parent groups, by Polansky *et al.*, Snygg, and Skodak and Skeels, the last two being foster studies and thus involving changes of environment unrelated to natural parent IQ.

Standardization mean regression and its relationship to group mean regression

If there are errors involved in the standardization means, the effect of these errors on regression estimates will be greatest for studies involving groups near the population mean. The results thus obtained in fact yield estimates ranging

Table 14.8 Group mean regression in non-IQ deviant groups				
	Group mean regression (%)			
Study	Single-parent–offspring	Mid-parent–offspring	Single-parent–offspring (SES)	Mid-parent–offspring (SES)
Cattell and Willson	26	—	—	—
Outhit	47	38	—	25 / 29 (corrected)
Conrad and Jones	49	—	—	—
Higgins et al.	54	—	—	—
Alström	56	37	—	—
Burks	65	53	—	—
Waller	67	—	49	—
Leahy	—	30	—	20 (indices, not %)
Jones	42	27	—	—

from −200 to +700 per cent. This suggests that standardization mean regression can only be sensibly assessed in groups that deviate substantially from the population mean. Data for the deviant groups are displayed in Table 14.9 and show little consistency. The sample in Gibson's study (Cambridge scientists) was in effect selected for high IQ and the figure shown denotes the *offspring–parent* regression.

As noted above, of the three studies involving low IQ mothers, in the case of two, the children were raised by foster parents, and thus in environments which were unrelated to natural parents' IQ. The comparability of the results of Polansky *et al.* and Snygg may seem surprising, since one is a foster study and the other is not. There are, however, two complications: first, the children in Polansky's study were in day care and it is possible that the effect of this was similar to fostering, and second, it is also possible that while the offspring are similar at their present low age, a difference may emerge as they get older. Other studies (Heber *et al.* 1968; Speer 1940) have reported progressive IQ declines in children reared by low IQ natural mothers.

Table 14.9 Regression in deviant IQ groups					
	Standardization mean regression			Group mean regression	
Study	Parent IQ	Offspring IQ	Regression (%)	%	Correlation
Polansky et al.	78M	94M	73	—	0.35
Snygg	78	95	78	89	0.13
Skodak and Skeels					
I	86	116	210	97	0.04
II	86	112	184	78	0.28
III	86	115	203	70	0.35
IVa	86	106	144	63	0.38
IVb	86	116	212	59	0.42
Terman/ Oden	152	133	36	91	0.08
As adults	134E	133	4	—	—

(Notes: M, median; E: estimate.)

The massive degree of regression (past the mean) in Skodak and Skeels's study must reflect considerable environmental influence, there being no reason to suppose that the genetic contribution of the fathers was abnormally high. Although the fathers' IQs were unknown, they were of similar SES and educational level to the mothers. In view of this systematic bias within the group, the disparities between the standardization mean and group mean regression are hardly surprising.

The only study of a deviant group appearing free of problems related to unusual rearing is that by Terman and Oden, which thus would seem to render it suitable for comparing standardization mean and group mean regression. Taken at face value this study shows that the IQ falls from 152 in the parents to 133 in the offspring, representing 36 per cent regression to the mean, and the result was obtained with very large ns. However, there are two possible errors in this result.

The quoted parent mean could be spuriously high due to test unreliability, because the group had been selected for high IQ largely on the basis of a single testing. The size of this error is a matter of conjecture since test reliability for such extreme IQs has not been established, but if one uses the quoted reliability for 'normally' high IQs (i.e. 0.9), then the expected unreliability error would be about 6 points. In addition, since most of the parents were tested on the 1916 Binet and the offspring presumably on the 1937, there are possibly errors arising from discrepancies between the two tests. Such evidence as is available suggests that, as age increases, the 1937 Binet provides higher IQs (Freeman *et al*.1928; Skodak and Skeels 1949).

It is unlikely that this degree of regression from the parents' IQs, measured as children, will also occur from their adult status. Longitudinal data on a sample of 72 from the Terman gifted group showed a drop from 150 to 141 from 6 to 12 years of age – less of a decrement than would be expected from our longitudinal data. Seven hundred 13-year-olds from the same sample showed a correlation of 0.66 with the Concept Mastery Test at age 34. This result corresponds to a drop to 134, and is a little lower than our longitudinal prediction. Using our data and the mid-range age for the Terman group, the predicted adult IQ would be 137. Using the performance on the Concept Mastery Test, McNemar (1947) estimated the IQ of the gifted group as 134 in adulthood. If these two separate lines of evidence are accepted as reasonable estimates of the adult IQs of this group, then near zero parents–offspring regression will have occurred.

To add to these two regression estimates, there is a third estimate – the group mean regression, which for this study is 90 per cent. This abnormally high figure indicates that there is a high degree of within-sample variation unrelated to parent IQ score. Even with random mating, the spouses could not produce more than 50 per cent and, in fact, the estimated spouses' mean IQ on the CMT was 125. We estimate the parent–parent correlation at 0.45 (based on parent IQ variances and the standard error of the difference between couples on the CMT). From the descriptions of the gifted group there is nothing to suggest abnormal within-group variability unrelated to intelligence, yet within this group an adequate degree of variation of intelligence in the parents (SD 14.7) does not transmit itself lawfully to the offspring, who, to make matters more puzzling, show an abnormally high degree of variability, significantly greater than that for the parents. This analysis of the complexities within the Terman and Oden study, together with the various estimates of regression (0, 33, 90 per cent) does not accord with the case advanced by Jensen (1973) and is difficult to interpret.

The effect of SES grouping on IQ regression

Three studies provided data which permitted comparisons of parent–offspring regression by IQ alone, by contrast with IQs resulting from SES grouping. If SES had no effect independent of parent IQ on offspring IQ, these two methods of ordering the parents should produce equivalent amounts of regression.

Outhit gives data for mid-parent and offspring IQ by social class which, when put into a regression equation with appropriate *ns*, shows 25 per cent regression by SES. A complication in the Outhit sample was the higher mean of the Alpha-tested children and their preponderance in the higher social classes. Correcting for this increased the figure to 29 per cent (the adjustment took into account the mean difference of the Alpha and Binet children, their proportions in each social class, and the mean differences of their parents, less regression), but even so this is less than regression by mid-parent IQ alone (38 per cent).

A similar analysis of Waller's data gave 49 per cent regression by SES and 67 per cent by IQ alone for single-parent–offspring. For Leahy, parent IQs were not available, but indices based on Otis raw scores gave a figure of 20 by SES and 29 by IQ alone for mid-parent data. Thus, consistently across three studies we found evidence for an effect of SES on child IQ, independent of parent IQ.

Variance

This has two aspects: (a) the overall population variance and (b) the relative contributions of different subgroups to this total.

OVERALL VARIANCE

The genetic model predicts increasing population variance from parents to offspring with non-random mating whereas the environmental model, in the absence of moderator variables, predicts a decrease. The majority of studies provide data on SDs (see Table 14.4) and, with the exception of Oden's, no study shows any appreciable increase in variance from parents to offspring; if anything, the trend is slightly in the reverse direction. Small differences in SDs, however, must be interpreted with caution, for tests do not always have exactly the same SDs at different ages. Further increments in variance will result from mean differences at various ages when such groups are mixed, particularly in the parent groups.

SUBGROUP CONTRIBUTIONS

1. *Parent deviation from the mean.* Three studies provide data about the effect of the parents' deviation from the mean on the variability of the offspring: Conrad and Jones group the parents into categories according to IQ and Leahy according to SES and thus also by mean IQ. Both of these studies show an essentially uniform child variance irrespective of parent IQ. For Outhit, we correlated mid-parent deviation with the variability of the first four children in each family and obtained a non-significant slightly negative correlation (−0.2). Overall, these results are inconsistent with the genetic model but fit an 'in ignorance' environmental one.

2. *Magnitude of IQ difference between husband and wife.* Cattell and Willson report a non-significant positive relationship, whereas both Jones and Outhit report slight negative trends.

Discussion

Taken in conjunction, the results presented in Table 14.4, and the summaries of the studies, indicate a considerable diversity of outcome and heterogeneity of populations sampled. There are substantial differences in degree of assortative mating, and this has been shown materially to affect variation in single-parent–offspring correlations. In addition, the abnormally low correlations in two of the deviant groups (Oden and Snygg) and, within non-deviant samples, the unusually high and low correlations of Cattell and Willson and Guttman, respectively, suggest within-study sampling variations. It is not possible to conclude with any degree of confidence that one investigation is more representative of a hypothetical 'general population' than is another, and indeed it seems sensible to question whether such a concept has any useful meaning with respect to genetic and environmental components in IQ variation.

In addition to differences in the way variables are distributed within studies, anomalies in the regression data suggest the existence of further overall differences between studies. Thus Burks's sample appears to show 65 per cent within-group regression to a mean of 115, whereas Waller's sample shows virtually the same within-group regression (67 per cent) to a mean of 103.

Without knowledge of the way relevant variables, other than parent intelligence, are distributed in different populations, generalizations, even from large bodies of data such as we have collected, cannot be made with any degree of confidence.

The correlation results indicate that the degree to which offspring IQ is attributable to the IQs of their parents is much less than that predicted on the basis of the genetic and environmental models, individually or combined. The mid-parent–offspring correlations (weighted average 0.57, unweighted 0.51) leave something like 70–75 per cent of the offspring variance not *directly* related to parent IQ. Even when allowance has been made for variance *indirectly* related to parent IQ (either due to random gene segregation or to 'capricious' or 'moderator' environmental variables) one is still left with 35–45 per cent unexplained.

Our analysis of Outhit's and Alström's data shows evidence for effects associated with families, yet unrelated to mid-parent IQ, and the regression data suggest that at least part of this effect is related to SES, again independent of parent IQ.

The possible contribution of test 'error' to the remainder is difficult to assess; it will be recalled that estimates were made of different types, and these may be present to varying degrees according to the design of the investigation. In particular, where studies varied with respect to age and test, it would be reasonable to expect a higher correlation between older children and parents on the same test than between the same parents and younger children, especially when the latter were assessed on a different scale.

Two studies (Outhit and Conrad and Jones), involving closely similar testing procedures, and containing both age and test changes, provide evidence on this point. In each, the children of young and intermediate ages were given the 1916 Binet, and the Army Alpha was used for the older offspring and parents. We estimated potential differences in correlation within these two investigations of up to 30 per cent. In fact, for Outhit, the older offspring–parent correlation was 0.65, and for the younger, 0.61; for Conrad and Jones both were 0.49. Manifestly the overall differences which exist between these samples are not due to variations in age and test. In Kagan and Moss's study, correlations span age 3–10 years, a range over which a difference in these of 50 per cent is possible; yet the results show uniformity. The evidence suggests that information from test equivalence and longitudinal stability may give little guidance for predictions outside these contexts.

Even for the older offspring in the studies discussed above, there was on average a large age disparity between parents and their children. It is possible that this in itself was a source of significant 'error', which further changes of age failed to increase. Of all the investigations, only one involved no age disparity: McCall compared parents tested as children with their offspring at exactly the same ages. The average correlation (0.32) is certainly no higher than those recorded by others, but it must be noted that this was a small select sample.

There remains, of course, the question of how far reliability and standardization errors may contribute to the unaccounted for variance: our crude estimates put these at between 10 and 20 per cent. Compensatory inflation of the mid-parent–offspring correlations to the extent suggested by our upper estimate, together with the corresponding rise in ' capriciousness', would explain all the variance within most studies. However, accounting for all the residual variance in this way ignores its differential distribution within and between families demonstrated in Outhit's and Alström's data. Hence, for these studies at least, such an estimate is obviously too large. Test error, it appears, remains something of an enigma.

On the whole, the data presented in this paper do not permit an assessment of how and to what extent parent intelligence operates environmentally to produce individual differences in IQ score. Certain conclusions can, however, legitimately be drawn. It will be recalled that one entirely unambiguous result was the lack of differential correlations by sex of parent or sex of offspring. It is clear from this that there is no *systematic* tendency for children of one sex to 'identify' intellectually with a parent of the same or opposite sex. Nor were Outhit or Jones able to demonstrate a relationship with the parent of higher or lower intelligence within a family. Assuming that mothers spend more time with their children than do fathers, one might expect a higher correlation with maternal than paternal IQ. Once again the results point to a negative conclusion.

The two foster studies yield lower natural parent–offspring correlations than do those in which children were reared by their own parents, but, as noted, this result is complicated by other factors. The Skodak and Skeels study does, however, indicate a clear environmental effect, which may or may not be related to the IQ of the foster parents, for whom no test data were available.

While we were unable to find, in this group of studies, any single piece of evidence unambiguously demonstrating an environmental effect directly due to parent intelligence, there is one showing a genetic effect, namely the set of natural mother–offspring correlations for ages over two, shown by Skodak and Skeels. However, whether these correlations denote a high or low genetic contribution cannot be assessed, since we do not know what the notional 'correct' parent–offspring correlation should be. In particular, while assortative mating is present in this sample, its degree is unknown; nor is it clear to what extent the children's rearing conditions were homogeneous.

However, good evidence for genetic transmission in one study does not necessitate acceptance of the genetic model, as currently conceived, which, as has been stated earlier, makes a number of precise predictions with respect to parent–offspring resemblances. For children reared with their parents, these predictions were in the main not clearly distinguishable from the environmental ones; however, the polygenic model does entail certain consequences with respect to variance, for which there appears to be no environmental counterpart.

The additive polygenic model predicts that, with assortative mating (which for intelligence is appreciable), the offspring variance should exceed the parent variance. However, only Burt (1955), with estimated parent IQs, was able to fulfil this promise, with an average population, and, as already stated, it is not possible to accept evidence from this source. Furthermore, if assortative mating persists over a number of generations, the trait distribution will become bimodal, and even dominance can only slow down the process. There is no reason to suppose that assortative mating for intelligence is of recent origin, and bimodality should thus have been found in the distribution of IQ scores for children, if not for adults. Test standardization procedures for adults could possibly obscure bimodality, but with children, since the test items are selected on the basis of performance differences *between* ages, bimodality *within* an age group cannot be masked. We have found no report of any such tendency.

The second variance prediction is that offspring variance will be greatest when mid-parent intelligence is average, and will reduce to zero for extreme high or low mid-parent IQ. The addition of other variables (whether environmental or non-IQ related genetic) would reduce, but not eliminate this effect. Three studies reporting variance according to parental level (Conrad and Jones, Leahy and Outhit) found uniformity across the IQ distribution.

The failure of these two genetic predictions is open to one or other of the following interpretations: that a suitable genetic model has been tested, in which case its failures point to an environmental interpretation; or that the particular genetic model is inappropriate and requires modification.

With regard to the latter possibility, geneticists have recorded a number of instances of failures of this model to account for the outcome of breeding studies. The expected reduction in phenotypic variability as selection proceeds is not observed. Admittedly, not all these experiments are suitable for such an analysis, on account of ceiling effects in the measurements used, but those we found which are adequate fail to show the reduction (De Fries *et al.* 1970; Robertson 1955).

Hirsch (1962) reports some failures of another prediction, namely that crossing opposite selected strains should produce reduced variance in the F generation, compared with a control group, followed by an increase in F. An even more surprising result was reported by Robertson (1955). Two separate strains of *Drosophila* were selectively bred for thorax length until improvement ceased, at which point it might be assumed that further increments were impossible. On crossing the strains, however, further improvement in response to selection over a number of generations was obtained.

A further problem with the present genetic model is its failure to account for the initial appearance of heterosis (hybrid vigour) and its subsequent decline after the F_1 generation (Jones 1924).

A common explanation for the unexpectedly high variability in the progeny of (non-human) homozygous parents is their increased susceptibility to the environment. However, the only author who cites direct evidence of relative phenotypic variance in response to known environmental changes is Lerner (1954), who analysed data presented by Heuts (1948) and Harvey (1939). Heuts measured the longevity of *Drosophila* in three temperature conditions, and Lerner's analysis showed less change in longevity across varying temperatures for hybrids than for homozygotes. Unfortunately he mistook weeks for days in part of the data, and use of the correct units give results which fail to support Lerner's conclusions. Harvey's data on corn give only incomplete support. It appears, therefore, that there are a number of findings in the field of experimental genetics for which it is not clear whether a genetic or environmental explanation is required.

Our finding of between-family variance unrelated to parent intelligence emphasizes that narrow and wide heritability are separate issues for human intelligence. Furthermore our review, which only concerns part of the evidence on narrow heritability, leads us to conclude that neither our understanding of the mechanisms involved in transmission, nor our knowledge about the origin and nature of sample differences, is adequate to make generalizations concerning parent–offspring resemblances with any degree of confidence.

The authors wish to express their gratitude to Dr Marion Outhit and Dr Marie Skodak for publishing their raw data; to Professor C.H. Alström for making his available; to Dr Marie Oden for data relating to the Terman Gifted Group; to Mr Arthur Royse and Drs D.C. Kendrick and D. Sewell for their valuable comments; to Mr John Devine and his staff for help in using the computer; and to Professor A.D B. Clarke for his encouragement and advice throughout the research project. We are most grateful to four referees for their helpful evaluations.

Notes

1   Narrow heritability refers to the effect of the additive genetic components of the parents, whereas wide heritability refers to the effects of all genetic components, additive and non-additive. Parent–offspring correlational studies detect the additive component; the normal analysis of MZ/DZ twin studies picks up the wide component *within* (but not *between*) families.

2   Isozygous, meaning the genes have the same value, is used in preference to homozygous which additionally assumes identity.

References

Adams, M.S. and Neel, J.V. (1967). 'Children of incest.' *Pediatrics 40*, 55–62.

Alström, C.H. (1961) 'A study of inheritance of human intelligence.' *Acta Psychologica et Neurologica Scandinavica 36*, 175–202.

Bayley, N. (1949) 'Consistency and variability in the growth of intelligence from birth to eighteen years.' *Journal Genetic Psychology 75*, 165–196.

Bayley, N. (1957) 'Data on the growth of intelligence between 16 and 21 years as measured by the Wechsler–Bellevue Scale.' *Journal of Genetic Psychology 90*, 3–15.

Bloom, B.S. (1964) *Stability and Change in Human Characteristics*. New York: Wiley.

Bradway, K.P. and Thompson, C.W. (1962) 'Intelligence at adulthood: a twenty-five year follow-up.' *Journal of Educational Psychology 53*, 1–14.

Brandon, M.W.G. (1957) 'The intellectual and social status of children of mental defectives.' *Journal of Mental Science 103*, 710–738.

Burks, B.S. (1928) 'The relative influence of nature and nurture upon mental development; a comparative study of foster parent–foster child resemblance and true parent-true child resemblance.' *Yearbook of the National Society for the Study of Education 27*, 1, 219–316.

Burt, C. (1943) 'Ability and income.' *British Journal of Educational Psychology 13*, 83–98.

Burt, C. (1955) 'Evidence for the concept of intelligence.' *British Journal of Educational Psychology 25, 158–177.*

Burt, C. (1961). 'Intelligence and social mobility.' *British Journal of Statistical Psychology 14*, 3–24.

Cattell, R.B. and Willson, J.L. (1938) 'Contributions concerning mental inheritance.' *British Journal of Educational Psychology 8*, 129–149.

Clarke, A.M. and Clarke, A.D.B. (1974) 'Genetic–environmental interactions in cognitive development.' In A.M. Clarke and A.D.B. Clarke (eds) *Mental Deficiency: The Changing Outlook* (3rd edn). London: Methuen.

Conrad, H.S. and Jones, H.E. (1940) 'A second study of familial resemblance in intelligence: environmental and genetic implications of parent-child and sibling correlations in the total sample.' *Yearbook of the National Society for the Study of Education 39*, 2, 97–141.

Dearborn, W.F, and Rothney, J. (1941) *Predicting the Child's Development.* Cambridge, Mass: Sci-Art Publications.

De Fries, J.C., Wilson, J.R. and McClearn, G.E. (1970) 'Open-field behaviour in mice: selection response and situational generality.' *Behavavior Genetics 1,* 195–211.

Doppelt, J.E. and Wallace, W.L. (1955) 'Standardization of the WAIS for older persons.' *Journal of Abnormal and Social Psychology 51,* 312–330.

Eaves, L.J. (1973) 'Assortative mating and intelligence: an analysis of pedigree data.' *Heredity 30,* 199–210.

Ebert, E. and Simmons, K. (1943) 'The Brush Foundation study of child growth and development. I. Psychometric tests.' *Monographs of the Society for Research in Child Development 8,* No. 2, 1–113.

Eckland, B.K. (1967) 'Genetics and sociology: a reconsideration.' *American Sociological Review 32,* 173–194.

Erlenmeyer-Kimling, L. and Jarvik, L.F. (1963) 'Genetics and intelligence: a review.' *Science 142,* 1477–1479.

Eysenck, H.J. (1973) *The Inequality of Man.* London: Temple Smith.

Foulds, G.A. and Raven, J.C. (1948) 'Normal changes in the mental abilities of adults as age advances.' *Journal of Mental Science 94,* 133–142.

Freeman, F.N., Holzinger, K.J. and Mitchell, B.C. (1928). 'The influence of environment on the intelligence, school achievement and conduct of foster children.' *Yearbook of the National Society for the Study of Education 27,* 1, 219–316.

Gibson, J.B. (1970) 'Biological aspects of a high socio-economic group. I. IQ, education and social mobility.' *Journal of Biosocial Science 2,* 1–16.

Guttman, R. (1974) 'Genetic analysis of analytical spatial ability: Raven's Progress Matrices.' *Behavior Genetics 4,* 273–283.

Halperin, S.L. (1945) 'A clinico-genetical study of mental defect.' *American Journal of Mental Deficiency 50,* 8–26.

Harvey, P.H. (1939) 'Hereditary variation in plant nutrition.' *Genetics 24,* 437–461.

Heber, R., Dever, R. and Conry, J. (1968) 'The influence of environmental and genetic variables on intellectual development.' In H. J. Prehm, L.A. Hamerlynck and J.E. Crosson (eds), *Behavioural Research in Mental Retardation.* Eugene, Oregon: University of Oregon Press, 1–23.

Herrnstein, R.J. (1973) *IQ in the Meritocracy.* London: Allen Lane.

Heuts, M.J. (1948) 'Adaptive properties of carriers of certain gene arrangements in *Drosophila pseudoobscura.*' *Heredity 2,* 63–75.

Higgins, J.V., Reed, E.W. and Reed, S.C. (1962) 'Intelligence and family size: a paradox resolved.' *Eugenics Quarterly 9,* 84–90.

Hirsch, J. (1962) 'Individual differences in behaviour and their genetic basis.' In E.L. Bliss (ed) *Roots of Behaviour.* New York: P. Hoeberg.

Hirsch, N.D.M. (1930) 'An experimental study upon three hundred school children over a six year period.' *Genetic Psychology Monograph 7,* 6, 493–546.

Honzik, M.P. (1957) 'Developmental studies of parent-child resemblance in intelligence.' *Child Development 28*, 215–228.

Honzik, M.P. (1972) 'Intellectual abilities at age 40 years in relation to the early family environment.' In F.J. Monks, W.W. Hartup and J. de Wit (eds) *Determinants of Behavioural Development.* New York: Academic Press.

Honzik, M.P., McFarlane, J.W. and Allen, L. (1938) 'The stability of mental test performance between two and eighteen years.' *Journal of Experimental Education 17*, 309–324.

Jencks, C. (1973) *Inequality.* London: Allen Lane.

Jensen, A.R. (1969) 'How much can we boost IQ and scholastic achievement?' *Harvard Educational Review 39*, 1–123.

Jensen, A.R. (1973) *Educability and Group Differences.* London: Methuen.

Jensen, A.R. (1974a) 'Cumulative deficit: a testable hypothesis?' *Developmental Psychology 10*, 996–1019.

Jensen, A.R. (1974b) 'Kinship correlations reported by Sir Cyril Burt.' *Behavior Genetics 4*, 1–28.

Jones, D.F. (1924) 'The attainment of homozygosity in inbred strains of maize.' *Genetics 9*, 405–418.

Jones, H.E. (1928) 'A first study of parent–child resemblance in intelligence.' *Yearbook of the National Society for the Study of Education 27*, 1, 61–72.

Kagan, J. and Moss, H.A. (1959) 'Parental correlates of child's IQ and height: a cross-validation of the Berkeley growth study results.' *Child Development 30*, 325–332.

Kamin, L. (1973) 'Heredity, intelligence, politics, and psychology.' Invited address to the Eastern Psychological Association Meetings, May 1973. Subsequently published in C.J. Karier (ed) *Shaping the Educational State: 1900–1970.* New York: The Free Press.

Kangas, J. and Bradway, K.P. (1971) 'Intelligence at middle age: a 38-year follow-up.' *Developmental Psychology 5*, 333–337.

Leahy, A.M. (1935) Nature–nurture and intelligence. *Genetic Psychology Monographs 17*, 4, 241–305.

Lerner, I.M. (1954) *Genetic Homeostasis.* Edinburgh: Oliver & Boyd.

McCall, R.B. (1970) 'Intelligence quotient pattern over age: comparisons among siblings and parent–child pairs.' *Science 170*, 644–648.

McNemar, Q. (1942) *The Revision of the Stanford–Binet Scale: An Analysis of the Standardization Data.* Boston: Houghton Mifflin.

McNemar, Q. (1947) 'Intellectual status of the gifted subjects as adults.' In L.M. Terman and M.H. Oden (eds) *Genetic Studies of Genius, IV.* Stanford, California: Stanford University Press.

Outhit, M.C. (1933) 'A study of the resemblance of parents and children in general intelligence.' *Archives of Psychology 23*, 1–60.

Penrose, L.S. (1933) 'A study of the inheritance of intelligence.' *Bristish Journal of Psychology 24*, 1–19.

Pinneau, S.R. (1961) *Changes in Intelligence from Infancy to Maturity.* Boston: Houghton Mifflin.

Polansky, N.A., Borgman, R.D. and De Saix, C. (1969) 'Mental organization and maternal adequacy in rural Appalachia.' *American Journal of Orthopsychiatry 39*, 246–247.

Reed, E.W. and Reed, S.C. (1965) *Mental Retardation: A Family Study.* Philadelphia: Saunders.

Robertson, F.W. (1955) 'Selection response and the properties of genetic variation.' *Coldspring Harbor Symposium on Quantitative Biology 20*, 166–177.

Schaie, K.W. and Strother, C.R. (1968) 'A cross-sequential study of age changes in cognitive behaviour.' *Psychological Bulletin 70*, 671–680.

Skodak, M. and Skeels, H.M. (1949) 'A final follow-up study of 100 adopted children.' *Journal of Genetic Psychology 75*, 85–125.

Snygg, D. (1938). 'The relation between the intelligence of mothers and of their children living in foster homes.' *Journal of Genetic Psychology 52*, 401–406.

Sontag, L.W., Baker, C.T. and Nelson, V.L. (1958) 'Mental growth and personality development: a longitudinal study.' *Monographs of the Society for Research in Child Develompent 23*, No. 68, 1–143.

Speer, G.S. (1940) 'The mental development of children of feeble-minded and normal mothers.' *Yearbook of the National Society for the Study of Education 39*, 2, 309–314.

Stanton, R.G. (1946). 'Filial and fraternal correlations in successive generations.' *Annals of Eugenics 13*, 18–24.

Waller, J.H. (1971) 'Achievement and social mobility: relationships among IQ score, education and occupation in two generations.' *Social Biology 18*, 252–259.

Wechsler, D. (1958) *The Measurement and Appraisal of Adult Intelligence* (4th edn). Baltimore: Williams & Wilkins.

Willoughby, R.R. (1928) 'Family similarities in mental test abilities.' *Yearbook of the National Society for the Study of Education 27*, 1, 55–59.

CHAPTER 15

The Burt Affair

Commentary

This commentary offers a unique, but incomplete, account of our part in exposing Sir Cyril Burt's fraudulent data in two classic studies. It precedes a brief published letter which summarizes some of our evidence.

Readers may remember a biographical note in Chapter 1 which included the fact that, although working under H.J. Eysenck's supervision for our PhDs at the Institute of Psychiatry, we had to register under Burt at University College, London. This was because Burt, whose enmity towards the Institute was well known, had blocked Eysenck's official university status. To us, this new situation was no more than a nuisance. We were expected to attend Burt's brilliant although highly egocentric lectures, to undertake a statistical analysis which he had invented, although an adviser had suggested another, and, reasonably enough, to report progress from time to time. However, he also demanded of one of us to add a critical chapter to our thesis concerning Eysenck's new statistical method which we had not used, nor did Burt discuss with Eysenck the appointment of external examiners. He was, however, always courteous and in many ways kind to us and we were pleased to have so grand a name as a referee for job applications.

Burt had asked us to approve or correct two thesis abstracts he had prepared. We did so, making minor changes, and it did not occur to us to ask why he had taken this trouble and had failed to use our submitted summaries. We were surprised a couple of months after our PhD success to find thesis summaries in print and to be greeted by a colleague who had found these reports to be slanted against Eysenck. On careful reading, we acknowledged this, having failed to recognize some of the contents. Much later we were to learn that insertions and corrections were part of Burt's repertoire, without consultation with the authors. We went to apologize to Eysenck who dismissed the problem with the statement that this sort of thing was to be expected of the old man.

Burt had had an amazingly productive and successful career. Starting in 1913 as the first educational psychologist in the world, he had been appointed by the London County Council (LCC). In this connection he had produced the first intelligence and attainment tests in England, and had worked to identify children in need of special education. In 1924 he was appointed to the Chair of Educational Psychology in what was then the London Day Training College. Gradually the LCC began to use IQ tests as part of the London Junior County Scholarship examination and ultimately Burt played a considerable part in various committees, and influenced the contents of the 1944 Education Act. He was knighted in 1946, the first psychologist to be so honoured.

In 1932 Burt had moved from education to take the Chair of Psychology at University College, London, the most senior chair of only five in Great Britain. He continued in the footsteps of his predecessor Charles Spearman, who had built up a small but powerful research school centring on the investigation of human abilities and personality traits, employing psychometric methods, especially the development of factor analysis.

Burt wrote distinguished articles on the factor analysis of human ability and became deeply interested in the genetic determinants of intelligence, among many other subjects. In this connection he published two seminal papers in retirement, one on ability and attainment (1961) and the other on identical twins reared together and separately (1966). In both cases Mendelian genetic models have precise predictions and amazingly Burt was able to record large groups of people who fulfilled them. In the case of ability and attainment he wrote about several hundreds of adults and their offspring, with IQ scores in six social classes, ranging from higher professional through managerial to unskilled manual. Many scholars wondered how he had obtained this precise material. So far as the twin study was concerned, Burt said that he had had the opportunity of collecting a large cohort of identical twins separated in infancy (often because parents could not afford to raise two children in addition to those they already had). These separations had often involved different social classes between twin pairs, and they were followed up with IQ tests many years later. In fact, he claimed to have access to more records than all the other twin studies of identical twins reared apart combined.

In 1974 we published a chapter, an enlarged revision of earlier chapters, for the third edition of a textbook. This concerned genetic–environmental interactions in cognitive development, and among other researches we had to review these articles. We noted that the findings were 'suspiciously perfect', contained 'puzzling features' and we identified many problems with the interpretation of the data. We wrote regretfully that Burt's work raised 'a number of important questions which unfortunately can never be answered now', Burt having died in 1971 (Clarke and Clarke 1974). How wrong we were! There began at this time to be stirrings of dissatisfaction with the general acceptance of Burt's work, particularly by those who disliked his very hereditarian stance, buttressed as it was by the largest, most perfect sample and the most extreme results pointing to a genetic determination of intelligence. American scholars were busy re-analysing the published output and in London Jack Tizard made it his business to enquire about two ladies who were intimately associated with Burt's data, who published jointly, or from his laboratory in University College. Perhaps it should be noted that after his retirement Burt had been denied access to his offices since he had proved to be too dominant in the department for his new successor to accept. It was also well known that Burt wrote what were termed 'spoof letters' to 'his' journal, under noms de plume, criticizing others and quoting himself as a part of the rebuttal. So Tizard, on approaching the British Psychological Society (of which he had just become President), was told that Margaret Howard and J. Conway were completely unknown and, with some amusement, that they were probably further noms de plume! At that time, one of us was working on a paper included in this book (Chapter 14) and had concluded that Burt's data were too unsatisfactory to be used in the analysis. A journalist (formerly a geneticist) from the *Sunday Times* became interested, came to Hull and told us that he could find no evidence for the existence of the two ladies anywhere (they were supposed to have gone to Australia) and it clicked in our minds that the answer to our puzzles was that the old man had invented the data. We allowed ourselves to be quoted in Oliver Gillie's article, initiating an enormous explosion in the scientific, educational and political worlds of knowledge.

Burt had been, as noted, the most eminent and honoured professor of psychology, whose past students were scattered all over the English-speaking world and were in many cases occupying Chairs. They were (mostly) horrified at our accusations, and assumed wrongly that our motivation had been a belief in the overwhelming importance of the environment, not heredity. In fact, our motivation was a feeling of horror that this man had abused the trust which is the bedrock on which scholarship exists.

There were vigorous arguments in *The Times* and elsewhere and various psychologists took up the cudgels on Burt's behalf; several 'remembered' Margaret Howard, and one thought that he had been tested by J. Conway. Most of the discussion was about Howard, clearly a mathematician of considerable talent, who had published with Burt and on her own, on the factor analysis of mental ability. However, in all the brouhaha one of us remembered that it was J. Conway who was thanked for testing the twins in the series of articles by Burt published over the years. She published herself in 1958 and 1959, although she was not, nor even had been, associated with the address whence she wrote. We undertook a close search of all the data, and wrote to the British Psychological Society's Bulletin as follows:

Letter to the *Bulletin of the British Psychological Society*

Sir Cyril Burt

Dear Sirs,

Professor Hearnshaw (*Bulletin*, January 1977) rightly states that the campaign against Burt cannot be dismissed simply as a politically motivated smear. Indeed, the three independent sources of academic criticism, all published at about the same time, came from psychologists of very different persuasions on the nature/nurture issue. Professor Kamin (1974) who gave a pre-view of his analysis in a September 1972 lecture, appears to be an extreme environmentalist. Professor Jensen's (1974) paper, which presents an important analysis of Burt's data, concluded that his correlations were useless for hypothesis testing, although his own hereditarian position remains unchanged. Finally, our very much less ambitious review (1974), confined to a few pages (pp.168–171) in a textbook, indicated our grave suspicions, later amplified (McAskie and Clarke 1976, pp.256, 269). Our position on the nature/nurture issue has been stated frequently; we have no doubt that genetic and constitutional factors play a significant role in determining intellectual differences.

All, then, whatever their persuasion, are at least agreed about 'worthlessness'. In this extraordinary situation, a major question arises. Was it merely carelessness on Burt's part, as some of his apologists maintain? Our colleague, Michael McAskie has pointed out in examining Burt's papers, that carelessness was in many important matters, unidirectional in favour of his own beliefs. We consider that, for those who have not exposed themselves to the tedium of checking and cross-checking the many publications, final judgements on Burt and all his work, as Professor Hearnshaw suggests, should for the time being be suspended, particularly since the contents of diaries and letters remain to be evaluated.

---

*   Reprinted from the *Bulletin of the British Psychological Society 30*, 1977, pp.83–84.

We are also in complete agreement with Professor Hearnshaw's implication that there remain a number of important matters yet to be elucidated. The status, qualifications, whereabouts in the 1950s and role of Miss J. Conway, first generally queried by Professor Tizard, are certainly among them. As just one example of these problems, it may be helpful to offer a very minimal documentation. Burt (1943) mentioned (p.91) a sample of 15 pairs of MZ twins reared apart. In the same paper Miss Conway is credited (p.91) with testing foster children. In 1955 (p.167) we find that she is noted as collecting data and undertaking the final computations, 'having been able to increase the number of cases, particularly for the small but crucial groups of monozygotic twins reared together or apart', the latter now numbering 21 pairs.

In 1957, Burt reported that nearly 30 pairs had been investigated. In 1958, this became 'over 30 such cases'. In the same year Conway, who unlike Margaret Howard, never published jointly with Burt, noted that 'Since the last review of our own cases was published' (reference to Burt 1955) 'our collection has been still further enlarged... The number of cases of this type – all identical twins reared apart from early infancy – now amounts to 42' (p.186).

In 1959, Miss Conway (p.7) refers to her 1958 article. During this period in the 1950s her address is given as either University College, London, or Psychology Department, University College, London. In 1966, Burt (p.141) reports that he had now studied 53 pairs of separated MZ twins, and Miss Conway's 1958 paper is referred to (p.140, where a detailed statement of the elaborate and unusual testing procedure is given, and in an important footnote p.141). Thus, by 1966 Burt and Conway had gathered the largest separated MZ twin sample in the world, appropriately and uniquely divided across different social classes and, incidentally exhibiting impressive normal distributions for IQ, with a range from 37 points below the population mean to 32 above. In her 1959 paper Miss Conway (p.11) presents data related to social class and intelligence of schoolchildren in London 'tested by Burt and myself in 1950'.

So Miss Conway was associated with University College, London, from at least 1950 to 1959 and was collaborating with Burt from some time prior to 1943. Her work was apparently majorly based on London. Yet she is not recorded as either a student or as staff in any institution in the University, including the Institute of Education (formerly the Day Training College), nor was she employed in any capacity that can be ascertained by the LCC. She was never a member of the BPS, and inquiries to other British universities for identification have so far proved fruitless (Dr O. Gillie, personal communication). Miss Conway was also unknown in the 1950s to those most closely and regularly in contact with Burt. His secretary, who worked for him from 1950 until his death, has stated that Burt in fact wrote the two articles of which Conway was the sole author, explaining that she had gone abroad without leaving an address. Yet between the 1955 and 1958 reports, Miss Conway had doubled the size of the separated MZ twin sample. These brief examples and many other problems concerning the data base of the Burt (1961) paper on intelligence and social mobility (in which results are reported from an extraordinarily large sample of fathers in different occupational categories and their sons) remain to be resolved.

It is, to say the least, unfortunate that so many questions have to be asked concerning the two most widely quoted papers (Burt 1961, 1966) hitherto taken on trust by scientists who had placed confidence in the statements of an eminent man, a confidence which reflected his reputation for scholarship and his erudition.

Yours faithfully,

Ann M. Clarke and A.D.B. Clarke
University of Hull
Hull HU6 7RX

Needless to say, Miss Conway was never identified, and the one individual who thought that he had been tested by her was wrong, according to May Davidson who was at Aberystwyth at the material time, undertaking testing for Burt. Nor is it necessary to indicate additional internal evidence for fraud, uncovered by R. Rawles (personal communication, 2002).

Burt's Edwardian prose, including an excessive use of elaborate footnotes, is easily identified without any need for computer analysis. So any reading of *the British Journal of Statistical Psychology* (of which Burt was the senior editor) enables one to identify the 'spoof letters' and the pseudonymous (and often savage) reviews which he had included.

To say more would constitute an overkill. The tragic fact remains that Burt was a brilliant deceiver, always arranging that his 'data' would be bigger and better than anyone else's. Readers wishing to learn more about Burt are referred to Hearnshaw's (1979) book. See also our Chapter 2 and our published correspondence with Burt.

References

Burt, C. (1943) 'Ability and income.' *British Journal of Educational Psychology 13*, 83–98.

Burt, C. (1955) 'Evidence for the concept of intelligence.' *British Journal of Educational Psychology 25*, 158–177.

Burt, C. (1957) 'Inheritance of mental ability.' *Eugenics Review 49*, 137–141.

Burt, C. (1958) 'The inheritance of mental ability.' *American Psychologist 13*, 1–15.

Burt, C. (1961) 'Intelligence and social mobility.' *British Journal of Statistical Psychology 14*, 3–24.

Burt, C. (1966) 'The genetic determination of differences in intelligence: A study of monozygotic twins reared together and apart.' *British Journal of Psychology 57*, 137–153.

Clarke, A.M. and Clarke, A.D.B. (1974) *Mental Deficiency: The Changing Outlook* (3rd edn). London: Methuen; New York: The Free Press.

Clarke, A.M. and Clarke, A.D.B. (1977) 'Sir Cyril Burt.' *Bulletin of the British Psychological Society 30*, 83–84.

Conway, J. (1958) 'The inheritance of intelligence and its social implications.' *British Journal of Statisitcal Psychology 11*, 171–189.

Conway, J. (1959) 'Class differences in general intelligence: II.' *British Journal of Statistical Psychology 12*, 5–14.

Hearnshaw, L.S. (1979) *Cyril Burt, Psychologist.* London: Hodder & Stoughton.

Jensen, A.R. (1974) 'Kinship correlations reported by Sir Cyril Burt.' *Behavior Genetics 4*, 1–28.

Kamin, L.J. (1974) *The Science and Politics of IQ.* Potomac, Md: Erlbaum.

McAskie, M. and Clarke, A.M. (1976) 'Parent–offspring resemblances in intelligence: Theories and evidence.' *British Journal of Psychology 67*, 243–273.

CHAPTER 16

Task Complexity and Transfer in the Development of Cognitive Structures

Commentary

The present chapter reviews and extends some ten years of experimental work on learning transfer, the facilitatory (or less often, inhibitory) effect of learning one task on another. The series began with an observation by D.O. Hebb that the classic work on this topic used adolescent or adult subjects. But transfer, if any, would have taken place earlier in life so that its later assessment would show minimal effects…shutting the stable door after the horse had bolted. The corollary of this view is that by the time adulthood is reached, nothing really new ever happens. A 'new' event is related to earlier experiences and conceptualized as such. For example, in meeting a Pekingese and then a Great Dane, these, though different, are automatically categorized as 'dog' and certain common characteristics inferred.

Initially studying learning disabled children and adults, Hebb's view was apparently confirmed, the younger gaining much more from one learning experience on another than did the adults. But ultimately this proved to have been the result of 'ceiling effects'. There was the problem of differing starting points in learning by adults versus children, so that the former had no possibility of improving their performance since this had already reached its limits, while the children had every chance of gaining from experiences which had previously been lacking in their young lives.

The problem was solved by equating the starting levels of adults and children, not only by holding the learning and transfer tasks constant, but above all equalizing their starting levels. We reduced the task by a third for the children, so that they and the adults started on the same footing. The transfer to the new task was then exactly the same (and considerable) for both groups. This suggested that complexity of the tasks was the important variable for eliciting transfer. This work was continued and the role of complexity confirmed in a set of tasks in which accurate sorting was needed for correct solution. Thus comparison was made between, at one extreme, the sorting of simple geometric shapes, and at the other, more complicated shapes, both in relation to the task on which transfer was measured, a set of photographs of common objects. These consisted of different examples in each of the following categories: furniture, clothing, tableware, animals and humans. Bruner had pointed out that categorization involves treating things as *equivalent*, even though discriminably *different*, and that such categorization reduces the complexity of the environment. For example, pictures of a chair, a table and a wardrobe can all, in certain predetermined circumstances, be treated as furniture. In life, common experiences thus build up innumerable concepts or mental structures which enable people to cope with the daily bombardment of different stimuli in generalized ways.

In rather complicated experiments the results gained from the study of severely learning disabled children and adults were confirmed with normal, equally naive, preschool children. Using several different and complicated learning and transfer tasks it became clear that those which demanded the formation of new rules to establish categorical equivalence yielded the most significant transfer results. The implications are that the exposure to complicated tasks (or events), which demand new psychological structures in coping with unusual complexity, is surely a basis for further individual development, a bit close to Vygotsky's 'zones of proximal development'. In plainer English, practice in categorizing particular tasks has effects more general in facilitating the learning of entirely different concepts. In a word, for the naive preschooler, practice in thinking facilitates thinking.

Ordinarily we build up a vast number of categories through the demands which life imposes on us. The advantages in studying our subjects is that one can track and anticipate the development of concepts as they occur. And in the naive, this may accelerate ordinary developmental processes.

The series of experiments recorded here was carried out under the auspices of the National Health Service, the Nuffield Foundation and the Association of the Aid of Crippled Children, New York. It was picked out for mention in an *Annual Review of Psychology*.

Task Complexity and Transfer in the Development of Cognitive Structures[*]

Ann M. Clarke, G.M. Cooper and Alan, D.B. Clarke[1]

An experiment with naive preschool Ss concerns transfer effects on a category sorting problem, induced by training on a variety of tasks differing from the former in perceptual and conceptual content. An attempt was made to control for the possibility that differing motivation might be responsible for differential transfer, and a cognitive theory is considered more appropriate in accounting for the results. Evidence indicates the presence of two forms of transfer, one relating to specific categories (even though different exemplars may be involved) and the other to an increasing capacity of the organism to structure variability after exposure to complex learning experiences.

A number of psychologists have argued that transfer of previous learning may play an important role in the development of cognitive abilities. McGeoch and Irion (1952) write 'after small amounts of learning early in the life of the individual, every instance of learning is a function of the already existent learned organization of the subject; that is, all learning is influenced by transfer'. Harlow has repeatedly stated his position that behaviour which appears in a mature person as reasoning ability is acquired on the basis of progressively formed learning sets; he states (1949) that 'a host of different learning sets may supply the raw material for human thinking'. Hebb (1949) also developed the notion that transfer might be highly important in cognitive development, and his view that transfer from early experience might be greater and more generalized than in adult life formed the basis for the early work in the series of experiments to be reported.

Starting with a hypothesis derived from this view, Clarke and his colleagues made a direct comparison of institutionalized retarded children and adults on visual discrimination tasks and found that significantly greater transfer was demonstrated by the younger subjects (Clarke and Blakemore 1961; Clarke and Cookson 1962). The tasks used included the sorting of typewriter key-tops bearing symbols unfamiliar to the Ss, and the formboards of the Minnesota Spatial Relations Test. In these investigations the measure used was time taken to complete the tasks, using a correction procedure. Clarke argued that the substantial transfer shown was due to learning set, improved perceptual

* This article first appeared in 1967 in the *Journal of Experimental Child Psychology 5*, pp.562-576.

discrimination and (since, as learning progressed more efficient strategies were demonstrated) improved conceptual discrimination. The latter notion implies the formation of structures, defined by Mandler (1962) as 'temporal and probabilistic linkages of inputs and behaviour which are available in functional units'.

In later experiments (Clarke and Cooper 1964, 1966a) adjustment was made for the different starting levels of the adults and children by increasing the complexity of the task for the former and decreasing it for the latter. In both cases similar learning and transfer curves resulted, leading to the hypothesis that task complexity might be a relevant variable in transfer studies.[2]

It seemed desirable to test this hypothesis, holding age constant and varying the complexity of the training tasks. In addition, since in these experiments tasks were used which, while differing in content, were sufficiently similar for there to be an obvious correlation between strategies, it was decided to investigate transfer across tasks in which both perceptual and conceptual components were dissimilar.

Task complexity and category learning

In the first of this series of experiments (Clarke, Cooper and Henney 1966) four groups of imbecile *Ss* were used, matched for age, sex, Binet IQ, and score on one trial of the transfer task, which consisted of photographs of objects within five common conceptual categories, to be matched to a sample from each. Two groups were given pretraining on complex sorting tasks involving categorizing geometric shapes; one group was trained to match simple shapes; one group received no training. Transfer was significantly greater for the groups which received complex training.

Similar results were obtained (Clarke and Cooper 1966b) from matched groups of intellectually normal preschool children aged between 33 and 60 months. Using a modified version of the transfer task (photographs of common objects) and three new training tasks (each based on different geometric shapes),[3] it was shown that the two groups trained on either of the complex problems, which differed from each other substantially in level of difficulty, were greatly superior in their learning to a control group and a group trained on a very easy sorting task. In addition, the level attained on shift to parallel versions of the transfer task (using the same categories but different pictures) was directly related to the rapidity of initial acquisition and thus to the amount of overtraining, and indirectly to type of pretraining. Nevertheless, the fact that there was, as in the previous study, no difference in the considerable amount of transfer shown by the two groups trained on the more complex tasks indicated that, at least within the limits of the experimental paradigm used, there was no monotonic relation between complexity of pretraining and amount of transfer. Since, however, the number of trials had been held constant for all groups, those trained on the easier complex task had reached their asymptote early and thereafter had been overtrained. A further group (matched with the others) was therefore trained to asymptote on this problem and then immediately switched to the transfer task; these subjects showed significantly less transfer than the two contrast groups. Thus, the transfer effect previously demonstrated appeared also to be related to the amount of time spent on the complex pretraining, although the precise interaction between these factors remains to be determined. Analysis of the responses made by the children trained on the complex material revealed that both for the training and the transfer tasks there was a significant tendency for categories to appear in a hierarchical order, with, however, a significant $S \times$ Category interaction.

The findings were related to Mandler's (1962) view of the formation of cognitive structures from overlearned associations. They also apply to some speculations by Bruner (1957) on factors underlying the emergence of coding systems. Defining a coding system as 'a set of contingently related, nonspecific categories' similar to Bartlett's (1932) idea of schemata, he proposes four general sets of conditions which may be relevant to the acquisition of coding systems: (a) set or attitude, (b) need state, (c) degree of mastery of original learning, and (d) diversity of training. He suggests that from a diversity of experience the organism develops generic codes which may have narrower or wider applicability. Elsewhere Bruner, Goodnow and Austin (1956) have pointed out that the learning and utilization of categories represents one of the most elementary and general forms of cognition by which man adjusts to his environment (p.2); and that 'by categorizing as equivalent discriminably different events, the organism *reduces the complexity of its environment*' (p.12, Bruner's italics). The assumption underlying the theoretical positions of Mandler, Bartlett and Bruner seems to be that the organism acquires a structure, schema or generic code in one or more situations which he can employ in different situations, accelerating his mastery of new problems.

In view of the results of these experiments, it may be important to distinguish between two levels of cognitive structure; on the one hand concepts or schemata developed in one situation will be readily available in another and may be extended to include new material (as in the shift from the transfer task to parallel versions using the same categories, but different exemplars). On the other hand, the gain demonstrated in the main experiment from the complex training tasks to the transfer task was clearly not related to specific behaviours, but rather to the cognitive organization of the material.

Thus, it is postulated that the experience of forming a set of rules for organizing one complex situation facilitated the formation of a different set of rules in another complex situation.

Before this hypothesis can be regarded as firmly established, however, some further factors must be considered. The present experiment was designed to test these.

Hypotheses arising from existing findings

(a) *Difficulty rather than complexity facilitated the transfer* demonstrated. It may be argued that in the experiments described so far two factors have been confounded: (1) difficulty which might give rise to increased attention and effort on the part of the *Ss*, altering their level of general adaptation, and (2) complexity, which relates to the number of dimensions (relevant and irrelevant) present in a configuration or task, which may require coding. Although as pointed out (Clarke *et al.* 1966) the terms 'difficulty' and 'complexity' are not necessarily synonymous, they are often used interchangeably and are normally related. It seemed important, however, to separate these factors in a new experiment and to contrast the transfer effect of complex tasks with a difficult task, similarly demanding of attention and effort but of lower complexity. In this way motivational factors might be controlled.

(b) *The differential transfer shown by complex as opposed to simple tasks was due to a specific set in the former to establish equivalence between different exemplars within categories.* On this hypothesis no transfer would be expected between a training task, however complex, in which exemplars did not differ from the stimuli (i.e. a matching task) and the transfer task in which differences between stimuli and exemplars were rather wide.

(c) *The transfer effects were in large part due to the fact that all material was visually presented and would not occur in conditions where the training was non-visual.* (d) *The demonstrated transfer effects were partly due to chance factors and would not stand the test of further repetition.* Five tasks were used to test these hypotheses: they are described in the following section. The transfer task was, of course, the same as that previously employed, and number of trials was held constant on each training task (24) and on the transfer task (10).

Method

Subjects

Forty-five intellectually normal preschool children, aged between 3½ and 4¾ years, were drawn from two state nursery schools. Initial selection was based on age, score, and errors on one trial of the transfer task, and the *S*'s willingness to co-operate. Five matched groups were thus obtained, with the additional constraints that an approximately equal number of children from each school should be assigned to each group, and that the number of boys and girls in each group was similar. Each group was then randomly allocated to one of four training conditions; Table 16.1 summarizes the data. Control data for 13 *Ss*, from a previous experiment (conducted in the same two schools), were available.

	Table 16.1 Data on four experimental groups on transfer task prior to training					
Statistics	Circles $n=9$	Quadri-lateral $n=9$	Words $n=9$	Simple matching $n=9$	Complex matching $n=9$	*F*
Mean score (out of 20)	7.55	7.55	7.44	7.55	7.33	<1
Mean errors	28.55	28.89	29.33	28.78	26.89	<1
Age in months	52.33	51.33	51.44	49.89	49.70	<1
Number of boys	6	5	6	5	6	

Note. Throughout this article the word Score relates to the number of cards placed correctly at the first attempt. The transfer task consisted of 20 response cards; each training task had 15 response cards.

The tasks

Transfer Task. The transfer task was the same as that used in one of the previous investigations (Clarke and Cooper 1966b), namely, a set of 25 photographs of common objects from five categories, five stimulus exemplars, and 20 response cards which had to be sorted to the stimuli. The stimulus pictures, which were placed in a different random order each trial, were: baby, pig, cup, sofa, dress. The 20 response pictures presented in the same random order each trial, were:

sheep, man, cupboard, knife, boy, bed, plate, shirt, girl, fork, cat, shoes, chair, spoon, hat, horse, table, dog, woman, gloves.

The *Shift Task*. Again the same as that used previously, given to all *S*s after initial training plus ten trials on the transfer task, consisted of outline drawings of objects on plain backgrounds. Most pictures in this condition represented new examples of the same five categories as those in the transfer task. The stimulus cards showed: a crocodile, a baby's cot, a little girl, a ski-jumper and a tea pot. The response cards were: shoe, woman's torso, desk, jug, kangaroo, boy's head, dressing-table, egg cup, tie, eagle, knife, TV set, deer, trousers, Indian fakir, armchair, hat, elephant's head and fore-legs, glass and a man.

Training Tasks. All training tasks consisted of five stimulus exemplars and 15 response cards. Each task related to one of the hypotheses already mentioned.

Hypothesis 1. The task designed to be difficult but not complex involved the discrimination of size of circles, differing in radius by $\frac{1}{12}$ inch. On each of five stimulus cards was drawn a circle with radii varying between $\frac{5}{12}$ inch and $\frac{9}{12}$ inch, inclusive; these were presented in different positions each trial. Response cards were made up of three identical exemplars of each stimulus object. Hereafter this is referred to as the Circles Task.

Hypothesis 2. Like the Circles Task, this problem consisted of five stimulus cards with three identical exemplars of each, presented in random order each trial. By contrast to the Circles Task, the Complex Matching Task consisted of five closely similar complex geometric figures, with some irrelevant details. The figures were as follows (actual height, $2\frac{1}{8}$ inch on 3 inch square cards):

Hypothesis 3. The Word Task was complex and fairly difficult. It consisted of five outline drawings to which verbs, spoken by *E*, had to be associated. In order to hold constant the motor act of card sorting in this condition, the words were each printed on a card and handed to the (illiterate) *S*s who placed them in the apparatus. The stimulus pictures for the Word Task were: a boy running, a girl sewing, a lady telephoning, a man driving a car, and a boy catching a ball. Words spoken by *E* were: knit, hop, clap, sing, ride, hit, jump, fly, mend, shout, skip, throw, whisper, cycle, darn.

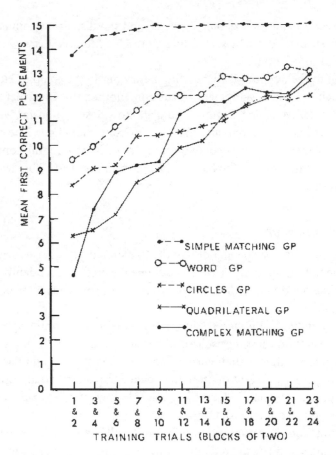

Figure 16.1 Mean first correct placement scores for matched groups under different training conditions over 24 trials

Hypothesis 4. Two tasks, slightly modified from earlier versions, were used. The Quadrilateral Task, which previously had yielded the greatest transfer effect, was difficult and complex, requiring the sorting of outline shapes of five different quadrilateral figures (squares, rectangles, parallelograms, trapezia and irregular shapes) differing in size, orientation, position on card, and internal relations of angles and lines. The Simple Matching Task was a slightly modified version of the task which previously had yielded slight negative transfer (compared with a control group). It required the sorting of five easily discriminable figures: cross, star, circle, equilateral triangle, and crescent. The stimulus figures were fairly small, while the response figures were approximately twice the size, but did not vary in any other respect. All figures in each category were the same. Thus, by comparison with the Quadrilateral Task, the distance between categories was much greater, and the distance within each category much smaller. As can be seen from Figure 16.1 this task was very easy for the children to perform.

According to the hypothesis that coding behaviour in the complex situation would facilitate the development of rules in another, the Quadrilateral, Word, and Complex Matching Groups should all show positive transfer, while the Simple Matching Task Group and the Circles Group should not. The performance of the latter two groups could be compared with that for the control *Ss* of the previous experiment, who had received no training at all before learning the transfer task.

Apparatus and procedure

The apparatus consisted of a panel holding the five stimulus cards, each with a box below, the floor (trap door) of which could be lowered independently, by levers at the side. A red light bulb was fixed in each box immediately beneath the stimulus card.

The *Ss*, seen individually each session, were seated in front of the apparatus. Two demonstration cards, not subsequently used in the experiment, were slowly placed one at a time in their correct compartment, the red light flashed and the card dropped from sight through the opened trap door. Verbal instructions were kept to a minimum. The subject was told 'I want you to put all the pictures I give you into their proper place.'

A correction procedure was used throughout as follows. In each case when a correct response was made the red light came on, *E* said 'Good' and the card disappeared. If the response was incorrect, *E* said 'No,' the red light failed to come on and the trap door remained closed. The card was handed to the *S* who was then required to try again. In the rare cases where a correct response was not obtained after five attempts, *E* placed the card in the correct compartment and the next response card was offered.

Note was taken of each response and the precise location of each error. Positions of stimulus cards on the panel were randomized under each condition on every trial. During the training trials the order of presentation of response cards was reversed every other trial. In the transfer and shift tasks a fixed random order was used from trial to trial.

Trials on the various tasks were given as follows: a single pretraining trial was given to all children on the transfer task, for matching purposes. Training on the five different tasks commenced two days later, and thereafter each group received two trials a day for 12 days (24 trials). After a further gap of two days following cessation of training the five groups proceeded to ten trials of

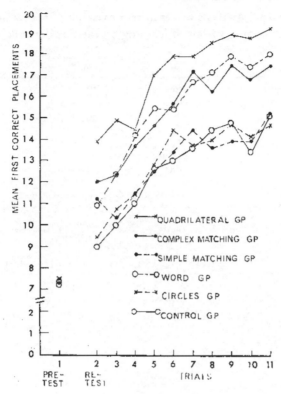

Figure 16.2 Mean first correct placement scores over 11 trials on the transfer task for originally matched groups trained under different initial training conditions

training on the transfer task (again two trials per day); after a further gap of two days all the *Ss* were given two trials on the shift task.

Results

Figure 16.1 shows the learning curves of each of the five groups on their respective training tasks; in all cases the score is the number correct out of 15. Figure 16.2 shows the performance of the same groups on trials of the transfer task; the score in this case is the number correct out of 20. It is obvious that the main hypothesis is confirmed: that, as before, the Quadrilateral Group emerges as very superior in performance to the Simple Matching Task Group, while the Circles Group resembles the latter. Analysis of variance of the scores for the latter two groups and the control group of 13 *Ss* over the ten trials on the transfer task yielded an *F*-ratio of less than 1 ($F = .23$, $df\,2/307$). It thus appears that a

Table 16.2 Analysis of variance for five groups (*n*=9 in each) over ten trials of learning on the transfer task

Source	df	MS	F
Occasions	9	167.57	17.56*
Groups	4	292.81	30.69*
Interaction	36	2.76	<1
Within cells	400	9.54	

	Tukey comparison of means				
Groups	Quadri-lateral	Words	Complex matching	Circles	Simple matching
	17.15	15.53	15.33	13.01	12.94
Quadrilateral	—	<.01	<.01	<.01	<.01
Words		—	NS	<.01	<.01
Complex matching			—	<.01	<.01
Circles				—	NS

*p <.001.

firm baseline had been established against which facilitation effects could be measured.

Analysis of scores over ten trials on the transfer task and Tukey comparison of means for the five experimental groups are given in Table 16.2.

Although it might not be immediately obvious how the sorting of different quadrilateral shapes is relevant to the classification of photographs of real objects, the fact that such a powerful facilitation effect is shown leads to the conclusion that the nature of the coding behaviour must be similar in both cases, and that the children had acquired a set to establish equivalence between different exemplars within categories.

By contrast to the above, the other two groups trained on complex tasks showed a significant superiority to the groups trained on an easy and a difficult non-complex task, but their gain was less impressive. The Words Group had moved from a situation where information was received auditorily to one where it was presented visually, while the Complex Matching Group had had no direct experience of making common responses to dissimilar stimuli.

Table 16.3 Analysis of variance of two trials on shift task			
Source	*df*	*MS*	*F*
Groups	4	42.09	4.44*
Residual	85	9.47	
	Tukey comparison of means				

Groups	Complex matching	Quadri-lateral	Words	Circles	Simple matching
	16.44	15.83	14.61	13.11	13.11
Complex matching	—	NS	NS	<.05	<.05
Quadrilateral		—	NS	<.05	<.05
Words			—	NS	NS
Circles				—	NS

*p <.005.

The results for the two trials on the shift task (outline drawings of different exemplars in the same categories as the transfer task) are given in Table 16.3.

In the previous experiment it was found that *Ss* who early attained high scores on the transfer task (and therefore had experienced more trials at a high level) showed greater efficiency on shift to the parallel version of the task than *Ss* who had learned more slowly. This finding was confirmed. Kendall's rank correlation was computed between the number of trials taken to reach a score of 18 on the transfer task and average score on the two trials of the shift task $\tau = .4755$; $z = 4.607$ $p < .00006$. It is clear from these results that members of the three groups originally trained on complex material maintained their superiority over those trained on non-complex material.

Finally, an attempt was made to discover something about the methods used by the children in the Quadrilateral Group to organize the material in this task. Although none of the *Ss* had shown any tendency to verbalize during their learning of the Quadrilateral Task, one obvious hypothesis was that they were using their own individual associations with objects.

At the end of the main experiment, therefore, these nine children were brought back to their original level on the Quadrilateral Task, after which the

Table 16.4 Words used by the two most consistent members of the Quadrilateral Group to describe the stimulus cards (one occasion) and response cards (two occasions)

Name given to stimulus cards

S I	(parallelogram) 'don't know what this is like'	(square) 'a box'	(rectangle) 'a stick'	(trapezoid) 'don't know what this is like'	(irregular) 'a tent'
Words given to response cards:					
Occasion 1	don't know	a box	a stick	don't know	a tent
	don't know	a box	a stick	don't know	don't know
	don't know	a box	a stick	don't know	don't know
Occasion 2	don't know	a box	a stick	don't know	a garage
	don't know	a box	a stick	don't know	don't know
	don't know	a box	a stick	don't know	don't know

Name given to stimulus cards

S II	(parallelogram) 'don't know'	(square) 'a window'	(rectangle) 'don't know'	(trapezoid) 'don't know'	(irregular) 'don't know'
Words given to response cards:					
Occasion 1	a mattress	a window	a mattress	a mattress	a mattress
	a mattress	a window	a door	a mattress	a mattress
	a door	a window	a door	a mattress	a mattress
Occasion 2	a plastic door	a window	a door	a plastic door	a door
	a plastic door	a window	a window	a path	a door
	a window	a window	a door	a path	a window[a]

Note. The responses are arranged per category; these latter being designated in parentheses. [a] Incorrectly sorted.

following procedure was used: (a) the five stimulus cards were presented individually and each S asked to say what it looked like. Thereafter, the 15 response cards were presented in random order, with the same question asked, and the S's responses recorded. (b) As a further check, a day later Ss were given one trial of the task with the apparatus, and as they sorted each response card to the appropriate stimulus card they were asked what it looked like.

No clear evidence emerged on the methods whereby the children differentiated between the categories. Only two Ss showed a tendency to apply consistently a verbal label to material within some of the categories. The remaining seven Ss showed no such tendency, and frequently either perseverated with one response or gave 'don't know' in reply to the request that they name the shapes. To illustrate the point, the responses of the two most consistent Ss are reproduced in Table 16.4.

When the child was forced to employ words in the experimental situation, the proportion of 'don't knows' was high. Moreover, when he did attempt to name the shapes, he commonly perseverated, using the same word for shapes in different categories and often inappropriately. Thus, if the explicit use of words is taken as a reflection of their possible implicit use during the main experiment, no support was given to the hypothesis that words played a significant role in category differentiation. On the contrary, there was an observable paradox between the smooth, efficient placement of exemplars in their categories and the inefficient use of overlapping verbal responses.

Discussion

The main results add support to the hypothesis that (at least in naive Ss) the learning of complex sorting problems requiring the formation of cognitive structures (or concepts) will facilitate the learning of other problems requiring the sorting of dissimilar material.

While all five training tasks involved category discrimination, the essential difference between the Quadrilateral, Words, and Complex Matching Tasks on the one hand, and the Circles and Simple Matching Tasks on the other, appears to lie in the fact that in the former new rules had to be developed to establish categorical equivalence among the exemplars, while the latter tasks made no such demand. In the case of the Circles Group, learning presumably depended on improved perceptual judgement (which would probably transfer to another task requiring perceptual judgement) while for the Simple Matching Group the shapes to be sorted were both sufficiently familiar and sufficiently well differentiated for the categories to be easily identified from the start without the necessity for forming new rules.

Thus, for a wide range of discrimination tasks (not as yet fully explored), a relation is postulated between the amount of transfer shown in learning certain new tasks and the complexity and amount of the original learning for a given organism, with the obvious proviso that both shall be within the *Ss'* capabilities. In a discussion of stimulus variability and cognitive change Munsinger and Kessen (1966) propose four factors which they assume to be relevant, and which fit closely the theoretical position developed here: (a) human beings are sensitive to stimulus variability; (b) there is an upper limit on the capacity of human beings to process independent environmental events; (c) human beings are able to break through this limitation on their capacity to process independent events by developing rules (structures) which reduce the effective stimulus variability; (d) a person will be most likely to change his cognitive structure if he is presented with a level of cognitive uncertainty just beyond his present processing ability. If he is presented either with cognitive uncertainty far beyond his ability to process, or no cognitive uncertainty at all, little or no change will take place. To these we would, in the light of our findings, add a fifth postulate: (e) change of cognitive structure in one situation may lead to a more rapid structuring of a different set of variable stimuli, provided there has been a sufficient degree of learning in the first case.

It may not be necessary to assume that these postulates must be confined to human behaviour. Mandler (1962) considers that there is evidence both from animal and human studies suggesting that cognitive characteristics of the organism may be developed out of associationist processes. He discusses the 'warm up' effect, learning sets, and overlearning and transfer, arguing that these three effects all have one characteristic in common: 'practice on one task may have a facilitating effect on another task even though the behaviour required in the two tasks is topographically different, and may even be incompatible.' During learning, simple stimulus-response sequences and previously learned units of behaviour become welded into analogic structures, which may be a basis for mediational activity.

An alternative hypothesis to the suggestion that categorizing structures (or 'abilities') are developed by exposure to complex learning situations is that such situations usually demand closer attention and a higher level of arousal and hence induce greater efficiency, than simpler tasks. Berlyne (1960) has shown a consistent relationship between the amount of information in stimulus objects and the degree of attention or curiosity which they evoke; more recently Munsinger and Kessen (1966 and Munsinger, Kessen and Kessen 1964) have shown that young children prefer figures of high variability to low, even though they cannot adequately process them. By the same token, members of our Quadrilateral, Words, and Complex Matching Groups might be said to have become more generally 'aroused' by their complex training in contrast to the monotonous conditions of training suffered by the Circles and Simple Matching Groups.

While the Quadrilateral Task may have provoked arousal and curiosity, assisting the learning process, members of the Circles Group also showed systematic learning of a difficult task demanding similarly close attention.

Nevertheless, they failed to exhibit any significant transfer compared with either a control group or a group whose training material was so readily categorized that it could not be said to evoke careful attention. Thus the findings cannot be explained in terms of motivational factors rendering the Ss differentially attentive to the tasks.

It has long been recognized that learning will be facilitated where either specific categories are relevant to different tasks (even when new exemplars may be involved) or where a principle or relationship in the solution of one problem is also relevant to another. The present evidence suggests that, in addition, there can occur in the naive organism an increasing capacity to structure variability after exposure to complex categorization experiences. The limits to such facilitation remain to be discovered, and the question whether such findings might be replicated with other cognitive operations remains open.

Notes

1   The researches reported have been made possible by a generous grant from the Nuffield Foundation. The authors are also greatly indebted to Mr A.B. Royse for critically reading an early draft of this paper and for many helpful suggestions. In addition we wish to thank the many who made research facilities available, particularly the staff and pupils of the nursery schools where much of the research was conducted, and Mrs J. Nettleton for technical assistance.

2   Complexity relates to the number of relevant and irrelevant dimensions present in a task to which an organism may be expected to attend. In discrimination-learning experiments it may be manipulated in a number of ways including the following: (a) by increasing (or decreasing) the number of different categories upon which judgement has to be made or the number of different exemplars to be ordered within a category, (b) by increasing (or decreasing) the 'distance' between exemplars within given categories, or the distance between categories, (c) or by a combination of several of these.

3   Details of the transfer task, the more difficult of the complex tasks and method employed are given later in this paper.

References

Bartlett, F.C. (1932) Remembering: *An Experimental and Social Study.* London: Cambridge University Press.

Berlyne, D.E. (1960) *Conflict, Arousal and Curiosity.* New York: McGraw-Hill.

Bruner, J.S. (1957) 'Going beyond the information given.' In *Contemporary Approaches to Cognition.* Cambridge: Harvard University Press, 41–69.

Bruner, J.S., Goodnow, J.J. and Austin, G.A. (1956) *A Study of Thinking.* New York: John Wiley.

Clarke, A.D.B. and Blakemore, C.B. (1961) 'Age and perceptual-motor transfer in imbeciles.' *British Journal of Psychology 52,* 125–131.

Clarke, A.D.B. and Cookson, M. (1962) 'Perceptual-motor transfer in imbeciles: a second series of experiments.' *British Journal of Psychology 53,* 321–330.

Clarke, A.D.B. and Cooper, G.M. (1964) 'Age and perceptual-motor transfer of training.' *Perceptual Motor Skills 19,* 849–850.

Clarke, A.D.B. and Cooper, G.M. (1966) 'Age and perceptual-motor transfer in imbeciles: task complexity as a variable.' *British Journal of Psychology 57,* 113–119.

Clarke, A.M. and Cooper, G.M. (1966) 'Transfer in category learning of young children: its relation to task complexity and over-learning.' *British Journal of Psychology 57,* 361–373.

Clarke, A.M., Cooper, G.M. and Henney, A.S. (1966) 'Width of transfer and task complexity in the conceptual learning of imbeciles.' *British Journal of Psychology 57,* 121–128.

Harlow, H.F. and Harlow, M.K. (1949) 'Learning to think.' *Scientific American,* August.

Hebb, D.O. (1949) *The Organization of Behavior.* New York: Wiley.

Mandler, G. (1962) 'From association to structure.' *Psychological Review 69,* 415–427.

McGeoch, J.A. and Irion, A.L. (1952) *The Psychology of Human Learning.* New York: Longmans.

Munsinger, H. and Kessen, W. (1966) 'Stimulus variability and cognitive change.' *Psychological Review 73,* 164–178.

Munsinger, H., Kessen, W. and Kessen, M.L. (1964) 'Age and uncertainty: developmental variations in preference for variability.' *Journal of Experimental Child Psychology 1,* 1–15.

CHAPTER 17

Editorial

The Later Cognitive Effects of Early Intervention

Commentary

The Commentary in Chapter 4 presented our thesis that although there might be a strong correlation between early experience and later personality attributes, we do not consider that there is a necessary *causal* link between them. In the present chapter we review the later effects of early intervention. Our analysis of their later outcome rests on the too-often forgotten methodological principle that unless it can be positively shown that there was a significant *discontinuity* between early and later environmental circumstances, no conclusions can legitimately be drawn concerning the effect of the former. That is, a continuity of experience gives no clue about the effect of any period within the continuity. The idea of educational intervention in the earliest years rested on the widespread belief in the 1950s and 1960s that this period was absolutely critical for later psychosocial development, and thus the best possible time for educational intervention. Evidence of the very modest gains among socially disadvantaged children has already been presented in connection with the Commentary in Chapters 10 and 11 on sleeper effects. Here we consider the case more extensively at the invitation of a distinguished American journal.

We present the results both for socially deprived children and also for the more damaged learning disabled youngsters in whom the general pattern is reproduced. There is a fairly significant gain measurable at the end of the programme, followed by a fading of effects which may be rapid or more slow until by the end of the second year there is no cognitive difference between those who had experienced the intervention and those who had not on tests of academic and scholastic achievement. However, there was a significant tendency for the intervention children to do better on teachers' assessments than those without intervention, being less likely to be retained in grade (i.e.

repeating a year) or assigned to special classes. Head Start parents also saw benefits to their children and to themselves. The results are therefore mixed.

Special mention should perhaps be made of the famous Perry Preschool Project which, although offering rather brief intervention between the ages of 3 and 4½, also involved the mothers and was conducted by exceptionally dedicated teachers. In this research, the IQ and scholastic achievement in school was very much the usual, including fewer intervention children in special classes, but later these were more likely to graduate from high school, go to college or vocational training, be employed and were less likely to be delinquent. The authors believe, with us, that the preschool programme, although not particularly useful in itself, set off a chain of positive transactional events which supported the young people through childhood and adolescence.

By contrast, the Abecedarian programme, mentioned both in Chapter 3 and here, was a very concentrated intervention, starting in infancy and offering enrichment all day, every day, until age 6. At 12 there was a highly significant effect on the intervention students as assessed on both standardized tests and also teacher assessment. At age 21, while there was considerable overlap between the intervention children and the comparison group, some important differences remained.

It may be concluded, therefore, that with excellent concentrated and costly preschool intervention, processes may be initiated where, with the help of parents, teachers and significant others, disadvantaged children may develop some way towards achieving their potential. It may be suggested, however, that for children from chaotic families and parents unable to cope, adoption is likely to be far more effective in the rescue process than shorter-term programmes. For additional information see Chapter 5 in Clarke and Clarke (2000).

Editorial: The Later Cognitive Effects of Early Intervention[*]

Ann M. Clarke and Alan D.B. Clarke

Early intervention typically yields short-term advantages, both for children and their parents, and these effects should not be undervalued. As time passes after programme termination, however, cognitive increments usually follow

---

[*]   This article first appeared in 1989 in *Intelligence 13*, pp.289–297.

the law of diminishing returns unless the intervention sets off a chain of ongoing, positive consequences. In effect, continuing interventions and maintenance of these changes is unlikely. It follows, therefore, that familial factors (including both unfolding genetic, as well as psychosocial influences) are more important for long-term outcome than brief interventions themselves.

The argument to be advanced here is a logical outcome of the authors' position stated over many years: early psychosocial experience *by itself* has no *necessary* long-term effect on later development (A.D.B. Clarke 1968; A.M. Clarke 1982, 1984; Clarke and Clarke 1976, 1986). The original formulation arose from observations made in controlled studies during the 1950s: among a group of adolescents and young adults compulsorily detained in an institution for mental retardates, it was shown that the *worse* the early social history the *better* the outcome in terms of IQ increments and positive educational and social advances following *removal* from the seriously adverse social conditions involving cruelty and neglect (Clarke, Clarke and Reiman 1958). Thus, the early experience of this population had not damaged them irrevocably for life, and these young persons had responded to fairly minimal rehabilitation within a low economy setting. The findings, replicated elsewhere, emphasizing the potentially transitory nature of the effects of early experience, ultimately suggested to us that brief periods of enrichment in early life, followed by years in socially disadvantaged settings, would equally exhibit only temporary gains.

Intervention may be defined as a systematic attempt to alter the course of development from its predicted path, or from an established path. Early intervention may include deliberate attempts to accelerate gifted children by parental or other teaching. It should perhaps not be exclusively reserved for the variety of psychological or therapeutic interventions provided for handicapped, at-risk or disadvantaged preschoolers, as suggested in the definition provided by White, Bush and Casto (1985), although in the minds of many it has become synonymous with these. Early intervention may aim to lay foundations for healthy social and emotional behaviour, although outcome studies have tended to emphasize the more cognitive aspects. It is to these latter, IQ and perhaps its more important relation, scholastic achievement, that this paper is in the main addressed.

Our analysis of the later outcome of early intervention with disadvantaged preschoolers rests on the too-often forgotten methodological principle that unless it can be positively shown that there was a significant discontinuity between early and late environmental circumstances, no conclusions can legitimately be drawn concerning the effect of the former. The vast majority of children experience considerable environmental continuity during their first years and middle and late childhood; in broad terms the advantaged 3-year-old is likely to remain favoured, while the disadvantaged infant is likely to grow up in unfavourable conditions. Assuming that the life path will be determined by constitutional and environmental factors in interaction over the whole period of development, it will be clear that the long-term effects of experimental interventions which subsequently cease and where the families concerned are not in a position to offer continuity provide an important test of the position outlined at the outset.

The idea of educational intervention in the preschool years as a way of ensuring normal cognitive development in socially disadvantaged children rested on a belief, widespread in the 1950s and 1960s, that the earliest years were critical for later psychosocial development, a view originating in modern times with ethological experiments, popularized by Konrad Lorenz and his followers and extrapolated from chicks, rats, dogs and monkeys to humans. As just one example, here is a quotation from J. P. Scott's *Early Experience and the Organization of Behaviour* (1968, p.152):

> What can we accomplish with our knowledge of early experience? For a laboratory rat we can prescribe an enriched physical environment which will enhance his ability to perform on certain intelligence tests and a regime of infantile stimulation that will make him a hardier and more emotionally stable adult. For a rhesus monkey we can provide the opportunity for social play during the first six months of life that will ensure the development of normal sexual behavior in both sexes and proper patterns of infant care in the females. For the dog we can give a prescription for the development of a well-balanced animal with satisfactory social relationship with both dogs and people, simply by recommending that he be taken from the litter between six and eight weeks of age and then adopted into human society.

The author suggests that due allowances should be made for human biological and cultural peculiarities, but that we ought to make similar concrete recommendations for human development. He writes that 'indeed some application of the findings from basic research in early experience is being made in the "head-start" programmes for children who are culturally deprived...'.

The importance of long-term social factors has become increasingly accepted over the years, perhaps partly as it became clear, on the basis of empirical evidence, that a single shot of educational experience, however apparently successful at its conclusion, would not ensure important lasting benefits to its recipients. Indeed, Entwistle, Alexander, Cadigan and Pallas (1987) writing on the effects of kindergarten, suggest that some of the positive effects attributed to Head Start may result from the children's experience in kindergarten. Schweinhart and Weikart (1980), authors and originators of the relatively successful Perry Preschool Programme, wrote, 'As data accumulate, it is clear that we are viewing a complex network of causes and effects. The preschool intervention has been successful over the years because its effects became the causes of other effects as well' (p.64). (See also Berrueta-Clement, Schweinhart, Barnett, Epstein and Weikart 1984).

Fowler (1986), whose book *Early Experience and the Development of Competence* is chiefly concerned with advantaged children, quotes a study by Swenson, who introduced intensive language stimulation to a group of infants beginning at 3 months and to another group at 8 months. The former showed a significant advantage which was, however, maintained only in those infants whose parents continued the intensive involvement in language interaction with their infants after the formal 12-month programme terminated.

Very recently, Ramey (1988), who has co-ordinated the well-designed Abecedarian project since its inception in 1972, has reported findings which support our thesis. Ninety children identified at birth as being at high risk for school failure and mild mental retardation had been randomly assigned in early infancy to educational intervention and control conditions (see Ramey and Campbell 1981, 1984; Ramey and Haskins 1981). At kindergarten they were again randomly assigned to a school-age intervention group or to a control condition. A special Home/School Resource programme was provided for the school-age intervention group during the first three years of elementary school, thus continuing the early intervention. One-half of each preschool group was so assigned. In addition, a comparison group of socially more advantaged classroom peers was selected. In terms of school achievement the results showed the positive effects of early and continuing educational programmes (birth to age 8) with the children who had received early but not continuing intervention next in the hierarchy, and the high-risk control group who had received no intervention at any time showing more evidence of school failure. It remains to be seen, however, whether those children who were twice lucky in the draw will retain their advantage over the adolescent years, and whether their later performance will justify the high costs of the Abecedarian programme. For an important analysis of the economics of early educational intervention, see Barnett and Escobar (1987).

The lack of enduring benefits on cognitive skills from preschool programmes has been documented so many times that it scarcely needs repeating here. However, recently there have been some valuable summary statements which it would be wrong to exclude.

One is the detailed evaluation of Head Start by the US Department of Health and Human Services abstracted in an Executive Summary (1985). Seventy-two studies provided data for meta-analyses of research into Head Start's effects on cognitive development. They were virtually unanimous in showing significant gains on cognitive tests at the termination of the programme, either by contrast with control groups or on the basis of a test–retest design. A gain of some 9 to 10 IQ points on average during preschool programmes is one of the most reliably established findings in the literature. Scores on tests of readiness or achievement were also significantly affected, and one year after programme termination, although the IQ differences tend to have washed out, differences in the other two measures continue to be in the educationally meaningful range. However, 'By the end of the second year, there are no educationally meaningful differences on any of the measures' (p.6). Nevertheless, in keeping with other research reports (e.g. Lazar and Darlington 1982; Royce, Lazar and Darlington 1983; or for summary see Clarke 1984; Clarke and Clarke 1986) the document cautiously maintains that 'Children who attended Head Start are less likely to fail a grade in school or to be assigned to special education classes than children who did not attend. *However, this finding is based on very few studies*' (p.8, italics added). In other words, children's ability to meet the minimum requirements of school, as judged by teachers, appears to be affected by inclusion in Head Start. Several sections of the excellent summary report are not particularly relevant to the present argument; nevertheless, a section at the end, based on 75 studies bearing on the impact of Head Start on families, should be mentioned. It is categorically stated that Head Start parents see benefits to their children and also to themselves; sizeable proportions participate in various paid and volunteer capacities; and children whose parents are highly involved perform better on cognitive tests than those whose parents are less involved, although, of course, the precise reason for this correlation is not clear. The impact of Head Start on child-rearing practices has been mixed, with some studies reporting small positive effects, but others none. A similar outcome is recorded for special programmes focusing on helping parents teach their children, and finally, perhaps surprisingly, it is stated categorically that Head Start has little effect on changing parents' attitudes to the value of education. Most studies find no difference in attitude between Head Start and non-Head Start parents. 'Children whose parents do value education score higher on cognitive tests and behavioral ratings' (p.16).

Proper evaluations of European attempts at compensatory education are rare. However, although not exclusively concerned with preschool programmes, the report commissioned by the Social Science Council of the Royal Netherlands Academy of Arts and Science presented by Scheerens (1987) is of relevance to the problem of boosting the educational achievement of socially disadvantaged children. Scheerens concluded as follows:

The results of the Dutch evaluations of compensatory education programs are in line with what has been found in other countries. Programs like these usually produce modest gains according to outcome measurements made immediately after program completion, while long-term effects are even smaller, if not altogether absent. (p.110)

Turning now to special programmes to help handicapped preschoolers, an impressive review article by Simeonsson, Cooper and Scheiner (1982) suggested that nearly half of the 27 studies they analysed gave inflated claims for their efficacy, a tendency not confined to researchers promoting the benefits of preschool programmes for mentally retarded children.

Casto and Mastropieri (1986) published a meta-analysis of 74 studies of early intervention with handicapped preschoolers. They found that early intervention produced an important positive effect; longer, more intense programmes are associated with efficacy; and there was little support for commonly held beliefs about early intervention, such as the age of start and the degree of parental involvement, matters which are cogently discussed by White (1986). So far as the long-term benefits of preschool education are concerned, the Utah group stated that there are as yet too few high-quality studies to say whether the clear immediate benefits will endure. One British study which has a bearing on this issue has recently been reported by Cunningham (1986, 1987). He led a team in the city of Manchester, England, which investigated a cohort of 181 families all of whom had a Down's Syndrome child born between August 1973 and August 1980, followed up between ages 5 and 10. Part of the study concerns the effects of an individually tailored, intensive and highly structured programme of intervention during the first two years of life, aimed at preventing the developmental deceleration typical of Down's Syndrome children. Sixty children (representative of the whole cohort) who had experienced early intervention were compared with a carefully matched contrast group from outside Manchester. The results indicated that although, as is usual, there were significant short-term benefits accruing to the intervention group, no major long-term effects were to be found on measures of child development or behavioural difficulties. Moreover, the study showed that the long-term predictors of development for these special children were the same as those found in the population at large, indicating that the enduring family ecology was more important in determining outcome than was the early intervention.

A somewhat similar finding is reported with a normal population by Lamb and his colleagues (Broberg, Lamb, Hwang and Bookstein, in press; Hwang, Lamb and Broberg 1989). They have demonstrated in a particularly elegantly designed study of Swedish preschool children that where parental ideology is not confounded with type of child care, the quality of home care predicted, from 16 months, intellectual development one and two years later, whereas out-of-home care did not. There was no differential effect of home care, family day care, or centre day care through the two years of the project. The authors attribute their results to the very high standards enjoyed by all the children, and the fact that no socially disadvantaged families were included.

Research across space and time indicates consistent correlations between developmental outcome and factors in the home environment. (The size of the correlations, of course, varies as a function of the degree of social homogeneity or heterogeneity). This universal law applies to families with Down's Syndrome children in England as it does to those without disadvantage in Sweden, or to members of the Colorado Adoption Project in America (Plomin, DeFries and Fulker 1988). Social factors can also be shown to correlate with differential recovery from the effects of low birth weight (Wilson 1985) or asphyxia at birth (Werner 1985). Further, recent adoption and twin studies have elaborated early findings of a very significant heritability of intelligence (e.g. Plomin 1989; Scarr and Weinberg 1983; Wilson 1983) and also the differential effects of widely different social rearing (e.g. Dumaret 1985; Schiff, Duyme, Dumaret and Tomkiewicz 1982). A relatively high heritability for IQ is entirely compatible with findings indicating a large effect of environmental differences, as Jensen (1981), for example, has shown. He goes on, however, to say that although intervention which might produce IQ changes of 45 points is not in the least incompatible with present estimates of broad heritability, the real problem is in bringing the environmental influences on IQ under control. He suggests:

> My hunch is that the nongenetic variance in IQ is the result of such a myriad of microenvironmental events as to make it extremely difficult, if not impossible, to bring more than a small fraction of these influences under experimental control. The results of all such attempts to date would seem to be consistent with this interpretation. (p.233)

We have to face the sad fact that an unknown number of children in advanced countries live in conditions which place them at risk for malevolent environments as well as suboptimal constitutions. They grow up in poor psychological and/or material surroundings, often in large families in which the regular intimate social interaction with intelligent family members is far less likely to occur than for children whose parents are better educated, more stable and less impoverished. Lengthy and wide-ranging interventions need to be prospectively planned, including especially those where total ecological change can occur. Where the latter does not take place, there needs to be an evaluation of whether family constellations are, as one suspects, more resistant to change than the mildly handicapped younger member. Probably those parents with 'subcultural' children are overwhelmed by personal disadvantages and are thus unable to respond effectively to help.

By contrast, throughout the ages, gifted children have been drawn disproportionately from families which have given them intellectual stimulation, starting at an early age (Fowler 1986), security, stability and individual attention. Family social factors were found to be among the only significant correlates of later achievement/underachievement among members of Terman's gifted group in adult life (Oden 1968), and more recently discriminated the backgrounds of High IQ and Moderate IQ children in a British study of giftedness (Freeman 1979). Anecdotally, it has also been noted by many workers in the field of retardation that unusual capability in Down's Syndrome children is often associated with the mother being a teacher or a nurse.

Moreover, evidence from the Colorado Adoption Project 'is impressive in suggesting substantial genetic influence on the relationship between environmental measures and children's IQ, evidence that has previously gone unnoticed' (Plomin, DeFries and Fulker 1988, p.292).

It should also be remembered that developmental changes during the life path, including in the mentally handicapped, are so vast that it is hardly surprising that different types of changing behavioural process may require different forms of skill training and periods of consolidation as each newly evolves. Those lucky enough to receive successive interventions at appropriate times, whether at home or in school, are likely to be more successful than those who do not. Development does not necessarily imply processes steadily incrementing within each individual. Rather, both unfolding genetic and environmental influences are likely to result in periods of static, or moderate, or surging growth. In addition, the individual to some extent both affects and chooses environmental influences, producing feedback which serves to maintain or modify personal characteristics, such as the gifted toddler whose desperate parents invented a math programme to cope with his hyperactivity, thus initiating a long process of cognitive enrichment.

In summary, it appears that early intervention typically yields concurrent advantages both for the child and the parents. Thereafter, as time passes, its effects are likely to follow the law of diminishing returns unless the intervention sets off an ongoing chain of consecutive positive influences. Without these, in effect, continuing interventions, desirable outcomes are unlikely. In brief, one needs to take account of the whole life span, and one should not, as

Zigler (Zigler and Valentine 1979) has put it, concentrate only upon one supposedly magical period in the child's development.

References

Barnett, W.S. and Escobar, C.M. (1987) 'The economics of early educational intervention: A review.' *Review of Educational Research 57*, 387–414.

Berrueta-Clement, J.R., Schweinhart, L.J., Barnett, W.S., Epstein, A.S. and Weikart, D.P. (1984) *Changed Lives: The Effects of the Perry Preschool Program on Youths through Age 19*. Ypsilan-ti, MI: Monographs of the High/Scope Educational Research Foundation.

Broberg, A., Lamb, M.E., Hwang, C.P. and Bookstein, F.L. (in press) 'Determinants of intellectual development in Swedish preschoolers.' *Journal of Child Psychology and Psychiatry*.

Casto, G. and Mastropieri, M.A. (1986) 'The efficacy of early intervention programs: A meta-analysis.' *Exceptional Children 52*, 417–424.

Clarke, A.D.B. (1968) 'Learning and human development – the 42nd Maudsley Lecture.' *British Journal of Psychiatry 114*, 161–177.

Clarke, A.M. (1982) 'Developmental discontinuities: An approach to assessing their nature.' In L.A. Bond and J.M. Joffe (eds) *Facilitating Infant and Early Child Development*. Hanover, NH: University Press of New England.

Clarke, A.M. (1984) 'Early experience and cognitive development.' In E.W. Gordon (ed) *Review of Research in Education 11*, 125–157.

Clarke, A.M. and Clarke A.D.B. (1976) *Early Experience: Myth and Evidence*. New York: The Free Press.

Clarke, A.M. and Clarke, A.D.B. (1986) 'Thirty years of child psychology: A selective review.' *Journal of Child Psychology and Psychiatry 27*, 719–759.

Clarke, A.M. and Clarke, A.D.B. (2000) 'Outcomes of less severe adversity.' In *Early Experience and the Life Path*. London: Jessica Kingsley Publishers.

Clarke, A.D.B., Clarke, A.M. and Reiman, S. (1958) 'Cognitive and social changes in the feebleminded: Three further studies.' *British Journal of Psychology 49*, 144–157.

Cunningham, C.C. (1986) 'The effects of early intervention on the occurrence and nature of behaviour problems in children with Down's syndrome.' *Final Report to the DHSS*. London: DHSS.

Cunningham, C.C. (1987) 'Early intervention in Down's syndrome.' In G. Hosking and G. Murphy (eds) *Prevention of Mental Handicap: A World View*. London: Royal Society of Medicine Services.

Dumaret, A. (1985) 'IQ, scholastic performance and behaviour of sibs raised in contrasting environments.' *Journal of Child Psychology and Psychiatry 26*, 553–575.

Entwistle, D.R., Alexander, K.L., Cadigan, D., and Pallas, A.M. (1987) 'Kindergarten experience: Cognitive effects or socialization?' *American Educational Research Journal 24*, 337–364.

Fowler, W. (ed) (1986) *Early Experience and the Development of Competence.* San Francisco, CA: Jossey-Bass.

Freeman, J. (1979) *Gifted Children: Their Identification and Development in a Social Context.* Lancaster, England: MTP Press.

Hwang, C.P., Lamb, M.E. and Broberg, A. (1989) 'The development of social and intellectual competence in Swedish preschoolers raised at home and in out-of-home care facilities.' In K. Kreppner and R.M. Lerner (eds) *Family Systems and Life Span Development.* Hillsdale, NJ: Erlbaum.

Jensen, A.R. (1981) 'Raising the IQ: The Ramey and Haskins study.' *Intelligence 5*, 29–40.

Lazar, I. and Darlington, R.B. (1982) 'Lasting effects of early education.' *Monographs of the Society for Research in Child Development 47*, 1–51.

Oden, M. (1968) 'The fulfillment of promise: A 40-year follow-up of the Terman Gifted Group.' *Genetic Psychology Monographs 77*, 3–93.

Plomin, R. (1989) 'Environment and genes: Determinants of behavior.' *American Psychologist 44*, 105–111.

Plomin, R., DeFries, J.C. and Fulker, D.W. (1988) *Nature and Nurture During Infancy and Early Childhood.* New York: Cambridge University Press.

Ramey, C.T. (1988) 'Educational intervention for high-risk children.' Abstracts of the programme on *Key Issues in Mental Retardation Research* for the 8th World Congress of the International Association for the Scientific Study of Mental Deficiency, Dublin, Ireland.

Ramey, C.T. and Campbell, F.A. (1981) 'Educational intervention for children at risk for mild retardation: A longitudinal analysis.' In P. Mittler (ed) *Frontiers of Knowledge in Mental Retardation. (Vol. 1): Social, Educational, and Behavioral Aspects.* Baltimore, MD: University Park Press.

Ramey, C.T. and Campbell, F.A. (1984) 'Preventive education for high-risk children: Cognitive consequences of the Carolina Abecedarian Project.' *American Journal of Mental Deficiency 88*, 515–523.

Ramey, C.T. and Haskins, R. (1981) 'The modification of intelligence through early experience.' *Intelligence 5*, 5–19.

Royce, J.M., Lazar, I. and Darlington, R.B. (1983) 'Minority families, early education and later life chances.' *American Journal of Orthopsychiatry 53*, 706–720.

Scarr, S. and Weinberg, R.A. (1983) 'The Minnesota Adoption Studies: Genetic differences and malleability.' *Child Development 54*, 260–267.

Scheerens, J. (1987) *Enhancing Educational Opportunities for Disadvantaged Learners: A Review of Dutch Research on Compensatory Education and Educational Development Policy.* Oxford, England: North Holland Publishing Company.

Schiff, M., Duyme, M., Dumaret, A. and Tomkiewicz, S. (1982) 'How much could we boost scholastic achievement and IQ scores? A direct answer from a French adoption study.' *Cognition 12*, 165–196.

Schweinhart, L.J. and Weikart, D.P. (1980) *Young Children Grow Up: The Effects of the Perry Preschool Program on Youths through Age 15.* Ypsilanti, MI: High/Scope Press.

Scott, J.P. (1968) *Early Experience and the Organization of Behavior.* Belmont, CA: Brooks/Cole.

Simeonsson, R.J., Cooper, D.H. and Scheiner, A.P. (1982) 'A review and analysis of the effectiveness of early intervention programs.' *Pediatrics 69*, 635–641.

U.S. Department of Health and Human Services (1985). *The Impact of Head Start on Children, Families and Communities: Head Start Synthesis Project.* Washington, DC: CSR, Incorporated. Contract No. 105-81-C-026.

Werner, E.E. (1985) 'Stress and protective factors in children's lives.' In A.R. Nicol (ed) *Longitudinal Studies in Child Psychology and Psychiatry.* New York: Wiley.

White, K.R. (1986) 'Efficacy of early intervention.' *Journal of Special Education 19*, 401–416.

White, K.R., Bush, D.W. and Casto, G.C. (1985) 'Learning from reviews of early intervention.' *Journal of Special Education 19*, 417–428.

Wilson, R.S. (1983) 'The Louisville Twin Study: Developmental synchronies in behavior.' *Child Development 54*, 298–316.

Wilson, R.S. (1985) 'Risk and resilience in early mental development.' *Developmental Psychology 21*, 795–805.

Zigler, E., and Valentine, J. (eds) (1979) *Project Head Start: A Legacy of the War on Poverty.* New York: The Free Press.

PART IV

Early Experience
and the Life Path

CHAPTER 18

Learning and Human Development
The 42nd Maudsley Lecture

Commentary

This 42nd Maudsley Lecture was delivered before the Royal Medico-Psychological Association (now the Royal College of Psychiatrists) in 1967. From a variety of research fields it outlined for the first time the notion that development involved learning in its broadest sense, including overlearning, reinforcement and extinction. Repetition of experience could be expected to reinforce the effects of early learning. Conversely, marked environmental change would involve unlearning and extinction of the previous behavioural repertoire.

The second, briefer, part of the lecture recorded a series of experiments with learning disabled and preschool normal children. These showed that present performance did not predict ultimate levels after training. Above all, practice in categorizing, especially if these activities were complex and demanding, carried over to the categorizing of new tasks. This transfer of training may be one of the ways in which cognitive abilities are built up. These studies raise the whole problem of under-functioning, a characteristic representative of a much wider population than learning disabled and preschool normal children. The researches took place over a ten-year period, firstly under the auspices of the National Health Service and thereafter supported by the Nuffield Foundation and by the Association for the Aid of Crippled Children, USA.

Learning and Human Development: The 42nd Maudsley Lecture, delivered before the Royal Medico-Psychological Association, 17 November 1967*

A.D.B. Clarke

Last December I received one of the most surprising letters of my life – an invitation to give the next Maudsley Lecture before this Association. I am deeply grateful for this honour, all the more so since I stand in considerable debt to the hospital which Henry Maudsley founded and which bears his name, having spent two fruitful years there as a research student.

A further reason for pleasure is that delivery of this lecture may extinguish in me a conditioned avoidance response established in the early 1950s. At that time I produced my first research paper of which I thought a great deal, but this was a view clearly not shared by the then editor of the *Journal of Mental Science* who rejected it with such rapidity that I never again dared to try to publish in it or in the *British Journal of Psychiatry*. I understand, however, that I may be more successful on this occasion.

I must admit that in recent months the rather grandiose title of my lecture has increasingly daunted me, although I believe that Henry Maudsley would at least not have disapproved of an attempt to discuss this broad topic. He foresaw very clearly that 'the study of the plan of development of mind, as exhibited in animals and in infants, would furnish results of the greatest value and be essential to a true mental science' (Lewis 1951). Now the field of learning and learning theory is immense, and any attempt to cover it would, in the time available, result in the most superficial survey; rather I want to do two things, first, broadly to re-examine the role of early experience, and second, more narrowly to outline some experiments which may have a bearing upon some of the processes involved in cognitive development.

Early experience

Psychological experience which has anything more than merely transitory effects must involve learning, that is, a modification of behaviour possessing some extension in time. While learning theories remain controversial, there are

*   This article first appeared in 1968 in the *British Journal of Psychiatry 114*, pp.1061–1077.

a number of well-established, if crude, facts about learning which enable us to examine the question of whether early experience is likely to possess a potent effect upon, or act as a crucial determinant of, adult behaviour, a view widely held by authorities from many different fields. I refer to such facts as the effects of repetition of learning sequences, of overlearning, of reinforcement and non-reinforcement leading to extinction, all of which are examined, albeit rather cursorily, in Part I of the Diploma in Psychological Medicine (DPM).

Obviously, development proceeds from the interaction of genetic and environmental influences. Those of us who choose to work on learning are, of course, as aware of the powerful influence of genetic factors as one hopes geneticists are of environmental influences. This afternoon I shall be merely examining some aspects of one half of the total developmental equation.

Now, at this point I must offer a hypothesis concerning the long-term effects of early experience. Early experience involving a modification of behaviour (learning) will by definition have immediate effects; the size and duration of these will, of course, depend partly upon the length and potency of the experience and the age of the learner, but more particularly on the amount, intensity and duration of subsequent reinforcement. Conversely, and in plainer English, early learning will have effects which, if unreinforced, will fade with time. It will not *per se* have any long-term influence upon adult behaviour, other than as an essential link in the developmental chain. I am not here referring to gross environmental effects such as early and prolonged malnutrition which may have long-term and serious sequelae; that is another and very interesting story (Cravioto, DeLicardie and Birch 1966; Dobbing and Widdowson 1965).

This over-simple hypothesis must at once be qualified by three further considerations. First, if there be critical periods of learning or critical periods of development, then we might have to modify this model. Second, since early learning involves first learning, it might not be unreasonable to believe that first learning, by pre-empting neural mechanisms, exercises particularly crucial and long-lasting effects (Fuller and Waller 1962). Third, we must not regard the child as a passive organism buffeted by the environment; rather it is an increasingly dynamic being able to exert reciprocating influences upon its surroundings (Kagan and Moss 1962; Rutter, Birch, Thomas and Chess 1964). There is thus the possibility that early experience may produce particular effects which, acting upon later environments, produce reinforcing feedback. Right from the start, therefore, we must fault my simple model; examination of research data will, however, indicate whether it will retain any merit.

I propose to examine under five headings the notion that early experience does not *per se* have long-term effects.

Animal studies

The results of numerous animal studies at first sight prove difficult for the survival of my hypothesis, so I must grasp this nettle firmly. Indeed, no one interested in the long-term effects of early human experience can afford to ignore this important body of evidence, particularly in the primate field, from studies which are so superbly controlled in comparison with human studies. I must, however, at the outset suggest several factors which warn against a too facile application of results to human development:

1. Many experiments on early animal learning use either a duration or severity of experience which could scarcely allow survival if analogously applied to human infants. In these cases, therefore, the findings may not apply to ordinary, less deviant, conditions. (On the other hand, animals, such as rats, which are very immature at birth respond with physiological and long-term behavioural effects even to minimal handling. The mechanisms are, however, unclear, and there is a need to investigate systematically the animal's physiological and behavioural responses during the handling process, as well as possible changes in maternal behaviour as a result of these brief separations. The former might indicate whether such experiences are indeed highly stressful, and the latter whether there is maternal reinforcement by additional stimulation of the very young animal.)

2. Few attempts have been made to find out whether any behaviour modifications may be reversible.

3. Few attempts have been made to find out whether similar effects can also be induced by similar methods later in life, i.e. whether or not such effects are specific to early experience.

4. It is possible that, with rapid maturation in a hostile natural world, early learning may have a very different function in animal as opposed to human development. I will return to this point later.

Let me begin by considering imprinting studies, which in the Sunday newspapers are so glibly related to human development, and even in more sober quarters are taken as the ideal and extreme paradigm for the disproportionate, long-term and irreversible influence of early experience. Recent work, however, suggests that the situation is rather less clear than might be supposed; critical periods, for example, can be artificially extended (Salzen and Sluckin 1959; Sluckin 1964) and are therefore not so intrinsically critical as was earlier believed. Or again, specificity of imprinted sexual attachment may not be as great as was earlier estimated (Schutz 1965). Moreover, the most comprehensive recent review concludes that 'our knowledge of the long-term effects of imprinting is no more than fragmentary' (Sluckin 1964). In this connection Haywood and Tapp (1966) state that imprinted behaviour has seldom been tested at any considerable temporal separation from the original imprinting experience in order to assess its permanence. Their study, in fact, showed a linear decay in per cent, following responses by strongly imprinted chicks, which reached zero after 21 days. This 'must call into question the frequent assertion of the permanence of responses which are dependent upon some occurrence during a critical period in development'. The strength of imprinting is anyway known to relate to the duration of exposure to appropriate stimuli, and it is also possible that the so-called permanence of imprinting effects may partly reflect the permanence of the environmental conditions which reinforce them. In any event, attempts to relate the notion of imprinting to human development, though extremely interesting, remain rather speculative. Salzen (1963), for example, has indicated that the classic work on smiling which studied the nature of releasing stimuli could not be accepted, if I may be permitted a *double entendre*, entirely at face value. Nevertheless, this may prove to be an important field for research.

Some of the classic deprivation studies hardly need detailed mention; for example, Harlow's work on isolated unmothered monkeys. These were described as 'heterosexually hopeless' when adults, and even after 'group psychotherapy' there were great difficulties in breeding from them. When these unmothered monkeys finally became mothers, their behaviour towards their offspring was 'enough to make strong men reach the point when they could hardly bear to observe this unmaternal behaviour' (Harlow 1963). With subsequent pregnancies, however, maternal behaviour became less abnormal.

Levine, in a number of very careful studies, made the surprising finding that early stress in rats had very considerable effects physiologically and behaviourally, accelerating maturation; and, in comparison with unstressed controls, these rats were more able in adult life to withstand emotion-provoking situations. It may well be, write Levine and Lewis (1959), that some degree of stressful experience in infancy is necessary for successful adaptation of the organism to the environment it encounters later in life.

Or again, Thompson and Heron (1954) and Melzack (1954) studied the effects of gross isolation of puppies during most of their first year of life, a very long period. In comparison with controls, these grew into immature, emotional animals with bizarre responses to pain and with poor intellectual capacities. There are, indeed, some dozens of similar researches which show, apparently unequivocally, the long-term and potent effect of early experiences. As I have already argued, however, these cannot necessarily be taken as indicative that infancy is the only period in which such changes may occur. Indeed, Peters and Murphee (1966) found a reversal from the usual expectancy. Rats aged 2 months and 7 months were exposed to a single traumatic 90-volt shock. As measured by brief exploratory activity and defaecation, most of the younger rats had recovered within five weeks, while the older had still not recovered after six months. The authors believe that their results indicate the greater resilience of young animals and the need for caution in interpreting research and theories on early experience.

In animal as with human studies, few attempts have been made to investigate the reversibility or modification of the effects of early learning. A few researches, however (e.g. Woods 1959), report that a later enriched environment can markedly reduce the effects of early sensory or motor deprivation, and, as noted, even the Harlow experiment using extreme and prolonged isolation of unmothered monkeys shows a later spontaneous shift in the degree of damage. Indeed, although research in the animal field has obvious attractions, at all points one is faced with complex problems of methodology, measurement and interpretation, highlighted by King (1958) who outlines no less than seven vital parameters and draws particular attention to the probable confounding of early and late experience because the later may either enhance or inhibit the effect of the earlier. Or again, Fuller and Waller (1962) suggested as a major possibility that early learning may be characterized by generality rather than specificity; in Hebbian terms, transfer may be greatest early in life.

Knowledge of environmental effects is, however, so considerable that Whimbey and Denenberg (1966) can speak of, and indeed claim to promote, the programming of life histories and the creation of individual differences by the experimental control of early experiences. They state that 'the results establish that stable and relatively permanent complex individual differences, of the sort often assumed to be genetically determined, can be generated by the appropriate manipulation of experiences during early life'. Let me hasten to reassure you that they were dealing with rats, but for rats the year 1984 has apparently come and gone.

In spite of the difficulties and complexities to which I have merely alluded, let us accept that there is undoubtedly evidence for the potent effects of early animal experience, although, as will be clear, almost every issue is clouded with uncertainty. In passing, I want at least to draw attention to some very important current work on the effects of early experience on brain chemistry and morphology (Bennett, Diamond, Krech and Rosenzweig 1964). I shall briefly return to this later.

There is one final point to be made about animal studies; the lower the phylogenetic status of the organism, the less the role of learning. But when periods of immaturity are short, if learning is to play a part at all it must do so quickly. It is no good in nature for the grey gosling gradually to learn to follow its mother, or for the rat slowly to learn cat avoidance. Single trial learning must be the order of the day if disaster is to be averted. In man the situation is entirely different; with a prolonged period of immaturity there might well be an advantage in early learning *not* fixing for the infant an immutable path. Hence in the present state of knowledge one can either press or dispute the relevance for human development of findings concerning early animal experience. For the purposes of the argument, therefore, we may still be at square one.

Human studies

Turning now to human studies, I want first to make some rather general points. There is a vast literature often cited as being germane to the problem of early experience. Much of this, however, is either of poor quality or of dubious relevance. For the present purpose we must at once note that all work, however good, on children reared by their natural parents may confound the facts of genetics and experience. Retrospective investigations, too, must be looked at with some doubt, and there are a number of complex problems associated with studies of twins or foster children. Research on the effects of major environmental change in young children, however, seems to me to possess fewer intrinsic difficulties, and I propose to examine the results of experimental and correlational studies under two headings.

The effects of short changes in early environment

Time does not allow more than a cursory glance at this topic, but, apart from one area, the findings of the better studies pose few difficulties for my hypothesis, so I will merely summarize.

Research by such workers as Schaffer (1958) or Prugh, Staub, Sands, Kirschbaum and Lenihan (1953) has concerned the reactions of children to short-duration hospitalization. The relationship of disturbance to pre-hospital adjustment has been shown, as well as to the child's age and the way in which the wards were organized. For us, however, the main interest lies in post-hospital follow-up. Here there is a steady decrease in behavioural disturbance as time goes on. Once again, then, the decay of non-reinforced learning is apparent.

At this point, such writers as Ainsworth (1962) argue that overt adjustment may well mask an underlying disturbance which may manifest itself later. One would be wrong to write off such a view as being of the 'have-your-cake-and-eat-it' variety, for it would certainly accord with the facts of extinction of learned responses, with subsequent revival when conditions reinforce. We need to know more about this possibility.

A tentative conclusion, however, must at this stage draw attention to the fading effects (at least overt) of short periods of unusual early experience. The possible exception, to which I have referred, relates to such conditioned responses as phobias, thought clinically to relate to a single incident, and which without *apparent* reinforcement resist extinction (Watson and Rayner 1920).

There are plenty of animal studies, but there is one recent Canadian investigation, using human subjects, in which a single and unexpected experience of respiratory paralysis, drug-induced and lasting about 100 seconds, was used to establish a conditioned response to a previously neutral stimulus (Campbell, Sanderson and Laverty 1964). This 'experience that was horrific to a degree', such that the subjects thought they were dying, set up a conditioned response which resisted extinction trials (100) over four weeks. It so happens that the subjects were *adult*, so it is possible that conditioned traumatic phobias involve processes which are not age-specific. For obvious reasons there is a dearth of such studies, and clinical reports relating to this type of behaviour may be unable to identify causal factors with any certainty.

Prolonged early experience

Prolonged early experience might well be expected to produce more powerful and more permanent effects. Let us examine the evidence.

Remembering Piltdown Man, I would normally be reluctant to discuss a single case-history. I do so for two reasons; the particular case was studied and reported independently by two different authors (Davis 1947; Mason 1942), and their testimonies are not discrepant. Second, it exhibits in a most extreme form the processes apparent in other individuals altering in response to smaller changes in early environment.

In the 1930s, two illegitimate children, each aged about 6 years, who had been kept locked in attics for virtually their whole lives, were discovered in different areas in the United States at about the same time. When rescued, neither could talk, both were rachitic and both functioned at imbecile level. The more deprived of the two did not receive any special treatment and her relative status did not alter; her mother was herself subnormal. The other had been with her deaf-mute mother alone in a darkened attic where both had been imprisoned by the mother's father. She received highly skilled treatment, learned to speak in sentences within two months, was reading and writing in nine months and had a vocabulary of 2000 words after 16 months. Her IQ trebled in 18 months, and after two years she was considered intellectually normal. Unfortunately, the authors of these studies were a speech consultant and sociologist and failed to ask the questions you and I would have asked, but there seems little doubt that on final follow-up at age 14 this girl was considered normal. It seems, then, that six years of considerable isolation (though not from a deaf-mute mother) resulting in gross retardation did not doom the child to an unalterable condition. Her progress was, indeed, remarkably rapid. The other case was unaltered, but whether because of severer isolation or lack of skilled treatment or because of congenital factors, or a combination of these, is unknown. Another descriptive study, probably of a highly selected sample, of Korean orphanage children adopted in the United States has similar implications to the first case above (Rathbun, Di Virgilio and Waldfogel 1958).

The main sources of evidence for the effects of prolonged early experience come from studies of institutionalization. Bowlby's (1951) monograph is too well known to need quoting here; and, of course, his thesis has subsequently been modified in the light of his own and others' work. Of those best known whom he quoted, and upon whose reports his thesis largely depended, I will single out Spitz and Goldfarb for brief mention. Spitz was one of the first to draw attention to the harmful effect of some institutions, but his theoretical orientation led him to overlook the wide range of deprivation and isolation experienced by these children, who lacked not only maternal care and attachment but also general care (Wootton 1959).

Interpretation of Goldfarb's work is similarly equivocal; why were the members of the control group fostered at birth, while those in the experimental group were not fostered until they were aged 3? Was Goldfarb's (1943) claim reasonable that three years of institutional experience had blunted cognitive and affective development even a decade later? If so, this would be a powerful support to the notion of the crucial importance of early experience. I submit that on the evidence one must be open-minded. There are, however, two series of studies which may have some bearing on this problem.

The findings of Trasler (1960) have by some been taken as confirmatory of Goldfarb, although Trasler himself is cautious. Investigating the causes of the high failure rate of foster-home placements in Britain, he found that more than three-quarters of those children admitted into public care before the age of 5 years, who subsequently failed in foster homes, had spent at least half of the first 3 years of life in institutions. Only 40 per cent of successful placements had this background. As Trasler asks, what selective factors delayed the differ-ent proportions of institutional children being fostered? In addition, however, a re-analysis of his data indicates that 44 out of 57 unsuccessful first place-ments were known to have been with foster parents who appeared to be unsuitable in a variety of ways. Have we not here a picture of early adversity followed by later adversity; hence a prolongation of adverse effects? This, then, could have a bearing upon studies of the sort reported by Goldfarb.

Another set of findings relevant to the Goldfarb studies emerged unex-pectedly in the work of my colleagues and myself in the 1950s. We found large IQ increments occurring in mildly subnormal persons aged between 15 and 30. To cut a long story short, it was possible to test several hypotheses, one of which was confirmed in each of four main studies. A record of early adversity, characterized by cruelty and neglect, was independently assessed and was found to be associated with later and very considerable IQ increments, again independently assessed. I stress independently, because in our main studies neither the social history rater nor the tester was allowed access to the other's data, or indeed to previous test data. Without such controls our research would have been largely worthless (Clarke and Clarke 1959, 1960; Clarke, Clarke and Reiman 1958).

Further evidence, contrary to our prediction, suggested that these large IQ increments were not so much a response to the present as a recovery from the past. Nor were they isolated phenomena in the lives of these individuals; on the contrary, they were associated with the emergence of other desirable traits. In brief, a fading of the effects of early adversity was demonstrated; this was probably by no means a complete reversion to what might have happened to these young people in happier circumstances, rather it represented a consider-able and spontaneous shift in the degree of damage as age increased. Now our studies began to follow-up grossly deprived young people at age 15, the time when Goldfarb's follow-up ended. It is therefore obvious that length of fol-low-up may be important in determining whether the effects of early experience are as permanent and immutable as some have believed.

Bowlby, Ainsworth, Boston and Rosenbluth (1956) also carried out a study of children who had spent an average of 18 months below the age of 4 years in a good but orthodox tuberculosis sanatorium. Contrary to expecta-tion, by the ages of 7–13 they had not become affectionless, warped dullards; their intelligence was average, as was their capacity for friendship. Sixty-three per cent were deemed to be maladjusted, but the criterion was a liberal one assessing 42 per cent maladjustment as an average for the general child popula-tion. And, as the authors say, the 21 per cent above expectancy might equally well have arisen from the circumstances that may be found in many homes from which the tubercular child is drawn.

Dennis and Najarian (1957) studied infant development in a foundling home in the Lebanon. Here little more than the most primitive physical care was provided, and from a normal developmental quotient (DQ) during the first two months of life, the average level had sunk to 63 in the period from 3–12 months. Between 4½ and 6 years, however, during which children were actively engaged in kindergarten training, the average DQs were in the low 90s. In this and the subsequent study, controls were excellent, and one's only regret is that the assessments were not comprehensive, including for example, verbal and personality measures. Dennis (1960) again demonstrated the resilience of children when moved from a bad into a good institution, that is, when early learning was not reinforced. Many other studies are similar in their implications, and here there is only time to mention Hilda Lewis (1954); Wittenborn (1956); Gardner, Hawkes and Burchinal (1961); Sayegh and Dennis (1965); Skeels (1966); and Skodak (1968).

To summarize this section, the papers quoted cast the gravest doubt on the notion that early experience without subsequent reinforcement necessarily lays down for the child a fixed and immutable path. So far, then, our simple learning model can be taken with some seriousness as providing a crude but better guide to interpreting the data than some other theories.

Miscellaneous studies

Several studies in entirely different fields may be worth a mention.

Recent work on the relationship between bereavement before the age of 15 and subsequent adult depression can be interpreted in a number of ways (Hill and Price 1967). One possibility is that the loss of a parent so modifies the future environment of the child that depressive tendencies are continually reinforced. It may not be the fact of bereavement, then, so much as the consequences which are operating. In any event, several studies show that the age of greatest vulnerability is (from the viewpoint of later depression) 10 to 14, and not the earlier years.

In an entirely different field, Schlaegel (1953) contrasted the imagery employed by blind and sighted adolescents. He quotes work which suggested that in studying visual dreams in the blind, the age of onset of blindness was important. Those who lost their vision before age 5 to 7 did not experience visual dreams. In other words, non-reinforcement of early experience resulted in extinction of visual imagery. Schlaegel himself studied 13 subjects blinded before the age of 6, only three of whom had any visual imagery. The loss was most pronounced in those subjects with the poorest vision.

An imaginative, yet little known, experiment was conducted by Burtt (1932) on the retention of early memories; he read aloud 20-line selections from Sophocles in the original Greek to his son, beginning at the age of 15 months. The sessions occurred daily, and every three months the material was changed to a different set of similar selections. The procedure was continued till the age of 3, when Greek disappeared entirely from the child's life. Testing for retention started at the age of 8½, when the boy learned some of the original material by a modified prompting method, and also material which he had never heard before. Similar experiments, using, of course, different selections, were conducted at ages of 14 and 18 years.

At the age of 8½ the boy learned the material heard in infancy significantly faster than new material of a similar nature. At the age of 14 only a slight effect could be discerned, and by the age of 18 the effect had altogether disappeared. Thus, daily experiences from the age of 15 months to 3 years had a significant effect five years later, but thereafter the results of this early learning faded.

The stability of personality characteristics

I now turn to the last area of study which may have a bearing upon the problem of the effects of early learning.

If in early life the basic characteristics of the individual are firmly laid down as a result of genetic and experiential factors in combination and interaction, then one would expect a high correlation between personality assessments of the very young child and those of the same individual when adult. The studies to be mentioned concern children in their own homes; if early learning as well as genetics do play a vital part in personality development then in these circumstances one would expect maximum support for the early determination of personality. How far do the data confirm or dispute this view?

The most ambitious work is by Kagan and Moss (1962), who report the results of a 30-year longitudinal study of normal persons from birth to maturity. A very large number of behavioural variables were investigated using techniques as widely different as projective tests, interviews, ratings and physiological measures.

The most dramatic and consistent finding was that many of the behaviours exhibited by the child during the period 6 to 10 years, and a few during the period 3 to 6 years, were 'moderately good predictors of later behaviours during early adult life'. This statement summarizes correlations averaging about 0.5, which are not very different from those found with intelligence test scores. Now 0.5 is not to be disregarded, it is a significant moderate correlation, but, after all, it does not represent a very large common variance. Kagan and Moss show a certain *näiveté* in their enthusiasm for these findings, which certainly show some continuity over development but also imply considerable variation. Note, however, that the period about which they are so enthusiastic is not the preschool years but the age range 6 to 10 years. Moreover, as the authors go on to indicate, not all of the childhood responses displayed long-term continuity. Compulsivity and irrational fears were not predictive of similar reactions at adulthood. And such measures as task persistence and excessive irritability during the first 3 years showed no relationship with similar responses during later childhood.

The findings closely parallel the results of longitudinal studies of intelligence, and, as in that field, the most reasonable explanation is that they represent the cumulative influence of nature and nurture. Moreover, it is the early school years and not the preschool period which is highlighted as being quite important.

Discussion

It has been my purpose to re-examine the common emphasis on the formative role of early experience, summarized typically and approvingly by Yarrow (1961), who states that 'the significance of early infantile experience for later development has been reiterated so frequently and so persistently that the general validity of this assertion is now almost unchallenged'.

There can be little doubt that we are immensely ignorant about the mechanisms of early behavioural development; nor can we doubt that for both psychiatry and psychology a better understanding could have considerable theoretical and practical repercussions. We cannot even be wholly confident about the intrinsic importance of behavioural milestones; how far do these reflect our own practices with children, and hence our own expectancies? In the educational field, for example, society is at great pains to fulfil its own predictions. I suppose my main contention about all such issues is that we cannot be dogmatic, and that open-mindedness about many questions which may have been prematurely answered is our main need.

Let me nevertheless summarize certain consistencies in the data from the better studies which permit the following comments:

1. There is little reason to suppose that infant learning is acquired more easily than later learning. Nor is there any indication that it is better retained or more resistant to extinction (Campbell and Campbell, 1962). In theory, therefore, we would not expect early learning to have profound long-term effects. This expectancy is confirmed in the studies of short-term hospitalization. In particular, for infants below the age of 7 months, overt effects appear very short indeed.

2. Longer term early learning can have very considerable effects, but if these are not subsequently reinforced they at least fade as time goes on. The extinction of non-reinforced early learning may perhaps never be complete when the experiences have been very adverse or prolonged but then even up to the age of 30 there is evidence for a shift in the degree of residual effects.

3. It is unwarranted to assume that all psychological processes are equally modified by particular experiences. Indeed, the violent disagreements in the 1930s between the nativist and environmentalist schools may have resulted from both sides tackling different problems – and both revealing part truths (Stone 1954). This problem deserves a lecture on its own.

4. Implicit in the belief that very early learning exercises a powerful adult effect is the view that personality characteristics must remain relatively stable. For normal children this appears not to be the case with most areas of behaviour until the early school years are reached. Only then do moderate correlations with adult behaviours emerge. An analogous situation exists with intelligence test scores. The common view that early characteristics remain relatively unchanged seems therefore either to be true only of a specially vulnerable section of the population, or to be the result of unwitting selection of evidence based on hindsight.

5. One way by which the effects of early experience may resist extinction is that, as Rutter et al. (1964) point out, environmental influences are to some extent shaped and modified by the child. Moreover, the *effective* environment is determined by those selectivities and susceptibilities which characterize him. Two-way feedback can thus be continually reinforcing.

6. Evidence suggests that early learning is of importance mainly for its foundational character. Development proceeds at different rates through a sequence of well-marked stages. Each stage depends on the integrity of previous stages, but it seems better to talk of optimal rather than critical periods of learning in man. Deficits arising from early environmental handicaps can to varying extents be made good sometimes apparently spontaneously. Nature interacting with nurture appears to exercise gradually cumulative effects.

7. As Huxley has pointed out, in science it is almost impossible to avoid teleological thinking. And in this sense, with man's slow maturation, some degree of plasticity and resilience in comparison with the animal kingdom would seem biologically desirable. Inadequate though much of it is, the data seem to be in correspondence with such a theory.

As I have tried to stress, these points are tentative, but they at least indicate that there exist some vital questions upon which much research is needed. This field then highlights the many difficulties and complexities facing the behavioural sciences. We are increasingly aware of the ease with which theories can be imposed on facts, of selection of evidence, and of man's great capacity for finding what he seeks. Is it possible that this is what has happened in ascribing such overriding importance to the early years? Since most children experience a continuity of similar influences during development, the small correlation of early and later effects in such individuals may not be a causal one, any more than the first rung of a ladder causes a higher rung to exist, although it certainly allows the higher to be reached. Moreover, we now have sufficient evidence on verbal conditioning to be sensitive to the possibility that clinician and patient may serve as mutual reinforcers in discovering early anomalies in development. And where such anomalies do in fact exist, are they perhaps only the first steps in a long process of personality distortion, without a causal role?

It has not been my purpose to put forward an all-embracing theory, nor does it fit all our meagre facts. In the present state of knowledge, and with the great complexity of human development, it is exceedingly unlikely that any one theory will do so. On the other hand, it fits many facts reasonably well, and a research assistant asked by me to 'break the hypothesis' by means of a detailed search in the literature was unable to do so. It is thus suggested that there is currently a very considerable over-emphasis on the role of early experience, and that reinforcement or non-reinforcement over long periods may be more important variables. It may well be that this comes as no great surprise to many psychiatrists and psychologists; Mayer-Gross, Slater and Roth (1954), for example, state that 'much that is impressed on the infant, if not re-impressed in later life, must become obliterated' (p.22). 'We must allow wide latitude for human plasticity, particularly in the years of infancy and childhood' (p.104). 'It is commonly assumed that the child is most susceptible in his earliest weeks, months and years, but this is at present pure assumption' (p.513). Apart from a few such brief comments, however, the literature is almost entirely one-sided on this issue, and the present viewpoint has received neither sufficient attention nor documentation.

Generalization of experience: some experimental studies

Now for the second part of my lecture; in it I want to illustrate the use of experimental method in shedding light upon problems of development. My theme concerns experimental studies on learning transfer, that is, on the effects of one learning experience upon another, discussed in the context of early development. My colleagues and I have concentrated on this and allied problems for the last six years, and although I will omit the details of most of the studies, I ought at least to indicate why we selected this area as potentially rewarding. There were three reasons: 1. that the increasing independence of the growing child from the specific logically demanded an important role for generalization, that is, transfer; 2. our observations of severely subnormal children and adults, as well as experimental studies by Tizard and by ourselves, indicated that transfer must be more important in the mentally handicapped than casual observation would suggest; 3. from Hebb (1949) we realized that the early work which had apparently closed the controversy on 'formal discipline' (that is that certain 'master' subjects such as Latin and arithmetic 'trained' the mind) possessed inherent weaknesses.

Our early work suggested that indeed there was something worth exploring, and that in subnormal adults and children the processes involved could be put under experimental control. In addition, as a by-product, a number of findings threw light both on some assets and deficits of such persons.

Transfer has been studied by experimental psychologists from three viewpoints: 1. the learning of specific 'elements' in one situation, which are present, and therefore useful, in a second situation; 2. the acquisition of principles in one situation which are also relevant to another (these two may be referred to as *specific transfer*); 3. the acquisition of learning sets (Harlow 1949) arising from frequent exposure to different stimuli in discrimination learning. Here the animal or the child 'learns to learn' (*non-specific transfer*).

From our earlier work and observations it seemed that the child's growing independence from the specific must be mediated by cognitive structures built up by experience (i.e. learning) which would be more general than any of the three modes of transfer outlined above. Accordingly, therefore, our studies aimed to explore this field early in life, using mentally subnormal children and adults as well as preschool normal children. In so doing we devised new techniques which appear to be of value in tracking the growth of cognitive skills in young children.

Recent work began with an attempt to make a direct and fair comparison between adult and child imbeciles, using the same or similar learning material. We had earlier failed to solve this problem because the age discrepancy had been reflected in ability discrepancy, and correspondingly by 'ceiling' effects for the adults. The solution, in the event, proved simple, either we could (a) increase the complexity of the adult task until it became as difficult for them as for the children, or (b) we could decrease the complexity of the child task until it became as easy for them as for the adults. In brief we equated children and adults by these two methods for similar starting points, and from both a substantially similar picture emerged. Adults and children given two tasks serially, which were of the same order of relative difficulty, showed similar learning curves and hence similar transfer. This was of interest *per se*, but suggested something much more important, namely that transfer might occur on the basis of task complexity (Clarke and Cooper 1966). It therefore seemed possible that, if we now held age constant and varied the complexity of training, differential transfer would occur.

The next major experiment was not only designed to check the point about complexity and transfer, using a different methodology and a new group of 36 subnormal subjects aged 12, but also to determine whether transfer could occur across tasks widely different in content. In other words, whether transfer could be very general.

The task on which transfer influences could be measured, that is the transfer task, consisted of five stimulus pictures exemplifying five common concepts (human beings, tableware, clothes, animals and furniture). Twenty response cards, bearing different exemplars of these concepts, had to be sorted out one by one on successive trials under the five stimuli which were mounted on a card-sorting apparatus.

There were three training tasks of different complexity, one for each group of nine subjects, and the fourth group operated without training as a control. Again the training problems involved sorting by shape various geometric designs under their five stimuli cards. One such task, for example, included the variables of shape, size, orientation and irrelevant content. The findings showed clearly that complex training yielded significantly more transfer than simple training or control conditions. This relation between complex training and transfer was further supported by the fact that those whose training scores were initially low, that is who found the tasks difficult, showed more transfer than those whose scores were high. Equally interesting was the clear indication that transfer could take place across tasks possessing no identical elements other than that, for the subject, they were intellectual problems demanding the formation of categories and concepts. Lastly, the differential effects of training were relatively persistent over ten learning trials on the transfer material (Clarke, Cooper and Henney 1966).

At this point I must say a little about the functions of concepts. 'The world of experience' (write Bruner, Goodnow and Austin 1956) 'is composed of a tremendous array of discriminably different objects, events, people, impressions. There are estimated to be more than 7 million discriminable colours alone, and in the course of a week or two we come in contact with a fair proportion of them... But were we to utilize fully our capacity for registering the differences in things and to respond to each event...as unique, we would soon be overwhelmed by the complexity of our environment.' Bruner *et al.* go on to argue that we solve the problem by categorizing as equivalent things which are discriminably different. Thus our use of about a dozen colour names categorizes 7 million hues. By forming concepts we thus reduce the complexity of our environment. Note the idea of complexity in this context and in our work on transfer. I shall come back to this point.

Our next main experiment used normal preschool children aged between 4 and 5, and was designed to discover whether our findings would be replicated on a normal sample. The paradigm for the experiment was identical with the last and the transfer and training material were similar. In brief, our results showed a similar pattern to those of the severely subnormal, although transfer was greater. Complex training induced much more transfer than simple or control conditions. And again, the transfer occurred across entirely different tasks. To test the strength of the categories acquired, the subjects were ultimately shifted to parallel versions of the transfer task, and the former differentials remained, indicating some strength possessed by the concepts which had clearly not been specific to the original material. It was also clear from a subsidiary experiment that overlearning a complex problem could yield as big effects as learning a very complex problem. So overlearning and complexity can interact in producing transfer.

We see then that the learning of a complex problem requiring a reduction in its complexity by categorization facilitates the learning of a different complex problem, which for correct solution also requires a reduction in

complexity. This is a roundabout way of saying that exercise in one form of categorization improved the ability to undertake a different system of
categorizing (Clarke and Cooper 1966).

So far I have merely offered the barest details of these experiments, but a
number of problems needed further elucidation, and I will outline these in an
account of the next main experiment. Several questions were asked; first, what
did we mean by complexity, and, linked with this, what was transferred
between the various tasks? Perhaps by complexity we meant difficulty, and
perhaps difficulty so aroused motivation and attention that these were the relevant qualities transferred?

Alternatively, perhaps the practice in categorizing, and thus reducing the
complexity of the problem, produced an ability or set to reduce complexity by
categorizing. Perhaps, too, the notion only related to visually presented
material and might not generalize to a different sensory modality. And further,
having already replicated the finding several times, there was nevertheless
every reason for trying yet again to see whether the relationships demonstrated
would survive further repetition. These, then, were the notions upon which a
complicated experiment using normal preschool children was founded (Clarke
et al. 1967).

We used 45 normal children aged between 3½ and 4¾ years, matching
five equal groups on pre-test in the usual way, and randomly allocating each to
a different training condition. We also used control data from a previous investigation. The paradigm below summarizes the experimental design.

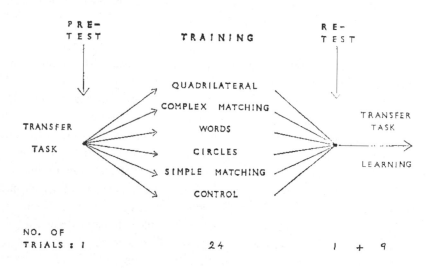

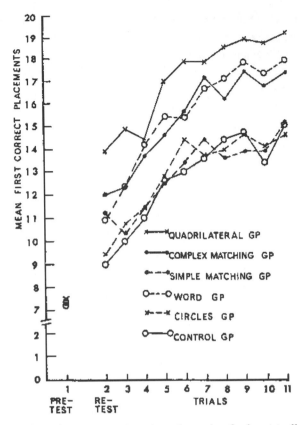

Figure 18.1 This shows the pre-test starting point and retest data for the originally matched groups which had experienced different forms of intervening training. Following retest, a further nine trials of learning on the transfer task were given

The transfer task was the same as one used previously. The training task which had previously yielded the greatest transfer, the Quadrilateral, was both difficult and complex, required the sorting of five different quadrilateral figures differing in shape, size, orientation, position on the card and internal relations of angles and lines. The Complex Matching training task was both difficult and complex. There were five closely similar geometric designs with some irrelevant details. Response cards had to be matched to these stimuli. The Word training task was complex and fairly difficult. It consisted of five outline drawings to which verbs spoken by the experimenter had to be associated. The training task, designed to be difficult but not complex, demanded the discrimination of circles differing in radius by $1/12$ inch. Response cards were identical and had to be matched to the stimuli. The learning of this Circles task demanded attention and motivation. The Simple Matching training task consisted of five easily discriminable figures to which corresponding figures had to be matched. Control subjects scores were also available.

Figure 18.1 shows the average transfer and subsequent learning scores for the five training groups and the controls.

Once again the Quadrilateral group shows a clear and significant (< .01) superiority over all others in transfer. The other two groups trained on complex tasks, that is the Complex Matching Group and the Words Group, showed a significant superiority to the groups trained on an easy matching task and a difficult but non-complex Circles Matching task, but their gain was less impressive. The Words Group had moved from a situation where information received auditorily was applied visually, while the Complex Matching Group had had no direct experience of making common responses to dissimilar stimuli.

There were a number of subsidiary findings, but the main result is clear: the learning of complex sorting problems requiring the formation of concepts, categories or rules facilitated the learning of different problems requiring different rules. The results of the Circles Group argues against attention/motivation as the transferred process, and the notion of practice in establishing similarities between dissimilar material – in a word, categorization – receives support.

Thus for a wide range of discrimination tasks, not yet fully explored, a relation is postulated between amount of transfer shown in learning certain new tasks and the complexity and amount of the original learning. Our data also yield information not here discussed on the transfer of specific learning but the main evidence suggests that, in addition, there can occur in the naive organism an increasing capacity to structure variability after exposure to complex categorization experiences. Of course the limits to such facilitation, and the question whether such findings might be replicated with other cognitive operations, remain open (Clarke, Cooper and Clarke 1967).

The last experiments to be mentioned attempted to provide further information on the persistence of the cognitive sets induced by complex training. Using complex tasks, one highly relevant to the transfer task and the other quite irrelevant, we interposed training on an easy task before testing for transfer. Not only were the effects of complexity not dissipated, but, surprisingly, the training relevant to the transfer task was no more powerful than the 'irrelevant' training.

Finally we aimed to discover how far the conceptual schemata formed in the experiment would be available in a different and much less structured situation. Initial performance, using the same categories as earlier, was very varied, suggesting that the change of context and instructions was damaging. Once the new situation was understood, however, the effects of earlier training became apparent (Clarke and Cooper 1967).

Summary

I have tried to show, in the first part of my lecture, the consequences which operate logically from acceptance of the truism that development is determined by the interaction of learning with congenital factors. This at once suggests that results of early experience which have anything more than merely transitory effects are likely by definition to exhibit the general phenomena of learning. In turn, the permanence of early learning will depend not only upon the age of the child and the duration and intensity of the experience, but more particularly upon its later reinforcement. Early learning will fade if not reinforced. At the outset I faulted this crude model and asked whether data from properly controlled studies would overthrow it. On the contrary, it seems to me that the data give moderate support to this notion, and cast doubt on some current views, which really imply an extreme environmentalism in relation to the age range 0 to 5 but not thereafter.

The formative years seem likely to be of much longer duration than some have thought, and it may well be that the relative stability of some human characteristics reflect environmental stability and continuity for the individual (Bloom 1964). Even so, under conditions of relative environmental stability there is some degree of variation of psychological characteristics over time. This must, therefore, reflect either the influence of genetic and maturational factors, or else subtle, as opposed to gross, environmental effects (Sontag, Baker and Nelson 1958), or an interaction of both. When larger alterations occur in the child's experiences, corresponding and larger changes occur in his personal characteristics.

The second part of my lecture related to transfer and categorization processes. I have tried to indicate that experimental method gives us a mode of attack in elucidating difficult problems, the solutions to which are only vaguely indicated by correlational studies. It has been shown that exposure to complex categorizing experiences facilitates categorizing different material and reveals transfer processes of far wider effect than the specific processes more commonly studied. Such effects have some persistence and do not easily extinguish, although doubtless they too would fade if not reinforced. It may be that our experiments have sampled the processes by which young children gain independence from the specific, and the means by which cognitive abilities are built up. Thinking is partly a matter of drills and skills (Ryle 1953); our experiments indicate that complex drills create both some specific and some more general skills. Certainly the notion of complexity fits quite well studies on the effects of enriched versus impoverished environments, and this in turn ties up with the first part of my lecture. Moreover, two other streams of research coincidentally focus upon the importance of complex experiences. The first is associated with the name of Rosenzweig, and shows in animals significant changes in brain chemistry and morphology as a result of complex experience (Bennett, Diamond, Krech and Rosenzweig 1964; Rosenzweig, Bennett and Diamond 1967). The second, by Munsinger, Kessen and Kessen (1964) and Munsinger and Kessen (1966), indicates that young children show a preference for complex over simple stimuli.

Taken together, both subjects I have discussed have in common an emphasis upon change in human characteristics, the one in the long term during development, and the other in laboratory conditions which seek to simulate some of the problems of real-life cognitive experience. Now, change in human characteristics is perhaps a more attractive notion than the predestinationism built into theories ascribing crucial importance to the preschool years. Crawshay-Williams (1947) has alerted us to the dangers of 'comfortable concepts', and I have therefore tried to examine my theme very critically.

Most aspects of behaviour, to a greater or lesser extent, possess learned components, and it seems that for man long periods of enduring experience are needed before personality and cognitive structures are so developed and shaped by overlearning that they attain that relative inflexibility, stability and autonomy in the face of changing circumstances which are characteristic of the mature person. By the age of 30, remarked William James, man's personality is set hard as a plaster cast.

From the practical viewpoint, and as I have indicated, there already exist some careful studies which reveal that some children and young people can respond dramatically to dramatic environmental change, usually from impoverished to enriched environments. The United States is currently basing its major attempts in the prevention of mild mental retardation on such studies (Gray and Klaus 1965). The Head Start programme will, however, stand or fall not on what it achieves in the preschool years, but on whether or not these diversions of development are subsequently reinforced.

Our major need now is to determine more precisely the factors that initiate, accentuate and maintain alteration in human characteristics, as well as to determine the ultimate limits of these effects and the causes of individual differences in responsiveness to change. For psychiatry and developmental psychology a formidable task lies ahead, but by now we have available sophisticated techniques and methodologies which may help to establish more fundamental principles than we yet possess.

Acknowledgements

The first part of this paper is based upon a chapter in *Foundations of Child Psychiatry* (1968) and I am grateful to Dr Emanuel Miller, the Editor, and Pergamon Press for permission to use this material. The second part concerns an experimental programme generously supported by the Nuffield Foundation from 1963 to 1967, and currently by the Association for the Aid of Crippled Children, New York, to both of which I am greatly indebted. These researches arose from the co-operative efforts of a research team to which my wife, Dr Ann Clarke, and Mr G.M. Cooper were the main contributors.

References

Ainsworth, M.D., Andry, R.G., Harlow, R.G., Lebovici, S., Mead, M., Prugh, D.G. and Wootton, B. (1962) *Deprivation of Maternal Care: A Reassessment of its Effects.* Geneva: World Health Organization.

Bennett, E.L., Diamond, M.C., Krech, D. and Rosenzweig, M.R. (1964) 'Chemical and anatomical plasticity of brain.' *Science 146,* 610–619.

Bloom, B.S. (1964) *Stability and Change in Human Characteristics.* New York: John Wiley.

Bowlby, J. (1951) *Maternal Care and Mental Health.* Geneva: World Health Organization.

Bowlby, J., Ainsworth, M., Boston, M. and Rosenbluth, D. (1956) 'The effects of mother-child separation: a follow-up study.' *British Journal of Medical Psychology 29,* 211–247.

Bruner, J.S., Goodnow, J.J. and Austin, G.A. (1956) *A Study of Thinking.* New York: John Wiley.

Burtt, H.E. (1932) 'The retention of early memories.' In W. Dennis (ed) *Readings in Child Psychology,* (2nd edn). Englewood Cliffs, NJ: Prentice-Hall, 341–352.

Campbell, B.A. and Campbell, E.M. (1962) 'Retention and extinction of learned fear in adult rats.' *Journal of Comparative and Physiological Psychology 55,* 1–8.

Campbell, D., Sanderson, R.E. and Laverty, S.G. (1964) 'Characteristics of a conditioned response in human subjects during extinction trials following a single traumatic conditioning trial.' *Journal of Abnormal and Social Psychology 68,* 627–639.

Clarke, A.D.B. and Clarke, A.M. (1959) 'Recovery from the effects of deprivation' *Acta Psychologica 16,* 137–144.

Clarke, A.D.B. and Clarke, A.M. (1960) 'Some recent advances in the study of early deprivation.' *Journal of Child Psychology and Psychiatry 1,* 26–36.

Clarke, A.D.B., Clarke, A.M. and Reiman, S. (1958) 'Cognitive and social changes in the feeble-minded – three further studies.' *British Journal of Psychology 49*, 144–157.

Clarke, A.D.B. and Cooper, G.M. (1966) 'Age and perceptual-motor transfer in imbeciles: task complexity as a variable.' *British Journal of Psychology 57*, 113–119.

Clarke, A.M. and Cooper, G.M. (1967) 'Conceptual transfer as a function of prior training.' *Psychonomic Science 9*, 307–308.

Clarke, A.M., Cooper, G.M. and Clarke, A.D.B. (1967) 'Task complexity and transfer in the development of cognitive structures.' *Journal of Experimental Child Psychology 5*, 562–576.

Clarke, A.M., Cooper, G.M. and Henney, A.S. (1966) 'Width of transfer and task complexity in the conceptual learning of imbeciles.' *British Journal of Psychology 57*, 121–128.

Cravioto, J., DeLicardie, E.R. and Birch, H.G. (1966) 'Nutrition, growth and neurointegrative development: an experimental and ecologic study.' *Pediatrics 38*, 319–372.

Crawshay-Williams, R. (1947) *The Comforts of Unreason*. New York: Humanities Press.

Davis, K. (1947) 'Final note on a case of extreme isolation.' *American Journal of Sociology 52*, 432–437.

Dennis, W. (1960) 'Causes of retardation among institutional children.' *Journal of Genetic Psychology 96*, 47–59.

Dennis, W. and Najarian, P. (1957) 'Infant development under environmental handicap.' *Psycholoical Monographs 71*, 1–13.

Dobbing, J. and Widdowson, E.M. (1965) 'The effect of under-nutrition and subsequent rehabilitation on myelination of rat brain as measured by its composition.' *Brain 88*, 357–366.

Fuller, J.L. and Waller, M.B. (1962) 'Is early experience different?' In E.L. Bliss (ed) *Roots of Behaviour*. New York: Harper and Bros.

Gardner, D.B., Hawkes, G.R. and Burchinal, L.G. (1961) 'Development after non-continuous mothering.' *Child Development 32*, 225–234.

Goldfarb, W. (1943) 'The effects of early institutional care on adolescent personality.' *Journal of Experimental Education 12*, 106–129.

Gray, S.W. and Klaus, R.A. (1965) 'An experimental preschool program for culturally deprived children.' *Child Development 36*, 887–898.

Harlow, H.F. (1949) 'The formation of learning sets.' *Psychological Review 56*, 51–65.

Harlow, H.F. (1963) 'The maternal affectional system.' In B.M. Foss, (ed) *Determinants of Infant Behaviour*. London: Methuen.

Haywood, H.C. and Tapp, J.T. (1966) 'Experience and the development of adaptive behaviour.' In N.R. Ellis (ed) *International Review of Research in Mental Retardation*, Vol. 1. New York: Academic Press.

Hebb, D.O. (1949) *The Organization of Behaviour.* London: Chapman and Hall.

Hill, O.W. and Price, J.S. (1967) 'Childhood bereavement and adult depression.' *British Journal of Psychiatry 113*, 743–751.

Kagan, J. and Moss, H.A. (1962) *Birth to Maturity.* New York: John Wiley.

King, J.A. (1958) 'Parameters relevant to determining the effect of early experience upon the adult behaviour of animals.' *Psychological Bulletin 55*, 46–57.

Levine, S. and Lewis, G.W. (1959) 'The relative importance of experimenter contact in an effect produced by extra-stimulation in infancy.' *Journal of Comparative and Physiological Psychology 52*, 368–369.

Lewis, A. (1951) 'The Twenty-Fifth Maudsley Lecture – Henry Maudsley: his work and influence.' *Journal of Mental Science 97*, 259–277.

Lewis, H. (1954) *Deprived Children.* London: Oxford University Press.

Mason, M.K. (1942) 'Learning to speak after years of silence.' *Journal of Speech and Hearing Disorders 7*, 245–304.

Mayer-Gross, W., Slater, E., and Roth, M. (1954) *Clinical Psychiatry.* London: Cassell and Company Ltd.

Melzack, R. (1954) 'The genesis of emotional behaviour: an experimental study of the dog.' *Journal of Comparative and Physiological Psychology 47*, 166–168.

Miller, E. (ed) (1968) *Foundations of Child Psychiatry.* London: Pergamon. In press.

Munsinger, H. and Kessen, W. (1966) 'Stimulus variability and cognitive change.' *Psychological Review 73*, 164–178.

Munsinger, H. Kessen, W. and Kessen, M.L. (1964) 'Age and uncertainty: developmental variations in preference for variability.' *Journal of Experimental Child Psychology 1*, 1–15.

Peters, J.E. and Murphee, O.D. (1966) 'Emotional trauma in rats: age as a factor in recovery.' *Condit Reflex 1*, 51–56.

Prugh, D.G., Staub, E.M., Sands, H.H., Kirschbaum, R.M. and Lenihan, E.A. (1953) 'A study of the emotional reactions of children and families to hospitalization and illness.' *American Journal of Orthopsychiatry 23*, 70–116.

Rathbun, C., Di Virgilio, L. and Waldfogel, S. (1958) 'The restitutive process in children following radical separation from family and culture.' *American Journal of Orthopsychiatry 28*, 408–415.

Rosenzweig, M.R., Bennett, E.L. and Diamond, M.C. (1967) 'Effects of differential environments on brain anatomy and chemistry.' In *Psycho-pathology of Mental Development.* J. Zubin and G. Jervis (eds) New York: Grune and Stratton.

Rutter, M., Birch, H.G., Thomas, A. and Chess, S. (1964) 'Temperamental characteristics in infancy and the later development of behavioural disorders.' *British Journal of Psychiatry 110*, 651–661.

Ryle, G. (1953) 'Thinking.' *Acta Psychologica 9*, 189–196.

Salzen, E.A. (1963) 'Visual stimuli eliciting the smiling response in the human infant.' *Journal of Genetic Psychology 102*, 51–54.

Salzen, E.A. and Sluckin, W. (1959) 'The incidence of the following response and the duration of responsiveness in domestic fowl.' *Animal Behaviour 7*, 172–179.

Sayegh, Y. and Dennis, W. (1965) 'The effects of supplementary experiences upon the behavioural development of infants in institutions.' *Child Development 36*, 81–90.

Schaffer, H.R. (1958) 'Objective observations of personality development in early infancy.' *British Journal of Medical Psychology 31*, 174–183.

Schlaegel, T.F. (1953) 'Visual experience and visual imagery.' *Journal of Genetic Psychology 83*, 265–277.

Schutz, F. (1965) 'Sexuelle prägung bei anatiden.' (Sexual imprinting in the *anatidae* (duck and swan family).) Zeitschrift fur Tierpsychology 22, 50–103.

Skeels, H.M. (1966) 'Adult status of children with contrasting early life experiences: a follow-up study.' *Monographs of the Society for Research in Child Development 31*, 3, No. 105.

Skodak, M. (1968) 'Adult status of formerly retarded individuals who experienced intervention in early childhood.' *Proceedings of the First Congress of the International Association for the Scientific Study of Mental Deficiency.* London: Jackson.

Sluckin, W. (1964) *Imprinting and Early Learning.* London: Methuen.

Sontag, L.W., Baker, G.T. and Nelson, V.L. (1958) 'Mental growth and personality development: a longitudinal study.' *Monographs of the Society for Research in Child Development 23*, 68, No. 2.

Stone, L.J. (1954) 'A critique of studies on infant isolation.' *Child Development 25*, 9–20.

Thompson, W.R. and Heron, W. (1954) 'The effects of early restriction on activity in dogs.' *Journal of Comparative and Physiological Psychology 47*, 77–82.

Trasler, G. (1960) *In Place of Parents.* London: Routledge and Kegan Paul.

Watson, J.B. and Rayner, R. (1920) 'Conditioned emotional reactions.' *Journal of Experimental Psychology 3*, 1–14.

Whimbey, A.E. and Denenberg, V.H. (1966) 'Programming life histories: creating individual differences by the experimental control of early experiences.' *Multivariate Behavioral Research 1*, 279–286.

Wittenborn, J.R. (1956) *The Placement of Adoptive Children.* Springfield, Ill: Charles G. Thomas.

Woods, P.J. (1959) 'The effects of free and restricted environmental experience on problem-solving behaviour in the rat.' *Journal of Comparative and Physiological Psychology 52*, 399–402.

Wootton, B. (1959) *Social Science and Social Pathology.* London: Allen and Unwin.

Yarrow, L.J. (1961) 'Maternal deprivation: toward an empirical and conceptual re-evaluation.' *Psychological Bulletin 58*, 459–490.

CHAPTER 19

How Modifiable
is the Human Life Path?

Commentary

This chapter is based on an invited lecture in a sponsored National Institute of Child Health and Human Development conference on 'Environmental Determinants on Nervous System Development', held at the Civitan Research Centre, Birmingham, Alabama. Its publication was invited by the then editor of the *International Review of Research in Mental Retardation*.

The article concentrates on the outcomes for four different groups of children: 1. those removed from conditions of very severe adversity, 2. children who experienced prenatal or perinatal biomedical problems, reared in different social classes, 3. those who exhibited childhood adjustment difficulties and 4. children escaping conditions of social disadvantage.

The concept of 'life path' is a broad one, representing multiple correlations of dozens of varying contributing components. Development over the life path is seen as reflecting a series of linkages in which characteristics in each period have a probability of linking with those in another particular period. But probabilities are not certainties, and deflections, for good or ill, are usually possible within the constraints of genetic, constitutional and social factors.

How Modifiable is the Human Life Path?*

Ann M. Clarke and Alan D.B. Clarke

Introduction

The origins of the stream of research to be reviewed are to be found in the authors' early studies of institutionalized mildly retarded adolescents and young adults (e.g., Clarke and Clarke 1953, 1954, 1959; Clarke, Clarke and Reiman 1958). Subsequent work showed that the findings generalized to different samples of children who, to varying extents, suffered disablement (in some cases temporary) arising from adversity (e.g. Kadushin 1970; Kagan and Klein 1973; Koluchová 1972, 1976). The present thesis therefore goes well beyond the field of mental retardation, but includes it. It challenges the view that experiences in the first few years of life predetermine the life path.

By *life path* we mean the biosocial trajectories of development from birth through childhood, adulthood and senescence. These complex processes affect and are reciprocally affected by the experiences of individuals. As implied, the whole of the life span is perceived as important and, to varying extents, formative. Such a view contrasts with earlier (but still common) notions that regarded the first few years of life as critical for later development (see Bowlby 1951, 1988).

To provide a historical context, it may be helpful to indicate briefly some autobiographical details in so far as these illuminate the origin of the authors' current attempts to understand human development better. In 1951 we were asked to reopen a psychology department founded and then abandoned by several psychologists in a very low cost institution. This hospital contained some 1400 persons compulsorily detained under legal order, some three-quarters of whom were mildly retarded or, in some cases, merely backward. These were mainly adolescents or young adults who either had caused social problems or were regarded as at risk of perpetrating maladjusted or criminal behaviour in the community.

Two apparently unrelated streams of research followed, both of which gave results in the teeth of received wisdom. The more important, relating to this article, was the accidental discovery that some of our mildly retarded individuals in adolescence and early adulthood showed marked increments in IQ

* This article first appeared in 1992 in the *International Review of Research in Mental Retardation 18*, pp.137–157.

and social adjustment. A number of hypotheses were examined; these included the possibility that younger members would have made greater increments, that test practice might be responsible, that to be a recent admission to the hospital might result in underestimation because of emotional upset, and that those with lower IQs might show greater improvements. None of these appeared potent; however, it was established that a record of earlier severe, prolonged social adversity predicted later improvement. The rating of severe adversity depended on the presence in the individual case-history of at least two of 12 specific criteria indicating an early record of cruelty and neglect that had led to official action to remove the child from the parents (Clarke and Clarke 1954). Conversely, less severe adversity or its absence in the background was associated with a poorer prognosis for IQ increments, social adjustment, and discharge from care. After a pilot study, a 'clean' series of studies were initiated, in which assessment was carried out independently by a colleague without knowledge of social history or earlier test scores, and another independent researcher without knowledge of the individual or test scores rated childhood history for the degree of adversity (severe or less severe).

Altogether we undertook four studies, although our results were recorded in a number of articles in addition to the primary sources. The first (Clarke and Clarke 1954) investigated the frequency of IQ changes over two-and-a-quarter years and their relationship to earlier severe adversity. The second, third, and fourth studies were all reported by Clarke et al. (1958). The second study employed a four-and-a-half-year test–retest time interval, confirming larger changes in relation to the longer time interval. The third increased the test–retest interval to six years. Some 78 per cent of the severely deprived group showed increments of 15 or more IQ points, compared with some 25 per cent of the less deprived group. The fourth study showed that changes were *not* related to differences in institutional programmes, but represented a fading of the effects of earlier adversity – a self-righting tendency. Finally, we studied a control group of consecutive new admissions, reassessed after three months, enabling an estimate to be made of the greatest possible effects of regression toward the mean and test practice. On average, these accounted for at the most only a quarter of the 6-year increments.

The late or delayed development occurring in the most deprived mildly retarded persons seemed to represent one of several factors accounting for the marked decrease in administrative prevalence from adolescence onward, which is common in epidemiological research. For example, Richardson (1985, p.374) reported some results from the Aberdeen study in which five birth-year cohorts were followed from ages 5 to 22. After school-leaving age

(15–16 years) the prevalence of those receiving mental retardation services decreased by more than half, a drop accounted for by formerly designated mild cases, there being no change in the number of more severely retarded.

Subsequently our four studies were replicated several times elsewhere. For example, Svendsen (1982, 1983) followed to adulthood a sample of educable mentally retarded and slow-learning children. Estimates of early family and personal problems showed that IQ changes were associated with the greater number of problems and with post-school education. Increments in the 'problems' group averaged 18 IQ points, compared with 5 points in the group with one or no problems and without further education. Somewhat similar findings are recorded by Roswell Harris (1958) and Brown (1972), among others.

This, then, was a problem that found the researchers rather than vice versa. It challenged the notion of a necessary developmental constancy, a view that has dominated developmental theory for most of this century (Brim and Kagan 1980; Clarke and Clarke 1984). It also challenged the idea, then recently revived (Bowlby 1951), that the events of the first few years have a crucially formative influence. The early experiences of our 'adverse' subjects could scarcely have been more damaging. Indeed, their compulsory incarceration provided testimony to their earlier disturbed behaviour and significantly subaverage intellectual functioning. But these effects had tended to fade. As noted, improvements were much less common in those with backgrounds of less severe or no adversity. We were soon to be greatly encouraged by the identification of the catch-up phenomenon in physical growth after illness or mild malnutrition which seemed to rather closely parallel our behavioural results. It seemed possible that these findings might generalize (e.g. Clarke and Clarke 1959, 1960).

During the 1960s most of the published evidence appeared to go against our hypothesis and to support the existence of psychosocial critical periods very early in life. The work of the ethologists was very influential; Harlow (1963), Levine (1960) and Scott (1963, 1968) all published experimental results showing the long-term adverse effects of early deprivation in animals. While accepting the usefulness of animal studies at neural levels, we were very sceptical about the extrapolation of some of the results to social and educational problems in disadvantaged children.

So far as Harlow's work on the later maladjustment of formerly isolated monkeys was concerned, we took this very seriously indeed, but lamented that an equal amount of ingenuity had not been spent constructing experiments that might reverse the damage. We argued that if, following isolation experiences, these monkeys had not been transferred to an improved, remedial situation, then a self-perpetuating cycle of maladjusted behaviour might be expected. There was no evidence that any such attempt had been made. Much later this problem was addressed by Suomi and Harlow (1972) and Novak and Harlow (1975) whose results were in keeping with our own hypothesis.

There was also the problem of the many human studies that showed merely a correlation between early environmental circumstances and later behavioural status, without demonstrating a clear environmental change inbetween, strictly speaking the only valid test of the crucial effect of the early period. Finally, to our great surprise, Skeels (1966) entitled his important monograph 'Adult status of children with contrasting *early* life experiences: a follow-up study' [our italics], again following the *zeitgeist* of the 1960s. This research seemed clearly to be a study of children who had been shifted around a good deal during the 'critical years' (Skeels and Dye 1939) and then fortunately had been adopted (albeit late) and remained in stable, accepting homes. The outcome in adult life was thus almost certainly as much a product of their happy adoptive status as of their early experiences (see Clarke 1982; Clarke, Clarke and Berg 1985, pp.9, 10).

By 1975 we believed that there was sufficient evidence to produce a book that suggested that early experiences, good or bad, did not in themselves set for the child an invariant life path. Contributions were included from such scholars as Urie Bronfenbrenner, Jerry Kagan and Michael Rutter. It was stressed that conclusions should not be interpreted literally as a counterbalance, which might be an equal and opposite extreme, but rather as an attempt to achieve a balanced view. With one or two discordant voices, reviewers seemed to feel that in *Early Experience: Myth and Evidence* (Clarke and Clarke 1976) a valid case had been made for a greater degree of potential open-endedness in human development than had until then been accepted.

Summarizing the main arguments, we indicated that there is no known adversity from which at least some children had not recovered if moved to something better and that the whole of the life path is important, including the early years. These are, of course, for most children, foundational – leading in most cases to confirmatory – influences, as age increases. Three additional points were also made. First, increasing age probably imposes constraints on potential responsiveness to environmental influences. This may be intrinsic to the aging process or may result from habit, forced or chosen life paths, and social pressures. For want of a better analogy we called this a 'wedge' model.

Second, one way in which early experience effects may be perpetuated, usually indirectly, is when one good or bad thing leads to another and a chain of good or bad events then follows. For example, a maladjusted child in care may not be considered for fostering or adoption and, therefore, will remain in a less than satisfactory institution. The maladjustment may remain, justifying on later review no new intervention.

Third, it seemed possible that early adversity, overcome by improved circumstances, might nevertheless leave the individual potentially more vulnerable to later stress. Experiences that affect the individual's behaviour in more than a transitory way must involve learning, broadly defined. Stress might reawaken earlier maladjusted behaviour in the same way that unused skills are more easily relearned after the passage of time.

Traditionally, researchers often sought powerful single main factors leading to single main effects; however, many variables may be involved in an outcome. These are not necessarily solely additive; some studies have shown potent multiplicative effects of two, three or four variables (Rutter, Yule, Quinton, Rowlands, Yule and Berger 1975). Identifying six risk factors in childhood, Rutter *et al.* showed that the occurrence of one yielded no greater risk than was evident in control children. Two resulted in a fourfold increase, and four factors produced a tenfold increase in emotional and conduct disorders.

Genetic factors, constitutional factors, and micro- and macro-environmental influences represent headlines for the complex processes involved in human development. One should also add transactions; there is empirical evidence that, to some extent, individuals create or choose their own environments, receiving reinforcing or modifying feedback (e.g., Bell 1968; Scarr and McCartney 1983; Thomas, Chess and Birch 1968). Finally, chance encounters or events sometimes potently alter the course of development.

Even an armchair analysis of these overly simple headlines would suggest enormous complexity in human development, and that the probable non-linearity of each variable, let alone in combination, would indicate some degree of unpredictability in the long term of *individual* (as opposed to group average) life paths. Indeed, this complexity suggests that the title of this article is overambitious, and that a choice of research data under just a few headings must represent an oversimplification. This criticism is both offered and accepted; however, it is hoped that some general principles will emerge.

Hundreds of correlational studies of intelligence, temperament, or attainment over long periods indicate that there is a range of individual change or non-change in ordinal position and relative level, with individual constancy at one extreme and marked change over time at the other. 'How modifiable is the human life path?' We can already answer that, for many individuals, behavioural characteristics alter differentially in natural circumstances, in spite of social and educational pressures that tend to keep a person on a self-fulfilling prophetic track. And these characteristics, in turn, may affect the person's life path for good or ill (Clarke and Clarke 1986).

Contributors to Brim and Kagan's (1980) *Constancy and Change in Human Development* offer a number of different ways of tracking development. Here perhaps the simplest has been chosen: investigations of changing or unchanging behavioural levels.

Empirical evidence concerning children with actual or potential problems is outlined; here the question of modifiability of the life path is at its most pressing and its test the most exacting. We discuss the outcome for four groups:

1. children removed from very severe adversity

2. children with prenatal or perinatal biomedical problems in different social classes

3. children with adjustment difficulties and

4. children escaping from disadvantage.

Finally, an attempt is made to draw the threads together in an overview.

Removal from isolation or very severe adversity

One test of human resilience is to be found in studies of children removed from isolation or very severe adversity. Legends about feral children date from Romulus and Remus; later 19th- and 20th-century cases suggest that these were recently abandoned autistic or retarded children. Davis (1947) provided the first modern studies concerning two children withdrawn from long isolation. With the help of a specialist, one made a remarkable recovery; without special attention, the other child did not. The latter may have been the victim of organic impairment.

The best documented study is by the Czech psychologist Koluchová (1972, 1976), who has provided the authors with recent unpublished material. Her successive follow-ups concerned monozygotic twin boys, born in 1960, who lost their mother soon after birth, were cared for by a social agency for a year, and were then reared for a further six months by a maternal aunt. Their development was normal. The father, who may have been limited intellectually, remarried, but his new wife proved to be extremely cruel to the children, banishing them to a cellar for the next five-and-a-half years and beating them from time to time.

On discovery they were dwarfed in stature, lacked speech, failed to recognize the meaning of pictures, and were severely malnourished and rachitic.

They were legally removed from their parents and, after a medical rehabilitation programme, were adopted by an exceptional lady and her sister. Scholastically, from a state of severe retardation they caught up with age peers and achieved intellectual and emotional normality. After basic education they went on to train as typewriter mechanics but later decided to go on to secondary school, specializing in electrotechnology. After military service, one now works as an instructor in vocational training and the other as a computer technician. Both are married; one has a child. They are said to be entirely stable emotionally, lacking abnormalities and enjoying warm relationships. Note that they are twins, that they were together in appalling circumstances, and that soon after removal from their parents they were adopted into an unusually warm and supportive home.

A second case, a girl adopted by the same lady at age 5½, was more problematical. She had been isolated on her own and had a psychopathic natural mother; no information was available on the father. Cared for by a social agency during infancy, she appeared mentally retarded. Later, she was restored to her mother, who concealed her existence and neglected the child. She suffered repeated otitis and may have had meningitis. She was difficult for some time in her new family, showing anxiety and, at school, poor peer relations. But gradually she improved, becoming average scholastically; she now works in a factory making handbags (J. Koluchová, personal communication 1991).

Thompson (1986, and personal communication 1990) has published the case-history of a little boy called Adam who was abandoned at the age of 4 months in Colombia and brought up in isolation in a reformatory for girls, where she first saw him. The conditions were appalling and the child was severely malnourished. He was removed to an orphanage at 16 months, at which time he weighed only 12 lb 12 oz (i.e. less than 6000 g). Emotionally he was completely withdrawn. He could not sit, walk or crawl. Adam was diagnosed as an extremely malnourished, mentally retarded spastic. Gradually he improved and, at 32 months, was adopted by a North American family, along with a little girl from the same orphanage. Initially, of course, there were problems. Adam was doubly incontinent and frequently bit his sister, but he has continued to improve in his adoptive family and, at age 8, his WISC-R was 113; his sister who was less severely deprived had an IQ of 102 at the same age. Both graduated from high school and are emotionally stable.

A useful review of most known and properly recorded cases (nine in number) has been provided by Skuse (1984). Certain clinical features in such isolated children are, on discovery, virtually ubiquitous: motor retardation, absent or rudimentary language, grossly retarded perceptuomotor skills, paucity of emotional expression, lack of attachment behaviour, and social withdrawal. If recovery is to occur, progress must be rapid at first. Skuse concludes that 'in the absence of genetic or congenital anomalies...victims of such deprivation have an excellent prognosis. Some subtle deficits in social adjustment may persist – most human characteristics, with the possible exception of language, are strongly "canalised" [in Scarr-Salapatek's (1976) conception] and hence virtually resistant to obliteration by even the most dire environments' (p.567).

If this is so, then the message is clear. Early behavioural development is not critical in the same way that, for example, early prenatal central nervous system damage can be critical. Gross deficits can be made good and the self-righting tendency suggested by Waddington (1957, 1966) appears strong.

Recovery from perinatal problems

Studies of some isolated children illustrate the gradual fading of physical and developmental problems granted special care in unusual circumstances. Is there evidence to support the idea that these ameliorative processes can take place without the removal of the child from the scene of his or her initial difficulties?

The best-known longitudinal study of children who suffered perinatal damage is, perhaps, Werner's (Werner 1985, 1989; Werner and Smith 1982). She and her colleagues studied a total birth cohort of Oriental or Polynesian descent on the island of Kauai. The sample included 698 children, followed from birth until 2 years 10 months, and in some cases until 18 and 32 years.

Neonatal and infant mortality rates were very low, but a number of infants experienced perinatal stress involving a variety of congenital disorders. 'At birth 9% of the cohort had some congenital defects, of which 3.7% were serious enough to require long-term, specialized care for either severe physical handicaps and/or severe mental retardation' (Werner 1985, p.337). Fourteen (or 2%) of the children surviving until 2 years had suffered severe perinatal stress; 69 (or 10%) had suffered moderate perinatal stress.

At each of the follow-up stages intellectual outcome was a function of a significant interaction between characteristics of the caretaking environment and degree of perinatal stress. As early as 20 months, the children growing up in middle-class homes who had experienced the most severe perinatal complications had mean scores on the Cattell Infant Scale almost comparable to those of children with *no* perinatal stress who were living in disadvantaged homes. The most developmentally retarded (in physical as well as intellectual status) were those who had both experienced perinatal stress and been reared in the poorest homes.

The impact of the caretaking environment appeared even more powerful at age 10 years. First, children with and without severe perinatal stress who had grown up in middle-class homes both achieved mean PMA (Primary Mental Abilities) IQ scores well above the average. Second, PMA IQ scores were seriously depressed in children from low SES [socioeconomic status] homes, particularly if they had experienced severe perinatal stress. Third, the family's socioeconomic status showed significant associations with the rate of serious learning and behavior problems. *By age 18 years, ten times as many youths with serious coping problems were living in poverty as had survived serious perinatal stress.* (Werner 1985, p.341)

The latest report (Werner 1989) focused on high-risk children, one-third of whom had in adult life made satisfactory adjustments despite a combination of moderate to severe perinatal stress, discordant or impoverished homes, and alcoholic or mentally disturbed parents. Many of the characteristics identifying the resilient children were already present at the age of 2. Pediatricians and psychologists noted their alertness, positive social orientation, and self-help skills. The author also drew attention to supportive social environmental factors that appeared to protect these young people at various points during their life span.

A less well-known but very elegant study was presented by Wilson (1985) as an offshoot of the famous Louisville Twin Study. This important prospective longitudinal research project included 494 pairs of monozygotic and dizygotic twins and their singleton siblings, demographically representative of the metropolitan borough of Louisville, Kentucky. These twins were tested at 3 months, 6 months, 12 months, 24 months, 3 years and 6 years. A vast amount of personal and demographic information concerning the children and their families is available.

The cohort yielded, naturally enough, babies who were small for gestational age and also twins falling below 1750 g birth weight. Would all these babies be at risk for slow mental development compared with the complete cohort of twins who as a group were somewhat premature, were somewhat smaller at birth and showed delayed development?

It turned out that the small-for-gestational-age infants later exhibited only a modest deficit in IQ scores (about 4 points) at age 6, reduced from a deficit of 16 points at age 3, when compared with the whole cohort. The statistical significance was greatly enhanced by the large numbers involved, outweighing their psychological importance. The author therefore concludes that small-for-gestational-age babies are at no special risk for later retardation.

The same, however, was not true of the very low birth weight babies, many of whom were also very premature. They showed a highly significant deficit at each test age throughout childhood, and although the initial deficit of 19 IQ points was eventually reduced to 9 points, there was no evidence of further recovery for this group. In contrast to the small-for-gestational-age twins, most, but not all, of these infants seemed to be at a long-term disadvantage. When the group was divided by social status, although the numbers were relatively small, 17 high versus 17 low, those in the high-SES group appeared to have recovered by age 6 with average IQs of 101, whereas those in the low-SES group were one standard deviation below them with average IQs of 86.

> Mother's education was significantly related to recovery from 24 months onwards, which suggests that maternal intelligence plays a prominent role in determining the level of recovery. When monozygotic twins of markedly unequal birth weight were compared, the twins who weighed less than 1750g attained the same level of IQ scores at 6 years as did their heavier co-twins. Among these genetic replicates, the initially powerful effects of low birth weight did not exert a long-term handicapping effect on mental development. The data argue for a high degree of resilience in mental development in the face of prenatal stress and for a powerful effect of heritage and home environment in guiding the recovery from early deficit. (Wilson 1985, pp.69, 70)

Wilson (1985) concludes:

> Although the prior analyses have dwelt on the predictions of which infants will recover fully and which ones will not, perhaps the most heartening feature of these data is the pronounced weight gain shown by *all* risk infants up to school age. The effects of risk are not immediately overcome in the first 2 years, but even the low-SES infants showed a substantial upward gain between 3 years and 6 years of age.

> There are recuperative capabilities and qualities of resilience even among risk infants that steadily compensated for the burden of prematurity. Such qualities bring into focus the fact that developmental processes are continuous and ongoing, and they possess intrinsic self-correcting tendencies. In fact, Waddington (1971) identified this as one of the cardinal properties of developmental processes. (p.84)

Adjustment difficulties

We now turn to studies of children who showed adjustment difficulties and disorders that are usually defined as maladaptive reactions to psychosocial stressors leading to impairment of functioning, or symptoms that are in excess of normal reactions. These include severe anxiety, sleep disturbances, phobias and depression, identified at different periods of childhood and adolescence. How do they fare in adult life? The answer, by contrast with many other psychiatric disorders, is *well*.

As with many abnormal conditions, adjustment disorders may arise from a variety of different, and sometimes overlapping, causes. There are a number of obvious variables: the family context, especially the quality of parenting; the degree of match or mismatch between parents and between parents and child; the qualities of individual vulnerability and resilience during or following stress; the enhanced probability of disorder in those with organic brain dysfunction (e.g. Rutter and Sandberg 1985); the doubled risk of emotional and conduct disorders in inner-city areas (London) compared with rural areas (Isle of Wight).

The New York Longitudinal Study, initiated in 1956 by Chess and Thomas, provides a careful prospective longitudinal study of childhood disorders, uniquely with data gathered in all cases before onset (Chess and Thomas 1984; Thomas *et al.* 1968). The sample consisted of 133 middle- to upper-middle-class subjects recruited through personal contact with parents during pregnancy or shortly after birth. An important incentive for joining the study and remaining in it was the promise of free high-quality medical care. There was no attrition among the 133 children whose families joined.

Adjustment disorders represent a wide range of very common behavioural problems, which, as Chess and Thomas note, in many cases represent age-specific behaviours that, though troublesome, are not suggestive of pathological deviation. Sometimes the issue is simple, involving inappropriateness of the routines employed by parents. Suggesting alternative ways of handling the child can be effective. When problems are not resolved, psychiatric evaluation and sometimes treatment are necessary. As is to be expected in this sample there were virtually no conduct disorders. Of 45 clinical cases in childhood, 40 exhibited adjustment disorders, the majority classified as mild. By adolescence 24 had recovered and two had improved; by adulthood 29 had recovered and five had improved their original childhood diagnostic status, two were unchanged, two were moderately worse, and two were markedly worse. In addition, of 12 cases with onset during adolescence, six were completely recovered in early adult life, including three with severe problems (Chess and Thomas 1984).

Two recent prospective longitudinal studies, one from Sweden (von Knorring, Andersson and Magnusson 1987) and one from Germany (Esser, Schmidt and Woerner 1990), confirm the fadeout of clinically diagnosed adjustment disorders with time. The von Knorring *et al.* study provided data on a large, representative sample, prospectively from 10 to 24 years and retrospectively from 0 to 9 years. In reviewing relevant literature these authors noted the higher incidence of childhood disorders in cities, compared with towns and rural areas, and the higher incidence in boys than girls, which, however, is reversed during adolescence. Conduct disorders may be dealt with other than clinically, but the authors underline the poor prognosis for these, with good outcomes for children with emotional disorders.

The criteria for inclusion in the von Knorring *et al.* (1987) sample were different from those of the Chess and Thomas research, as von Knorring *et al.* depended on the rather tough criterion of psychiatric referral during childhood through early adulthood. The findings endorse other work, however; only three of 28 children exhibiting anxiety and emotional disorders before 9 years of age remained in psychiatric care in early adulthood, whereas a quarter of a large group with onset at 10 to 14 years and almost half of those with onset between 15 and 19 years were still in psychiatric care between ages 20 and 24. Males who had attended special classes were at particular risk for developing these disorders.

Esser *et al.* followed a random sample of 356 eight-year-old children in West Germany until the age of 13. Although the overall prevalence rate of 16 per cent for all psychiatric disorders remained constant across the two ages, the persistence of conduct disorders in individual cases was very much greater than that of emotional disorders.

A related topic concerns the life path of children removed from problem families. Two recent studies reported by Quinton, Rutter, Dowdney, Liddle, Mrazek and Skuse (1982) complement one another and illustrate an important principle. Prospective and retrospective studies on the same theme and with similar populations normally yield different answers to the same question. A major reason is that an identified adult deviant group may enable a continuous deviant past history to be revealed in a retrospective investigation, whereas there is no way of knowing how many had similar early histories yet escaped unscathed. The research by Quinton *et al.* has a bearing on both intra-individual and intergenerational constancy and change.

Both projects studied current parenting and associated psychiatric problems, relating these to past and present circumstances. The authors sought to assess the effects on child rearing of early emotional deprivation, as predicted by early learning theorists (Quinton et al. 1982). The first, a retrospective study, evaluated histories of parents whose children had been removed from home and placed in residential care. The second, a prospective study, examined the adult outcome of children originally assessed by the late Jack Tizard and colleagues in the 1960s when they were in residential care, having been themselves removed from home. In both investigations, appropriate carefully chosen comparison groups were used. Important differences emerged between the findings of these two studies: 'our data…show that the picture of intergenerational continuities looking forwards is quite different from that looking backwards' (Quinton et al. 1982, p.293).

The retrospective sample of adults with children in care exhibited a strong link between their parenting breakdown and their own adverse childhood experiences; however, comparison group data showed that quite severe early adversities seldom led directly to such problems. Thus, an additional linking mechanism must be invoked in the former sample. Multiple personal and material circumstances seem to have been involved (see also Quinton and Rutter 1984a, 1984b).

The second, prospective sample of adults who as *children* had been assessed in care indicated that the experience of serious adversities in childhood or of seriously maladaptive and disruptive parenting does not always lead to parenting and other breakdown in the next generation. There is certainly an increased 'risk' but this is not a 'probability'. Many comparison children had also experienced severe adversity but had survived. Indeed, 'intergenerational discontinuities outweigh continuities' (Quinton et al. 1982, p.293). Nearly a third of the women removed from their parents and reared in institutions showed good parenting, and a further quarter displayed only moderate difficulties of a type also shown by 40 per cent of the comparison group (for an overview, see Rutter, Quinton and Liddle 1983).

The general point here is that early adversity can set up a chain of consequences. The effects of early adversity can produce new environmental effects; there also appears to be an increased personal vulnerability to later adversity. Later events in adolescence or adulthood can be potent agents of amelioration or added difficulties. For example, indirect selective factors may lead to choosing a stable and supportive marriage partner or an unstable, equally damaged spouse. Once again, the cumulative and transactional nature of development is implied by these important findings. One small subgroup showed up as particularly vulnerable (Rutter et al. 1983). Ten children had been admitted to institutional care before the age of 2 years and had remained there continuously until 16 years of age or older, inevitably experiencing the relatively detached, multiple-person caretaking that characterizes institutions. Eight of the ten showed later problems, and although this subgroup difference fell short of statistical significance, it is possible that detached, multiple-person caretaking commencing in infancy may be as unsatisfactory in its consequences as rearing in seriously discordant multi-problem situations.

Escape from disadvantage

Our theme, that the life path is modifiable whether through internal or external factors, or both, may be further illustrated by reference to studies, often prospective surveys, that indicate that some individuals escape their adversities. This can occur without any special intervention. For example, a small British study (Tonge, Lunn, Greathead, McLaren and Bosanko 1983) indicated that at adulthood one-third of those reared in problem families achieved normal adjustment, one-third made marginal adjustment, and one-third remained clearly disadvantaged, like their parents.

Many other studies show that there are always some children who escape the dire predictions suggested by their early circumstances. In 1972, Sir Keith Joseph initiated what became known as the Transmitted Deprivation Programme. He had asked why it was that in spite of major social improvements since the end of the Second World War, 'deprivation and problems of adjustment so conspicuously persist? ...social attitudes and ways of life tend to recur in some families from one generation to the next. But what is more surprising (is that) this does not always happen'. In *Cycles of Disadvantage* (Rutter and Madge 1976) and *Despite the Welfare State* (Brown and Madge 1982) the field was reviewed at the beginning and end of the programme, respectively. The 23 studies supported and the more than a dozen commissioned reviews of relevant world literature endorsed the view that cycles of deprivation do exist but do not inevitably recur between generations. These books offer a very comprehensive account of the problem under discussion.

The Newcastle Study, one example of a late funded project, began well before the Transmitted Deprivation Programme. In 1947 Sir James Spence and colleagues undertook what was initially envisaged as a one year investigation into the ecology of infant illnesses in a total sample of 1142 infants born to Newcastle families in two months of that year. Successive follow-up studies, with much broader developmental concerns, led to a final report by Kolvin, Miller, Scott, Gatzanis and Fleeting (1990), who used baseline data from the 1952 assessments. The original sample had by then shrunk to 847, largely due as a result of movement out of the city, presumably of the less deprived.

The final follow-up took place in 1979 – 1980; three randomly selected groups, comprising 264 families, were chosen from the 1952 cohort: 1. a non-deprived sample (14% of the original), 2. a deprived group (50% subsample) comprising those who met one or two of the criteria of deprivation, 3. a *multiply* deprived group (68% subsample) with three or more indices of deprivation. By determined efforts 96 per cent of the sample was traced and 92 per cent interviewed, more than 15 years (age 32) after the last contact.

Among the more salient findings, it emerged that there were degrees of movement both into and out of deprivation. Indeed, as Kolvin *et al.* (1990, p.167) indicate, 'change is the dominant feature'. Thus, of the sample of 62 children whose families did not show any deprivation in 1952, only 43.5 per cent of the families of formation remained non-deprived in 1980, nearly 5 per cent being multiply deprived. Escape from 1952 multiple deprivation was equally evident. Only 43.6 per cent remained in the same situation; the remainder mostly shifted to lesser degrees of adversity, and almost 13 per cent escaped completely.

Kolvin *et al.* believe that deprivation increases personal vulnerability, modifiable, however, by such protective factors as intelligence, equable temperament, scholastic ability and social skills. There is a degree of specific intergenerational transmission via marital disruption and poor quality of physical and emotional care of children. More general transmission, reflected in the sum of individual adverse factors, appears more potent.

The findings of this study are, in general, congruent with the conclusions of other research. This work spans a period of immense social change perhaps somewhat attenuated in northeast England. It emphasizes what Rutter (1989) has termed chain effects. These can persist along the life path or, in certain circumstances, can be broken by environmental influences and personal qualities.

The National Child Development Study (NCDS) has followed the development of all children born in the United Kingdom during one week in March 1958. Various subsamples, as well as the whole cohort, have been the subject of separate analyses. Here the study of only one subsample is mentioned.

In *Born to Fail?* Wedge and Prosser (1973) underlined data on 11-year-olds in the NCDS, the already robust findings concerning the physical and psychological correlates of socioeconomic status. They had a widespread impact, drawing public attention to 'the massive accumulation of burdens afflicting disadvantaged children and their families, and which they are frequently expected somehow to overcome. Yet it should cause no surprise that so many of these children fail to "behave," fail to "learn" and fail to succeed...one in sixteen, the disadvantaged group, suffered adversity after adversity, heaped upon them from before birth; their health was poorer, their school attainment lower and their physical environment worse in almost every way than that of ordinary children' (p.59). So the question for the future becomes: did they all fail in later development?

Fortunately, this study was continued by Essen and Wedge (1982), as part of the Transmitted Deprivation series. It concerned children in the NCDS who were identified as socially disadvantaged at 11, 16, or both 11 and 16. These data, together with earlier information, were designed to represent the ecology of these children at different stages of development. One of the main aims was to determine whether families experience long-term or transitory difficulties, and how these bear on outcome. Such families could at the same time be compared with ordinary families.

The criteria of disadvantage were threefold: rearing in atypical families, poor housing, or low income. At ages 11 and 16, the percentages for the whole NCDS sample were, for the first criterion, 19.8 and 19.3; for the second, 14.7 and 10.2; and for the third, 13.1 and 11.9, respectively. Those who fulfilled all three criteria at age 11 constituted 4.5 per cent, but by age 16 this had declined to 2.9 per cent. Although the findings show some continuities between ages 11 and 16, marked discontinuities were also evident. Of all the disadvantaged at either age, about a quarter were disadvantaged at both ages, half at age 11 only, and a quarter at age 16 only. It is therefore clear that a larger group suffered disadvantage at some stage in childhood than is indicated by the cross-sectional findings at ages 11 and 16 (Essen and Wedge 1982, p.46). This underlines the fact that even an extreme ecology is not necessarily static. From the detailed findings, it became clear that those who at 11 or 16 years were multiply disadvantaged were found to show poorer achievement and behaviour and to be shorter on average than ordinary children. Multiple disadvantages at either age were equally damaging to the children's life chances. It is of interest that for outcome measures at age 16, those who were multiply disadvantaged at that age were at no greater disadvantage than those who had experienced such problems at age 11. 'Neither of these ages appears to be particularly critical…[in] that multiple disadvantage of either, and therefore perhaps any, age is equally damaging to the children's life chances' (p.166).

Recently this NCDS was followed up with interviews at age 26–27 of an educationally successful sample and a comparison group, both of whom had been disadvantaged during one or more periods in childhood. The former were somewhat less disadvantaged than the latter, and certain parental and adolescent aspirations for the future seemed relevant. It was already known that such qualities as easy temperament and good motivation were relevant to escape. This final study confirmed the importance of such factors, and indicated that the achievers had better relationships in their homes than did the comparison subjects. The strongest predictors related to parental interest in the child's education, and of course educational achievement is the key to a better adult life (Pilling 1990).

Discussion

It has been argued that the various behavioural characteristics may severally or in combination affect the direction of the individual life path. Of course, this concept of a life path, or what Rutter (1989) calls life pathways, is a broad one. It represents multiple correlations of dozens of contributing components, which may vary over time.

This article has summarized some of the best recent evidence available. The implications of these studies could suggest a totally unrealistic proposal, namely, that to be absolutely safe so far as the environment is concerned, *all* the world's children should from conception be cared for in well-educated, economically secure, stable and loving families that will support them in times of special need, discipline them, and engender self-discipline to meet life's problems, ensuring that emerging talents are encouraged. Even so, it must be noted that some children reared in these ideal circumstances would still lead troubled lives. Conversely, some children with early problems and reared in dire circumstances will escape and achieve normal adult adjustment.

Why do some succeed and others fail? Attempts will be made to answer this difficult question. Bear in mind, however, that no prospective study as yet conducted, no matter how carefully designed and or how many measures used, can give us detailed answers in individual cases. Nevertheless, there are some clues, culled from numerous studies, including those reviewed by Rutter *et al.* (1983) and Werner (1989), already discussed. Several factors seem to be protective:

1. Constitutional dispositions that will render some children attractive even to the most depraved parents and probably to other members of the family and to a wider community These include sociability, problem-solving ability and planning ability, leading gradually to an internal locus of control. Such children are likely to attract the positive attention of teachers in school; to acquire self-esteem and self-confidence; and to believe both in their own ability to adapt to changing circumstances and in their ability to change circumstances themselves.

2. Some network of affectional support, which may be absent even in the best institutions but may be present in very disadvantaged homes.

3. Schools in which children are valued and encouraged to learn. There are by now massive research data supporting the view that schools may differentially enhance both achievement and adjustment.

4. A peer group, probably based in school, that is prosocial. This means that individual children need to be sufficiently attractive in positive ways to be chosen as friends.

5. An ability to plan purposefully, which Rutter (1989) believes will make a big difference to choice of career and/or choice of continuing education and to delaying marriage and childbearing until an appropriate time.

All these factors have been found to be protective of children at risk, in large-scale studies based in ordinary communities. In addition, there are accounts of rare intervention programmes that start in the preschool period and either maintain their hold over certain children (as in Ramey and Campbell 1987) or initiate a sequence of positive, ongoing events, as in the well-publicized Perry Preschool Programme (Berrueta-Clement, Schweinhart, Barnett, Epstein and Weikart 1984; Schweinhart and Weikart 1980, 1981).

Several factors mitigate against positive personal development:

1. Temperamental irritability and lack of sociability, often combined with some degree of mental retardation. Infants growing up in large, chaotic, discordant families may not have the opportunity to gain an understanding of social cause and effect, nor to develop planning ability or knowledge of the desirability of delayed gratification and an internal locus of control.

2. Lack of emotional security and strong affectional ties with any one person, be it a sibling, grandmother, neighbour, or other significant individual.

Children who lack these supports are likely to be rated *troublesome* by teachers and later by peers in school, to be unpopular with peers, and to seek attention and emotional support in socially undesirable ways. If they are unlucky they will find themselves in schools that lack the necessary tranquillity and academic press to enable them to learn, returning to large, affectionless families that are unable to exercise kind but firm control. They may grow up in a social situation characterized by poverty and lack of hope, from which they lack the personal resources to escape. Problems of inner cities give rise to what Haggerty, Roughman and Pless (1975), followed by Baumeister (Baumeister and Kupstas 1990), term *the new morbidity*. This concept is not entirely new; it is the considerable increase in earlier well-known hazards that has prompted the evolution of the term. It includes behavioural and school problems among children and adolescents, environmental risks, drug and alcohol abuse, accidents, violence, adolescent pregnancy, psychiatric disorders and family disruption (Baumeister and Kupstas 1990, pp.50–51).

The theme addressed in this article is one that is beginning to attract attention from some unexpected quarters. The late John Bowlby, who in 1951 was primarily responsible for reviving the belief that the life path was predetermined in the very early years, wrote in 1988 that:

> the central task...is to study the endless interactions of internal and external (factors), and how the one is influencing the other not only during childhood but during adolescence and adult life as well... Present knowledge requires that a theory of developmental pathways should replace theories that invoke specific phases of development in which it is postulated that a person may become fixated and/or to which he may regress. (pp.1–2)

It may be also worth recording an example of psychoanalytic commentary and surprise at findings like these, which in its original, orthodox view should not be possible. Moskovitz (1985) followed up a small number of child survivors of the Holocaust who had been brought to England at the end of the war. Noting that in the late 1970s the picture often presented suggested a grim outcome of irreparably damaged people 'what (now) became apparent...was the wide range of adaptation when there was theoretically no reason to expect to see anything positive... Many made adaptations that are not only impressive but inspiring' (p.407).

Conclusions

Our thinking about the effects of early social experiences started in the 1950s in a large institution for the mentally retarded in which we were surprised to observe positive cognitive and social changes in adolescents and young adults who had previously experienced exceptional adversity. Explanations were sought and, at first, tentative hypotheses raised. The results of our early studies have been shown to generalize widely and to be relevant to other socially disadvantaged children in whom, for a variety of reasons, intellectual or emotional under-functioning has been manifested. The results suggest that one cannot necessarily take at face value, and as of predictive accuracy, personal levels measured in the context of seriously adverse past or present circumstances.

Rutter (1989) points out that 'chain effects' during development are common. 'Life transitions have to be considered both as end products of past processes and as instigators of future ones...as both independent and dependent variables' (p.46). Similarly, we see development as a series of linkages in which characteristics in each period have a probability of linking with those in another particular period. But such probabilities are not certainties, and deflections, for good or ill, are possible, but always within limits imposed by genetic, constitutional, and social trajectories. Although increasing age appears to diminish the possibility of alterations in the life path, the point where no modification is possible may be extreme old age.

Acknowledgements

This article is based on a joint lecture delivered in October 1990 at a meeting organized by the National Institute of Child Health and Human Development (NICHHD), held at Birmingham, Alabama. The authors are very grateful to Dr Phillip Nelson, Chief, Laboratory of Developmental Neurobiology, NICHHD, National Institutes of Health, Bethesda, Maryland, and to Dr Craig Ramey, Co-director of the new Civilian Research Center, Birmingham, Alabama, for their generous invitations to attend and contribute to the conference on 'Environmental Determinants on Nervous System Development'.

References

Baumeister, A. and Kupstas, F. (1990) 'The new morbidity; Implications for prevention and amelioration.' In P.L.C. Evans and A.D.B. Clarke (eds) *Combatting Mental Handicap*. Bicester: AB Academic, 46–72.

Bell, R.Q. (1968) 'A reinterpretation of effects in studies of socialization.' *Psychological Review 75*, 81–95.

Berrueta-Clement, J.R., Schweinhart, L.J., Barnett, W.S., Epstein, A.S. and Weikart, D.P. (1984) *Changed Lives: The Effects of the Perry Preschool Program on Youths Through Age 19* (Monographs of the High/Scope Educational Research Foundation). Ypsilanti, MI: High/Scope Press.

Bowlby, J. (1951) *Maternal Care and Mental Health*. Geneva: World Health Organization.

Bowlby, J. (1988) 'Developmental psychiatry comes of age.' *American Journal of Psychiatry 145*, 1–10.

Brim, O. and Kagan, J. (eds) (1980) *Constancy and Change in Human Development.* Cambridge, MA: Harvard Educational Press.

Brown, M. and Madge, N. (1982) *Despite the Welfare State.* London: Heinemann.

Brown, R.I. (1972) 'Cognitive changes in the adolescent slow learner.' *Journal of Child Psychology and Psychiatry 13*, 183–193.

Chess, S. and Thomas, A. (1984) *Origins and Evolution of Behaviour Disorders.* New York: Brunner/Mazel.

Clarke, A.D.B. and Clarke, A.M. (1953) 'How constant is the IQ?' *Lancet 2*, 877–880.

Clarke, A.D.B. and Clarke, A.M. (1954) 'Cognitive changes in the feebleminded.' *British Journal of Psychology 45*, 173–179.

Clarke, A.D.B. and Clarke, A.M. (1959) 'Recovery from the effects of deprivation.' *Acta Psychologica 16*, 137–144.

Clarke, A.D.B. and Clarke, A.M. (1960) 'Some recent advances in the study of deprivation.' *Journal of Child Psychology and Psychiatry 1*, 26–36.

Clarke, A.D.B. and Clarke, A.M. (1984) 'Constancy and change in the growth of human characteristics.' *Journal of Child Psychology and Psychiatry 25*, 191–210.

Clarke, A.D.B., Clarke, A.M. and Reiman, S. (1958) 'Cognitive and social changes in the feebleminded: Three further studies.' *British Journal of Psychology 49*, 144–157.

Clarke, A.M. (1982) 'Developmental discontinuities: An approach to assessing their nature.' In L.A. Bond and J.M. Joffe (eds) *Facilitating Infant and Early Childhood Development.* Hanover, NH: University Press of New England, 59–79.

Clarke, A.M. and Clarke, A.D.B. (eds) (1976) *Early Experience: Myth and Evidence.* London: Open Books; New York: The Free Press.

Clarke, A.M. and Clarke, A.D.B. (1986) 'Thirty years of child psychology: A selective review.' *Journal of Child Psychology and Psychiatry 27*, 719–759.

Clarke, A.M., Clarke, A.D.B. and Berg, J.M. (eds) (1985) *Mental Deficiency: The Changing Outlook* (4th edn). London: Methuen.

Davis, K. (1947) 'Final note on a case of extreme isolation.' *American Journal of Sociology 45*, 554–565.

Essen, J. and Wedge, P. (1982) *Continuities in Childhood Disadvantages.* London: Heinemann.

Esser, G., Schmidt, M.H. and Woerner, W. (1990) 'Epidemiology and course of psychiatric disorder in school-age children – Results of a longitudinal study.' *Journal of Child Psychology and Psychiatry 31*, 243–263.

Haggerty, R.J., Roughman, K.J. and Pless, I.V. (1975) *Child Health and Community.* New York: Wiley.

Harlow, H.F. (1963) 'The maternal affectional system.' In B. M. Foss (ed) *Determinants of Infant Behavior.* London: Methuen, 3–33.

Kadushin, A. (1970) *Adopting Older Children.* New York: Columbia University Press.

Kagan, J. and Klein, R.E. (1973) 'Cross-cultural perspectives on early development.' *American Psychologist 28,* 947–961.

Koluchová, J. (1972)' Severe deprivation in twins: A case study.' *Journal of Child Psychology and Psychiatry 13,* 107–114.

Koluchová, J. (1976) 'A report on the further development of twins after severe and prolonged deprivation.' In A.M. Clarke and A.D.B. Clarke (eds) *Early Experience: Myth and Evidence.* London: Open Books; New York: The Free Press, 56–66.

Kolvin, I., Miller, F.J.W., Scott, D. Mcl., Gatzanis, S.R.M. and Fleeting, M. (1990) *Continuities of Deprivation? The Newcastle 1000 Family Study.* Aldershot: Gower House.

Levine, S. (1960) 'Stimulation in infancy.' *Scientific American 202,* 80–86.

Moskovitz, S. (1985) 'Longitudinal follow-up of child survivors of the Holocaust.' *Journal of the American Academy of Child Psychiatry 24,* 401–407.

Novak, M.A. and Harlow, H.F. (1975) 'Social recovery of monkeys isolated for the first year of life: I. Rehabilitation and therapy.' *Developmental Psychology 11,* 453–465.

Pilling, D. (1990) *Escape From Disadvantage.* London: Falmer Press.

Quinton, D. and Rutter, M. (1984a) 'Parents with children in care: I. Current circumstances and parenting.' *Journal of Child Psychology and Psychiatry 25,* 211–229.

Quinton, D. and Rutter, M. (1984b) 'Parents with children in care: II. Intergenerational continuities.' *Journal of Child Psychology and Psychiatry 25,* 231–250.

Quinton, D., Rutter, M., Dowdney, L., Liddle, C., Mrazek, D. and Skuse, D. (1982) *Childhood Experience and Parenting Behavior.* Final Report to the Social Science Research Council, UK.

Ramey, C.T. and Campbell, F.A. (1987) 'The Carolina Abecedarian Project: An educational experiment concerning human malleability.' In J.J. Gallagher and C.T. Ramey (eds) *The Malleability of Children.* Baltimore, MD: Paul H. Brookes.

Richardson, S.A. (1985) 'Epidemiology.' In A.M. Clarke, A.D.B. Clarke and J.M. Berg (eds) *Mental Deficiency: The Changing Outlook* (4th edn). London: Methuen.

Roswell Harris, D. (1958) *Some Aspects of Cognitive and Personality Test Changes in a Group of 100 Feebleminded Young Men.* Unpublished MA thesis, University of Reading.

Rutter, M. (1989) 'Pathways from childhood to adult life.' *Journal of Child Psychology and Psychiatry 30,* 23–51.

Rutter, M. and Madge, N. (1976) *Cycles of Disadvantage.* London: Heinemann.

Rutter. M., Quinton, D. and Liddle, C. (1983) 'Parenting in two generations: Looking backwards and looking forwards.' In N. Madge (ed) *Families at Risk.* London: Heinemann, 60–98.

Rutter, M. and Sandberg, S. (1985) 'Epidemiology of child psychiatric disorder: Methodological issues and some substantive findings.' *Child Psychiatry and Human Development 15*, 209–233.

Rutter, M., Yule, B., Quinton, D., Rowlands, O., Yule, W. and Berger, M. (1975) 'Attainment and adjustment in two geographical areas: III. Some factors accounting for area differences.' *British Journal of Psychiatry 126*, 520–533.

Scarr, S. and McCartney, K. (1983) 'How people make their own environments: A theory of genotype-environment effects.' *Child Development 54*, 424–435.

Scarr-Salapatek, S. (1976) 'An evolutionary perspective on infant intelligence: Species patterns and individual variations.' In M. Lewis (ed) *Origins of Intelligence.* New York: Plenum, 165–197.

Schweinhart, L.J. and Weikart, D.P. (1980) *Young Children Grow Up: The Effects of the Perry Preschool Program on Youths Through Age 15* (Monographs of the High/Scope Educational Research Foundation). Ypsilanti, MI: High/Scope Press.

Schweinhart, L.J. and Weikart, D.P. (1981) 'Perry preschool effects nine years later: What do they mean?' In M.J. Bejab, H.C. Haywood and H. Garber (eds) *Psychosocial Influences on Retarded Development Vol. 2.* Baltimore, MD: University Park Press, 113–125.

Scott, J.P. (1963) 'The process of primary socialization in canine and human infants.' *Monographs of the Society for Research in Child Development 28*, 1–47.

Scott, J.P. (1968) *Early Experience and the Organization of Behavior.* Belmont, CA: Brooks/Cole.

Skeels, H.M. (1966) 'Adult status of children with contrasting early life histories.' *Monographs of the Society for Research in Child Development 31*, 3, No. 105, 1–65.

Skeels, H.M. and Dye, H.B. (1939) 'A study of the effects of differential stimulation on mentally retarded children.' *Proceedings of the American Association on Mental Deficiency 44*, 114–136.

Skuse, D. (1984) 'Extreme deprivation in early childhood: II. Theoretical issues and a comparative review.' *Journal of Child Psychology and Psychiatry 25*, 543–572.

Suomi, S.J. and Harlow, H.F. (1972) 'Social rehabilitation of isolate-reared monkeys.' *Developmental Psychology 6*, 487–496.

Svendsen, D. (1982) 'Changes in IQ, environmental and individual factors. A follow-up of educable mentally retarded children.' *Journal of Child Psychology and Psychiatry 23*, 69–74.

Svendsen, D. (1983) 'Factors related to changes in IQ: A follow-up study of former slow learners.' *Journal of Child Psychology and Psychiatry 24*, 405–413.

Thomas, A., Chess, S. and Birch, H.G. (1968) *Temperament and Behavior Disorders.* New York: New York University Press.

Thompson, A. (1986) 'Adam – a severely deprived Colombian orphan.' *Journal of Child Psychology and Psychiatry 27*, 689–695.

Tonge, W.L., Lunn, J.E., Greathead, M., McLaren, S. and Bosanko, C. (1983) 'Generations of problem families in Sheffield.' In N. Madge (ed) *Families at Risk*. London: Heinemann, 37–59.

Von Knorring, A.-L., Andersson, O. and Magnusson, D. (1987). 'Psychiatric care and course of psychiatric disorders from childhood to early adulthood in a representative sample.' *Journal of Child Psychology and Psychiatry 28*, 324–341.

Waddington, C.H. (1957) *The Strategy of Genes*. London: Allen & Unwin.

Waddington, C.H. (1966) *Principles of Development and Differentiation*. New York: Macmillan.

Waddington, C.H. (1971). 'Concepts of development.' In E. Tobach, L. R. Aronson and E. Shaw (eds) *The Biopsychology of Development*. New York: Academic Press, 17–23.

Wedge, P. and Prosser, H. (1973) *Born to Fail?* London: Arrow Books.

Werner, E.E. (1985) 'Stress and protective factors in children's lives.' In A.R. Nicol (ed) *Studies in Child Psychology and Psychiatry*. London: Wiley, 335–355.

Werner, E.E. (1989) 'High-risk children in young adulthood; A longitudinal study from birth to 32 years.' *American Journal of Orthopsychiatry 59*, 72–81.

Werner, E.E. and Smith, R.S. (1982) *Vulnerable but Invincible: A Longtiudinal Study of Resilient Children and Youth*. New York: McGraw-Hill.

Wilson, R.S. (1985) 'The Louisville Twin Study: Developmental synchronies in behavior.' *Child Development 54*, 298–316.

CHAPTER 20

Contrary Evidence?

Commentary

This chapter, reprinted from *Early Experience and the Life Path* (2000), examines possible reasons for disputing our general theme that, on their own, early experiences (unreinforced) do not predestine future development. Studies of early attachments have revived the view that early life has crucial long-term effects, but raise more questions than answers. Four problems are identified; nevertheless, we point out that an extinction of early effects might later be reactivated under stress. Moreover, rates of attachment stability are not impressive, even within the same families. We conclude, therefore, that attachment measures are likely to be similar to other early psychological characteristics in having poor long-term predictive power. In cases of very severe global privation, however, recent evidence underlines the lingering effects on attachment which may persist for some children. These were not the usual insecure attachments as commonly measured. Rather, disinhibited or 'indiscriminately friendly' behaviour was manifest some years after early adoptive placement with sensitive caregivers. The authors point out that there is considerable variation between children. 'This variation implies that institutional deprivation is not sufficient for the development of attachment disturbances...' (O'Connor *et al.* 2001, p.57). They emphasize that such findings contain important lessons for understanding resilience.

Next, we examine in greater detail the very important prospective study of Romanian adoptees brought to this country before 2 years of age. From very retarded development, physically and psychologically, these children made on average huge gains in IQ and health, once again the 'catch-up' phenomenon. But those adopted before 6 months made the most spectacular gains, compared with older adoptees, suggesting a sensitive period for cognitive resilience.

Elsewhere we have noted three criteria for scientific veracity: 1. *replicability*. There have been many replications of resilience as a very important factor in development through the life span, so there is no problem here. 2. Could there be *alternative explanations* for the widespread catch-up phenomenon? No, and early attempts to promote the constancy model suggesting that first assessments or diagnoses were wrong, so that an 'improvement' was spurious, led the proponents into ridiculous, circular arguments. 3. Is our thesis *falsified?* Again, for reasons just given, 'no', but might it need to be modified? Yes, perhaps, there may well be a watershed around six months, after which resilience might be attenuated but not extinguished. We need much more information on this problem and on why some children do spectacularly well even though environmental change came long after 6 months.

The age 11 follow-up of the Romanian and British adoptees studied by Rutter and his colleagues is awaited with great interest, for surely this research on severe global privation is the most important over the last decade or two.

Contrary Evidence?*

A.M. Clarke and A.D.B. Clarke

Signpost: Studies of adopted Romanian orphans may suggest some modification to our thesis

In seeking evidence which might throw doubt on our thesis, a number of common findings, sometimes thought to be relevant, can be shown either to be irrelevant or at least dubious. For example, although institutions can vary considerably, it is often indicated in general that institutional rearing is damaging to children. Usually such rearing is consequent upon early adversity, but the poor outcome for children must be ascribed both to that and to subsequent, prolonged institutional influences. In any event, outcome, good or bad, can itself be influenced by post-institutional experiences (Quinton *et al.* 1982; Rutter *et al.* 1983).

In a useful review, Wachs and Gruen (1982), in noting what they describe as 'a highly stimulating exchange' between themselves and ourselves, go on to say that 'neither one of us convinced the other' (p.viii). Yet there seems to be

---

*   This chapter first appeared in A.M. Clarke and A.D.B. Clarke (2000) *Early Experience and the Life Path*. London: Jessica Kingsley Publishers, pp.83–98.

little to quarrel with in their review, especially when they write: '…with certain exceptions, the vast majority of early experiences, *taken in isolation*, will not have long lasting effects unless later experiences occur which stabilize the effects of the initial experiences. These…may occur naturally, as a result of transactions set up by the initial early experiences, or they may be built in to intervention strategies' (p.207). Wachs and Gruen have some useful things to say about early intervention and processes underlying continuities/discontinuities in development, and there is much less disagreement with aspects of our theme than these authors seem to believe. Skuse (1984) has, as noted earlier, shown that the prognosis is excellent for many very severely deprived children placed after rescue in better circumstances. But some do not do well, and this he ascribes to the presence of organic factors. It is, however, possible that without very strong intervention to overcome early developmental retardation, whether intellectual, emotional or both, a poorer progress would result. If so, such cases have not been reported.

A further point needs recognition: there is always a wide range of individual differences following intervention after adverse early experiences; some do very well, some quite well and some less well. What is it that characterizes the latter group? It may be an extreme vulnerability which later support can do rather little to minimize; or it may be that other aspects of the child's temperament (with its substantial genetic component) is also unfortunate, prompting adverse transactional feedback which in effect continues adversity. As Tizard (personal communication 1999) points out, there may also be differences in the adequacy of the intervention where, for example, new foster or adoptive parents are unresponsive or hostile. In any event, the correlated influences of biology, psychosocial environment, transactions and chance occurrences account for the inevitability of individual differences in outcome.

We turn now to more cogent evidence which may suggest modifications to our theme.

Attachment

Attachment studies have become more and more prevalent over the last two decades. They have their origin in Bowlby's initial interest in mother–child separation which logically developed further into research on attachment to a single figure (monotropy) which, in turn, merged into a recognition that multiple attachments normally occur. These researches gave rise to the view that the quality of early attachment produced internal representations, working models which would affect the nature of subsequent relationships, yet another variant of the early experience model. The family is now seen as the 'secure base' providing a reliable and readily available network of attachment relationships (Byng-Hall 1997).

Probably the most relevant and ingenious set of studies with an implication of supporting an early experience determinism have been undertaken by Fonagy, Steele and Steele (1991), Fonagy et al. (1994) and Steele, Steele and Fonagy (1995); these claim an intergenerational transmission of attachment behaviour.

During first pregnancies, mothers and fathers-to-be were asked to describe their own childhood relations with their parents, and were classified as secure/insecure via the Adult Attachment Interview (AAI). After the birth of their babies the children were assessed at 12 and 18 months, enabling them to be classified as secure or insecure in the Strange Situation. Maternal perceptions of their own childhood attachment predicted subsequent infant–mother secure/insecure attachment patterns around 75 per cent of the time. Thus a high level of prediction was confirmed. Not only do the authors discuss their successful predictions, but also consider the 25 per cent 'error', examining cases where prenatally reported early attachment security coincided with insecurely attached children, as well as prenatally reported attachment insecurity related to securely attached offspring. Various speculative explanations, including some environmental circumstances, were offered. Such findings illustrate our view that a single criterion (in this case, early attachment) is unlikely to provide a wholly satisfactory account of complex behaviour, even when predictively powerful. Although Steele et al. (1995) discuss temperament briefly, this factor may well be of importance in the Strange Situation, especially at extremes of temperament. This characteristic, with its substantial genetic influence, may well be one of the mediating variables between parents and offspring (see also Benoit and Parker 1994; Fox, Kimmerley and Schafer 1991; Goldsmith and Alansky 1987).

Fonagy's work is particularly useful in the present context, suggesting that early attachment may have long-lasting effects, although, as we shall see, it is an open question whether early security/insecurity is a direct *causal* influence on adult outcome, or whether it is a marker for ongoing influences throughout childhood and adolescence. After all, the parents-to-be were asked to reflect on their whole childhoods, not just the very earliest years, of which memories would be fragmentary. If temperament is, indeed, one of several mediators, its ongoing continuity in some cases may reflect indirectly from early attachment. In a notable review, Rutter (1995) believes that 'we are very far from having reached an understanding of the development of relationships or of the ways in which distortions in relationships play a role in psychopathology ... attachment is not the whole of relationships' (p.566).

Commenting on Fonagy's work, Holmes (1998) refers to the Adult Attachment Interview, believing that the way people talk about themselves manifests an inner representation of self–other relationships, and that these derive from early parent–child interaction. 'Narrative patterns are thus both an effect of parental handling in childhood and a cause of future patterns of relationship with intimates' (p.279). Earlier, Holmes (1993) had commented upon the Adult Attachment Interview as 'revealing feelings about current and past attachments and separations, and [tapping] into emotional responses to loss difficulty. Interviews are rated not so much for their content as for the way in which the subject describes their [sic] lives and losses' (p.433). As outlined, this technique does not only reveal early responses, but also later ones. In any event, the Adult Attachment Interview presumably cannot possibly capture the origins of individual attachment, only the later relations which, of course, may, or perhaps may not, directly follow from the earlier situation.

Kagan (1998) offers several examples of problems in the interpretation of the Strange Situation in measuring early attachment. For example, attachment classifications are not very stable over periods as short as six months, although a number of studies claim greater stability (see review by Melhuish 1993). Is it likely, he asks, that any 20-minute observation can uncover psychological products created over 6000 hours of parent–child interaction? More important, 15 to 20 per cent of children are genetically programmed to become fearful in novel situations, including therefore the Strange Situation. Labelled insecurely attached, many will have had sensitive, predictable mothers. Or again, infants who have experienced day centres are used to separation, and are less likely to cry when the mother leaves. They continue to play when the mother returns, but they, too, are labelled insecurely attached. Kagan offers many more research findings which lead him to question the view that the Strange Situation can capture accurately the infant's emotional relationships over the previous 12 months. He questions, too, the interpretations usually offered about the Adult Attachment Interview. This method implies a belief that the infant's attachment quality is transformed into a 'Working Model' of future relationships, detectable in adults when they reminisce about their childhoods. In turn, this may affect the way in which parents respond to their own child. Few psychologists would believe that an adult's conception of friendship derives from his or her early experiences of a day-care centre, nor would they think that early speech had profound effects on adult linguistic competence. And few have questioned whether the mother's verbal sophistication, temperament and ease or tension with an unfamiliar interviewer might influence the form of her narrative (Kagan 1998).

Kohnstamm and Mervielde (1998) ask:

> What is cause and what is effect? Is the attachment relation with the child really influenced by the parents' thoughts about their own past, as most researchers in this area seem to think, or is the present quality of the relation with the child actually influencing the parents' memories? Or are both true? As long as this is unclear it would perhaps be better to use the phrase *intergenerational concordance* or *congruence* instead of *intergenerational transmission* of the quality of attachment relations. The latter phrase suggests a one-way causal pathway only. (p.433)

One awaits with interest further work in this area. Summarizing so far, to some of the objections to the above one-way (and powerful) causality, one notes that 1. most outcomes are influenced by multiple, interacting factors, not just by one; 2. the Adult Attachment Interview assesses memories of the whole of childhood, not merely the very early years; 3. temperamental differences are likely to be one of the many mediating factors between memories of early attachments and later parental behaviour as assessed intergenerationally via the Strange Situation; and 4. the direction of causality, if indeed causality is involved, is unclear.

Sroufe, Egeland and Kreuzer (1990) have reported part of an ambitious prospective longitudinal study of children drawn from lower socioeconomic groups. They used a range of measures, including assessments of the home environment; quality of attachment at 12 and 18 months (in the Strange Situation); tool problem assessment (graded problems with mother's assistance) at 24 months; teaching tasks with mother's direction at 42 months; curiosity box (child's readiness to explore) at 54 months; teacher rankings and behaviour problems (at kindergarten); home evaluation (30 months and 6 years); and counsellor ratings (age 10). One small group ($n=11$) out of a large set showed consistent positive adaptation from 12 to 24 months, then showed poor adaptation during the 42- to 54-month period. However, these children showed the greatest capacity for later rebound in the elementary school years, despite poor functioning in the preschool period.

The issues are complex, write the authors, but one possibility is that the impact of early experience may remain dormant in certain contexts, only to be expressed later, as shown in some research using animals. We anticipated this general view (1968) in suggesting a possibility that the effects of early experience might be overcome but under stress might be reactivated. However, much later we examined critically the concept of 'sleeper effects', raising doubts whether this was a useful model (Clarke and Clarke 1981, 1982). Overall, Sroufe *et al.* believe that the results indicate that adaptation is always a product of both developmental history and current circumstances. In so far as this is a study of children who did not experience major life changes, the finding that early adaptation plays some part in later functioning is by no means inconsistent with our theme. See also Carlson and Sroufe (1995), however, who now believe that attachment organization provides the basis for personality functioning.

Belsky *et al.* (1996) have reported on two very much larger samples in an effort to assess the stability of early infant–parent attachment security. They recall that 'according to attachment theory, the infant during the second half of the first year of life develops an internal representation of the attachment relationship. Once found this representation is relatively stable (although still subject to modification based on subsequent experience) and guides the infant's behaviour in new situations' (p.921). Both samples were assessed at 12 and 18 months, and one further evaluation included infant–father attachment at 13 and 20 months. Rates of stability were no more than would be expected by chance, averaging about 50 per cent. The authors indicate, critically, that nearly a decade had passed since data on stability had appeared, that samples were modest in size, that corrections for chance associations had not been made and that much had changed in the way that Strange Situations are scored, and that there have also been changes in the ecology of infancy. This study underlines the complexity of the whole field of attachment classification. The question about chance associations is a very important one. For example, between two-thirds and three-quarters of non-risk samples can be expected to have participants classified as secure. By randomly assigning secure classifications to this percentage of members at two times of assessment, a high level of concordance will be achieved, inflating the appearance of stability (p.923). For a further overview, see Melhuish (1993).

Summing up, in view of the poor predictive quality of other early life characteristics, it seems unlikely that early attachment is an exception, on its own, in predicting the quality of later relationships. But the nature of early attachment can, of course, set in train ongoing consequences if there are environmental continuities. However, for an 'orthodox' view of attachment, see Steele (2002).

Romanian adoptees

In the area with which this book is concerned the most important research of the decade has been carried out by Rutter and the English and Romanian Adoptees (ERA) Study Team, for example, O'Connor *et al.* (2000); these articles are very detailed and complex. Selected from a larger group on carefully described criteria, 111 Romanian orphans who had been brought to England before the age of 2 years were followed up to age 4. They had all been victims of severe global privation and on arrival had entered adoptive homes. At the same time, 52 within-country UK adoptees, placed before six months, formed a comparison group, again studied at age 4 and later by O'Connor *et al.* (2000) at age 6.

Romanian records on the children were rather skimpy, but in most cases yielded information on height, weight and head circumference. Within the UK, apart from physical measures, reliance for the initial assessment was placed on adoptive parents' retrospective reporting, from which Denver developmental quotients were derived. The children proved to be severely developmentally impaired and severely malnourished on arrival, with almost half below the third percentile on height, weight, head circumference and IQ, this latter giving a mean of 63 (i.e. mild retardation, but with a wide range). Many suffered recurrent intestinal and respiratory infections. Here it should be noted that children placed before the age of 6 months were of initially higher status than the remainder of the cohort. This will be discussed later.

The authors offer a brief picture of conditions in the Romanian orphanages. These varied from 'poor' to 'appalling'. The infants were in most cases confined to cots, there were few if any playthings, little talk from 'carers' and no personalized caregiving. They were fed with gruel from propped-up bottles with large teats. Washing often involved the child being hosed down with cold water. Half the group had been institutionalized for the whole of their lives, the remainder having spent varying periods within families or at least half their lives in an institution.

From time to time (e.g. Clarke and Clarke 1976) we have indicated that across a wide age range for adoptive placement, the older members of all adoptive samples always, on average, do less well than the younger. We have attributed this to selective factors in the later adoptions. In the present study, the authors point out that selective factors on age of adoption (between 6 months, or above that figure) are very unlikely to have occurred. Hence any differences to be found at the age 4 follow-up must have arisen from differing pre-adoption experiences. This is undoubtedly correct. For us, the main finding (among several interesting subsidiary ones) is the initial average difference on the Denver Scale between the earlier (before 6 months) and later adopted (76.5 and 48.1, a difference of 28.4 points).

By age 4, an immense catch-up had taken place, as measured on the McCarthy Scale. The mean for the whole group had risen by 36.2 points, being by now 99.2 (with a large standard deviation of 19.2 points). The within-UK comparison group, by contrast, now had a mean of 109.4 (with a smaller SD of 14.8). Physically, too, there had been great improvements.

Whereas originally 51 per cent of the Romanian adoptees were below the third percentile for weight, only 2 per cent were so impaired at age 4.

Both the Denver and McCarthy scales showed that children adopted before the age of 6 months (n=56) were closely comparable to the development of the within-UK sample, in spite of the severe physical and developmental retardation on entry to the UK. Their mean scores (age 4) lay between 106 and 116, depending on the scale used – that is, spanning the average of the within-UK adoptees.

The mean scores of those adopted between 6 and 24 months were, however, at age 4 below 100 (92 and 97, respectively), so they were very significantly lower than the before age 6 months and the within-UK adoptees. These later adopted children were, on average, within the normal range, although about a standard deviation below the early adopted children. Their relatively depressed scores were related partly to the presence of seven intellectually impaired children not found in the within-UK sample, and partly to an overall smaller catch-up of their group. The authors' general inference is that the deficit probably reflects the influence of some aspects of institutional rearing. They also indicate from physical data that the differential catch-up did not simply reflect the level of malnutrition which was therefore not a major determinant of cognitive outcome.

A number of qualifications were pointed out. For example, in almost all cases, psychological privation was accompanied by malnutrition. Thus, it could be that the effects of such privation are increased by the co-occurrence of malnutrition, a multiplicative effect.

In summarizing some aspects of this important study we note:

1. On average, by age 4 the Romanian adoptees had made dramatic gains, both physically and cognitively.

2. Their average status at four years was nevertheless significantly below the average of the controls, the within-UK adoptees. This is perhaps unsurprising because it seems possible that the parents of such children, in the very adverse conditions in Romania, would themselves be below average. Less able parents would presumably be more likely to abandon their children than more gifted families.

3. Although the initial developmental quotients of the Romanian adoptees came from baseline adoptive parent reports which were perhaps less reliable accounts than the physical measures, both sets of data were reasonably confirmatory of each other.

4. For us, a major finding lay in the differences between those aged below 6 months on entry to the UK, and those who were older. These differences were apparent both initially and again at age 4. Part of this relative deficit reflected the presence of seven severely intellectually impaired children.

5. Those adopted before 6 months, as well as those adopted later, made massive gains on average, but the smaller gains in the later adopted group (from a lower baseline) must have arisen from the longer period of privation. This suggests a sensitive (but not critical) period in children who experienced privation, both physically and psychologically. It is of interest that, overall, adoptive breakdown was only 1.8 per cent, below that of within-UK adoptees, so it seems that emotional damage which usually leads to breakdown had in most been sufficiently repaired to allow adoption to proceed without insuperable problems.

A further and even more recent report has come from Rutter *et al.* (1999). Pointing out that in earlier studies of deprived, institution-reared children there have been no comments on the occurrence of autism, and that the same applies (with just two exceptions) to case studies, the senior author became aware of autistic-like development in some of the Romanian adoptees. The total sample includes the 111 already referred to, and a further group of older children not discussed here. Qualitative analyses have focused on the 111, for whom data were available both at age 4 and 6. There was also a contrast group of 28 'ordinary' autistic children, as well as a further group of 52 UK-adopted children placed before 6 months.

Autistic-like features were most marked at age 4 but tended to diminish greatly over the next two years. Eleven children were identified, showing difficulties in social relationships and in communication (e.g. problems in social reciprocity, eye-to-eye gaze, impaired language development). In most, too, there were preoccupations with sensations and intense, narrow interests; these came to a peak well after arrival in the UK. The behavioural patterns of these 11 were not identical. One child who arrived before the age of 6 months progressed well, lost language at about 20 months, became socially unresponsive, but within the next year language returned, normal social behaviour was regained and at school age he appeared completely normal. He was then excluded from further comment. The remaining ten divided into three children whose autistic features were associated with severe learning disablement and seven whose general cognitive score exceeded 50 (average score 57). Of these, six children had been assessed at both 4 and 6 years, and thus formed the basis of the analysis which is of particular interest.

The first three (learning disabled children) came late to the UK (between ages 21 and 34 months), all having experienced extremely poor institutional rearing, one being exceptionally severely malnourished. All three had something unusual in their histories, one being very premature at birth (weighing 2 lb); another had a high-tone hearing loss and came from an orphanage with a record of high infant mortality; and the last had been isolated in a single room because of racial discrimination and illegal status. Two had a head circumference below the third percentile at age 6. While these three showed behaviour close to classic autism, nevertheless all had learned Makaton sign language, two made considerable social approaches, though deviant in quality, and one had improved greatly, halving his autistic score in two years. So there were quite a number of features uncharacteristic of autism.

Turning to the subgroup of six children without severe cognitive impairment, but with quasi-autistic behaviour, how did they differ from the contrast group of 'ordinary' autistic children? First, at 4 years there were no apparent differences. Second, by age 6 the situation was quite different in that the diagnostic scores were by then significantly lower (i.e. better) than in the contrast group. So, third, the improvements over a comparatively short time were atypical. The contrast children had become worse, while the Romanian quasi-autistic orphans had improved, including a tendency for IQ increment averaging 20 points. Even so, they still averaged 32 points below the rest of the sample at age 6. Note that early in their development there had been nothing especially different from the also unusual behaviour of the other adoptees. The quasi-autistic behaviour, as indicated above, had developed between arrival and 4 years of age.

In discussing the causes of quasi-autistic behaviour, the authors offer three possibilities. First, there might have been some deviant development of attachment relationships, also noted by Chisholm *et al.* (1995) and Chisholm (1998). Second, the greater degree of cognitive impairment in these children, compared with their non-quasi-autistic peers, perhaps reflected an extreme lack of active experiences, social and non-social, resulting from prolonged confinement to cots, lack of toys and of linguistic exchanges with adults. Third, as with blind children who have a higher than usual incidence of autistic behaviour, especially if also retarded, perhaps their isolation played a comparable role. But it is important to remember that the great majority of adoptees did not respond in this way; only some 6 per cent did.

As noted earlier, across a wide age range at which adoption takes place, older adoptees tend to do less well than younger ones. In the case of Rutter and

Chisholm studies, selective factors which may have been relevant in other studies do not appear probable. Tizard (personal communication 1999) suspects that the nature of the earlier deprivation or privation, and the characteristics of the new environment, are important in outcome. Abuse and cruelty may have different effects than institutional neglect, and many parents who adopt older children are totally ill-prepared for, and horrified by, the problems they meet. Transactional effects then follow.

A further follow-up of the whole age 4 cohort of Romanian orphans took place at age 6, and the report awaits publication (O'Connor and the ERA Team 2000). The senior author has kindly provided a preprint. To recapitulate, 111 Romanian orphanage children, suffering from global severe privation, were adopted in the UK before the age of 2 years. On the whole, after two years in adoptive homes (at age 4) they had shown, on average, dramatic improvement, and many continued to gain cognitively until the second psychometric test at 6 years. Within this large cohort there were, of course, differences in outcome. Children adopted after 6 months (59 altogether) included seven who at the age of 4 were found to be seriously mentally retarded, but even making allowances for these children, these differences remained at age 6, so that the gap between the pre- and post-6-month-old adoptees was maintained rather than closed. Even so, within the later (7–24 months) children there were 28 out of 59 who scored 100 or above, of whom seven gained 120 or more.

A number of even later adopted children admitted after the age of 2 years had been too old to be tested at the first follow-up (at age 4), but were available at age 6. These late-placed adoptees included 26 adopted between 24 and 30 months, 16 between 31 and 36 months and six between 37 and 42 months. Thus by the age 6 follow-up, there were available the adoptees first assessed at age 4, plus a further 48 adopted after age 2. The large differences in length of severe privation enable one to estimate its effects upon recovery from the impaired level at arrival.

An important investigation of subsamples of the whole age six cohort is recorded in an Appendix. In this study, children admitted to the UK between 0 and 18 months were compared with those adopted very late, after 24 to 42 months in the institution. These two samples had each experienced roughly two-and-a-half to four years in adoption – that is, duration of adoption was the same. For the purposes of the study it had been held constant, the main difference being the time spent in severely deprived circumstances. A very large average cognitive difference was recorded in favour of the earlier (to repeat, 0–18 months) adopted group, even though a number of these children would have passed the six-month sensitive period.

The article includes a scattergram showing the relation between the children's ages at entry to the adoptive home, against their age 6 general ability scores. Taking age 8 months or later adoption (that is, well clear of the six months watershed), 11 children scored 120 or above, with four of 130 or above, very superior ability. Against this, some 25 children scored below 85, the arbitrary borderline for well below average ability. Among these were the seven referred to earlier who were probably constitutionally learning disabled. The majority of the eight months or later adopted subsample scored between 85 and 119. We see, then, very large differences in age 6 cognitive outcome, and that late and sometimes very late (e.g. age 3½) adoption neither precludes superior ability, nor significantly below average functioning. Hence factors other than prolonged, severe privation must be involved. What these might be is a matter for speculation, but one obvious candidate is the genetic differences between individuals.

The authors conclude that duration of severe global privation was the more powerful predictor of individual differences in outcome than was the time spent in the adoptive home, beyond approximately the two years in which recovery took place. In view of these dramatic gains, it cannot be concluded that there is a critical period for cognitive ability around six months, but one must keep open the possibility that for many there may be a sensitive period around this time, as many writers have suggested. In view of the number of later adopted children who were of average to superior ability at age 6, it is clear that the sensitive period failed to have universal effects.

Chisholm et al. (1995) and Chisholm (1998) have reported a study with similar implications to those of Rutter et al. (1999) Measuring security/insecurity of attachment and indiscriminate friendliness to previously unknown adults, their sample of adopted Romanian orphanage children showed differences between those adopted before 8 months and others adopted between 8 months and 68 months (median length of time in an orphanage, 17.5 months). Security of attachment was assessed in the child's own home; some 35 per cent of the early adoptees versus 58 per cent of later adopted showed insecure patterns of behaviour. However, on parent report, the early adopted did not differ from later adopted, nor from controls, on this type of behaviour. Parent report nevertheless indicated that the later adopted showed more indiscriminately friendly behaviour than the early adopted. So there is a degree of similarity between Rutter et al.'s (1999) cognitive studies and the attachment research of Chisholm.

These ongoing studies have been considered at length because they may suggest some modification to our theme. It has, of course, been known for many years that around 6 to 7 months of age there comes a profound psychological change (e.g. the sudden tear of strangers' and 'six-month anxiety'). This was shown empirically in Schaffer's (1958) study of the later effects of hospitalization in infants. Below the age of 6 months, the children showed brief 'global' disturbance on returning home. Above this age, the older children were 'over-dependent' on their mothers for a much longer time.

In a different research area a study of full-term singletons by Skuse *et al.* (1994) included a group of children with serious growth-faltering in their first year of life. The authors point out several possible influences, ranging from under-nutrition, congenital factors, child characteristics and inadequate parenting, as well as interactions between some of these. For example, the authors suggest that poor nutrition early in life may make a child more vulnerable to low levels of stimulation. The main general conclusion of this study is that growth-faltering in the first 6 months of life is associated with poorer mental and psychomotor development measured in the second year. This, then, is additional evidence for a sensitive period in the first year of life. However, it is probable that such children almost certainly experienced continuities in whatever aspects of child rearing which may be assumed to have played some part in growth-faltering. It is well known that the brain in the third trimester of pregnancy and the first year of post-natal life is especially vulnerable during its major growth spurt. One notes that growth deceleration in those where it first appeared after the age of 6 months showed no difference from a comparison group in the assessment measures used.

In spite of the above suggestion of a sensitive period, many of the studies quoted in this book relate to the outcome for older (and sometimes much older) children whose lives had altered radically for the better. These, too, exhibited considerable catch-up. Even so, their outcome might have been even better had the life changes occurred early. However, considering such studies as those by Koluchová (1972, 1976, 1991) where the privation, both physically and psychologically, was surely at least as great as that suffered by the Romanian adoptees, it seemed that total recovery had taken place. In this study, however, the children's first year was spent in care, followed by six months with an aunt, after which five-and-a-half years of gross privation took place. But the twins were together (see pp.51–52). So there remains a puzzle, and further follow-up of the Romanian group may – or may not – show a closing gap between the early and later adopted children. See Note 1, p.28. Bruer (2002) argues that 'maybe the Clarkes have conceeded too much too soon...'. We shall see in due course!

Summary

Among the several research areas reviewed in this chapter, only studies of adopted Romanian orphans may suggest modification to our thesis. Following conditions of severe global privation, those babies rescued before the age of 6 months made, on average, spectacular gains in development by age 4, maintained at age 6. The children adopted after the age of 6 months also made massive average gains, though not as great, from an initially lower level, even though they included seven who were functioning as almost certainly permanently learning disabled. But the difference between before and after 6 months must have reflected lengthier institutional privation, suggesting a sensitive (but not critical) period in their lives. But this sensitive period was not universal; some children did well or very well cognitively, even though adopted after (and sometimes long after) 6 months, both at age 4 and 6 follow-up. Genetic differences could be one of several possible factors explaining these outcomes. Results with similar indications were reported by Chisholm. Will these differences be maintained, or will the gap close as the children age, as has apparently happened in other cases? There is, however, a paradox in that many other studies show immense resilience in children rescued from very prolonged adversity at sometimes much later ages.

References

Belsky, J., Cambell, S.B., Cohn, J. F. and Moore, G. (1996) 'Instability of infant-parent attachment security.' *Developmental Psychology 32*, 921–924.

Benoit, D. and Parker, K.C.H. (1994) 'Stability and transmission of attachment across three generations.' *Child Development 65*, 1444–1456.

Byng-Hall, J. (1997) 'The secure family base: some indications for family therapy.' In G. Forest (ed) *Bonding and Attachment: Current Issues in Research and Practice.* Occasional paper No.14. London: Association for Child Psychology and Psychiatry.

Carlson, E.A.A and Sroufe, L.A. (1995) 'Contributions of attachment theory to developmental psychopathology.' In D. Ciccheti and D.J. Cohen (eds) *Developmental Psychopathology, Volume 1.* New York: Wiley.

Chisholm, K., Carter, M.C., Ames, E.W. and Morison, S.J. (1995) 'Attachment security and indiscriminately friendly behaviour in children adopted from Romanian orphanages.' *Development and Psychopathology 7*, 283–294.

Clarke, A.D.B. (1968) 'Learning and human development – the 42nd Maudsley Lecture.' *British Journal of Psychiatry 114*, 1061–1077.

Clarke, A.D.B. and Clarke, A.M. (1981) 'Sleeper effects in development: Fact or artefact? *Developmental Review 1*, 344–360.

Clarke, A.M. and Clarke, A.D.B. (eds) (1976) *Early Experience: Myth and Evidence.* London: Open Books. New York: The Free Press.

Clarke, A.M. and Clarke, A.D.B.(1982) 'Intervention and sleeper effects: A reply to Victoria Seitz.' *Developmental Review 2,* 76–86.

Fonagy, P. Steele, H. and Steele, M. (1991) 'Maternal representations of attachment predict the organization of infant–mother attachment at one year of age.' *Child Development 62,* 891–905.

Fonagy, P., Steele, M., Steele H., Higgit, A. and Target, M. (1994) 'The Emanuel Miller Memorial Lecture, 1992. The theory and practice of resilience.' *Journal of Child Psychology and Psychiatry 35,* 231–257.

Fox, N.A. Kimmerley, N.L. and Schafer, W.D. (1991) 'Attachment to mother/attachment to father: A meta-analysis.' *Child Development 62,* 210–225.

Holmes, J. (1993) 'Attachment theory: A biological basis for psychotherapy?' *British Journal of Psychiatry 163,* 430–438.

Holmes, J. (1998) 'Psychodynamics, narrative and intentional causality.' *British Journal of Psychiatry 173,* 279–280.

Kagan, J. (1998) *Three Seductive Ideas.* Cambridge, Massachusetts and London: Harvard University Press.

Kohnstamm, D. and Mervielde, I. (1998) 'Personality development.' In A. Demetriou, W. Doise and C. van Lieshout (eds) *Life-Span Developmental Psychology.* Chichester: John Wiley.

Koluchová, J. (1972) 'Severe deprivation in twins: A case study.' *Journal of Child Psychology and Psychiatry 13,* 107–114.

Koluchová, J. (1976) 'A report on the further development of twins after severe and prolonged deprivation.' In A.M. Clarke and A.D.B. Clarke (eds) *Early Experience: Myth and Evidence.* London: Open Books. New York: The Free Press.

Koluchová, J. (1991) 'Severely deprived twins after 22 years' observation.' *Studia Psycholgica 33,* 23–28.

Melhuish, E. (1993) 'A measure of love? An overview of the assessment of attachment.' *ACPP Review and Newsletter 15,* 269–275.

O'Connor, T.G. and the English and Romanian Adoptees Study Team (2000) 'The effects of global severe privation on cognitive competence.' *Child Development 71,* 326–390.

O'Connor, T.G., Rutter, M., Beckett, C., Brophy, M., Castle, J., Colvert, E., Gregory, A., Groothues, C. and Kreppner, J. (2001) 'Early deprivation and later attachment related behaviour: Lessons from the English and Romanian Adoptee Study.' In W. Yule and O. Udwin (eds) *Parenting: Application in Clinical Practice.* Occasional Papers No. 18, Association for Child Psychology and Psychiatry. London: ACPP.

Quinton, D., Rutter, M., Dowdney, L., Liddle, C., Mrazek, D. and Skuse, D. (1982) *Childhood Experience and Parenting Behaviour.* Final Report to the Social Science Research Council, UK.

Rutter, M. (1995) 'Clinical implications of attachment concepts.' *Journal of Child Psychology and Psychiatry 36*, 549–571.

Rutter, M. Quinton, D. and Liddle, C. (1983) 'Parenting in two generations: Looking backwards and looking forwards.' In N. Madge (ed) *Families at Risk.* London: Heinemann.

Rutter, M., Anderson-Wood, L., Beckett, C., Bredenkamp, D., Castle, J., Groothues, C., Kreppner, K., Keaveney, L., Lord, C., O'Connor, T.G. and the ERA Study Team (1999) 'Quasi-autistic patterns following severe early privation.' *Journal of Child Psychology and Psychiatry 40*, 537–549.

Schaffer, H.R. (1958) 'Objective observations of personality development in early infancy.' *British Journal of Medical Psychology 31*, 174–183.

Skuse, D. (1984) 'Extreme deprivation in early childhood: II. Theoretical issues and a comparative review.' *Journal of Child Psychology and Psychiatry 25*, 543–572.

Skuse, D., Pickles, A., Wolke, D. and Reilly, S., (1994) 'Postnatal growth and mental development: Evidence for a "sensitive" period.' *Journal of Child Psychology and Psychiatry 35*, 521–545.

Sroufe, L.A., Egeland, B., and Kreuzer, T. (1990) 'The fate of early experience following developmental change: Longitudinal approaches to individual adaptation in childhood.' *Child Development 61*, 1363–1373.

Steele, H. (2002) 'Attachment theory.' *The Psychologist 15*, 519–522.

Steele, H. Steele, M. and Fonagy, P. (1995) 'Associations among attachment classifications of mothers, fathers and infants.' *Child Development 67*, 541–555.

Wachs, T.D. and Gruen, G.E. (1982) *Early Experience and Human Development.* New York: Plenum Press.

PART V

Epilogue

CHAPTER 21

Human Resilience and the Course of Human Development

Commentary

In this book we have tackled not only our own thesis, but some broader issues in life-span development. Our reliance on what must be some hundreds of studies by other researchers must be obvious, for we have benefited from their data and ideas in firming up and supporting our general conclusions.

There are two aspects in tracing the life course, the absolute changes in functioning and the relative changes in ordinal position with respect to age peers. In the former case, development is often regarded as only incremental, but can also be decremental as particular processes are replaced by others. Then there are decrements in some functions associated with aging. Where relative changes in ordinal position are concerned, one noted the poor prediction from the early baselines. This notion, however, must not be pressed too far. For some, the outcomes are eminently predictable from the context continuing from birth (e.g. parents addicted to hard drugs and in poverty), but for others rescued from dire circumstances, an early baseline may have little predictive power. And the majority of people in stable, humane environments will vary within their own broad bands of functioning.

The chapter briefly reviews some of the main principles reflecting life-span development. It concludes with an examination of factors affecting the expression of resilience.

As noted in Chapter 1, the initial findings from which much of our later research was derived caused us great surprise since we had been reared, like everyone else, with the constancy model. This suggested that with respect to age peers, people do not change much, particularly with cognition in which they tend to remain within a narrow band.

After a pilot study we were able to set up 'clean' research, with independent evaluation of current status, and independent assessment of social history. The results caused us to examine the constancy model and to find it lacking so far as our population of socially deprived persons was concerned. Then began a long process of seeking generalization to other groups, since we thought it unlikely that the changes we had recorded were unique. By 1958, however, a growing confidence prompted us to write about resilience and vulnerability and to raise, probably for the first time, the question of why some children seemed overwhelmed by apparently minor problems, while some others appeared to have escaped unscathed from dire backgrounds. This argued for an important research area. A year later, our then publisher encouraged us to write a book on the problem of deprivation. We began writing it but, ever cautious, felt that as yet there was insufficient evidence to proceed, abandoning our work and waiting 16 years before fully tackling it again. By this time we were able to enlist some of the writings of eminent authors such as Bronfenbrenner, Chess and Thomas, Kagan, Rutter and B. Tizard, who allowed us to reprint their contributions. The purpose of our evolving aims was first, to show that resilience is important and that its effects could be measured, and second to record its prerequisites, both internal and contextual, its antecedents and outcomes. Needless to say, these aims were only partially achieved!

This book has tackled the growing knowledge of some broader issues in life-span developmental psychology. The selected reprints, which allow access to hundreds of studies, provide a window on the influences which shape development, but also indicate their continuing relevance.

Interacting influences

From time to time we have found it useful to distinguish four major, interacting influences on human development:

1. *Biological trajectory*. This includes genetic factors as well as acquired damage, and of course both have effects which unfold over time. They provide a framework of possibilities, dependent on interaction with other influences: the obvious is worth stating here! Our very existence is dependent on biological factors. The important problem is to assess the extent to which genetic influences are responsible, partly or solely, for *differences* between individuals. Genetic effects on behaviour cannot be measured directly because of their interactions with other factors to produce a 'phenotype'. Such interactions imply that heredity cannot be

solely responsible for the end product. Moreover, these influences unfold over time, with genes switching on and off as in (by analogy) the physical growth spurt at adolescence which terminates in the late teens.

2. *Environmental trajectory.* As with the biological trajectory, social and related influences unfold over time. They may be material, psychological or biological (substandard housing and poverty, cruel parenting or brain injury from disease or accident, respectively). And the place of a particular environment within its historical and economic context is obviously relevant (Elder 1998).

3. *Interactions and transactions.* The interactive nature of developmental influences has already been stressed. Transactions occur when personal characteristics affect the environment in such a way that feedback from the latter tends to reinforce the personality of the individual. We have further suggested (and there is some evidence now for this) that the more extreme the psychological features of the individual, whether of intelligence or temperament, the stronger their effect on the environment and therefore directly back on to the individual. The very bright person will have very little in common with the dullard, and the very shy person will avoid novel social situations; in both examples people will seek and find circumstances in which they feel comfortable and unthreatened. Thus people to some extent create their own environments.

4. *Chance events.* The role of chance in individual development is far too often ignored. A very few researchers note that chance can sometimes radically alter an individual life path. For example, a modest study of mature students returning to higher education after earlier 11-plus failure showed that about 70 per cent cited some chance event as directing them to a chosen university and of these around half cited 'pure' chance as the decisive factor. Moreover, sudden 'chance' historical or economic events can set off a cycle of ongoing consequences. The Great Depression was one such catastrophe for many families (Elder 1974). Rutter (1999, p.125) points out that sometimes such serious events can have a strengthening effect, and certainly Elder's older children were strengthened by having to cope with the extra family

responsibilities in their disrupted situation. Younger children found their experiences more difficult to handle (see also Elder 1998).

From all the foregoing one notes a high degree of complexity in development across time. Of course, all psychological characteristics will show *absolute* developmental change. Such growth is usually thought of as incremental, but may also be decremental (e.g. the fadeout of crawling in infancy, or the personality disintegration in schizophrenia). We have also stressed the *relative* changes in comparison with age peers. Some show minor changes, others larger. In the normal population, however, such relative increments and decrements will in most cases be small; remaining in the same broad band of personal possibilities is the norm. But the situation is entirely different in two circumstances. First, behavioural constancies will be much more apparent in abnormalities than in normality. There are three reasons for this: 1. some abnormalities may have been largely caused by abnormal conditions of rearing, which are likely to persist, with real difficulties in breaking the ongoing chain of events; 2. the abnormality may impinge strongly on the social environment, producing reinforcing feedback of a transactional nature (e.g. conduct disorder which produces antagonistic responses which serve only to strengthen the behaviour); 3. where strong genetic influences relate to the behaviour, these may be maintained; 4. the abnormality may be the consequence of serious biological insult.

The second area in which there can be strong differences in outcome relates to those rescued from severe adversity and placed in better circumstances. On average, these show very great improvements. On the other hand, if such unfortunates remain in adversity their problems are likely to be intensified. So again we stress that in development there may be individual constancies and individual changes.

Some research problems

The last 50 years have witnessed a growing sophistication in research methodology. Problems of measurement have been addressed, so too a growing awareness of 'experimenter effects' is now catered for in research design. There is a need for data to be collected by those without a knowledge of the hypothesis and 'blind' to individual membership of a particular group. The importance of long-term prospective ('follow-up') studies cannot be over-emphasized but there are problems of ongoing cost and the potentially distorting influences of sample wastage. Similarly there is now greater awareness of snags with retrospective ('follow-back') research, valuable as this can be; in particular one cannot know whether there is a significant 'escape' by those with similar early histories; these will not be members of the identified sample.

We have briefly considered some of these issues in Chapter 12. In addition there are two concepts which obtruded in relation to our analyses of developmental research. They were 'regression to the mean' and also 'sleeper effects'. Both struck us as catch-phrases, perhaps descriptive, but lacking any indication of the processes involved. We discussed the former (Chapter 9), the tendency of extreme scores to be less extreme on reassessment and showed that behavioural processes are involved, not statistical artifacts.

Then in our investigation of 'sleeper effects' (Chapters 10 and 11) we argued that this concept was also used uncritically to describe positive relations between early and later measures but with a total absence of any correlation in between. At first the early effects were said to become dormant, yet like a submerged submarine broke surface later. We were reminded of our present incompetent use of French which is somewhat resurrected during a holiday in France...a 'sleeper effect'? This term could be used in describing any thought or activity not at the moment in consciousness, but which is re-activated by some change in thinking or by circumstances.

Predictions

In studying the course of human development, there are available different types of measurement. First there are possibilities of tracking apparently unitary scores (e.g. IQ or shyness) and establishing their stability or change over time. Then there are broader measures, such as 'success' or 'least successful' in life as in the famous Terman study of gifted children (see Elder 1998; Oden 1966). But closer examination of these broader categories usually reveals them to be aggregates of correlated single factors. They do, however, offer a more rounded view of individual development.

Consider whether the course of human development is predictable. If one uses broad criteria, then prediction from the early years is reasonably accurate in the main. But using narrower criteria, growth is sometimes unpredictable because of the multiplicity of interacting influences and chance throughout the life path. But there are notable exceptions and here we take two extreme examples. The life course of a child born to stable, economically secure and bright parents seems in broad terms eminently predictable: good schooling, a prosocial peer group, higher education and prospects of fulfilling employment are usually the norm. But in the classic Terman study of very bright children, with its unusually long follow-up to middle age, a significant minority fell by the wayside for such reasons as alcoholism or mental health problems which seemed to have their origins in the family background. This latter group therefore escaped their likely destiny (Oden 1966).

A second extreme example relates to a child born to a teenage, dull mother living singly and in poverty. Truancy and an antisocial neighbourhood leads to delinquency, drug taking, criminality and prison. Again, a predictable life path, but there are still those few, seemingly against all odds, who escape the prediction (see Chapter 4).

To summarize, the prediction of psychological growth depends first on the breadth or precision of the criterion. If the latter is broad (e.g. scholastic success versus failure) then prediction of individual development is reasonably accurate. If narrow, then there will be a much greater error in charting this aspect of the life course, partly because of the interaction of personal variable factors (e.g. motivation) and partly because the social context is itself changing. The second problem can be seen in those reared in abnormal conditions, which if continued will lead to distorted development. But a radical change of environment can alter this. The issues are complex (see Chapters 2 to 8), but our oft-repeated bottom line remains that the life course is *potentially somewhat* open-ended, with the italicized words as important qualifications.

Human resilience

A few years after our initial study had been published, we came upon research on the retarded physical growth of previously malnourished German wartime orphanage children (see Chapters 3 and 18). When these were provided with a balanced diet their growth accelerated much more rapidly than under normal conditions and they achieved their normally expected stature – a 'catch-up' phenomenon. This exactly paralleled what we had observed behaviourally in formerly deprived adolescents and young adults. At the same time an eminent geneticist, Waddington, began to talk about a fundamental 'self-righting' tendency which promotes a reversion towards or into normality whenever changed circumstances allowed this. So the stage was set for a belated recognition of a potentially powerful characteristic, human resilience.

It seems therefore that resilience is built into the human system, but as with other characteristics there are wide differences between individuals in the strength of its expression, which anyway is modulated by experience. While the phenomenon can be manifest during a catastrophe or other adversity, it is more usually apparent after such events, the effects of which then in a supportive environment begin to fade. The diagram below illustrates the interaction of the three most potent influences: personal characteristics, external support and duration of such support (see Figure 21.1).

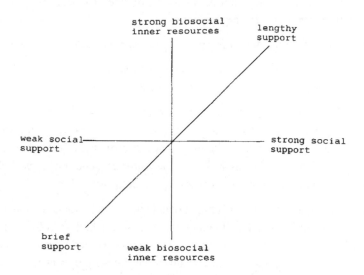

Figure 21.1 indicates the three major influences on the expression of resilience. This classification must not be regarded as necessarily static for the individual if one or more of these variables change; the complex, interacting and multiple influences on development can shift functioning from one quadrant to another, for good or ill

The inner resources, or personal characteristics, shown in Figure 21.1 seem to be largely constitutional in origin and include sociability, problem-solving ability and the development of self-esteem. Support involves some affectional network and/or some deliberate attempt to help the child, whether through an educational programme, or long-term fostering or adoption. This links with duration of support ranging from brief to lifelong improvements in personal circumstances (see Chapter 19).

Those who can be classified in the upper right quadrant have the best prognosis after rescue, in that strong personal qualities interact with strong external support of long duration. Next come those in the lower right quadrant; even though their inner resources are weak, they enjoy strong, long-term support and have a good prognosis. At the upper left, prospects are less good; they have brief, weak interventions but may be partially compensated by strong personal resources. Finally, those at the lower left have poor prospects.

Many findings can be summarized concerning the aftermath of adversity and the intervention possibilities that can be present:

1. Psychological changes tend always to move on average in the direction of environmental shift but, as Rutter (1999) has indicated, much depends on what preceded the change, as well as its present and future contexts.

2. Their amount depends on *the degree, nature and duration of shift*.

3. However, there is always an array of *individual differences* around average changes, probably constitutional in origin.

4. Amounts of change may not be primarily related to the age of the child, although for a variety of reasons age is likely to impose growing constraints, due to the aging process, to habit and to social constraints, as well as to ongoing cause–effect cycles where effects in turn become causes of the next responses.

There is a general issue in applying research findings to social problems. It is clear that continuing social influences, whether good, bad or indifferent, have a powerful role in shaping individual development. Hence to undo the effects of the many ongoing malevolent circumstances bearing upon those in adversity must be of high priority. But here, while we may know what *should* be done, this is far from being what *can* be done. There is a lack of resources, both human and financial, to follow the implications of the many studies we have quoted. However, currently the most obvious and, at least partially, achievable field of application is that of adoption or fostering of children in care ('looked after' in politically correct parlance), in spite of the immediate problems experienced by such children and by their adoptive parents. Once again resilience is deeply involved.

Fostering is usually perceived as second best for deprived children. This is by no means so, and there are several excellent studies which reveal the therapeutic strength of long-term fostering, as well as fostering in preparation for adoption. As with adoption, much depends on enlightened agencies, careful training and continuing support for foster parents.

It is, of course, obvious that vast numbers of the world's population are under-functioning, whether physically, emotionally or cognitively, for the sorts of reasons we have indicated. As noted, nearer to home we can point to children in care. These usually leave their period of being 'looked after' without qualifications, with poor self-images and prospects of lowly, dead-end employment, assuming that they have sufficient motivation to retain their jobs. In turn there can be a rapid descent into drugs, crime and prison. Yet this gloomy scenario could have earlier been interrupted by adoption or fostering. There has until recently been a failure of local authorities and social workers to face these problems and this is one of the scandals of our time. This is not to say that adoption is an easy solution, either for the adoptee or for the adoptive parents of the necessary calibre. Children have to unlearn behaviour which was adaptive to the tragic circumstances in which they lived, and at the same time learn new acceptable behaviour. Adoptive parents face lengthy challenges, yet long-term outcome is in most cases favourable. The cost of inaction for deprived children probably vastly outweighs the cost of action. Current government interest in this area is beginning to shake the more tardy local authorities into facing the issues.

Most researchers, including ourselves, have tended to treat resilience as a unitary process. It seems probable, however, that different facets of personality may have different 'natural histories' when confronted with situations requiring resilience. For example, intelligence is apparently well buffered against mild or moderate adversity, while emotions are probably more labile; Rutter (1999) has pointed out that children 'actively process their experiences, adding meaning to what has happened to them' (p.134). We note that some have little difficulty in coming to terms with past problems, while others ruminate to such an extent that the problem may become self-reinforcing and even lifelong. Rutter, too, points to the vast range of outcomes after adversity, but says of his now famous English and Romanian adoption study (see Chapter 20) that while the catch-up cognitively was not complete in the group as a whole, it was very impressive. 'It would be very difficult to find a more striking example of what is meant by resilience' (p.122). Equal or more striking gains for individuals (as opposed to groups) are also to be found in our reviews of literature (see Chapters 18, 19 and 20).

The Department of Health (1999, pp.10–18) has summarized research indications of the factors affecting the vulnerability of adoptive children. For example, the age of the child at placement is important; those who are younger have a better outcome. Correlated with this, the child's past experience is also crucial; the longer in care or adversity, the greater the later risk of poor outcome. So, too, with behaviour problems. The composition of the adoptive home is relevant; the presence of birth children increases risks. Parenting styles, as one might expect, are important; expressed warmth, emotional involvement and sensitivity and the way in which these are combined are powerful. These are of course statements of averages to which there may be exceptions. However, one should add the obvious point that on occasion genetic risks which in the mother gave rise to the offer of the child for adoption may well be hugely important in later adoptive failures, since the child shares the biological mother's genetic make-up. One can also add that currently some advanced social workers are looking at ways in which resilience in damaged children can be encouraged (Clarke and Clarke 2001).

Frequently personal and contextual factors interact to prevent the expression of resilience and accentuate vulnerability. Just as one good thing leads to another, so one bad thing (or things) can set off cycles of disaster over time. Rutter and colleagues (1995), for example, show that childhood problem behaviour (e.g. conduct disorder) leads to further adversities, and these feed back and reinforce problems. Or again, there are childhood antecedents to disaster-prone marriage with a deviant spouse, and then to childhood and adolescent behaviour. The contexts of the latter strongly predict adult exposure to situations promoting risks of psychiatric disorders. All this underlines our oft-expressed view that it is to *continuing influences* that importance must be ascribed. Cycles of both individual vulnerability and resilience undoubtedly exist and transactional processes seem always to be involved, especially at extremes of personality.

This book has, in summary, tracked not only our growing awareness of major influences in the life span, but also the ways in which the researches of others impinge upon, confirm or modify our own thinking. Underpinning all the successful long-term studies of rescue from deprivation is the process of resilience, a quality of obvious evolutionary advantage. As noted, the geneticist Waddington (1966) indicated that there is a strong restitutive process at work, which allows a return towards normality whenever later circumstances permit this; no better example is, as noted, Rutter and colleagues' English and Romanian adoption study (Chapter 20). Here the 'self-righting' tendency interacted with good living conditions after severe privation. Contrast this with our own findings (Chapters 2 and 3). From a background of cruelty and neglect, a switch to an austere but orderly institution permitted much later IQ and social increments. Large differences in the programmes within that situation had no differential effect, so we concluded that it was primarily *withdrawal from* rather than *response to* a better situation. In other words this was a 'purer' version of the powerful 'self-righting' tendency.

While this book has been concerned with resilience after adversity, sometimes very severe, this process is equally obvious in both children and adults, in coping with bereavement, divorce, great disappointments, frustrations and the conflicting demands of ordinary life. The same principles are likely to apply to a happy outcome, namely strong biosocial internal resources with often the added bonus of a long-term supportive background.

The individual who does not need at some stage to benefit from resilience must have experienced a tranquil and unchallenging life. It is most needed (and most obvious) during, or more likely after, some catastrophe or other adversity.

We have stressed the qualities of the subsequent supportive environment. In rare cases, the child will seek this out; more often it will be provided with varying degrees of adequacy. Such interventions may be time-limited for reasons of inadequate resources. The problem, therefore, is to set in motion ongoing restitutive processes which might include using mentors and which in effect continue the intervention. Conversely, a brief programme not followed by changed circumstances is likely to fail. The need now is to mobilize support for children leaving care or other unfortunate situations, and indeed to prevent the cycle ever occurring, or at least to break it much earlier. This would be both humane and make long-term economic sense, provided the human resources are available to take up the challenge.

Finally, what of the future in research on resilience? Among the questions which for us seem unresolved are whether there are different processes involved in its expression, and whether these have different developmental histories. Second, is it possible that successive but successful adaptation to adversity strengthens future resilience, while unsuccessful transactions increase personal vulnerability? A number of studies suggest that this may be so. In any event, this field looks likely to continue to be rewarding, and of course the later development of Romanian orphans will be especially revealing.

References

Clarke, A.M. and Clarke, A.D.B. (2001) 'Early adversity and adoptive solutions.' *Adoption and Fostering 25*, 24–32.

Department of Health (1999) *Adoption Now: Messages from Research.* London: Department of Health.

Elder, G.H. Jr (1974) *Children of the Great Depression: Social Change in Life Experiences.* Chicago: University of Chicago Press.

Elder, G.H. Jr (1998) 'The life course as developmental theory.' *Child Development 69*, 1–12.

Oden, M.H. (1966) 'The fulfilment of promise: 40 year follow-up of the Terman Gifted Group.' *Genetic Psychology Monographs 77*, 9–93.

Rutter, M. (1999) 'Resilience concepts and findings: Implications for family therapy.' *Journal of Family Therapy 21*, 119–144.

Rutter, M., Champion, L., Quinton, D., Maughan, B. and Pickles, A. (1995) 'Understanding individual differences in environmental risk-exposure.' In P. Moen, G.H. Elder Jr, and K. Luscher (eds) (1995) *Lives in Context.* Washington, DC: APA.

Waddington,C.H. (1966) *Principles of Development and Differentiation.* New York: Macmillan.

By the same authors

A.D.B. Clarke and A.M. Clarke (1966, 1969, 1975) *Recent Advances in the Study of Subnormality*. London: NAMH

A.D.B. Clarke and A.M. Clarke (1973) *Mental Retardation and Behavioural Research*. London: Churchill Livingstone.

A.M. Clarke and A.D.B. Clarke (eds) (1958, 1965, 1974) *Mental Deficiency: The Changing Outlook* (4th edn with J.M. Berg [1985]). London: Methuen. New York: The Free Press.

A.M. Clarke and A.D.B. Clarke (eds) (1976) *Early Experience: Myth and Evidence*. London: Open Books; New York: The Free Press.

A.M. Clarke and A.D.B. Clarke (2000) *Early Experience and the Life Path*. London: Jessica Kingsley Publishers.

Index